Best Places to Stay in America's Cities

THE BEST PLACES TO STAY SERIES

Best Places to Stay in America's Cities
Second Edition/Bruce Shaw, Editorial Director

Best Places to Stay in Asia
Jerome E. Klein

Best Places to Stay in California
Second Edition/Marilyn McFarlane

Best Places to Stay in the Caribbean
Second Edition/Bill Jamison and Cheryl Alters Jamison

Best Places to Stay in Florida
Second Edition/Christine Davidson

Best Places to Stay in Hawaii
Second Edition/Bill Jamison and Cheryl Alters Jamison

Best Places to Stay in Mexico
Bill Jamison and Cheryl Alters Jamison

Best Places to Stay in the Midwest
John Monaghan

Best Places to Stay in the Mid-Atlantic States
Dana Nadel

Best Places to Stay in New England
Fourth Edition/Christina Tree and Kimberly Grant

Best Places to Stay in the Pacific Northwest
Second Edition/Marilyn McFarlane

Best Places to Stay in the Rocky Mountain Region
Roger Cox

Best Places to Stay in the Southwest
Second Edition/Anne E. Wright and Gail Barber Rickey

Best Places to Stay in America's Cities

SECOND EDITION

Bruce Shaw, Editorial Director

Houghton Mifflin Company
Boston • New York • London

For information about permission to reproduce selections
from this book, write to Permissions, Houghton Mifflin
Company, 215 Park Avenue South, New York, New York 10003.

ISSN: 1048-5481

ISBN: 0-395-62226-3

Illustrations by Chris Schuh
Maps by Charles Bahne
Design by Robert Overholtzer

This book was prepared in conjunction
with Harvard Common Press.

VB 10 9 8 7 6 5 4 3 2 1

Contents

Tucson, Arizona

Washington, D.C.

Best Places to Stay in America's Cities

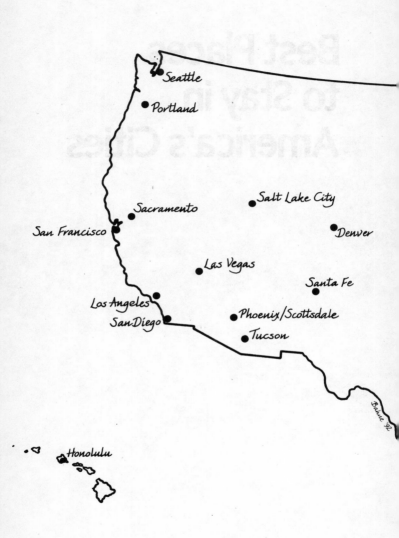

Introduction

For too long, people traveling to cities in the United States on business and pleasure have felt squeezed into staying at hotels whose biggest attraction was predictability. They all looked alike and offered the same impersonal services. The occasional maverick—distinctively appointed and staffed by people who pride themselves on going the extra mile to make guests feel at home—has been lost in the avalanche of advertising and in guidebooks that focus only on the safe choices, the standard fare.

Tastes have been changing, though, and it is becoming more common to find guest houses and small, service-oriented hotels in urban areas. Many larger hotels as well have responded to a traveling public that increasingly seeks personal attention and warm surroundings. Now travelers have a guide to many styles of outstanding lodgings in *Best Places to Stay in America's Cities*.

Small hotels, guest houses, bed and breakfasts, and exceptional larger hotels were chosen for this book because they provide guests with much more than simply a bed to sleep in. Whether furnished in European antiques or the latest Los Angeles designs, one thing nearly all the Best Places pride themselves on is an aesthetically pleasing and comfortable environment, unlike the cookie-cutter approach to decorating that most chains take. These hoteliers may hang regional artwork on the walls, display a personal collection of Native American sculpture, or place a whimsical stuffed animal in every room.

But beyond decor and furnishings, perhaps the most significant offering of the of the Best Places is service. Many model their hospitality on the European tradition, employing a concierge who stands ready to recommend a restaurant, get tickets to a show, or lend an umbrella. If something can't be provided from the hotel's own resources, the concierge will usually be able to provide it from some other source.

Other establishments, most often guest houses or B&Bs, bring country inn hospitality to city townhouses or Victorian mansions, pampering visitors with afternoon tea and cordials, breakfast in bed, fireplaces, and comfortable living rooms. Bathrooms may come stocked with fine toiletries, double-thick towels, built-in hairdryer, and, for those with pressing business, a telephone.

Business travelers will find this new breed of hostelry a welcome — and not necessarily expensive — change from week after week of bland high-rise hotels. Many are equipped for business meetings and can provide catering and clerical services, as well as teleconferencing, fax, and modem facilities. All-suite hotels are included for travelers who need to spread out or settle in. The book even covers resorts within city limits and country inns within a short drive of downtown.

In all, 315 hotels and inns in 40 urban areas were selected for *Best Places to Stay in America's Cities*. Each establishment was visited and inspected by one of the eleven professional travel writers who have contributed to this book. (Hundreds of other establishments were visited but deemed unworthy of inclusion.) The writers have chosen the most distinctive places to stay — not always the most famous or glamorous, not the ones with the biggest atriums, never simply the biggest. No establishment made its way into the book by making any kind of payment.

While many of the hotels and inns described in these pages offer extraordinary creature comforts, *Best Places to Stay in America's Cities* is not simply a guide to the nation's most luxurious lodgings. The establishments in this book are not ranked or rated according to any one set of criteria. Instead, we have sought to recognize the diversity in style, cost, and size of lodgings in this country and to identify the best entries in a great variety of categories.

Contributing Writers

The contributing writers to this volume are: Roger Cox (*Denver, Las Vegas, Salt Lake City*); Christine Davidson (*Miami, Orlando, Tampa/St. Petersburg*); Kimberly Grant and Christina Tree (*Boston*); Bill Jamison and Cheryl Alters Jamison (*Honolulu*); Marilyn McFarlane (*Los Angeles, Portland, Sacramento, San Diego, San Francisco, Seattle*); John Monaghan (*Chicago, Cincinnati, Cleveland, Columbus, Detroit, Indianapolis, Kansas City, Milwaukee, Minneapolis/St. Paul, St. Louis*); Dana C. Nadel (*Baltimore, New York, Philadelphia, Pittsburgh, Washington*); Carol Timblin (*Atlanta, Memphis, Nashville, New Orleans*); and Anne E. Wright (*Austin, Dallas/ Fort Worth, Houston, Phoenix/Scottsdale, San Antonio, Santa Fe, Tucson*).

Atlanta

Ansley Inn
253 15th Street, N.E.
Atlanta, Georgia 30309
404-872-9000
800-446-5416
Fax: 404-892-2318

General manager: Tim Thomas
Accommodations: 12 rooms (all with private Jacuzzi baths)
Rates: $100–$250
Included: Continental breakfast, afternoon tea, and parking
Payment: Major credit cards
Children: Welcome
Pets: Discouraged
Smoking: Allowed
Open: Year-round

Corporate travelers love this Tudor brick bed-and-breakfast inn in Ansley Park near midtown Atlanta, a MARTA station, and Peachtree Street. Built in 1907 by the founder of Muse's department store, an Atlanta establishment, the 17,000-square-foot house was constructed of the finest materials—ceramic tile fireplaces, heavy molding in all the rooms, and a ballroom. After the Muses ceased to live here, the building became a respectable boarding house for a while but ended up as a flop-house before it was bought by several partners and restored in 1985. They plan to add twenty more rooms sometime in the future.

With its heavy, dark molding, the house has a very masculine appearance. A pair of Regency leather sofas form a conversation area around the big fireplace in the parlor, and the dining room features a barrel-vaulted ceiling, crystal chandeliers, and English Chippendale table, where breakfast is served. (The dining room often doubles as a meeting room; three other large rooms are also available to groups.) Local artists are invited to exhibit their work on the walls.

Guest rooms, named for neighborhood streets, are very large and feature four-poster rice beds, hardwood floors, and Oriental rugs. All the rooms have individual Jacuzzis (except for one that is double) and are equipped with individual climate control, cable television, direct-dial telephone, wet bar, and other extras such as terrycloth robes. The Inman Room on the third floor has a small refrigerator.

Great attention is given to personal service, including a concierge available 24 hours a day. Several restaurants in the area will deliver to the inn.

Hotel Nikko Atlanta

3300 Peachtree Road, N.E.
Atlanta, Georgia 30305
404-365-8100
800-NIKKO-US (outside Georgia)
Fax: 404-233-5686

General manager: Klaus Mennekes
Accommodations: 440 rooms, including 22 suites (all with
   private baths)
Rates: $165–$1,200
Included: Continental breakfast and afternoon cocktails with
   hors d'oeuvres on concierge floors
Payment: Major credit cards
Children: Welcome
Pets: Not allowed
Smoking: Nonsmoking rooms available
Open: Year-round

Though the exterior of Hotel Nikko Atlanta has a classic Georgian look, the name is definitely from another place. Opened in 1991 in the Buckhead area, Hotel Nikko Atlanta is the city's first all-Japanese hotel — a veritable showcase for Japanese art, food, furniture, and horticulture. The hotel's art collection includes 125 paintings, sculptures, ceramics, and paper works, representing 43 different artists and spanning three and a half centuries. (Pick up a guide and take the self-guided tour.)

The Japanese theme is carried even further in the three-level garden with its 45-foot waterfall. Kamogawa, one of two restaurants in the hotel, offers authentic Japanese cuisine and private dining in its tatami rooms. (By contrast, Cassis serves French cuisine, and afternoon tea in the lobby lounge is definitely British.) The hotel also a Japanese suite where you take off your shoes at the door, don your kimono, and then relax in a totally Japanese atmosphere. Most rooms in the hotel have standard beds.

There is an emphasis on the business traveler here. The business center offers full secretarial services, and the hotel can accommodate up to a thousand people. For the exercise-minded, the fitness center and outdoor pool offer ways to relax.

The Ritz-Carlton Atlanta
181 Peachtree St., N.E.
Atlanta, Georgia 30303
404-659-0400
800-241-3333
Fax: 404-659-7821

General manager: Paul Giovanini
Accommodations: 447 rooms and 24 suites (all with private baths)
Rates: $150–$685
Included: Complimentary food and beverages on the Club floors
Payment: Major credit cards
Children: Welcome
Pets: Not allowed
Smoking: Nonsmoking rooms available
Open: Year-round

A sister to the Ritz-Carlton Buckhead, this downtown glass and marble property is just as impeccable in its ambience and service. Much of the hotel's character, even its name, is patterned after the Ritz-Carlton, Boston, which was purchased by W. B. Johnson Properties, Inc., in 1983, the year before this property opened.

Compared with other downtown hotels, known for their vast, multi-story atrium lobbies, the 25-story Ritz-Carlton Atlanta appears small and unassuming but is the most elegant hotel around. Dark mahogany public interiors, Oriental carpets, and fine traditional furnishings create an intimate, comfortable setting, much like a quiet den where you might gather with friends. Fresh flowers (about 2,500 daily), original art, and fine silver and china add to the atmosphere.

The Ritz-Carlton Atlanta is also known for its outstanding food, including Sunday brunch, considered one of the city's best. The Restaurant, one of only four four-star, four-diamond restaurants in the state, serves international delicacies such as scallop raviolis with fine herbs and mushrooms, guinea hen supreme with crème fraiche and Calvados, and Grand Marnier chocolate torte. Food is also available in the Café, which offers menu selections for the fitness conscious, and the Bar, where you may order from the Gold Medal wine list. In the Café, the chef Efrem Cutler will create an individualized five-to seven-course meal upon request for about $40 per person, or guests may choose his three-course dinner for around $30. It's considered the "best dining value in Atlanta." The Lobby Lounge is the setting for the complimentary Continental breakfast, afternoon tea, and evening cocktails; a pianist entertains throughout the day.

The hotel offers concierge service and room service 24 hours a day, valet parking, safety deposit boxes, and other amenities. Special services such as secretarial help, portable typewriters, and international telex and fax are geared to the business traveler. The executive fitness center, open daily, offers massage therapy and personalized fitness programs.

The rooms are special as well, with extras such as marble bathrooms, refreshment cabinets, plush terrycloth robes, fresh flowers, and maid service twice a day. In keeping with the classic style of the hotel, they are furnished in 18th-and 19th-century reproductions. The 24th and 25th floors of the hotel are Club floors, accessible by elevator key only. The concierge staff provides a Continental breakfast, light lunch, afternoon tea, evening hors d'oeuvres, and late night cordials and chocolates. The Presidential Suite and the Ritz-Carlton Suite, with its baby grand piano, are located here.

While rates at the Ritz-Carlton Atlanta may seem a little steep, weekend packages are very affordable and offer good value. The basic Refresher package is $99 and includes the room and valet parking; the Special Occasion Celebration package for $169 includes the room, champagne and truffles, a gourmet breakfast, and valet parking.

The Ritz-Carlton Buckhead

3434 Peachtree Road, N.E.
Atlanta, Georgia 30326
404-237-2700
800-241-3333
Fax: 404-239-0078

General manager: Ed Staros
Accommodations: 524 rooms and 29 suites (all with private baths)
Rates: $149–$685
Included: Complimentary food and beverages on the Club floor
Payment: Major credit cards
Children: Ritz-Kids program offering special foods, amenities, and services
Pets: Not allowed
Smoking: Nonsmoking rooms available
Open: Year-round

Very few hotels have their own symphony orchestra, art curator, and food and wine university, not to mention a recycling program that has been adopted by all other hotels in the company. The Ritz-Carlton Buckhead does; perhaps that's why it's the flagship of the company and rated as one of the top twenty hotels in the world. Built in 1984, the hotel is one of two Ritz-Carltons in the Atlanta area and one of several worldwide. It is also a member of Leading Hotels of the World. The entire chain takes its name from the Ritz-Carlton, Boston, purchased by W. B. Johnson Properties of Atlanta in 1983.

From the moment of arrival until departure, guests feel they are special, for service is the watchword. Horst M. Schulze, president of the company, has developed a training program that stresses the importance of perfect service, and he hires employees with no hotel experience so they can be properly trained. They must learn how to set and wait tables, be hospitable and friendly rather than arrogant, address guests properly by name, and say things such as "Good morning" and "My pleasure." Schulze often reminds his staff that they are "ladies and gentlemen on stage." Every service imaginable has been thought of and offered—from international currency exchange to concierge.

The public rooms of the 22-story hotel, with its tiered bay windows, are exquisitely done. The walls of the lobby feature Honduras mahogany moldings and African Sappele hardwood paneling; the floors are Italian Botticino classic white marble with inlaid Continental mahogany marble from Tennessee. There are cut-crystal chandeliers from Europe and sparkling wall sconces. The rooms are furnished in classic 18th-and 19th-century styles and include works of art from the hotel's outstanding collection. Art tours are scheduled regularly. The Ritz-Carlton also has five Steinway grand pianos, often used for special concerts at the hotel.

The rooms at the Ritz-Carlton Buckhead are impeccable. Among the special features are Brunschweig & Fils fabrics used in the window treatments and bedspreads, marble baths, terry-cloth robes, full toiletries, twice-a-day maid service, and other luxuries. Guests in the suites and on the Club level are given hair dryers and shoeshine service. Of course, nightly turndown service is always offered. Guests also may take advantage of the 60-foot indoor lap pool and the fitness center.

Food is given the utmost attention by the Ritz-Carlton Buckhead staff. The hotel is the only one in the chain and the only hotel in America to have a Michelin chef. Guenter Seeger presides in the hotel's main dining room, where meals are presented on the Ritz-Carlton china, complemented by the blue cobalt glassware that has become a trademark of the hotel. Menus are handwritten each day. (Grits at the Ritz are delicious!) The Café offers all-day dining, including "fitness cuisine." Food is also available in the Bar, and afternoon tea is always served in the Lobby Lounge. Sunday brunches are very popular.

Throughout the year the hotel stages special events for the enjoyment of guests. In July the hotel pulls out all the stops to celebrate the Fourth. Another time the focus might be on the Vidalia onion. Mozart is celebrated in March. Shopping is always a big pastime, with the hotel's convenient location to Lenox Square and Phipps Plaza.

Stouffer Waverly Hotel
2450 Galleria Parkway
Atlanta, Georgia 30339
404-953-4500
800-HOTELS-1
Fax: 404-953-0740

General manager: Joe Guilbault
Accommodations: 521 rooms and 24 suites (all with private
  baths)
Rates: $170–$1,200
Payment: Major credit cards
Children: Welcome
Pets: Not allowed
Smoking: Nonsmoking rooms available
Open: Year-round

Whether or not you spend the night at the Stouffer Waverly, you should try the Sunday brunch, the largest in Georgia and voted "Atlanta's Best" by several local publications. Between 600 and 1,000 people show up every week, and as many as 3,000 dine here on holidays. The brunch, which features more than 150 different items, including eggs Benedict, wild game dishes (blackened alligator, venison, and quail with blackberry sauce), ethnic specialties, seafood, French pastries, gourmet ice cream, and complimentary champagne, is served over the entire marble-tiled lobby. A musical trio provides entertainment. Children under age 12 are given their own space in the Lobby Bar during the Sunday event.

The four-diamond Stouffer Waverly Hotel has also become quite famous for its big band Friday night dances, held in the atrium lobby between 7 P.M. and 10 P.M. and open to singles and couples. For about $10, one enjoys dancing, hors d'oeuvres, champagne and $3 off the Friday night Brasserie Buffet—a deal that's hard to find elsewhere in town.

There are six restaurants on the property, including the Waverly Grill, which is known for its prime aged beef and fresh seafood, and the New York–style deli Alfresco, open 24 hours a day. And can you think of a better way to wake up than with a pot of fresh coffee and a newspaper delivered to your door immediately after your wake-up call? The hotel also provides nightly turndown service upon request.

If you stay on the Club floor, expect even more extras—a concierge staff on hand to serve the complimentary Continental breakfast, afternoon tea with petits fours, evening hors d'oeuvres, and coffee. The lounge is stocked with all kinds of reading material and has a large-screen TV. Rooms on the Club floor feature mini-bars, bathrobes, electric shoe buffers, hair dryers, and other amenities.

Rooms on the other floors are very spacious and have a residential look. Each one has a sitting area and is well equipped with telephones, television options, and in-room movies. All the rooms and suites, as well as several meeting rooms, have been renovated within the last three years. The Presidential Suite, which Ronald Reagan stayed on two occasions when he was president, has been completely refurbished. It yields seven rooms, including a living room and a master bathroom with a two-person Jacuzzi. The carpet in the foyer of this ultimate suite features the presidential seal, and space has been allocated for the Secret Service.

The recent renovation also added several pieces of art to the hotel's outstanding $6 million collection, established by Trammell Crow, a real estate developer and art aficionado, when he opened the property in 1983. The new additions include works by southeastern and Georgian artists. The centerpiece of the lobby is a collection of sixteen hand-carved teakwood bells, each seven feet tall.

As for recreational options, there are plenty. The hotel has both an outdoor pool and an indoor pool with a whirlpool, racquetball courts, a fully equipped exercise room, steam room, sauna, aerobics studio, and other amenities, not to mention the health lounge with its snack bar and wide-screen TV. You can also get a massage at the hotel.

The hotel offers a number of special weekend packages designed around romance, dancing, and the Sunday brunch. Regular weekend rates are considerably less than the standard weekday rates.

Near Marietta and about 11 miles from downtown Atlanta, Stouffer Waverly Hotel is the focal point of the Atlanta Galleria shopping and office complex. Construction on Galleria Centre, a convention complex, is scheduled for completion in early 1994.

Swissotel Atlanta
3391 Peachtree Road, N.E.
Atlanta, Georgia 30326
404-365-0065
800-637-9477
Fax: 404-365-8787

Owner: Swissair and Ackerman and Company
Accommodations: 348 rooms (all with private baths) and 17
  suites (some with Jacuzzis, fireplaces, and full kitchens)
Rates: $170–$900
Included: Continental breakfast, afternoon tea, and hors
  d'oeuvres provided on concierge floors
Payment: All major credit cards
Children: two children under 17 years free with parents
Pets: $50 deposit charged for small pets
Smoking: Nonsmoking rooms available
Open: Year-round

Opened in 1991, Swissotel Atlanta adds another international
dimension to the South's largest city. The first European hotel
in Atlanta, the ultramodern 21-story high-rise is in Buckhead,
the city's most affluent neighborhood, and overlooks Lenox
Square, Peachtree and Georgia 400, and the Atlanta skyline.
The Bauhaus architecture features white porcelainlike tiles
with blue granite accents and an all-glass facade. The marble
lobby is 45 feet high, and its focal point is the Grand Staircase
leading to the mezzanine and grand ballroom.

Designed for the business traveler, the guest rooms feature
Beidermeier-style furniture, purple and red color schemes,
three telephones with call waiting, in-house movies, mini-bars,
and extra-large desks. Gucci amenities are used in all rooms.
The hotel also has a business and communications center and
several meeting rooms. Guests staying on the concierge floors
(21 and 22) receive a Continental breakfast, afternoon snack
and tea, hors d'oeuvres, desserts, and cordials. The Presidential
Suite, encompassing 2,300 square feet, has two bedrooms, an
outdoor patio with Jacuzzi, a full kitchen, two fireplaces, a
music room, and a boardroom.

Guests have two dining options—the casual Café Gamay
and the more upscale Opus, famous for its whole wheat rolls
and varied Continental dishes. There are also a piano bar and
lounge, health and fitness club, indoor pool, sauna, steam bath,
gym, and sundeck.

Swissotel Atlanta is a joint venture of Swissair and Ackerman
and Company, an Atlanta real estate development company. In
the hotel business since 1980, Swissair owns thirteen properties
worldwide.

Austin

Doubletree Hotel
6505 I-35 North
Austin, Texas 78752
512-454-3737
800-528-0444
Fax: 512-454-6915

General manager: Carl McKee
Accommodations: 335 rooms and 15 suites
Rates: $125; double, $145; suites, $350
Added: 13% tax
Payment: Major credit cards
Children: Free in room with parents
Pets: Not allowed
Smoking: Nonsmoking rooms available
Open: Year-round

A Spanish colonial–style lodging built in 1984 on the northern edge of Austin, the Doubletree has quiet charm. Its focal point is a peaceful inner courtyard with waterfalls, fountains, and a swimming pool shaped like a shell. Nearly half of its guest rooms open onto galleries overlooking the courtyard— sanctuary from the bustling city beyond.

The rooms are spacious and comfortably furnished. Some have French doors opening onto small balconies. All have dressing areas next to the bathroom and bath telephones. Two styles of suites are on the premier floor, where guests are pampered with Continental breakfast and afternoon cocktails. All guests are treated to fresh chocolate chip cookies the night they arrive.

The second-floor fitness room has a sauna and exercise equipment. In addition to the outdoor pool, there's a whirlpool spa.

The hotel's restaurant is the plant-filled Courtyard Café, which looks out onto the garden. The menu runs from seafood to steak, and dinner entrées range from $8 to $20. Dover's Lounge is a cozy bar with overstuffed chairs and a large stone fireplace.

Guest parking in the hotel's garage is free. Complimentary transportation is offered to both the airport and downtown Austin. And on top of the hotel is a heliport for quick arrivals and departures.

The Driskill Hotel
604 Brazos
Austin, Texas 78701
512-474-5911
800-223-0888
Fax: 512-474-2188

General manager: Mike Kolanek
Accommodations: 177 rooms and suites
Rates: $109–$119; double, $119–$129; suites, $200–$500
Added: 13% tax
Payment: Major credit cards
Children: Under 18 free in room with parents
Pets: Not allowed
Smoking: Nonsmoking rooms available
Open: Year-round

Built in 1886 by a Texas cattle baron, the Driskill is an architectural treasure, with an immense arched entrance and ornamented balconies. Its history is intertwined with that of the Lone Star State. Walk through its doors and you know you're in Texas. Above the registration desk hangs a portrait of Colonel Jesse L. Driskill, watching over his creation. In the lobby, there is a massive bronze sculpture depicting a dramatic moment in the lives of two cowboys. Portraits of the state's governors line the walls of the handsome lobby bar, and LBJ often made the hotel his campaign headquarters.

Throughout, there's a feeling of openness and space, a fitting style for a hostelry that is Texas to the core. The guest rooms occupy two connecting buildings: the 1880s hotel, with high ceilings and several room configurations, and the 1930s tower, with lower ceilings and a more uniform room design.

All the rooms are spacious and tastefully decorated, with touches of grandeur such as border designs on the walls and crystal drawer pulls on the period furniture. The baths in the tower rooms have an adjacent dressing area.

One of the hotel's banquet rooms is designed around eight mirrors framed in gold leaf—the wedding gift of Mexico's Maximilian to his bride, the Empress Carlotta of Belgium. At the top of each mirror is a gilt medallion likeness of the empress, said to be the most beautiful woman in Europe.

Guests may use a health club across the street whose facilities include a workout area with Universal and Nautilus equipment, racquetball courts, a lap pool, a whirlpool, and a sauna.

The Driskill Dining Room, romantically decorated with mirrors and a carved white ceiling, serves nouvelle American cuisine with a southwestern bent.

In the heart of downtown Austin, the Driskill opens onto Sixth Street, a lively entertainment area with restaurants, bars, and specialty shops. Sightseeing trolleys stop right in front of the hotel. The Driskill is also just a few blocks from the capitol and the University of Texas.

Four Seasons Hotel Austin
99 San Jacinto Boulevard
Austin, Texas 78701
512-478-4500
800-332-3442
Fax: 512-477-0704

General manager: Tom Kelly
Accommodations: 292 units
Rates: $148–$168; double, $168–$190; suites start at $200
Added: 13% tax
Payment: Major credit cards
Children: Free in room with parents
Pets: Small ones on leash accepted
Smoking: Nonsmoking rooms available
Open: Year-round

On the shores of Town Lake, ten blocks south of the capitol, the Four Seasons Austin is a first-class hotel with a southwestern flair. Opened in 1987, it's a bright new star in the capital, setting a new standard for downtown lodgings.

Outside the entrance, lifelike statues of a gardener bending over a flowerbed, a fresh pot of flowers in his hand, and a businessman absorbed by the daily newspaper (and it will be that day's paper) warrant a second look. The lobby, with a stone fireplace and leather chairs, suggests the home of a wealthy rancher instead of a city hotel. Southwestern art, tastefully arranged, adds to the residential feeling.

Luxury is the tone here, with touches like terrycloth robes and hair dryers, pressing within the hour, and maid service twice a day. More important, the staff is genuinely friendly and eager to please. The guest rooms are attractive, decorated in soft earth tones. Although not especially large, they offer comfort with such conveniences as three phones and digital clocks. "Four Seasons" rooms are more like suites than standard hotel rooms.

The hotel's lakeside setting is used to full advantage. It is so serene, it's almost like being in a private park. Whether you're eating in the café, lounging by the pool, or working out in the health club, the lake is the focal point. Jogging trails line its banks. The health club is far above average, with good exercise machines, nicely appointed locker rooms, saunas, and a whirl-pool.

The Riverside Café, at lake level, serves new American cuisine with southwestern and Cajun influences. There's an emphasis on robust sauces, freshness, and innovative combinations. Dinner entrées range from $15.50 to $22.50. Lunch buffets are served upstairs in the Lobby Lounge.

Self-service parking is free; valet parking is also available at $8 per day.

Lake Austin Resort
1705 Quinlan Park Road
Austin, Texas 78732
512-266-2444
800-847-5637
Fax: 512-266-1572

Executive director: Deborah Evans
Accommodations: 40 units
Rates: 4-day fitness program, $500–$640; 1-week program, $875–$1,120; 10-and 14-day programs available
Included: All meals
Minimum stay: 4 nights
Added: 6% tax and a $22 per day service charge
Payment: Major credit cards
Children: Allowed during family weeks only
Pets: Not allowed
Smoking: Nonsmoking rooms available
Open: Year-round

On the shores of Lake Austin just outside Texas's capital, there's a spa dedicated to fitness education and conditioning. Its atmosphere is unpretentious and friendly; its program is comprehensive. The program includes exercise, nutrition, wellness classes, and beauty services. In a peaceful setting and with personal attention, participants work to achieve their goals, especially weight loss and a more healthful lifestyle, with the help of a physical fitness staff, a dietitian, and an exercise physiologist.

Guests can choose from twenty daily workouts, including hill country walks, low to high power aerobics, and an 18-station Swiss Parcourse. Classes on such subjects as relaxation, skin care, and nutrition are integral to the program. For relaxation as well as exercise, there's an outdoor and an indoor pool, a jogging track, paddleboats, and shuffleboard. All exercise facilities are available around the clock.

The guest rooms, in a low building facing the lake, have two double beds, TVs, and phones. The dining room is pleasant and casual. Guests are served a thousand-calorie-per-day menu. The emphasis is on wholesome food, featuring fresh vegetables and herbs grown at the resort. For those wishing to continue their healthful eating habits at home, the resort sells its own cookbook, with more than 450 low-fat recipes.

Pampering services, available at an extra charge, include skin analysis and facials, massages, manicures, and hair and skin treatments. Special spa packages are offered throughout the year.

Lakeway Inn
101 Lakeway Drive
Austin, Texas 78734
512-261-6600
800-LAKEWAY
Fax: 512-261-7322

General manager: Toby June
Accommodations: 138 units
Rates: $130–$160; suites, $140–$170; weekend packages available
Included: Breakfast
Added: 6% tax
Payment: Major credit cards
Children: Free in room with parents
Pets: Not allowed
Smoking: Allowed
Open: Year-round

On cliffs overlooking Lake Travis about 20 miles west of Austin, Lakeway Inn is at the center of a huge resort and residential community. There are many recreational choices here—two 18-hole championship golf courses, a marina with lots of boats for rent (fishing, sailing, ski, pontoon, and deck boats), 32 tennis courts (the renowned World of Tennis Club), horseback riding on 25 miles of trails, and several swimming pools.

The guest rooms and suites are spread out in low buildings near the main lodge or in two-to four-bedroom villas next to the World of Tennis complex (about a 5-minute drive from the lodge). Single bedrooms or bedrooms joined by parlors (you can rent one to three segments of a unit) are very spacious and modern, with private balconies overlooking the lake. Many have big stone fireplaces. The villas have fully equipped kitchens and fireplaces. Each cluster of villas has its own tennis court, supplementing the complex a few hundred yards away. There's a dining room and lounge at the main lodge and at the World of Tennis.

Some sample fees are: greens fees for 18 holes of golf, $44–$50; cart rental, $20 for shared use; tennis at Lakeway Tennis Center, $15 per day, per court, per player; World of Tennis courts, $20 per hour (indoor); fishing boat, $18 per hour; fishing boat with guide, $120 per half day; ski boat, $72 per hour with driver; pontoon boat with a 12-person capacity, $54 per hour; sailboat, $18 per hour; horseback riding, $15 per hour; parasailing, $35 per person per trip. For children aged 5 to 12, there's a supervised day camp during the summer with sports, nature walks, movies, and arts and crafts. The daily fee, $25, includes lunch, a camp T-shirt, and all camp activities.

Southard House

908 Blanco
Austin, Texas 78703
512-474-4731

Innkeepers: Jerry and Regina Southard
Accommodations: 5 rooms (all with private bath)
Rates: $49–$79; double, $59–$89; suites, $119–$129
Included: Continental breakfast on weekdays, full breakfast on weekends; beverages available
Minimum stay: Two nights on special Austin weekends
Added: 13% tax
Payment: Major credit cards
Children: Under 12 not allowed

Pets: Not allowed
Smoking: Prohibited
Open: Year-round

On a quiet, tree-lined residential street just minutes from downtown Austin, Southard House is an attractive 100-year-old Greek Revival and Victorian structure with large, inviting front porches. Inside, it is warmly furnished with antiques and original artwork by one of the owners.

The guest rooms have white wrought-iron beds with brass accents and are covered with elegant lace bedspreads and a profusion of pillows trimmed in lace. Antique washbasins, mirrored wardrobes, clawfoot tubs, wicker chairs, ceiling fans, sheer lace curtains, and flowered wallpaper give the rooms a Victorian flavor. The Treaty Oak Room Suite has a sitting room with a foldout sofa, TV, refrigerator, telephone, and fireplace.

On weekends, guests can expect breakfast dishes such as Belgian waffles with raspberry sauce, eggs Benedict with chile-hollandaise sauce, and a crustless quiche. During the week, Continental breakfasts consist of cereal, fresh fruit, and homemade cinnamon rolls and breads. Although generally served in the dining room, which has an interesting dragon chandelier, the morning meal moves to the pleasant outdoor gazebo in nice weather.

Off-street parking is available free of charge, and complimentary wines, juices, and soft drinks are also served. Southard House offers a Honeymoon Delight package.

Stouffer Austin Hotel
9721 Arboretum Boulevard
Austin, Texas 78759
512-343-2626
800-HOTELS-1
Fax: 512-346-7953

General manager: Jacques Van Seters
Accommodations: 478 units
Rates: $99–$169; double, $99–$189; suites start at $195
Added: 13% tax
Payment: Major credit cards
Children: Free in room with parents
Pets: Not allowed
Smoking: Nonsmoking rooms available
Open: Year-round

In the rolling countryside north of downtown, 15 minutes from the capitol, the Stouffer Austin is a retreat from the city yet near many business addresses, notably the high-tech companies for which Austin is now known. The hotel is part of the Arboretum, a 95-acre development with fancy shops and restaurants as well as sleek office towers. The entire complex sits on a hillside overlooking the Texas hill country, with its cedar forests and limestone cliffs.

An atrium-style hotel, the Stouffer has a distinctive look. At its center is an expansive marble plaza with sculptures, dining kiosks, and sitting areas. Large teak bells hang from above while bronze birds, remarkably lifelike, appear to soar overhead. Natural plants surround the atrium on every level.

The Pavilion, in the center of the atrium, serves deli sandwiches, salads, fruit, pastries, and beverages around the clock. The Garden Café serves breakfast and lunch, with a pianist to entertain at noontime. On one side is the Trattoria Grande, a northern Italian bistro with excellent food and service. Arched windows offer unobstructed views of the scenic terrain. The lobby bar has live entertainment in the evenings.

The guest rooms, decorated in subtle greens and beiges with Queen Anne furniture and Oriental art, are luxurious and large (some of the largest in the city). Many of the rooms have pastoral valley views. Atrium suites have small balconies opening onto the atrium, mini-bars, and separate sitting areas. Conference suites have beds that fold out of sight so that meetings can be held at the suite's own boardroom table. Guests on the private-access Club Floor enjoy concierge services from 6:30 A.M. to

10:00 P.M., complimentary breakfast, evening hors d'oeuvres, a lounge bar, and bathrobes and shoe polishers in their rooms. For luxury, the Presidential Suite is truly royal. Chinese palace lions guard the entrance. Inside, giant Oriental vases hold citrus and palm trees. Original oil paintings line the walls, and expansive windows provide a fine view. There's a full kitchen and a separate dining room that seats ten, but perhaps the most sumptuous room of all is the bath. A small Sony TV with microcassette recorder lets you watch your favorite program or dictate notes from the double Jacuzzi tub set in marble. The fixtures are all brass, and the satin-lined antique wooden vanity case, fully stocked, adds a special touch.

All guests are treated to complimentary coffee, a newspaper, and the daily weather report with their wake-up call. Other amenities include 24-hour room service, free parking, and free transportation to the airport, about 20 minutes away. Valet parking is available at the cost of $7 per day.

For relaxation, there's an especially wide range of choices for a city hotel — an oval outdoor pool (with an appealing hillside setting), an indoor pool, a sauna, hot tub, game room, well-equipped exercise room, jogging path, short nature trail, and picnic tables tucked among the trees. A separate elevator takes guests to the pool area; both pools are heated.

Next door are the upscale Arboretum shops, which range from Banana Republic to fancy boutiques, a four-screen movie theater, and the hotel's club, Tangerines.

Wyndham Austin Hotel at Southpark

4140 Governor's Row
Austin, Texas 78744
512-448-2222
800-433-2241
Fax: 512-448-4744

General manager: Dave Hansen
Accommodations: 313 rooms and suites
Rates: $119; double, $129; suites start at $350
Added: 13% tax
Payment: Major credit cards
Children: Under 18 free in room with parents
Pets: Allowed, with deposit
Smoking: 66 nonsmoking rooms
Open: Year-round

South of downtown Austin, the Wyndham Austin Hotel has a relaxing atmosphere, outstanding recreational features, and a hospitable staff. The 14-story hotel, opened in 1983, has a contemporary design. Just outside the lobby is an indoor-outdoor pool (shaped like a horseshoe) and recreation area. A bridge leads across the pool into the fitness center, which has an attractive deck, whirlpool, sauna, and weight and exercise room. Nearby is the hotel's sports court (basketball or volleyball), jogging track, and shuffleboard.

The rooms have luxurious, modern furnishings—rich fabrics, plush carpeting, and colorful artwork. Comfortable seating, TVs with in-house movies, and digital clock radios add to the pleasure. Some of the ground-floor rooms open out onto the pool. The Executive suites have a parlor with a conference table, a sitting area with a foldout couch, and one or two connecting bedrooms. Both the Presidential and the Governor's suites have a large parlor and two bedrooms; the former has a whirlpool tub.

Onion Creek Grill, a casual dining room, has all-day service. Pasta and pizza are featured, as well as steak and seafood. Sweetwaters Lounge is the hotel's friendly bar.

Airport transportation and hotel parking are free.

Baltimore

Admiral Fell Inn
Fell's Point, 888 South Broadway
Baltimore, Maryland 21231
410-522-7377
800-292-INNS
Fax: 522-0707

General manager: Dominik Eckenstein
Accommodations: 38 rooms, 4 with Jacuzzi
Rates: $105–$125
Included: Continental breakfast, free off-street parking
Minimum stay: None
Added: $10 each additional guest
Payment: Major credit cards
Children: Welcome
Pets: Not allowed
Smoking: Nonsmoking rooms available
Open: Year-round

With the intimacy and originality of a bed-and-breakfast and the sophistication of a luxury hotel, the Admiral Fell Inn is a unique property that epitomizes the rich history of its Fell's Point neighborhood. The inn sits on the oblique corner of South Broadway and Thames Street, with an unobstructed view of the historic waterfront docks. A microcosm of its eclectic neighborhood, the Admiral Fell comprises four joined buildings that were built between 1720 and 1910: the northernmost, the oldest, was the home of Baltimore's first mayor; the second is a three-story red brick building with a cast-iron Victorian facade; and the two that stand in between them are four tall stories with Georgian detailing in red brick. In former lives, some of these buildings served as the Anchorage Hotel, a YMCA, and a vinegar bottling plant. The buildings were vacant between the mid-1970s and 1984, when the property was bought with the intent of creating a deluxe country inn.

Decorated with period reproductions and occasional antiques, the rooms are an intriguing array of shapes and sizes, so be sure to inquire thoroughly. Some are large with harbor views; others are small or have odd angles. The double beds have fishnet canopies on four-poster rice beds; king-size beds have crown canopies that fall from ceiling moldings. There are always two telephones, a writing desk, and ample lighting. Often a television is hidden in an armoire. Either the walls or the trim is painted in traditional Williamsburg rusts, yellows, or greens, and the rooms are decorated with floral or period prints that pick up the tones of the carpet.

Guests entering from the corner find a pleasant foyer with seating areas on either side. To the right is a reception desk and a lovely forest green paneled fireplace, with faux marble, which reaches to the crown molding. Comfortable sofas and chairs gather by hunting and sailing prints on the walls. Visitors relax here, in the atrium, the brick courtyard in the quiet back of the inn, or in the heart pine–floored library, where they serve Continental breakfast. Guests will be grateful for the proximity of the fine restaurant on the lower level and for its separate entrance. The several rooms include a cozy pub with a tartan rug, a dining room with exposed brick walls, and another with exposed stone walls. The low ceiling lends a romance to the setting. Lunch and dinner are served daily, brunch on Sundays. The dinner entrées range from $15 to $21, and a sample meal might come as follows: crab, corn, and jalapeño bisque; an appetizer of baby crabcakes; and an entrée of pork tenderloin, rack of New Zealand baby lamb, or swordfish tropique served with pineapple-mango salsa; all followed by a long list of desserts.

The Admiral Fell is a busy place in the heart of a busy neighborhood—which gets quite lively on weekends—with surprisingly friendly service.

Ann Street Bed and Breakfast

804 South Street
Baltimore, Maryland 21231
410-342-5883

Proprietors: Joanne and Andrew Mazurek
Accommodations: 3 rooms, including 1 suite, all with private bath, 2 with fireplace
Rates: $75–$85
Included: Full breakfast
Minimum stay: None
Added: $15 each additional guest; 12% tax

Payment: No credit cards
Children: Check with innkeeper
Pets: Not allowed
Smoking: Prohibited
Open: Year-round

For those ardent bed-and-breakfasters who have come as far as Baltimore's Fell's Point for a taste of history, the Ann Street Bed and Breakfast will authenticate the experience. Just around the corner from harborfront Thames Street is the Mazurek home, opened to overnight guests in 1988. Theirs is a beautiful marriage of two colonial houses, mirror images in brick, four windows across, with dormer windows peeking out from the fourth-floor rooftop, centered with a tall chimney that services an incredible twelve working fireplaces.

The houses were built in the 1790s, and Joanne and Andrew have decorated faithfully, using Williamsburg trim, pewter light fixtures, dried wreaths, candles on the windowsills, and 18th-century reproduction furniture where they could not find antiques. What cannot be seen from the street is the charming backyard, a small garden with patio furniture accessible to guests.

The left house is devoted entirely to guests. The dining room is the fireside setting for the large breakfasts, which include a hot entrée. The common room is furnished in primitive country decor and also is warmed by the fireplace. The accommodations are on the second floor. The suite has a sitting room with a blue-checked sofa bed and blue wing chairs, and the wall is enlivened by an antique quilt. The trim is traditional green and maroon. The other guest room is furnished with a crewel wing chair and a four-poster fishnet curved canopy bed.

The right house, which is also the Mazureks' home, has one large guest room that is quite notable not for its antique rope bed but for the impressive bath, with a working cast-iron fireplace and whitewashed brick walls. Most striking is the cleanliness of the rooms, including the wide-planked original pine floors and the original mantels in deep Williamsburg colors. Flannel sheets and antique quilts dress up the beds.

While the accommodations in the Mazurek home might seem intimate, the other house offers a great deal of independence. The young couple is ever present to answer questions and recommend activities, yet they are respectful of their guests' privacy. This is a wonderful home for bed-and-breakfast enthusiasts: historic, immaculate, and very pretty.

Celie's Waterfront Bed and Breakfast

1714 Thames Street
Baltimore, Maryland 21231
410-522-2323

Proprietor: Celie Ives
Accommodations: 7 rooms, all with private bath
Rates: $95–$140; handicapped-accessible room, $85
Included: Continental breakfast
Minimum stay: 2 nights in some rooms on weekends
Added: $12 tax
Payment: Major credit cards
Children: Age 10 and over welcome
Pets: Not allowed
Smoking: Not allowed indoors
Open: Year-round

Celie Ives opened a single room in her private home to overnight guests several years ago and liked the bed-and-breakfast business so much that she decided to expand. Around the corner from her Fell's Point home, she built an old-looking new Federal rowhouse on cobblestoned Thames Street, which would be right across from the water but for the Fells Point Recreation Center, which sits just opposite. Her three-story inn, opened in February 1990, is gray brick with wine-colored trim and old detailing, quite a complementary addition to its historic neighbors.

While many a bed-and-breakfast is characterized by old moldings, Victoriana, and slanted wood floors, Celie's is a fresh haven of clean lines, cream-colored walls, low nap carpeting, and traditional antiques and furnishings. There is some historic detailing, for example, three wood-burning fireplaces, built-in bookshelves, mullioned windows, French doors, and window seats. These are done in crisp, contemporary comfort.

The first floor comprises the neat-as-a-pin living room and a tiled breakfast room where guests enjoy freshly squeezed orange juice and baked goods in the morning. In warmer months, the French doors of the breakfast room open to the brick patio, furnished with wrought-iron café tables. There is a handicapped-accessible room on the first floor and three rooms on each of the two upper floors.

Celie is adamant about down comforters, cotton linens, full bath sheets (not towels), and fresh flowers. The finest room is the third-floor king suite, with a fireplace and a whirlpool bath, which overlooks the harbor from three large mullioned windows topped by chintz swags and underscored by a long window seat filled with cushions. The king-size bed has a crown canopy. The room directly below shares the same view; two rooms have views of the back gardens, and two more face the atrium in the middle of the house. All the rooms are decorated in light colors, with soft-bordered beige duvets, a single-color trim, alcoves with refrigerators and coffeemakers, and sparkling new baths.

Celie is a gregarious hostess who heartily enjoys her guests and sharing her knowledge of Baltimore and the historic neighborhood of Fell's Point.

The Harbor Court Hotel
550 Light Street
Baltimore, Maryland 21202
410-234-0550
800-824-0076

Proprietor: David H. Murdock
General manager: Werner R. Kunz
Accommodations: 178 rooms, 25 suites
Rates: $165–$210; suites, from $235
Added: $15 each additional guest; 12% tax
Payment: Major credit cards
Children: Welcome
Pets: Not allowed
Smoking: One nonsmoking floor
Open: Year-round

Since the summer of 1985, Baltimore's premier hotel has been the Harbor Court. It was built shortly after owner David Murdock completed the restoration of the gorgeous Hay-Adams Hotel in Washington, DC. His wife, Gabriele, fresh from her work designing the Hay-Adams, conceived of the Harbor Court's interior design. Not only is the Harbor Court stunningly appointed with unusual Old World antiques and beautiful accommodations, but it is magnificently located.

The hotel shares its Inner Harbor waterfront location with the Baltimore Science Center, shop-filled Harborplace, and the National Aquarium, and it is within a short walk of the business district and the Baltimore Convention Center.

The seven-story brick building has a dignified, postmodern exterior, the second floor an array of floor-to-ceiling arched windows under which billowing flags mark the entrance. Cars drive into a courtyard that encircles a fountain. Through the entrance is the sweeping lobby, its marble floor inlaid with red and green geometric marble. The marble used extensively throughout the hotel was excavated from eleven countries. Circular tables and urns, between overstuffed armchairs, are adorned with floral arrangements.

Two stories above, a brass chandelier hangs from a round mural of ivy, approached by a grand red-carpeted circular staircase. Follow this to the second-floor Explorer's Lounge and the Harbor Court's luxurious restaurant, Hampton's. The Explorer's Lounge decor was inspired by safari and African themes: huge murals of an elephant and monkeys grace the walls, and architectural drawings and African sculpture catch one's eye. Above the crown molding, the ceiling is painted brightly. Plants suggest the feel of the tropics, though the overwhelming elegance rests in the classic furnishings.

Taking advantage of the floor-to-ceiling windows trimmed in combed wood, Hampton's restaurant provides postcard views of the Inner Harbor. Columns, exposed ceiling beams, and crown molding are done in rich wood. Rust damask silk wall coverings complement the heavy drapes that frame the windows. Guests dine in modified wing chairs in a room that feels overwhelmingly English. Also the setting for a brunch that has been called Baltimore's best, Hampton's is renowned for its fine dinners. Entrées range from $18 to $37 for exotica like Cajun seared and spiced blackened buffalo served with mushroom and shallot marmalade, or grilled breast of pheasant with Michigan dried cherries and bourbon sauce. Upwards of two hundred wines are available from Hampton's extensive cellar.

Brighton's, an exceptionally cheerful garden room that shares the arched-window view of the Inner Harbor, serves lighter fare and afternoon high tea. The room has a crystal chandelier and sunny yellow walls adorned with floral prints.

Gabriele Murdock's design for the guest rooms is beautiful, reminiscent of an English country home. Those rooms blessed with a harbor view have enchanting floor-to-ceiling windows in a keyhole shape, masked by either chintz or gold drapes, offering nonpareil views. The furnishings are classic Chippendale reproduction. Most beds are king-size with a canopy, some with a beautiful Chinese pattern of yellow and beige with splashes of colors, others in a chintz on a gray backdrop. Rooms have televisions in armoires and green marble-top mini-bars. The lovely baths are the height of luxury, with marble vanities, Neutrogena amenities (including a sewing kit), telephones and televisions, and five-foot bathtubs. Fluffy robes are presented on satin hangers.

The Harbor Court has a third-floor atrium garden atop the two-story lobby. On the seventh floor, the Harbor Court Fitness Center has a heated indoor swimming pool and saunas, whirlpool, racquetball, and a tennis court. Boat cruises on the *Lady Baltimore* and the sailboat *Clipper City* leave from the dock in front of the hotel daily.

Service is outstanding at this rare, glamorous property. A stay at this sophisticated hotel is quite worth a trip in itself, simply to experience such elegance.

The Inn at the Colonnade
4 West University Parkway
Baltimore, Maryland 21218
410-235-5400
800-456-3396

Managing partners: Howard and Richard Rymland
Director of sales: Antony M. Gross
Accommodations: 125 rooms, including 36 suites
Rates: $115–$125; suites, $160–$460
Minimum stay: None
Added: $10 extra person; 12% tax
Payment: Major credit cards
Children: Welcome
Pets: Allowed
Smoking: Nonsmoking rooms available
Open: Year-round

For convenience to Johns Hopkins University with Inner Harbor elegance, Baltimore visitors stay at the Inn at the Colonnade. This new property opened in early 1990 and has already received a four diamond award from AAA. The Inn, a tall brick condominium building with two floors that accommodate hotel guests, devotes special attention to overnighters, given the personable nature of the property.

Across the street from John Hopkins's lacrosse field, the Inn sits behind a surprisingly elegant portico supported by two-story cement pillars, introducing the colonnade concept echoed throughout the property. A semicircular drive is a grand introduction. The main sitting room is lovely, octagonal with formal paneled walls made of satinwood from Sri Lanka, and a round mural overhead painted by local artist Janet Pope, suggesting the feel of an open-air rotunda and a Greek architectural influence. Underneath, the octagonal carpet, handmade in a neoclassic pattern, follows the lines of the walls. The floor is mahogany inlaid with redwood, and the columns that support the rotunda and the subsequent hallway are a burnished maple with painted capitals. To one side of the rotunda are several gift shops, a salon, and the Polo Grill. Down the hall is reception and the neoclassic elevators.

The unique and tasteful 18th-century Beidermeier-style furnishings of the guest rooms result in a commanding, masculine decor. The headboards of the beds look like pediments trimmed in black, flanked by bedstands supporting interesting neoclassic lamps in three varieties. Televisions and VCRs are tucked into Beidermeier armoires, and each room has two telephones, with a third in the bath. Luxury services include nightly turndown, room service until 1 A.M., and same-day valet. The baths are grandly appointed with floor-to-ceiling light-colored marble, brass fixtures, and Estuary amenities. Some have Jacuzzis and separate vanities outside the baths. The original artwork and architectural drawings are beautiful.

In the back courtyard is the glass-domed pool house, with deep Italian marble walls interrupted by picture windows, sparkling Tivoli lights, and two hot tubs. Below, guests may use exercise equipment and rowing machines in a newly appointed fitness room walled in pink marble.

The favorably reviewed Polo Grill offers eclectic American cuisine from chef Harold Marmulstein in an intimate setting. Entrées range from $14 to $29 and may include interesting dishes like pan-fried farm-raised Mississippi catfish in cornmeal crust with chili beurre blanc; grilled duck breast with glazed apples, oyster mushrooms, and tangerine sauce; or medallions of buffalo on potato cake, creamy wild mushrooms, amd Italian mustard fruit on peppered red wine sauce.

Inn at Government House

1125 North Calvert Street
Baltimore, Maryland
410-539-0566
Fax: 410-539-0567

Proprietor: Baltimore International Culinary College
Managing director: Mariana Palacios, assisted by Meg Daly
Rates: $100–$125
Included: Continental breakfast, high tea
Minimum stay: None
Added: 12% tax
Payment: Major credit cards

Children: Welcome
Pets: Check with manager
Smoking: Prohibited
Open: Year-round

The Inn at Government House, for years the leading property in the Society Hill Hotels, is now home to the Baltimore International Culinary College, which has another branch in Ireland, founded in 1991. Not only do guests have the privilege of staying at this magnificent house, they are also treated to fresh-baked croissants and sticky buns cooked each morning by the students, as well as an elaborate high tea.

The Government House is composed of three connecting townhouses in the elite Mount Vernon district. Dating to the 1880s, the grand corner Government House with its three-story turret was built for William Painter, the inventor of the bottle cap. Today, the Government House is where political royalty often stay or entertain. In addition to being furnished with beautiful period antiques, the house has been impeccably restored, with faux wood graining on original wood and millwork, and wood flooring patterns unique to each room. The Anglo-Japanese sitting room has a Renaissance Revival parlor set and such treasures as Ming Dynasty temple jars on bookcases. The dining room has a stunning Renaissance Revival chandelier, an electrified gasolier from 1843 with original glass shades. The ceiling paper is typical Victorian elaborate découpage in seventeen patterns. Guests may explore the Edwardian library with its unusual paneling, original marble fireplace, and stained glass windows.

The guest rooms, accessible by a luscious wood elevator or a walk up a light-filled atrium staircase, are blessed with original stained glass, woodwork, molding, some marble mantels, and unusual spaces. Certainly, two of the finer ones rest in the turret. Unusual is the lush quality of the fabrics and window treatments framing lace panels. Reproduction patterns of Victorian wallpaper decorate each room in interesting patterns. The baths are nicely updated, with bonuses like hair dryers and personalized bath grains. The Government House is notably stocked with a beautiful collection of original lithographs.

Mariana and Meg are consummate, gracious hostesses who revere this wonderful building. Guests receive a museum-type tour of the house upon check-in. As well, the innkeepers are quite enthusiastic about the school and its sister property, the Park Hotel in County Cavin, 50 miles northwest of Dublin.

The Inn at Henderson's Wharf
1000 Fell Street
Baltimore, Maryland 21231
410-522-7777
800-522-2088

General manager: Linda Lowe
Accommodations: 39 rooms, including 1 suite
Rates: $115–$125
Included: Continental breakfast, evening reception
Minimum stay: None
Added: $15 each additional guest; 12% tax
Payment: Major credit cards
Children: Welcome
Pets: Not allowed
Smoking: Prohibited
Open: Year-round

Nestled into Baltimore's Harbor, Fell's Point is a curving shore lined with historic brick buildings that date to the early 18th century. However nautical this district may be, no property in Fell's Point has water views like Henderson's Wharf. Half of the thirty-nine guest rooms look out over the water to the planked boardwalk that scurries around the harborfront. Belying its history, which is more than a century old, Henderson's Wharf opened as an inn quite recently, in the summer of 1991.

The end of cobblestoned Fell Street looks like it might tip right into the harbor, as a huge and heavy brick building sits at its peninsular tip. This is Henderson's Wharf, a seven-story pentagonal brick structure trimmed with light blue wood plank shutters. Built as a tobacco warehouse in the 19th century by the Baltimore and Ohio Railroad, Henderson's Wharf was restored in 1990–91 and placed on the National Register of Historic Places.

There are two faces to its entrance, and three more sides complete the pentagon. Visitors enter a large, long, traditionally appointed lobby dressed in French furnishings, with Oriental rugs thrown over the highly polished wood floors. One entire side is walled with mullioned French doors overlooking the formal English garden and brick patio, allowing light to sweep into the long, narrow lobby.

The guest rooms radiate from the center corridor of the lobby in several wings. Half rest around the perimeter, with views of the water through sliding doors behind floor-to-ceiling plantation shutters that are custom-made and set into a brick archway; the other rooms have views of the English garden or of cobblestoned Fell Street. Decorated in two different nonhistoric schemes of formal and country, the rooms have blue or seafoam carpeting, and all have televisions hidden in single pine or mahogany armoires. The beds are brass and black wrought-iron or oak spindle sleighs, and the wing chairs complement the bedspreads, in tapestries or black chintz. Some rooms have blanket chests and dressers painted with historic murals. The baths are elegant, with ceramic tiles, brass fixtures, and Dickens-Hawthorne amenities, including mouthwash.

Guests may take a Continental breakfast to their rooms or eat in the lobby or gardens. Service is that of a deluxe hotel, discreet and formal. Because the property is largely a condominium, overnight guests at Henderson's Wharf have a feeling of independence and privacy. Active guests may use the exercise studio. There is a 200-slip marina, and plans are under way for a dockside pool. Courtesy van or water shuttle service to the business district is provided.

Peabody Court
612 Cathedral Street
Baltimore, Maryland 21201
410-727-7107
800-732-5301

Proprietors: Grand Heritage Metropolitan
General manager: Russell Conoglio
Accommodations: 104 rooms, including 20 suites
Rates: $132–$152; suites, from $158
Added: $20 each additional guest; 12% tax

Payment: Major credit cards
Children: Welcome
Pets: Not allowed
Smoking: One of twelve floors nonsmoking
Open: Year-round

The clear choice in Baltimore for Old World elegance is the Peabody Court in the historic Mt. Vernon district. The neighborhood, marked by a 178-foot monument to George Washington, was established in 1827 and reigned as the city's most fashionable for years, evidenced today by the charming rows of restored townhouses, the world-renowned Peabody Conservatory of Music, and the Walters Art Gallery.

The hotel is Baltimore's second oldest, built in 1927–1929. It served as an apartment house for years before it was reintroduced as a grand hotel in 1985. The highly polished marble floors and elevators, the 6-foot, 500-pound Baccarat crystal chandelier, and the valuable French antiques and the hand-loomed carpets throughout the public spaces suggest the intimate luxury of a European boutique hotel. In addition, the Conservatory, with its panoramic city view from the top floor, offers some of Baltimore's finer food and has one of the loveliest dining rooms anywhere.

The first four stories of this 13-story brick edifice are brightened with light stone and maroon awnings. The inset two-story entrance is supported by four grand pillars, and guests are welcomed to a small, dark lobby, plush with antiques, artwork, and tapestries. Two marble elevators whisk guests to rooms or to the Conservatory, or one might glide up a curved set of marble stairs to the clubby Bistro, with green marble walls, darkly stained wood paneling and exposed floors, elaborate crown molding, and forest green leather tooled chairs.

The guest rooms are decorated with European and Empire reproduction furnishings in strong masculine tones of modest, neutral colors and patterns. Structured drapes fall from the ceiling, matching the bedskirt pattern. Remote cable televisions are hidden in dark wood armoires, and all rooms have stocked mini-bars. Though the suites have separate parlors, even the standard guest rooms have plush sitting areas. Imported lamps on marble-top bedstands were hand-painted to complement the room's hues. All guest rooms are blessed with good bathrooms, marble floors and walls, towel warmers, hair dryers, and separate vanities with makeup mirrors.

Thirteen stories above the city, the Conservatory is a glass-enclosed atrium that has the feeling of a Victorian greenhouse. Swirling low nap Victorian carpeting muffles one's steps past green faux marble pillars, lit by winged brass gasoliers. Black wrought-iron supports curve gracefully along the ceiling like an ivy-filled trellis, echoing the lines of the plants in the sills and filling the corners. Sweeping drapes are ingeniously gathered up the curving glass depending on the time of day, filling the room with light or enclosing it in the warmth of evening. Heavy velvet and tasseled drapes soften the passageways. The food is elegant French, with dinner entrées from $26 to $30. A $32 prix fixe menu is available weekdays.

When the service is not invisibly discreet, it is friendly and soft-spoken. Guests at the Peabody Court have complimentary passes to the Downtown Athletic Club.

Boston

Boston Harbor Hotel at Rowes Wharf
70 Rowes Wharf on Atlantic Avenue
Boston, Massachusetts 02110
617-439-7000
800-752-7077
Fax: 617-330-9450
Telex: 920027

Managing director: François-Laurent Nivaud
Accommodations: 230 rooms and suites
Rates: $220–$340 per couple; suites, $390–$1,290; holiday
  and weekend packages available
Added: 9.7% tax
Payment: Major credit cards
Children: Welcome
Pets: Allowed
Smoking: Restricted
Open: Year-round

Boston's most impressive luxury hotel is part of the Rowes
Wharf Harbor complex, which includes offices, residences,
shops, and a marina. The elegant architecture, with an 80-foot
arch and copper-domed rotunda, was called "a triumph of
urban design" by the *New York Times.* Come for the view.

No expense has been spared inside, either. Marble floors,
fabric-covered walls, museum-quality art, and small-scale public spaces create the feeling of an elegant private club, much like
the small, great hotels of London. There is a high employee-
guest ratio, resulting in excellent service.

The rooms have sweeping views of the harbor (and the vessels
that ply the water) or the glittering city skyline. They are decorated with rich flowered fabrics and chintzes, crystal lamps,
and Chippendale furniture. Fresh flowers, bathrobes, a mini-
bar, a television, and three telephones in each room are standard. Swiss Institute toiletries are provided in the bathrooms.

The Rowes Wharf Restaurant is very much like a smart Boston club. Overlooking the water, its two sections offer both a

formal and an informal atmosphere with similar menus of regional American cuisine and seafood. The salad niçoise, with grilled fresh tuna, is a culinary masterpiece. The bar, which has an entrance from the street as well, has become a meeting spot for financial district workers waiting for the commuter ferry. Afternoon tea, authentically set and served in the Harborview Lounge, is fast giving the other hotels in Boston a run for their money.

A health club and spa has a 60-foot lap pool, a whirlpool, sauna, steam room, and massage, exercise, and treatment rooms. A marina allows guests to arrive by boat, even if it's a dinghy (this is the first public dinghy dock in Boston).

A comfortable, stress-free water shuttle takes you directly from the airport to the hotel in 7 minutes, departing every 15 minutes Sunday through Friday. If you come from South Station or the Southeast Expressway, the hotel couldn't be more convenient. It's also within easy walking distance of the Aquarium, Faneuil Hall Marketplace, the North End, and the Tea Party Ship, Computer, and Children's museums.

The Bostonian Hotel

Faneuil Hall Marketplace
Boston, Massachusetts 02109
617-523-3600
800-343-0922
Fax: 617-523-2454

Managing director: Ladislav Brank
Accommodations: 140 rooms, 12 suites
Rates: $205–$575 per couple; weekend packages include breakfast
Included: All meals served; lunch served only to Bostonian Club members on weekdays
Minimum stay: None
Added: 9.7% tax
Payment: Major credit cards
Children: Welcome
Pets: Not allowed
Smoking: 1 nonsmoking floor
Open: Year-round

The Bostonian, more a sophisticated inn rather than a city hotel, is an intimate, newer (1982) place that incorporates two historic buildings in a predominantly modern structure. Across from Faneuil Hall and Quincy Market in Boston's oldest commercial district, the hotel blends well with its neighbors.

Both businesspeople and vacationers appreciate the proximity to the festive atmosphere at Faneuil Hall and the fruit and vegetable vendors at Haymarket.

Guests enter the red brick building through a porte cochere and a circular cobblestone driveway. Luggage is taken directly to the guest rooms via a service elevator. Inside, the lobby has been designed specifically for house guests, combining traditional and contemporary elements to create the intimate feeling found in small private clubs and guesthouses. For instance, a roaring fire and bowls of apples await guests in the winter. There isn't a typical registration desk and cashier, either; transactions are conducted discreetly behind a mahogany desk.

A glass elevator connects the separate public lobby with the hotel's nationally acclaimed rooftop restaurant, Seasons. Enclosed in glass with an arched ceiling, many angles, and wood beams, it offers a broad view of Faneuil Hall Marketplace. The food here is among Boston's best; the kitchen has spawned some of Boston's most creative chefs, including Jasper White, Lydia Shire, and Gordon Hammersley. Anthony Ambrose is now in charge, and if history is to repeat itself, you'll want to keep an eye out for him. (Classically trained, Ambrose is renowned for an excellent 3-minute egg.) The menu changes four times a year—with the seasons. Season's superb and extensive wine list is exclusively American.

Four color schemes and two types of furnishings are used for the rooms. Those in the new sections of the hotel follow a contemporary style, while a more traditional approach (French country provincial) has been taken in the historic Harkness wing. Hallways zigzag and corners don't always form right angles in this more interesting half of the hotel. Room 734 has a beamed ceiling, a water view, and French reproduction furniture. Suite 735 has a two-story room with a fireplace and is decorated in warm brown tones.

Most of the rooms have French windows opening onto small balconies with wrought-iron railings and flower boxes filled with seasonal plantings year-round. Most suites have a Jacuzzi; many have oversize oval tubs; all have VCRs. The bathroom amenities are unusual: small packets of Woolite, Roger et Gallet products, silk sachets, and terrycloth bathrobes. Other nice touches include a morning newspaper at your door as well as shined shoes (a complimentary service) if you leave them out the night before. The Bostonian doesn't have a health club on the premises, but a Nautilus facility is available.

The Atrium Lounge is a great place for people-watching, away from the hustle and bustle of the Marketplace.

The Charles Hotel
One Bennett Street
Cambridge, Massachusetts 02138
617-864-1200
800-882-1818
Fax: 617-864-5715

General manager: John Daily
Accommodations: 252 rooms, 44 suites
Rates: $199–$1,400 per couple; weekend packages available
Included: All meals served
Minimum stay: None
Added: 9.7% tax
Payment: Major credit cards
Children: Welcome
Pets: Allowed
Open: Year-round
Smoking: Not permitted in public spaces and in some rooms

Built in 1985 of brick to match Harvard's buildings and the sidewalks of Cambridge, the Charles fits in quite well. Its many large windows permit views of the river, the university, and its own square, a brick plaza with a café, street vendors, and a cluster of classy shops. Inside, the walls are hung with paintings of Cambridge and exquisite quilts. The square, modern lines of the public rooms set off the New England country antiques.

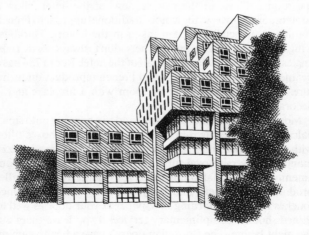

The guest rooms, many of which are decorated with blond, Shaker-style simple furniture, all feature down quilts and have three telephones and two cable TVs (one in the bathroom and one in a tasteful armoire that also hides an honor bar). The baths have terry robes and scales. Some rooms are equipped with computer modems, and computers may be rented. Every night there's turndown service, and every morning a newspaper is waiting outside your door. Room service, from an array of hors d'oeuvres to full dinners and late snacks, is available 24 hours a day.

The hotel's two restaurants quickly earned a strong local following upon opening. The bright, informal Bennett Street Café has outside seating in warm weather, a varied menu, crayons for drawing on the tablecloths, and a popular Sunday brunch ($24.50). The much-acclaimed Rarities, moderately to expensively priced, serves fine American cuisine. Also very popular among young professionals is the Regattabar, a jazz club that attracts top national and international ensembles Tuesday through Saturday evenings.

An elaborate spa, Le Pli, offers a pool, solarium, Jacuzzi, sauna, splash pool, exercise room, massage, and hair and skin salon.

The Charles caters largely to Harvard's visiting academics, benefactors, alumni, friends, and international VIPs. Guests have easy access to Boston via the Harvard Square subway station. And with a luxuriously late check-out time of 1:00 P.M., guests can enjoy the Cambridge shops, restaurants, bookstores, and street life, attractions in themselves, just that much longer.

Copley Plaza Hotel
Copley Square
Boston, Massachusetts 02116
617-267-5300
800-826-7539
Fax: 617-247-6681

General manager: Joseph Phillips
Accommodations: 373 rooms and suites
Rates: $190–$260; suites, $375–$1200; $20 for extra person
over 18 in the same room; special packages and weekend rates
Included: All meals served
Minimum stay: None
Added: 9.7% tax
Payment: Major credit cards
Children: Welcome
Pets: Small pets allowed
Smoking: 2 nonsmoking floors
Open: Year-round

The Copley Plaza, Boston's "grande dame," has just completed a refurbishing project encompassing all the guest rooms, public spaces, and restaurants. The magnificent building dates from 1912 and closely resembles New York's Plaza both physically and in atmosphere, with a marble lobby with a frescoed blue sky ceiling. Beyond lies Copley Square, the centerpiece of the Back Bay, with its blocks of town houses and Boston's smartest galleries and shops. The John Hancock, at 60 stories Boston's highest building (its rooftop Observatory is the best spot for a historical as well as geographic overview of the city), happens to be next door.

Since 1987, under local ownership, the guest rooms have been totally renovated. All have superb vintage 1912 mirrored closets and wall detailing as well as tasteful carpeting and reproduction furniture, TVs hidden in armoires, mini-bars, marble bathrooms, luxurious robes, and makeup mirrors.

Room layout varies widely, so guests may choose from a wide array to suit their needs. Many "superior" (medium price) rooms are actually two-room suites, with daybeds that fold out to accommodate a couple of children. The hotel also supplies cribs complete with cuddly animals, television with special cable channels for children, and a special children's guide to museums, events, and restaurants. Guests have access to the Spa at the Heritage, Boston's newest and most elegant fitness center, a short walk on Boylston Street, by the Public Garden.

The public spaces in the Copley Plaza represent the true heart of the Back Bay. The Plaza Bar, richly paneled and dimly lit, with deep leather seats, evokes an exclusive Fifth Avenue men's club—until the evening, when the room becomes Boston's premier jazz piano bar. The Copley Bar is another scene altogether: a central bar invites singles and couples alike to gather. Copley's, serving simple meals, is moderately priced yet opulent. The Tea Court in the lobby is a convenient (6:30 A.M.– 9:30 P.M.) source of scones, sandwiches and expresso as well as tea. The Plaza Dining Room, one of the grandest rooms in the country where the public may dine, rivals any restaurant in Boston, both in ambience and quality. Executive chef Gerard Thabius is the brains behind the unusually varied cuisine. This is truly one of Boston's most romantic spots.

The Eliot

370 Commonwealth Avenue
Boston, Massachusetts 02115
617-267-1607
800-443-5468
Fax: 617-536-9114

General manager: Fred V. Sherman
Accommodations: 84 suites and 12 rooms
Rates: $135; double, $145; suites, single, $165; double, $175; 2-bedroom, 2-bath, $265
Included: Continental breakfast
Minimum stay: None
Added: 9.7% tax
Payment: Major credit cards
Children: Under 12 free in room with parents
Pets: Not allowed
Smoking: Nonsmoking suites available
Open: Year-round

The Eliot, renovated and reopened as an all-suites hotel in 1990, is a gem. From the small but elegant lobby to the typical suite —two rooms furnished in Queen Anne mahogany and hung with fine prints—the feeling here is of a small London hotel. But the prices are scarcely Boston, let alone London.

Charles Eliot, one of Harvard University's most famous presidents, built the hotel in 1915 next to the Harvard Club, another brick building that it resembles architecturally and with which it shares an ornate black iron fence that used to be a hallmark of Back Bay.

At the time, Back Bay was filled with similar hotels, all now vanished or converted to dormitories. Timing was initially against the Eliot. The last of its genre to be built, it never quite caught on and foundered in the Depression. By 1939, when Nathan Ullian purchased it, the property was already a seedy "residential" hotel. It's been in the family ever since and is now closely monitored by Arthur and Dora Ullian, who have resurrected it in the conviction that its time has come.

The two rooms are separated by French doors and each has a color TV. The fully equipped kitchenette includes a microwave, coffeemaker, and fridge. The sitting room includes a desk, a wet bar, and a couch that converts to a queen-size daybed. The bathrooms have Italian marble walls.

At the corner of Massachusetts Avenue and Commonwealth Avenue, the Eliot is a short walk from Symphony Hall, the Hynes Auditorium, and a subway stop that leads to all parts of Boston and Cambridge. It's also a pleasant walk along Massachusetts Avenue and across the Charles River to MIT.

The Eliot is a shade easier to reach by car than many downtown hotels, and the bellman will stow your car in a nearby garage for about the same fee most hotels charge for parking. A Continental breakfast is served in an elegantly appointed dining room on the lobby level. A light room service menu is also available. While no other food is offered in the hotel, restaurants of every kind, including the Eliot Lounge around the corner in the same building, abound nearby.

The Four Seasons
200 Boylston Street
Boston, Massachusetts 02116
617-338-4400
800-332-3442
Fax: 617-426-7199

General manager: Robin Brown
Accommodations: 288 rooms, 80 suites, 11 rooms with
    wheelchair access
Rates: $225–$355 per couple midweek, $160–$250 weekends;
    packages available
Included: All meals served
Minimum stay: None
Added: 9.7% tax
Payment: Major credit cards
Children: Welcome; special children's program
Pets: Accepted with prior approval
Smoking: Designated nonsmoking floors
Open: Year-round

Less formal and much newer (1985) than the Ritz-Carlton, the Four Seasons is also more welcoming, despite the crystal chandelier in the porte cochere and the grand staircase. With a warm assurance that he is happy you have come, the doorman whisks your luggage away. The bellhop carefully outlines all the hotel's facilities, which include a spectacular eighth-floor pool and a full spa; 24-hour room service and an overnight shoeshine are also available.

If you are going to stay here, do it right and book a room overlooking the Public Garden. A Four Seasons Executive Suite ($250 a couple on weekends) is as luxurious as you need to go: the bedroom is separated by French doors from an elegant little sitting room with a table by the window that's perfect for breakfast. Of course, there's a wet bar, cable TV, fresh flowers, bottled water, and a marble bathroom with a hair dryer, robe, soaps, creams, and shampoo.

For New Englanders who live outside the city, the Four Seasons also makes a great "Gourmet Getaway." Its formal, second-floor dining room, Aujourd'hui, is arguably the best restaurant in town. It is spacious, richly paneled, and decorated with beveled mirrors and old prints. While the menu changes seasonally, you might begin with a charlotte of Louisiana crab with bell peppers followed by a peasant salad; the peppered Maine lobster with spring rolls is exquisite. The combination of ambience, food, and deft personal service is difficult to beat. Request a table with a view of the Public Garden. A less expensive menu is available, for both lunch and dinner, in the attractive Bristol Lounge, off the lobby. Post-theatre, on weekends, the Bristol hosts a delightfully sinful Viennese dessert buffet. For $7.50 you can choose from a diverse selection that may include fruit flan, hazelnut torte, strawberry roulade, or a Grand Marnier soufflé.

The dining room aside, the hotel is comfortably informal. Even children feel welcome; babysitters are available and there are videotapes to amuse youngsters, who can eat in their room while their parents dine in style.

The Four Seasons is within walking distance of shopping districts in Back Bay and downtown; if you don't want to take the subway to a business appointment or the waterfront, a complimentary limousine is provided.

The Inn at Harvard

1201 Massachusetts Avenue
Cambridge, Massachusetts 02138
617-491-2222
800-528-0444
Fax: 617-496-5020

General manager: Richard Carbone
Accommodations: 113 rooms, 1 suite
Rates: $99–$175
Included: Breakfast and dinner
Minimum stay: 3 nights during Harvard's commencement
Added: 9.7% tax
Payment: Major credit cards
Children: Welcome
Pets: Not allowed
Smoking: 2 nonsmoking floors
Open: Year-round
Handicap access: 6 rooms

Just four short blocks east of Harvard Square, the Inn at Harvard is the latest addition to the area's lodging scene. Though geared to and owned by Harvard University, the inn appeals to anyone who appreciates understated elegance. Designed by Graham Gund Associates, the four-story brick building, like much of the Square, was inspired by the many 18th-century Georgian buildings on campus.

A dramatic glass-roofed common space, the Atrium, serves as the hotel's living and dining room. By day the room is infused with soft, natural light from above; by night it is romantically lit with candles and dim lamps. Bookcases, filled with reading you'd expect to find in a summer cottage, line one wall. The multihued walls are set off by magnificent cherrywood moldings and arches.

Handsome cherry tables for four, some of which double as backgammon or chess tables, flank two sides of the room. The rest of the room is filled in with comfortable groupings of sofas, wing chairs, and marble-topped tables that create the feeling of a private club. This seems appropriate, since dining is available only to guests.

At mealtime, the tables are covered with white linen. For breakfast, try the stuffed French toast with maple syrup. A Continental breakfast buffet is available in addition to the regular menu when the hotel is full. The evening meal is beautifully presented, and features such dishes as grilled lime-marinated swordfish, an autumn salad of grilled scallops with a warm bacon dressing, and an Indian summer salad of tomatoes, shrimp, and feta cheese with a tapenade vinaigrette.

In the guest rooms, the beds and armoires are carved from the same cherrywood found in the Atrium. All of them have large windows that actually open, a writing table, fine art on the walls, and cable televisions hidden in the armoires. The bathrooms, with night lights, are done in gray and white tiles. Some rooms overlook the Old Cambridge Baptist Church, some have balconies facing Harvard Square, and others have French doors that open into the Atrium.

Affiliations with Harvard are readily apparent: there is direct access to the university telephone system, and guests may eat lunch at the Faculty Club and charge it to their hotel bill. But the hotel is also geared to working travelers; each room has a computer modem hook-up and voice mail.

Hotel Meridien
250 Franklin Street
Boston, Massachusetts 02110
617-451-1900
800-543-4300
Fax: 617-423-2844

Manager: Hugues Jaquier
Accommodations: 269 rooms, 57 suites

Rates: $205; double, $230; suites, $350–$800; weekend
  packages available from $109 per night
Added: 9.7% tax
Payment: Major credit cards
Children: One child under 12 free in room with parents; over
  12, $25 extra, only three permitted per room
Pets: Small animals accommodated
Smoking: Three nonsmoking floors
Open: Year-round

Without question, you come to the Meridien for the service,
which is not to be outdone in New England, and for the superb
French cuisine.

This is Boston's former Federal Reserve Bank, a 1920s Renaissance Revival structure of granite and limestone modeled on
a Roman palazzo. When it reopened in 1981 as the Meridien
Hotel, three stories and a glass mansard roof had been added as
well as other modern touches, like a six-story atrium and sloping glass walls in many guest rooms. But despite its size, it
conveys the ambience of a small hotel.

The magnificent public spaces are on the floors above the
vehicular entrance. There is the former members' court, now
the Restaurant Julien, with its vaulted, gold leaf–edged ceiling.
You have the sense of dining in a very elegant courtyard, one
with upholstered wing chairs. The food is a perfect blend of
contemporary and traditional French fare, and you're likely to
be served by four or five different service people.

On a level above the restaurant is the Julien Lounge, a truly
luxurious space with coffered ceilings, N. C. Wyeth murals on
paneled walls, and piano music. Enjoy your morning croissants, Sunday brunch, or light dinner in the smaller Café
Fleuri, in the soaring atrium.

The guest rooms, in contrast, are light and modern. Because
most of them have been carved from former office space, they
come in more than 150 different sizes and shapes. Toiletries,
bathrobes, roses in the bathroom, chocolate truffles, and tomorrow's weather forecast are among the small niceties.
Rooms also have live plants, mini-bars, sofas, radios, bathroom
scales, hair dryers, and telephones.

Guests can enjoy Le Club Meridien, a third-floor health club
with a 4-foot-deep lap pool, a whirlpool, aerobic exercise equipment, and saunas.

The Meridien is in the heart of Boston's financial district;
during the week, most guests are here on business. On weekends, when packages include free parking, tourists account for

most of the clientele. Faneuil Hall Marketplace and Filene's Basement are both within a few blocks.

The Meridien has an unusually large staff (326 for 326 rooms), and you can't help but notice. The French management is apparent from the moment you are greeted with "bonjour." But there is nothing at all stuffy about the Meridien, and an unusually friendly atmosphere prevails.

The Ritz-Carlton Boston

15 Arlington Street
Boston, Massachusetts 02117
617-536-5700
800-241-3333
Fax: 617-536-9340

General manager: Sigi Brauer
Accommodations: 278 rooms, 48 suites
Rates: $250–$700 per couple; weekend packages available
Included: All meals served
Minimum stay: None
Added: 9.7% tax
Payment: Major credit cards
Children: Welcome
Pets: Smaller pets welcome
Smoking: Designated nonsmoking floors
Open: Year-round

"We are not merely surrounded by traditions, we have become one," says the Ritz-Carlton's promotional material. It's true. Despite the flood of new luxury hotels, the Ritz-Carlton remains the place to stay in Boston.

The 16-story hotel was built in 1927, and an addition, which includes 52 condominiums, was completed in 1981. From inside the hotel, it is extremely difficult to distinguish between the two. While the new rooms have the same careful detailing found in the old ones, the bathrooms in the new wing are roomier and modern; the old ones (newly refaced in Vermont marble) have their original porcelain fixtures. The most handsome rooms are the suites, with elegant mirror-topped mantels (there are 42 fireplaces at the Ritz-Carlton) and fine antique breakfronts, desks, and sofas. All the rooms are large, have closets that lock, a safe, refrigerator, and honor bar. Most have fine views, either of the Public Garden or over the rooftops of Newbury Street.

The elevators are run by white-gloved operators, and many of the hotel's 570 employees have worked here for more than five years—a few have been here since the 1940s. A pantry on each floor, open 24 hours a day, provides superb service.

The second-floor Dining Room is very formal, with tall, mullioned windows overlooking the Public Garden and a menu offering Continental cuisine. The Lounge (with no windows) is a gathering place rather like a drawing room and is popular for tea. Downstairs, on the entry floor, The Café is a less formal spot for breakfast and lunch (with entrées such as grilled baby flounder with lemon butter and champagne by the glass). The Ritz Bar, a popular meeting spot, has recently acquired the look of a richly paneled club, complete with a fireplace.

A full range of health and fitness facilities, ice skates (to use on the pond in the Public Garden), walking shoes (for a walk along the Esplanade), and a chauffeured limousine (for morning appointments) round out the facilities of this full-service hotel.

Royal Sonesta Hotel
5 Cambridge Parkway
Cambridge, Massachusetts 02142
617-491-3600
Telex: 275293
Fax: 617-661-5956
Reservations: 800-SONESTA in the U.S. and Canada

General manager: Michael Levie
Accommodations: 371 rooms, 29 suites
Rates: $140–$160; suites, $270–$635; packages available
Included: Use of indoor pool and health club
Added: 9.7% tax
Payment: Major credit cards
Children: Age 18 and under free in room with parents
Pets: Not permitted
Smoking: 4 nonsmoking floors; restricted in public places
Open: Year-round

The Sonesta's location is both its beauty and weak point. The beauty is, of course, its view: directly across the Charles River to Beacon Hill and the downtown high-rises and down the curve of the river along the length of Back Bay.

This is, moreover, one view in which guests can participate, strolling or jogging along the riverside promenade. Hardy souls can walk over the Longfellow Bridge to the Massachusetts General Hospital, Massachusetts Eye and Ear Infirmary, and the rest of Boston. The Museum of Science and MIT are also within walking distance, and the Cambridgeside Galleria, the city's newest, glitziest shopping mall, is just across the street.

Still, despite the hotel's courtesy van, which runs more or less frequently from 7:00 A.M. to 10:00 P.M. daily, carrying guests to Harvard Square, MIT, Faneuil Hall and other points in Boston and Cambridge, the Sonesta lacks effortless access to public transport enjoyed by most of the Boston hotels included in this book. But this Sonesta, the jewel of a national hotel chain based in Boston, is outstanding: it is composed of two 200-room towers—one built in the 1960s, the other in the 1980s—connected by an attractive lobby and a public area that includes two restaurants and a bar. A spectacular pool, with a retractable roof and outside sunning deck as well as a full-service spa, is in the East Wing.

The guest rooms in the old tower have been renovated to match those in the new one. While not particularly large, they are decorated in soothing colors, and each has a piece of art from the Sonesta's unusual collection. Downstairs the halls are brightened with works by such artists as Andy Warhol, Jasper Johns, and Roy Lichtenstein. Many of the most interesting paintings and prints are by lesser-known local artists.

The Sonesta makes an unusual effort to woo summer vacationers, especially families. For the past few years its reasonably priced summer packages have included perks like boat rides on the Charles River, the use of bicycles and Polaroid cameras (Polaroid's headquarters are next door), and organized spa activities like aerobics and water aerobics, not to mention all the ice cream you can eat.

Davio's, the hotel's dining room, is actually an offshoot of one of the city's prima Italian restaurants, specializing in dishes like pollo al ripieno (roast chicken, garlic, Bel Paese stuffing, and sherry tomato sauce, $13.95). The decor is art deco and the view downriver. The Charles Bar and Grille, a sports bar, and a less formal, moderately priced café are also on the river.

Terrace Townehouse
60 Chandler Street
Boston, Massachusetts 02116
617-350-6520

Innkeepers: Bob and Gloria Belknap
Accommodations: 4 rooms (all with private bath)
Rates: $95–$140 in season, $105–$125 December through April
Included: Expanded Continental breakfast and afternoon tea
Minimum stay: 2 nights on weekends May through November
Added: 9.7% tax
Payment: MasterCard, Visa
Children: Over age 12 welcome
Pets: Not allowed
Smoking: Not permitted inside
Open: Year-round

This elegant bed-and-breakfast is in a brick town house, meticulously restored to its original elegance, on a tree-lined street in Boston's South End, only a few blocks from Copley Square. The small entrance is finished with a black and white marble floor, and there are wide-planked hardwood floors throughout. The hall and stairwell are painted a striking peach and accented with antique French prints, white woodwork, and brass sconces.

The China Trade Room, with cheery yellow walls, is furnished with an 1820s bed made in Salem, Massachusetts, and decorated with Clarence House and Pierre Deux prints. It has both the comforts of a luxury hotel and the cozy feeling of a private home. Another room, the Drawing Room, seems like an English club, with dark brown woodwork and warm brown colors. It has a four-poster canopy bed and a love seat by the bay window.

The British Officer's Room on the first floor is decorated in a turn-of-the-century style, right down to an 1897 issue of *Punch*. This smaller room has a wall of books, a sink built into a bureau, and a tiny but well-planned bathroom. The French

Dining Room, which has a very comfortable king-size bed, a crystal chandelier, dark green lacquered walls, and French antiques, looks down on a handkerchief-size garden with a fountain and flowering plants. Each room has its own telephone line.

The common space includes a thousand-volume library on the third floor where afternoon tea is served. (Gloria graduated from La Varenne in Paris and used to be a caterer in California, so this is special.) In good weather, tea is held on the landscaped roof deck.

Breakfast is served in each room on antique china. It may include yogurt, scones, fresh fruit or Scottish oatmeal, smoked salmon, cream cheese, and bagels; a Boston Globe always accompanies it.

Terrace Townehouse doesn't have space to store luggage during the day, but the nearby Back Bay Amtrak station can provide this service. And while there is no parking on the street, three parking garages are within a few blocks.

Tremont House

275 Tremont Street
Boston, Massachusetts 02116
617-426-1400
800-228-5151
Fax: 617-482-6730

Manager: Jay Polimeno
Accommodations: 281 rooms and suites
Rates: $115 per couple; special theater and other packages available
Included: All meals available
Minimum stay: None
Added: 9.7% tax
Payment: Major credit cards
Children: Under 18 free in room with parents
Pets: Not allowed
Smoking: Nonsmoking rooms available
Open: Year-round

Come to the Tremont for the location and reasonable rates. In the heart of the theater district, this twelve-story hotel is also within walking distance of Chinatown, Downtown Crossing (the pedestrian shopping district), and the Boston Common and Public Garden.

Constructed in 1925 as the national headquarters of the Benevolent Protective Order of the Elks, it became the Bradford

Hotel just a year later. In 1987 it was handsomely renovated as a Quality International property and is independently owned today. The lobby is grand and spacious, with high ceilings, a 16-foot chandelier, marble columns, and a marble stairway.

Furnished in Thomasville reproductions, the standard rooms are quite standard but nice, even if on the small side. The suites are one large room that accommodates a king-size bed and fold-out couch. All have a writing area and TV.

In the 1940s, the hotel's rooftop club held live radio broadcasts of the era's leading big bands. Today, two popular dance clubs, serving all age groups, are on the premises. The Roxy alternates live big band and swing music from the 1930s and 1940s and pop music, and NYC Jukebox spins 1970s disco and rock from the 1950s and 1960s.

With provisions trucked in straight from the Big Apple, the popular and glitzy Stage Deli specializes in high-rise sandwiches and is open for late breakfasts, lunch, dinner, and after-theater snacks. It also provides room service. The hotel's Encore Lounge offers early breakfasts and a nice place for quiet conversations in the evenings.

Chicago

The Drake
Lake Shore Drive and Michigan Avenue
Chicago, Illinois 60611
312-787-2200
800-55-DRAKE
Fax: 312-787-1431
Reservations: 800-HILTONS

General manager: Victor T. Burt
Accommodations: 535 rooms and suites
Rates: $185–$240; double, $215–$270
Included: Morning newspaper
Minimum stay: None
Added: 12.4% tax
Payment: Major credit cards
Children: Welcome
Pets: Not allowed
Smoking: Nonsmoking rooms available
Open: Year-round

One Sunday morning, police officers and hotel employees rope off a path from the elevators to the lobby entrance. The curious gather to watch Mary Robinson, the president of Ireland, casually sweep through and enter the motorcade that will whisk her to the airport. In a moment, the ropes are down and the lobby is back to business as usual.

This scene is not uncommon at the bustling Drake Hotel. After all, it is the favorite spot of Britain's royal family and other celebrities when they visit the Windy City.

The Drake opened on New Year's Eve, 1920, and except for a few shaky years during the Depression and its occupation by the military during World War II, it has remained open ever since. You can't get much closer to Chicago's center than at this Gold Coast hotel overlooking Lake Michigan.

Set off spacious wainscoted hallways, the guest rooms are attractively decorated with floral print draperies and over-stuffed couches. All the rooms have telephones, clock radios, remote control televisions, mini-bars, magnifying mirrors, and bathrobes. Nightly turndown service with bedside chocolates is a nice touch. The keys to the 30 executive-floor rooms allow access to the Panorama Lounge.

The hotel is famous for the Cape Cod Room, whose mounted stuffed sailfish, red checked tablecloths, and copper pots suspended from beamed ceilings evoke the New England coast. Diners often start with the Bookbinder Red Snapper Soup, followed by lobster, scallops, and shrimp entrées. When the restaurant considered replacing its oyster bar a few years back, loyal diners threw a fit. In the course of sixty years, visitors such as Marilyn Monroe, Jack Benny, and Joe DiMaggio carved their names into the rough wood countertop. Needless to say, the bar is still there.

The Oak Terrace dining room is another restaurant possibility, with popular prime rib carved tableside, while the Palm Court continues the tradition of midafternoon high tea with scones, pastries, and a harpist.

The guest shops include florists, a drugstore, men's and women's apparel stores, a barber shop, confectionary, airline ticket office, jewelry store, and art gallery. You are within steps of the Magnificent Mile and Water Tower Plaza and just minutes away from River North jazz and Rush Street blues.

Four Seasons Hotel

120 East Delaware Place
at 900 North Michigan
Chicago, Illinois 60611
312-280-8800
Fax: 312-280-1748
Telex: 00-214923
Reservations: 800-332-3442

General manager: Hans Williman
Accommodations: 313 rooms, 31 suites
Rates: $195–$235; double, $215–$265; suites, single,
  $275–$750; double, $305–$750
  Packages available
Included: All meals available
Minimum stay: None
Added: 12.4% tax
Payment: Major credit cards
Children: Welcome
Pets: By arrangement
Smoking: Nonsmoking rooms available
Open: Year-round

Late Sunday morning at the Four Seasons. What has been called the best brunch in Chicago attracts everyone from overwhelmed out-of-towners to three rich Chicago widows, who try to talk a fourth into picking up the $14,000 necklace she has been eyeing in a Michigan Avenue shop window.

Both groups agree that brunch in the 124-seat Seasons Restaurant lives up to its reputation. Men in tall chefs' hats prepare waffles and omelettes while you wait. Another cuts slices of rare roast beef. Buffet tables present a complete variety of oysters, clams, smoked salmon, whitefish, ham, chicken, lamb, along with pasta, vegetable, and seafood salads. A glass of fresh orange juice doesn't stay empty for long before the wait staff has it filled again. For dessert, there are peaches topped with Grand Marnier or a creamy chocolate mousse. A pianist offers soothing renditions of George Gershwin and Cole Porter.

Brunch is usually the cap to an unforgettable weekend at the Four Seasons, which rivals its sister hotel across the street, the Ritz-Carlton, as the city's most luxurious. Part of a 66-story, mixed-use skyscraper that also houses Bloomingdale's department store, the hotel blends English antiques and reproductions, fine woods and marbles, and an extensive art collection.

Guests enter the hotel off Delaware Place, where a small elevator whisks them to the large 7th-floor lobby. Crystal chandeliers and Georgian furnishings set the tone here, with opulent touches that include 18th-century marble fireplace mantels, a 15-foot marble fountain, and tapestry fabrics. The Seasons Restaurant is here, along with an adjacent bar and café.

The guest rooms, on floors 30–46, offer spectacular views of Chicago's lakefront and skyline. The large rooms combine a bedroom and sitting room; one-and two-bedroom suites, along with a Presidential Suite (at $2,500 per night) mix antiques, chintzes, and porcelains. Every room has three two-line telephones, twice-daily maid service, remote control televisions and radios, fully stocked mini-bars, and 24-hour room service. Ask for a room ending with 01 if you want more space. And you may prefer a city to a lake view, since you can't see much of the water after dark.

Unlike the Ritz-Carlton's, the room rate here includes access to the Spa, a fitness center complete with Roman columns as well as saunas, whirlpool, massage and steam rooms, exercise equipment, and a pool beneath a skylight. Where many hotels try to tap into current design fads, the Four Seasons succeeds in creating a luxury hotel whose classic accents and attention to service make it truly timeless.

Hotel Inter-Continental
505 North Michigan Ave.
Chicago, Illinois 60611
312-944-4100
800-628-2468
Fax: 312-944-3050
Telex: 62654670
Reservations:
  Inter-Continental Hotels
  800-332-4246

General manager: Rex Rice
Accommodations: 338 rooms, with 19 suites
Rates: $145–$239; double, $145–$279; suites, $250–$500;
  packages available
Minimum stay: None
Added: 14.9% tax
Payment: Major credit
Children: Welcome
Pets: Not allowed
Smoking: Nonsmoking rooms available
Open: Year-round

The 41-story tower, with its Indiana limestone facade crowned
by a Moorish-styled dome, was built as the Medinah Athletic
Club, just six months before the stock market crash in 1929.
Bankrupt by 1934, it spent the following years as a Sheraton and
Raddison before Inter-Continental Hotels Corporation added
it to their growing list of restored hotel properties. Lido Lippi, a
world renowned fine art conservator and a key figure in the
restoration of the Sistine Chapel, assisted in the project.

Returned are the painted ceilings, winding balustrade staircases, arched entryways, marble inlays, detailed bronze and
brass highlighting, and murals and friezes. The restorers relied
on old blueprints and photographs along with the cherished
memories of former guests. The imposing Hall of Lions is an
extension of the main lobby, with two Assyrian lions carved in
marble guarding each side of a staircase.

The lion motif carries into the guest rooms, decorated in the
classic Biedermeier style of the 19th century, which relies on
simple lines and designs in light-colored fruitwoods. Dark-
colored inlays of ebony and maple along with Axminster carpets and bold patterned wallpapers create striking contrasts.
Griffins remain a key ornamental motif for guest room furniture, while some chairs have Egyptian female figures carved

into the arms. From some windows you can see the exterior stone-cut details of mythological creatures. The spacious rooms are equipped with mini-bars, two-line telephones, and bathrooms with separate tubs and showers.

While The Hotel Inter-Continental shows off its stunning restoration in virtually every corner, its mosaic-tiled junior Olympic-size swimming pool remains the showstopper. Shimmering beneath a two-and-a-half-story atrium, it was used often by Olympic gold medalist Johnny Weismuller. This is all that's left of the old Athletic Club facilities, which once boasted a running track, gymnasium, bowling alley, and boxing ring. There are now state-of-the-art exercise machines, massage facilities, and an aerobics room available for guests.

The Inter-Continental has executive floors, providing such extras as a Butler's Service and access to an Executive Lounge on the 32nd floor. Here you'll find coffee, tea, and pastries served throughout the day. Limousine service shuttles guests to and from the airport. The hotel contains some 20,000 square feet of meeting and banquet space, including a 600-seat grand ballroom whose ornate marble balcony and decor recaptures the hotel's Egyptian-inspired elegance.

The Boulevard Restaurant overlooks the lobby rotunda at the head of a graceful stairway. Two sides of the horseshoe-shaped restaurant offer views up and down Michigan Avenue. The hotel is conveniently located near Water Tower shopping and the Magnificent Mile.

The $130 million renovation and restoration project also includes an adjoining tower, built in 1961. It houses the Forum Hotel Chicago, which caters to a large business clientele.

Hotel Nikko
320 North Dearborn
Chicago, Illinois 60610
312-744-1900
800-NIKKO-US
Fax: 312-527-2650

General manager: Peter Dangerfield
Accommodations: 396 rooms, 25 suites
Rates: $205–$225; double, $225–$245; suites, $300–$2,500
Included: All meals available
Minimum stay: None
Added: 12.4% tax

Payment: Major credit cards
Children: Welcome
Pets: By arrangement
Smoking: Nonsmoking rooms available
Open: Year-round

From a distance, the Nikko looks like any other high-rise glass tower in Chicago. Up close, it's another picture entirely. Elegant landscaping with boulders and flowers decorate the area around the circular driveway. The lobby's polished granite walls and floors are accented by Japanese ash and African mahogany furnishings. Bamboo rods crisscross the ceilings while a paneled Oriental screen decorates a wall. Opened in 1987, the Nikko exemplifies Japanese efficiency and attention to detail, both in room decor and guest services.

The standard guest rooms carry on the plain lines and flat black surfaces found downstairs. The spacious rooms feature large bay windows, marble baths, custom-made cabinetry, three telephones, and televisions enclosed in armoires. The bathrooms are modern, with terrycloth robes. Even the toiletries are elegant, with the black and white packaging a work of art in itself. Tea, coffee, and a morning newspaper are included as part of the wakeup call. Guests entering the Japanese suites are kindly asked to slip out of their shoes and into slippers supplied by the hotel. Traditional mats serve as seating around a low dining room table. At bedtime, the table is set aside and a futon is removed from the closet and spread on the floor. Deep soaking tubs with separate showers and Japanese rock gardens are part of the bathroom decor.

The Nikko offers plenty of extras for the executive. The rooms on the top three floors have access to a two-story executive lounge. Aside from beverage and concierge service, guests also receive a complimentary Continental breakfast. There is also an executive fitness area, with sauna and massage facilities, and an executive business center, with computers, fax machines, dictating equipment, and secretarial services available.

There are six conference rooms on the lower floors of the Nikko as well as Benkay, a 150-seat restaurant that offers traditional Japanese cuisine, including sushi, sashimi, tempura, and teriyaki. The restaurant features a main dining area, a sushi bar, and private tatami rooms, where diners enjoy a traditional Japanese experience on low tables in addition to lovely views of the Chicago River. If you're not in the mood for sushi, Les Celebrités offers contemporary American cuisine.

Mayfair Regent Chicago

181 East Lakeshore Drive
Chicago, Illinois 60611
312-787-8500
800-833-9884
Fax: 312-664-6194
Telex: 256266
Reservations:
  Leading Hotels of the World
  800-223-6800

General manager: Rita Lau
Accommodations: 201 rooms, 30 suites
Rates: $200–$250; suites, $300–$425; packages available
Minimum stay: None
Added: 14.9% tax
Payment: Major credit cards
Children: Welcome
Pets: Small pets allowed
Smoking: Nonsmoking rooms available
Open: Year-round

Built in the 1920s as a residential hotel, the Mayfair Regent was reopened in 1980 after a $12 million renovation. Most rooms have stunning views of Lake Michigan. Spacious suites, decorated with floral pastels in peach and gold color schemes, come with butlers' pantries and kitchenettes. Marble bathrooms, stocked mini-bars, bedside, bath and desk telephones, and an on-premises seamstress complete the picture of luxury. There is also 24-hour room service and a salon that provides massages, facials, nail care, and hair care. Ask the concierge for a complimentary pass to visit the Art Institute of Chicago.

Dining options here begin with Le Ciel Bleu, a rooftop restaurant specializing in French cuisine. Menu items include sautéed tenderloin of veal served with a truffle sauce or peppered filet of venison with lingonberry-balsamic glaze. The Palm restaurant features steak and lobster dishes. Afternoon tea, with scones, finger sandwiches, and homemade pastries, is served in the Mayfair Lounge.

The hotel always keeps the complimentary fruit bowls overflowing and even supplies them in the rooms for return guests. You'll usually find shiny red apples in the lobby.

On the second floor, the Exercise Room is open 24 hours and is equipped with weights, stair climbing and rowing machines, and exercise bicycles. Note that the Mayfair Regent is a luxury lodging, not a convention hotel, so meeting rooms are equipped for less than 100 people.

On some floors the Mayfair serves as apartments, where celebrities still reside. Sir George Solti, who calls the hotel "highly civilized and unpretentious," lives here when he's in town. Carol Burnett, Luciano Pavarotti, Liberace, Audrey Hepburn, and Bill Blass have either lived here or signed the guest register.

The Palmer House Hilton
17 East Monroe Street
Chicago, Illinois 60603
312-726-7500
Reservations: 800-HILTONS

Manager: Ted Ratcliff
Accommodations: More than 1,600 rooms, 88 suites
Rates: $139–$179; double, $164–$204; suites, one-bedroom,
    $295–$710; two-bedroom, $615–$865; packages available
Included: All meals available
Minimum stay: None

Added: 12.4% tax
Payment: Major credit cards
Children: Welcome
Pets: Allowed
Smoking: Nonsmoking rooms available
Open: Year-round

The original Palmer House, constructed in 1871, burned to the ground only 18 days after its grand opening. Rebuilt in 1873, it enjoyed a celebrity clientele that included Ulysses S. Grant, Mark Twain, Rudyard Kipling, and the queen of England. Today, with more than 1,680 guest accommodations along with restaurants, shops, and conference facilities, the hotel, now called the Palmer House Hilton, is a beautifully restored city within the city.

The lobby is a marvel in itself. The ceiling mural, a composite of twenty-one separate paintings by the French artist Louis Regal, was installed during another rebuilding of the hotel in the late 1920s. It blends mythical Greek subjects rendered in an Italian style. On the ground level of this two-story wonder are crystal light fixtures, velvet cut brocades, moiré taffetas, and cherry furnishings. French and English antique furniture lines the walls.

The traditional guest rooms have custom-made cherry armoires, wooden luggage racks, and marble-topped gaming tables and nightstands decorated in what the hotel calls "residential palatial" style. Almost 400 of the rooms have two full baths.

If you're overwhelmed by the hotel's size, visit the Palmer House Towers. Accessible only by private elevator on the 22nd and 23rd floors, almost 200 Tower Rooms are served by their own lobby and concierge. The rooms are decorated in jewel tones, with king-size beds or a pair of double beds piled high with pillows. Many Tower Rooms have two baths and two closets; they all have bathroom telephones, fancy toiletries, and retractable clotheslines.

Six restaurants are on the premises, including Trader Vic's, Palmer's Steak and Seafood House, the French Quarter, Palmer's Coffee Shop, and Windsor's Lobby Lounge and Café, which serves a buffet lunch. A popular Sunday brunch is served in the Empire Room, which has 24-karat gold leaf French chandeliers. Another banquet facility, the Crystal Room, resembles an intimate French salon, with a marble fireplace and Louis XV furnishings creating a bright aristocratic feel. Together, the banquet facilities here can accommodate up to 2,000 guests.

The Ritz-Carlton Chicago

At Water Tower Place
160 East Pearson Street
Chicago, Illinois 60611
312-266-1000
800-621-6906 outside Chicago
Reservations: 800-332-4222

General manager: Nicholas Mutton
Accommodations: 346 rooms, 85 suites
Rates: $210–$250; double, $240–$280; suites, $450–$750;
  packages available
Included: All meals available
Minimum stay: None
Added: 12.4% tax
Payment: Major credit cards
Children: Welcome
Pets: By arrangement
Smoking: Nonsmoking rooms available
Open: Year-round

For the past two decades, the Ritz-Carlton Chicago has more or less defined luxury lodging in the Windy City. Now, after a $16 million renovation, the 22 floors at the top of Water Tower Place offer even more spectacular accommodations. Rich mahogany or cherry headboards and armoires have been added to a Georgian-style bedchamber, complemented by chintz draperies and Bavarian diamond-cut crystal lamps. Many rooms also feature VCRs and CD players. More than 277 tons of rich Verde marble have been laid in the bathrooms. Even the names used to describe the room colors bespeak luxury: oyster, soft coral, and green celadon.

The attention to detail is evident the minute you enter the lobby. Inserts of imported Scottish carpet are tucked between squares of Italian marble. A seating area near the elevators features baroque wing chairs, exquisite brass and glass end tables, and plush damask sofas. The reception desk has even more creamy Italian marble, enhanced by floral displays and oil paintings.

Next to the lobby, the Café recalls an English dining room, though the atmosphere remains casual. You can enjoy all three meals and even a late snack since the restaurant stays open until 1:30 A.M. It now serves chicken and pasta dishes along with standard club sandwich fare. The acclaimed Dining Room offers a more luxurious setting and French cuisine. A piano player provides music beneath crystal chandeliers. The Greenhouse serves a light luncheon, afternoon tea, then cocktails in an atrium setting with a striking view of the lakefront. Evening piano entertainment is also offered here while the Bar provides dancing and live entertainment nightly.

Business guests and lavish weddings fill six major banquet and meeting facilities. The 9,000-square-foot Grand Ballroom accommodates up to 1,200 beneath its dramatic crystal chandelier. Corporate guests will appreciate that portable fax machines can be provided in their rooms.

There are other extras, most of them standard with a quality hotel. Complimentary beverages are set up in the morning while newspapers are delivered on request. The concierge staff claims to speak nine languages, including Japanese, while staff members always number more than one person for each guest. You will have to pay extra (about $6 per day) to use the 11th-floor Carlton Club, with its skylighted swimming pool, whirlpool, and separate men's and women's athletic departments with exercise equipment, steam rooms, saunas, and massage facilities.

Swissotel Chicago

323 E. Wacker Drive
Chicago, Illinois 60601
800-65-GRAND
312-565-0565
Fax: 312-565-0540
Reservations:
  COVIA
  800-637-9477

General manager: Richard Bayard
Accommodations: 636 rooms, with 41 suites
Rates: $175–$220; double, $195–$240; suites, $300–$900;
  packages available
Minimum stay: None
Added: 14.9% tax
Payment: Major credit cards
Children: Welcome
Pets: Not allowed
Smoking: Nonsmoking rooms available
Open: Year-round

Swissotel brings to Chicago the same European blend of service and style that distinguishes its chain of worldwide hotels. The oversize rooms and suites are decorated in pastel hues and floral print fabrics. Many have spectacular views of Lake Mich-

igan and the Chicago River. Marble-lined bathrooms have separate glass-enclosed showers.

Regional American cuisine is offered in the Land of Plenty,
where chef David Zozak prepares such dishes as roasted Maple
Creek pork loin and roasted free range chicken with garlic and
herb sauce. The East Side Terrace is the hotel's European-style
outdoor café, boasting beautiful views of the city and lakeshore
from café-style tables and chairs. Café Suise has an international bill of fare in a bistro setting, while the Americus Bar
offers lunch specials, appetizers and beverages. Afternoon tea
is also served daily in the lobby.

The hotel can accommodate meetings from 5 to 500 people.
In addition to 14 hospitality suites, 12 meeting rooms, two board
rooms and a 60-seat theater, there are also a junior ballroom
and a Grand Ballroom. The penthouse health spa, on the 42nd
floor, has a full-size pool, sauna, whirlpool, massage, steam-
room, weight equipment, and aerobic facilities.

Cincinnati

The Cincinnatian Hotel
6th and Vine Streets
Cincinnati, Ohio 45202
513-381-3000
800-332-2020 in Ohio
800-942-9000 in U.S.
Fax: 513-651-0256
Reservations: 800-323-7500

General manager: Denise Vandersall
Accommodations: 139 rooms, 8 suites
Rates: $160–$195; suites, $250–$750; weekend, $99; packages available
Included: All meals available
Minimum stay: None
Added: 10% tax
Payment: Major credit cards
Children: Welcome
Pets: Not allowed
Smoking: Nonsmoking rooms available
Open: Year-round

The Cincinnatian, built in 1882 and renovated in 1987 into a sleek contemporary hotel, lies just a short walk from business and tourist attractions in the heart of downtown Cincinnati.

The decor is decidedly modern in the guest rooms and common areas. Tall ferns, comfortable stuffed art deco chairs, and touches of neon decorate the Crickets lounge, beneath the eight-story atrium. But there are occasional reminders of the past, for example, the French Second Empire exterior. As you ascend the staircase to the second floor, you can see how the marble steps have been worn from a century of use.

The guest rooms are decorated with coordinated fabrics and furnishings, some in shades of gray and black, others in peach tones. All the rooms have access to a complimentary overnight shoeshine and a full-time concierge. Weather information for the following day is reported during the nightly turndown.

The Palace ranks among the city's finest restaurants, decorated in creams, burgundies, and periwinkle blues. The dishes have an artistic flair and are presented under glass domes. A talented chef, Anita Hirsch-Cunningham, is also a painter whose work appears on the menu covers. Diners return here for the rack of lamb, swordfish, and beef tenderloin; each is prepared differently depending on the season. The popular Sunday brunch and elegant picnic baskets prepared by the kitchen are also options here. Afternoon tea is served in the Crickets lounge on weekdays. Patterned after similar presentations at the Dorchester Hotel in England, it includes finger sandwiches, scones, tea breads, and pastries. Reservations are advised for this popular event.

Business travelers fill the hotel during the week. International guests can easily exchange currency or order a traditional Japanese breakfast. Honeymoon and shopping packages help make the Cincinnatian appealing to weekend guests.

The Omni Netherlands Plaza

35 West Fifth Street
Cincinnati, Ohio 45202
513-421-9100
Fax: 513-421-4291
Reservations:
   Omni Hotels
   800-THE-OMNI

General manager: Mark Kenney
Accommodations: 621 rooms, including 12 suites
Rates: $135–$145; double, $165–$175; suites, $285–$800;
   packages available
Minimum stay: None
Added: 10% tax
Payment: Major credit cards
Children: Welcome
Pets: Not allowed
Smoking: Nonsmoking rooms available
Open: Year-round

When the Netherlands Plaza Hotel opened in 1931, it was hailed as an art deco masterpiece, ranking with the Waldorf-Astoria in New York. Some even said it "challenged the splendor of Solomon's Temple." Tastes changed over the years, leaving the hotel's elegance hidden beneath layers of paint and off-the-rack carpeting. A massive restoration and renovation in the early 1980s brought the hotel back to its original grandeur, and an updating in 1991 added world-class facilities for an impressive blend of old and new.

The Netherlands Plaza is true art deco: a number of the bold patterns came directly from the famed Paris Exposition Internationale des Arts Décoratifs et Industriels Modernes in 1925. The impressive foyer, fashioned of Roman Breche marble, leads to a lobby lined in rare Brazilian rosewood. Herons are featured in the designs on the etched Benedict metal elevator doors.

The breathtaking Hall of Mirrors ballroom is a two-story version of its namesake in Versailles. It seats 900 theater-style or 500 at a banquet amid gold-lined mirrored arches and peach marble. The Hall of Nations, with its own impressive medley of decorating styles, offers as many as twelve smaller conference rooms. Other meeting rooms on the property can accommodate meetings for 10 to 1200 people.

In its early years, the hotel welcomed countless presidents and entertainers. Winston Churchill is said to have been so enamored with his Netherland Plaza bathroom that he had it duplicated in his country home.

Not nearly as ornate, the guest rooms have traditional wood furnishings and brightly patterned bedspreads and window treatments. Individually controlled heating and air-conditioning units, expanded bathroom shelving, and personal computers and fax machine hook-ups are just a few of the niceties added in recent years.

Hotel guests also have access to a 13,000-square-foot health club. The Carew Tower Health and Fitness Center features high-tech weight training and cardiovascular equipment, an aerobics studio, a lap pool, whirlpool, steam room, and sauna.

The grand-scale Palm Court section of the hotel offers formal dining at Orchids or more casual fare at the Palm Court Café. The Café has its own flourishes, including Egyptian detailing and a fountain guarded by two handsome seahorses with lotus crowns. Overhead is a mural of Apollo, the god of sunlight, painted in baroque style.

Prospect Hill B&B

408 Boal Street
Cincinnati, OH 45210
513-421-4408

Owners/innkeepers: Tony Jenkins and Gary Hackney
Accommodations: 3 rooms (1 with private bath)
Rates: $69–$79

Included: Continental breakfast
Minimum stay: None
Added: No tax
Payment: Visa, MasterCard
Children: Under 12 not allowed
Pets: Not allowed
Smoking: Prohibited
Open: Year-round

Prospect Hill B&B perches high upon a hill overlooking downtown Cincinnati. In the foreground you see the old section of town, reminiscent of an antique German village, and beyond it towering skyscrapers. Its views, fireplaces, and proximity to downtown have made Prospect Hill one of the city's most popular inns. The gray Italianate townhouse with sandstone trim was built around 1867 for Jacob Deboor, a successful flour and grain merchant. Gary Hackney and Tony Jenkins have been running Prospect Hill as a bed-and-breakfast since 1989. The other houses in the area, which were once run-down, have been reclaimed in recent years.

The Victorian-style 1870s room, in the home's original front parlor, has an Eastlake walnut bedroom set. The 1940s room, decorated with traditional furnishings and lace curtains, has the best views. Both rooms have fireplaces. The 1920s room has a three-piece walnut veneered bedroom set that was in the house when they bought it. It is the only room with a private bath, and the innkeepers made the most of it, with sparkling fixtures and a large Victorian clawfoot tub. There is also a shower.

Breakfast, including homemade coffee cakes, muffins and several varieties of fruit, is served buffet-style in the oak-lined dining room downstairs. French toast, pancakes, waffles, or scrambled eggs are also set out.

A second-floor common room, painted hunter green, is outfitted with comfy wing chairs and antiques. Guests often plot out dinner or day trips with the menus and literature provided by the innkeepers.

Cleveland

The Baricelli Inn
2203 Cornell Road
Cleveland, Ohio 44106
216-791-6500
Fax: 216-791-9131

Proprietor: Paul Minnillo
General manager: Bridget Assing-Svoboda
Accommodations: 4 rooms (all with private bath), 3 suites
Rates: $95–$105; suites, $125
Included: Continental breakfast
Minimum stay: None
Added: 10% tax
Payment: Major credit cards
Children: 12 years and older welcome
Pets: Not allowed
Smoking: Allowed
Open: Year-round

The Baricelli Inn, a brownstone in the heart of Cleveland's Little Italy, was built in 1896 for the Dutch architect John Grant, who lived here until 1913. In 1986, the Baricelli opened as an intimate country inn with elegant cuisine. It is owned by the Minnillo family, which is known in the area for sophisticated restaurants like Bella Luna, the Greenhouse, and Ninth Street Grill.

Paul Minnillo is the chef. He combines French and Italian influences in popular duck and veal entrées. A house specialty is a lobster and crab ravioli with a lemon butter and chive sauce. A pastry chef attends to fresh breads, rolls, and desserts. The Continental breakfast, which is served on the original glassed-in sun porch overlooking a private garden, includes croissant and brioche, fresh fruit, fresh juices, and Royal Kona coffee.

The guest rooms have 19th-century armoires, writing desks, and four-poster beds, accented by an array of chintz fabrics and subtle pastel color schemes. All the rooms have cable television, telephones, hair dryers, and European shower gels and shampoos.

While architectural touches like bay windows and cathedral ceilings give the feeling of an elegant residence, there are also modern details like fax machines, 24-hour desk service, and a lobby reminiscent of a small luxury hotel. This is the only common area available to guests, though in the summer they can use the spacious patio area surrounded by gardens.

The inn lies on a quiet street surrounded by two-family homes. Little Italy's shops and restaurants are within walking distance, and the Cleveland Museum of Art and Case Western Reserve University are less than a mile away.

The Glidden House
1901 Ford Drive
Cleveland, Ohio 44106
216-231-8900
Fax: 216-231-2130

General manager: Sharon Chapman
Accommodations: 52 rooms, 8 suites
Rates: $88; double, $98; suites, $135–$145
Included: Continental breakfast
Minimum stay: 2 nights on graduation weekend
Added: 13% tax
Payment: Major credit cards
Children: Welcome
Pets: Not allowed
Smoking: Nonsmoking rooms available
Open: Year-round

Built in 1910 for Francis Kavanaugh Glidden, this imposing French-style mansion remained in the paint manufacturing family until 1953, when it was purchased by Case Western Reserve University. A new wing was added in 1988 for the building's current use.

Ornate beamed ceilings with a hand-painted filigreed G and original carved woodwork act as a backdrop for the turn-of-the-century American antiques, Oriental rugs, and Victoriana found throughout the inn. The guest rooms and suites are done in soft pastels, with lace curtains and Laura Ashley wall coverings. Coffee and tea greet guests upon arrival, and each room has a telephone, cable television, and clock radio. One room has a woodburning fireplace.

Breakfast, a buffet, includes bagels, homemade muffins, fresh fruit, and cereal. A new restaurant in the carriage house, Miracles, serves lunch and dinner. Try the special sandwiches, which wedge roast beef or turkey between potato cakes instead of bread.

Because the Glidden House is right on campus, it is within walking distance of many cultural activities, including the Cleveland Museum of Art. It also borders Cleveland's Little Italy, with antiques shops, galleries, and more restaurants. At the inn, Glidden House mystery nights have become popular with both weekend and business guests.

The Ritz-Carlton Cleveland

1515 West Third Street
Cleveland, Ohio 44113
216-623-1300
Fax: 216-623-0515
Reservations:
    Ritz-Carlton Hotels
    800-241-3333

General manager: Cheryl O'Donnell
Accommodations: 208 rooms, including 19 suites
Rates: $160–$200; suites, $235–$2,000; packages available
Minimum stay: None
Added: 13% tax
Payment: Major credit cards
Children: Welcome
Pets: None
Smoking: Nonsmoking rooms available
Open: Year-round

Cleveland's addition to the Ritz-Carlton family of hotels won't disappoint in its decor and service. In the heart of Cleveland's bustling business and historic district, it has helped to fuel the city's renaissance.

The fineries here include crystal chandeliers and 18th-and 19th-century oils and antiques. Handwoven rugs grace marble floors. Guest rooms have marble baths with telephones, plush terry robes, and honor bars with refrigerators. There is round-the-clock room service and housekeeping twice daily. On the upper floor, the Ritz-Carlton Club offers elegantly appointed guest rooms and spacious suites with dramatic views of the Cauyahoga River and Lake Erie. The concierge staff is available to assist with the coordination of dinner, theater, and travel reservations. Complimentary food and beverages are offered here.

Dining options at the Ritz-Carlton Cleveland include the Restaurant, with its own a panoramic view, where Sunday brunch is especially popular. The Grill, serving meats, seafood, and shellfish, is richly appointed with mahogany and Italian marble for the look of an English club. The Café serves break-fast, lunch, dinner and a spectacular Sunday brunch. A harpist accompanies afternoon tea in the Lobby Lounge. On Sundays, there's a special childrens' tea with peanut butter and grape jelly pinwheels, and mouse-shaped American Cheese sand-wiches.

The Fitness Center, on the seventh floor, has an inviting indoor pool and spa beneath an atrium skylight. Business meetings are held in conference rooms, board rooms, and the elegant Ballroom. The hotel also adjoins the over 120 shops at the Avenue at Tower City Center.

Columbus

50 Lincoln
50 East Lincoln Street
Columbus, Ohio 43215
614-291-5056
Fax: 614-291-4924

Innkeepers: Zoe and Jack Johnstone
Manager: Kris Miesel
Accommodations: 6 rooms (all with private bath), 3 suites
Rates: $89; double, $99; suites, single, $109; double, $119
Included: Full breakfast
Minimum stay: None
Added: 15.75% tax
Payment: Major credit cards
Children: Welcome
Pets: Not allowed
Smoking: Allowed
Open: Year-round

Jack Johnstone and his wife, Zoe, both professional musicians, have created the closest thing the Midwest offers to a well-run European pensione, with lots of art, eccentricity, and a darned good cup of morning coffee. Jack doesn't only tolerate smoking at the inn—he encourages it.

The Johnstones don't go in for fancy Victorian headboards and armoires, but you can be sure the queen-size mattresses are firm and comfortable. Telephones, televisions with cable, and desks are found in each room. An exposed brick chimney creates the charming centerpiece in Room 8, a large suite under the sloped ceilings of the attic. Works of local artists appear in all the rooms, including gravestone etchings and hand-painted firescreens. Note, however, that the fireplaces are just for show.

The downstairs parlor is especially inviting, with wicker furniture, floral print curtains, and pink and peach hues. The breakfast room is attached, where guests choose between bacon and eggs or French toast, with side dishes of granola, cantaloupe, juice, and coffee. A bay window looks out on the brick-lined street.

50 Lincoln is in Columbus's Short North district, a mile from both Ohio State University and the heart of downtown. Ethnic restaurants and taverns fill the storefronts, as do artists who paint right in the windows.

Jack and Zoe, former Californians, are active members of this funky urban neighborhood (Jack even puts out a newsletter). The gentrification has been slow going, however. Some of the other Italianate homes on the same block are still boarded up, so it's not a good spot for a stroll after dark. It is an excellent place, however, to come home to after dinner, play a board game, and have a smoke. If Jack's around, he'll probably join you. Or perhaps Zoe or a guest musician will take a turn on the grand piano.

The Great Southern Hotel
310 South High Street
Columbus, Ohio 43215
614-228-3800
800-228-3789 in Ohio
800-328-2073 elsewhere
Fax: 614-228-7666

General manager: Steve Kovatz
Accommodations: 186 rooms, 10 suites
Rates: $90–$110; double, $100–$120; suites, single, $110;
   double, $120
   Packages available
Included: All meals available
Minimum stay: None
Added: 15.75% tax
Payment: Major credit cards
Children: Welcome
Pets: Upon special arrangement
Smoking: Nonsmoking rooms available
Open: Year-round

From the minute you step into the lobby of the Great Southern Hotel, you'll understand the labor of love that went into its restoration. The marble floors, polished brass, and magnificent stained glass ceiling speak of turn-of-the-century opulence, when the Great Southern Fireproof Building and Opera House had a theater, restaurants, shops, and residential space under its roof.

The guest rooms hold to the antique theme, with traditional cherry furnishings, high ceilings, and floral wallpaper. Vintage Visit and Southern Hospitality packages offer roses, champagne, and a $15 voucher that can be used in the restaurant and lounge or for room service.

The hotel's restaurant, Chutney's, serves slow-roasted prime rib and chicken Washington State topped with sun-dried cherries and a rich Marsala cream sauce. Sebastian's, an English pub with a center island bar and wood booths, offers lighter meals and drinks. Thurber's, an elegant restaurant decorated with illustrations by the humorist James Thurber, has now become a meeting facility, one of seven on the premises.

The grand ballroom has stained glass windows and can accommodate wedding receptions of up to 500 people. If you want a respite from the hustle and bustle of the cavernous main lobby, try the cozy overstuffed chairs and couches that line the mezzanine.

While on the mezzanine, note the exhibitions by local artists, which change monthly. The building's link with the arts community goes back to the 1930s, when the Great Southern was the hub of Columbus's cultural scene, welcoming Lillian Russell, John Barrymore, and Sarah Bernhardt among its guests. Ask George Dill, a local historian who runs the flower shop, to tell you more about the hotel's history. He can also keep you updated on the progress of the opera house restoration, which is still seeking financial backing.

The Worthington Inn
649 High Street
Worthington, Ohio 43085
614-885-2600

General manager: Shirley Black
Accommodations: 26 rooms, 4 suites
Rates: $85–$95; double, $95–$105; suites, $120–$150
Included: Continental breakfast; all meals available
Minimum stay: None
Added: 9.7% tax
Payment: Major credit cards
Children: Welcome
Pets: Not allowed
Smoking: Nonsmoking rooms available
Open: Year-round

Established as a stagecoach stop in 1831, the Worthington Inn was added onto several times before the most recent renovation in 1983. The brick inn now boasts a handsome mansard roof and romantic balconies. While its service and decorative touches are reminiscent of the best bed-and-breakfasts, the inn caters to wedding parties and business travelers who enjoy the relative peace and quiet of this historic village just 15 minutes from downtown Columbus.

The Continental breakfast is served in one of the four dining rooms. At dinner, fresh seafood and exotic salads are the specialties. Three second-floor meeting rooms cater to family gatherings or small meetings, and the third-floor Van Loon Ballroom boasts a huge Czechoslovakian chandelier hanging from a cathedral ceiling. This is a popular spot for weddings and banquets.

Though motel-like in design, the rooms have early American and heavy Victorian motifs. Antique and quality reproduction beds almost reach the 8-foot ceilings. One room has a pair of rope beds with mattresses raised high off the floor. Hand stenciling includes a stagecoach silhouette, in honor of the inn's origins. They all have telephones, televisions, wet bars, desks, and Caswell-Massey toiletries.

Four more suites are in the 1817 Snow House down the street. Where some of the historic charm has been renovated out of the Worthington, these rooms have retained their 19th-century character with slightly off-kilter brick walls and staircases, the product of almost 175 years of settling. They also have queen-size antique oak and walnut bedsteads.

The Worthington Inn is in a tiny historic village full of New England–style craft and antiques shops, stately homes, and churches. Golfing, fishing, boating, and fishing are nearby, as is Ohio State University, about five miles away.

Dallas/Fort Worth

The Adolphus
1321 Commerce
Dallas, Texas 75202
214-742-8200
800-441-0574 in Texas
800-221-9083 in U.S.
Fax: 214-747-3532

Managing director: Garvin O'Neil
Accommodations: 431 rooms and suites
Rates: $156–$220; double, $176–$240; suites, $350–$1,150;
   weekend packages
Added: 13% tax
Payment: Major credit cards
Children: Welcome
Pets: Not allowed
Smoking: Nonsmoking rooms available
Open: Year-round

Built in 1912 by the beer baron Adolphus Busch, Dallas's grand and glorious landmark hotel was totally renovated in 1981, combining the grandeur of an earlier era with the comforts of a modern luxury hotel.

The exterior is an extravagance of ornamentation—sculptures, bas-relief figures, gargoyles, heraldic characters, even a corner turret shaped like a beer stein. The interior is opulent, with a wealth of antiques from Europe and Asia as well as the United States. The interior looks like a museum, with two huge 1660s Flemish tapestries, a six-foot-tall portrait of Napoleon in coronation robes, and carved English Regency oak furniture.

The centerpiece of the Adolphus is the French Room, a dining room with a vaulted ceiling, columned walls, and rococo murals. On the ceiling, cherubs holding floral garlands fly beneath a pale blue sky.

Unlike those in new hotels, the guest rooms come in more than thirty configurations. Retaining their original high ceilings, they are warm yet elegant, decorated in reproduction antique furniture, matching draperies and bedspreads, and touches of lace. All the rooms have refrigerators, multiple phones, and TVs in armoires. Down comforters and terrycloth robes add an extra touch of luxury.

Terrace suites have an expansive sitting area, two baths, and a large terrace. Skylight suites, on the nineteenth floor, have slanting glass exterior walls, a large wet bar, and Asian accents mingled with reproduction period furniture.

Club Adolphus rooms, on the top three floors of the hotel, are geared towards the corporate traveler. Guests staying in Club Adolphus rooms have exclusive access to the hotel's penthouse suite, once Mr. Busch's own private residence, now staffed with its own concierge and outfitted with business machines such as a fax, credit card phone, typewriter, and personal computer.

Oriented to service, the Adolphus has a concierge, multilingual staff, 24-hour room service, and valet parking ($10). The French Room serves dinner only: entrées start at $22; prix fixe dinners are $48.50. The Bistro, with country French decor, offers Continental fare for all three meals and a late evening supper. The Lobby Living Room is open for afternoon tea and cocktails and has entertainment in the evening. The Walt Garrison Rodeo Bar is open for lunch and cocktails.

For light workouts the Adolphus has a fitness room with treadmills, stair machines, a stationary bicycle, rowing machine and free weights. Guests in need of more extensive athletic facilities can use the Texas Club a block away for $10 per day. The Club has an indoor lap pool, racquetball, squash, an indoor track, a gym, Nautilus equipment, and a steam room.

Fairmont Hotel
1717 North Akard Street
Dallas, Texas 75201
214-720-2020
800-527-4727
Fax: 214-720-5282

General manager: Ray Tackaberry
Accommodations: 551 rooms including 51 suites
Rates: $125–$215; double, $150–$240; suites, 325–$1,000
Added: 13% tax

Payment: Major credit cards
Children: Welcome
Pets: Seeing eye dogs and hearing dogs only
Smoking: Nonsmoking rooms available
Open: Year-round

The Fairmont is a sophisticated downtown hotel next to the Dallas Arts District. A new Texas marble exterior was just one of the changes made as part of the 1989 multimillion-dollar renovation. With sweeping public areas and one of the best-known restaurants in town, it makes an excellent base for seeing the city of Dallas.

The lobby lounge is dominated by stunning floral arrangements and an eye-catching contemporary work of art celebrating Cabeza de Vaca, the first European to see the interior of Texas, New Mexico, and Arizona.

The Pyramid Lounge, also distinctive, has a bright mural depicting events and figures of the 1960s. The Venetian Room is especially dramatic, with deep slate–colored walls, red chairs, wall sconces, and Spanish arches. Once a supper club, the room now serves an abundant Sunday brunch in a gondola buffet. Its hallmark dish, pancakes Oscar, — buckwheat pancakes sprinkled with brown sugar, covered in meringue, and topped with a strawberry sauce—will satisfy the sweetest of sweet tooths.

But it's the Pyramid restaurant, with its intimate settings and award-winning cuisine, that draws the most attention. Entrées, from $19 to $27, include grilled rack of lamb with crab flan and curry sabayon, roast maple leaf duck with essensia wine, orange peel, and black beans; and grilled Dover sole with citrus compote and black chanterelle mushrooms. A harpist adds to the ambience, and a Spanish guitarist entertains in the late evenings.

The guest rooms are in two towers. The furnishings are attractive, with such luxuries as down pillows and Irish linens. Amenities include round-the-clock room service, nightly turndown, and twice-daily housekeeping.

The sunny Brasserie restaurant is open 24 hours a day. There is also a sports bar that serves deli lunches on weekdays and is decorated with sports paraphernalia lent by hotel employees. The Olympic-size pool and surrounding patio is big enough to satisfy the needs of such a large hotel, and the views of downtown Dallas from the pool deck are terrific. Guests can also use the facilities at the YMCA, next door.

Valet parking is $12 per day.

The Grand Kempinski Dallas
15201 Dallas Parkway
Dallas, Texas 75248
214-386-6000
800-426-3135
Telex: 795515
Fax: 214-386-6937

Managing director: Michael Spamer
Accommodations: 529 rooms and suites
Rooms: $125–$145; suites, $250–$1,200
Added: 13% tax
Payment: Major credit cards
Children: Free in room with parents
Pets: Not allowed
Smoking: Nonsmoking rooms available
Open: Year-round

In 1987 Kempinski Hotels, a West German luxury hotel chain, took over this modern property, its first venture in North America. Actually in Addison, about 15 minutes north of central Dallas, the Grand Kempinski has a spaciousness most downtown hotels can't achieve. A glass atrium adds to the lofty quality, while Italian marble throughout provides elegance.

With 37 suites (18 on two levels) and a concierge floor in addition to the standard rooms, there are plenty of choices. The rooms, with French provincial, English country, or Oriental furnishings, all have a decidedly masculine air. Special touches include turndown service, fresh flowers, and telephones in the bathrooms.

Not to be missed on a Sunday morning is the champagne brunch in the Malachite Showroom. The vibrant green and black surroundings are striking. The brunch runs about $21 for adults, $13 for children under 12.

Monte Carlo is the hotel's fine restaurant. With silk bougainvillea vines overhead and mosaic floors, it has a Mediterranean bistro flavor. Crab and spinach lasagna with crustacean sauce and boneless quails stuffed with spinach and mushrooms in a phyllo pastry are examples of the creative fare. Dinner entrées range from $20 to $25, while the restaurant's brasserie serves lighter meals at lower prices.

Le Café also has a pleasant atmosphere and inventive menu. A rose on every table compliments the rose and green decor. Dinner may feature pecan smoked shrimp salad ($12.50) and sirloin chablisienne with white wine mirepoix and shallot sauce ($14.50). English teas are served in the Bristol Lounge, and the

Atrium Bar has a piano player and complimentary hors d'oeuvres in the evening.

After dinner you can dance the night away in Kempi's, the hotel's nightclub, complete with neon lights and fog. If the dancing doesn't burn off enough calories, there are four lighted tennis courts, two racquetball courts, two heated pools with adjoining hot tubs—one inside, one outside—and a fitness club.

Concierge, room, laundry, dry cleaning, telex, and fax services are available 24 hours a day. The hotel also offers an executive business center—secretarial support, complimentary limousine service within three miles of the hotel, and free transportation to the nearby Galleria mall. Valet parking is $7; self-parking in a covered lot is free.

Hotel Crescent Court

400 Crescent Court
Dallas, Texas 75201
214-871-3200
800-654-6541
Fax: 214-871-3272

Managing director: Seamus McManus
Accommodations: 188 rooms and 28 suites
Rates: $220–$310; double, $250–$340; suites, $425–$1,250
Added: 13% tax
Payment: Major credit cards
Children: Free in room with parents
Pets: With approval
Smoking: Nonsmoking rooms available
Open: Year-round

Opened in late 1985, the Crescent Court is a Rosewood Hotel, a sister property to the Mansion on Turtle Creek, a mile up the road, and the Bel Air in California. Unlike the other Rosewoods, however, this hotel is designed for the business traveler. But even if you're in Dallas just for pleasure, it is a hotel well worth discovering.

Although its architect, Philip Johnson, was inspired by the Royal Crescent in Bath, England, the Crescent Court, with its light gray exterior and mansard roof, bears more of a resemblance to a Loire Valley château. Inside you are treated like the château's lord; the ever-dutiful staff seem to appear magically just when you need them, then discreetly fade and let you have the run of the manor.

Staying here is an immersion in beauty. Every sense is stimulated from the time you enter the lobby. Arched windows, Spanish and Italian marble floors, Louis XV furnishings and European art, massive floral arrangements and airy palms set the tone. In the background is classical music. The bellman, the desk clerk, and the concierge are more than attentive. Soon you've forgotten the traffic and daily hassle. You can relax. Somebody else will take care of everything.

Make no mistake, however; this is not a retreat. There's a vibrancy about the place, a mood that flows from the lobby to the restaurant to the courtyard beyond. The Beau Nash restaurant and bar, named for the arbiter of taste in 18th-century England, is done in hunter green marble with floral motifs. It has a lively bistro atmosphere and excellent food—southwestern and California cuisine dominate—and is popular with residents as well as guests. The brasswork on the wood bar is said by some to resemble the hotel itself. Prices run about $6.50 for breakfast, $9–$12 for lunch, and $12–$16 for dinner.

In 1990 the hotel opened the Conservatory, an elegant dining room. Entrées include grilled sea bass with sorrel sea urchin sauce, roast Peking duck with sun-dried cherries, and grilled shrimp with lobster sauce and lemon fettuccine. For special occasions, the hotel's wine cellar can be rented by small parties (up to sixteen). Seated under arched brick ceilings and surrounded by hundreds of vintage wines, a candlelit dinner here is memorable.

The rooms are just as beautiful as the public areas. With a residential feeling, they're spacious and aesthetically pleasing in subtle pastels and rich earth tones. French windows open to the courtyard below. The furnishings are comfortably elegant—easy chairs and sofas with down cushions, armoire desks, and original works of art.

Above all, it is attention to detail that sets this hotel apart. In your room, expect fresh flowers, three phones, the newspaper, hooded terrycloth robes, and brass and marble fixtures in the bathroom. Some suites have wet bars and refrigerators. If you want to be truly pampered, a maid will unpack your luggage. When you need a hem repaired, a seamstress will help. Laundry comes back in a lined wicker basket. Turndown service includes a fresh orchid on your pillow and the weather report for the following day.

The hotel is part of a project called the Crescent. Off the lobby, a courtyard leads to a three-level marketplace of chic shops and galleries; on the other side of the hotel are three 18-story office towers.

The Spa at the Crescent, a luxurious private health and fitness club, is also part of the complex. Rose marble floors surround the whirlpools, and there are plush sofas in the locker room. The wooden lockers are so well equipped—including designer workout clothes—that guests need only bring their athletic shoes. European treatments are combined with America's zest for fitness. Beauty treatments, water therapy and massage, exercise facilities, and nutrition are all included. The Spa also has a Food and Juice Bar, with naturally healthy lunches and snacks. Hotel guests can use the workout area for $20 per day and, for an additional $20, can work with a private trainer. Wet area usage is $25. A 1-hour European facial is $60. Packages are also available. The hotel's outdoor swimming pool is separate from the spa and is free to all guests.

The Crescent Court complex stands on a hilltop on the north side of the city. Between the hotel and Dallas's downtown skyline lies the West End Historical District. The hotel is also near the Arts District and Dallas Market Center. Dallas/Fort Worth International Airport is a 20-minute drive, while Love Field is only 10 minutes away. There is free transportation to the downtown business district aboard the Crescent Trolley on weekdays.

Hotel St. Germain
2516 Maple Avenue
Dallas, Texas 75201
214-871-2516
Fax: 214-871-0740

Proprietor: Claire L. Heymann
Accommodations: 7 suites
Rates: Suites, $200-$600
Included: Breakfast
Added: 13% tax
Payment: Major credit cards; no personal checks
Children: Discouraged
Pets: Not allowed
Smoking: Allowed
Open: Year-round

Located in the McKinney Avenue section of Dallas—a shopping, dining, and entertainment area near downtown—the St. Germain is a 1906 Victorian mansion beautifully converted into a small luxury hotel by owner Claire Heymann. Named for Heymann's French grandmother and the left bank of Paris (Heymann studied at the Sorbonne during college), the St. Germain opened in late 1991, making it one of the newest additions to the Dallas lodging scene, and certainly one of the most unique. With only seven suites, the feeling is intimate, yet the St. Germain has many services offered by larger hotels such as nightly turndown (complete with a chocolate), valet parking, room service, and a round-the-clock concierge.

The suites themselves are tastefully appointed with fine antiques, elegantly draped canopy beds, and fireplaces. Many of the furnishings came from the owner's years in New Orleans. All suites have cable television, Jacuzzi or deep-soaking tubs, terrycloth robes, and top-of-the-line toiletries in the baths. Two of the guest suites have their own porches, accented with fanciful wrought iron railings. Outside there's an inviting courtyard for guests to enjoy.

In the morning, a silver bread basket arrives at your door filled with brioche, croissants, sticky buns, fruited danish, and other tempting pastries, along with café au lait. On Friday and Saturday evenings, meals are served in the hotel's dining room, which is graced by a magnificent crystal chandelier. The four-course prix fixe dinner is $65 per person, and entreé choices range from poached salmon and julienne of truffle, leek, and radicchio in a champagne butter sauce served with a baked dumpling and asparagus tips, to seared sirloin of beef with a dijon garlic crust and topped with a chanterelle sauce. Dinners are open to the public, and since seating in the dining room is limited, reservations are required.

Loews Anatole Hotel
2201 Stemmons Freeway
Dallas, Texas 75207
214-748-1200
800-23-LOEWS
Fax: 214-761-7520

Managing director: John Thacker
Accommodations: 1,620 units
Rates: $135–$145; double, $160–$170; suites, $250–$1,150
Added: 13% tax
Payment: Major credit cards
Children: Under 18 free in room with parents
Pets: Not allowed
Smoking: Nonsmoking rooms available
Open: Year-round

Loews Anatole is so large, you need a map to get around. Spread over 45 acres, it's a city unto itself, with nine restaurants, eight lounges, more than a dozen shops, and a huge health spa. Downtown Dallas is about a 5-minute drive away.

The largest hotel in the Southwest, the Anatole is primarily geared to conventions. But individuals and smaller groups can enjoy its many services. It's worth a stop just to see the public areas—parking is free, so pull off Stemmons Freeway and take a look. Two enormous elephants, carved from monkey pod wood by entire villages in Thailand, stand guard inside the tower section. Behind them is an 18th-century white marble Hindustani pavilion from a royal palace in India.

Inside Atrium II hang five fantastic batik banners, created in Ceylon especially for the hotel. The Jade Room, used for receptions, has a magnificent collection of jade artistry. Outside the Wedgwood Ballroom, with its collection of pieces dating from the 18th century, is a rare Wedgwood vase nearly five feet tall. And so the collection continues—much of it inspired by Trammell Crow, who developed the hotel as well as the innovative Infomart across the freeway.

Behind the hotel in a southern mansion–style building is the Verandah Club, a health spa with indoor and outdoor jogging tracks; indoor and outdoor pools; tennis, racquetball, and squash courts; a full-size basketball court; exercise rooms; and a sauna, steam room, and whirlpool section. A private club, Verandah, is available to guests for about $12 a day. Extra fees are charged for racquetball. Outdoor swimming is free.

The guest rooms are in two atrium high-rises and a 27-story tower. The traditional furnishings are comfortable if not distinctive. The 70 tower suites have small parlors and elegant baths with marble vanities and a phone. A variety of other suites are also available. Two concierge floors provide Continental breakfast, afternoon wine and cheese, and a full-time concierge.

Guests can dine at the Anatole any hour of the day. There are eight restaurants on the premises; several are open 24 hours. Room service is also available round-the-clock.

The Mansion on Turtle Creek

2821 Turtle Creek Boulevard
Dallas, Texas 75219
214-559-2100
800-527-5432
Fax: 214-528-4187

Managing director: Jeff Trigger
Accommodations: 142 rooms and suites
Rates: $215–$305; double, $255–$345; suites, $685–$1,200
Added: 13% tax
Payment: Major credit cards
Children: $40 extra in room with parents
Pets: Not allowed
Smoking: Allowed
Open: Year-round

The only problem with staying at the Mansion is that it spoils you for staying anywhere else. It's a world of quiet opulence — a combination of aesthetic beauty and attentive service. Beginning at registration, guests' preferences for everything from newspapers to wine are noted and attended to, with records filed for future visits. Best of all, the staff's hospitality seems genuine.

The hotel is indeed a mansion, once the home of the millionaire Sheppard King, set on a terraced hillside in one of Dallas's most prestigious residential areas. Built in 1925, it has a 16th-century Italianate design with imaginative spires and turrets. In 1981 Rosewood Hotels restored the original building, converted it into a fine restaurant, and built a complementary hotel tower next door.

At this hotel, the concierge wears a suit, not a uniform. There are no shops off the lobby, no hints of the commercial world. Instead, there's soft music, handsomely arranged fresh flowers, and a bevy of employees (more than two staff members for every guest) to satisfy every whim. The lobby resembles a fine living room, accented with antique mirrors and a Chippendale breakfront.

The guest rooms are exquisite. Decorated in peach, gold, or beige, they have four-poster beds, overstuffed chairs with ottomans, love seats, armoires with TVs, and French doors opening onto small balconies. (Although the rooms are all the same size, they cost more on the upper floors because of the view.) The bathrooms are not only luxurious but pleasing to the eye, decorated in marble and brass. Terry robes, bathroom telephones, and turndown service add to the feeling of luxury. In the evening, a special treat is delivered, perhaps spice tea or cookies and milk. Other courtesies include overnight shoeshine and 24-hour pressing and room service.

Three guest rooms open onto the hotel's attractive pool, which is heated in cooler weather. Guests also have complimentary use of a nearby health club, with transportation provided.

One of the highlights of staying at the Mansion is dining at its restaurant, an architectural treasure as well as a culinary delight. Much of the grandeur of the original home, such as carved fireplaces and imported marble floors, has been retained in its restoration. A dramatic wrought-iron staircase spirals up from the foyer. The ceiling of the main dining room is a composite of 2,400 pieces of enameled and inlaid wood. A set of stained glass windows depicts British barons signing the Magna Carta, and two pairs of early-19th-century Spanish cathedral doors lead to one of the dining areas.

The cuisine does justice to its surroundings. Nouvelle American dishes with a southwestern flair are well prepared and attractively presented. Rack of lamb roasted with rosemary and mustard sauce, Louisiana crabcakes, and lobster tacos are popular favorites. The service is polished but unpretentious. Elaborate weekend brunches are popular with residents as well as hotel guests.

Like its sister hotel, the Crescent Court, the Mansion has a wine cellar stocked with more than 28,000 bottles of vintage wine; it seats up to twelve for guests' private dinner parties. Breakfast and lunch are served in the cheerful Promenade.

About five minutes from downtown Dallas, the Mansion is near many business, cultural, and shopping areas. Dallas/Fort Worth International Airport is a 30-minute drive. Valet parking costs $10.85; there is no self-parking.

Radisson Plaza Hotel Fort Worth

815 Main Street
Fort Worth, Texas 76102
817-870-2100
Fax: 817-870-2100, ext. 1555

General manager: Armel Santens
Accommodations: 517 rooms
Rates: $128–$140; double, $143–$160; suites, $225–$1,000;
   weekend rates available
Added: 13% tax
Payment: Major credit cards
Children: Free in room with parents
Pets: Accepted with deposit
Smoking: Nonsmoking rooms available
Open: Year-round

Today's Radisson Plaza Hotel opened in 1921 as the Hotel Texas. At one end of downtown Fort Worth, it reigned for years as the city's social center. Big dance bands played in its ballroom, and the rich and famous stayed in its guest rooms. One of its most noteworthy guests was John F. Kennedy, who spent his last night in the hotel before going to Dallas.

The hotel closed in 1979, reopening in 1981. By then it had been named to the National Register of Historic Places.

The 14-story hotel is a rectangle of red brick and terra cotta. While its exterior was virtually unchanged in the renovation, the interior was gutted and is now totally modern. The lobby is soothing, with waterfalls, lush plants, exotic cockatoo, and reflecting fish ponds.

There are two restaurants. The Café Centennial is casual and relaxed, and the Crystal Cactus serves southwestern cuisine. In the evenings, a piano player entertains in the lobby bar beneath a glass atrium.

The rooms, traditionally furnished in blues, burgundies, and beiges, are masculine and spacious, but not particularly distinctive. The plaza level has such extras as Continental breakfast and afternoon hors d'oeuvres. The health club, in an adjacent office tower, has a heated pool, sauna, and exercise room.

The concierge and staff make every effort to attend to each guest's needs. Room service operates from 6:00 A.M. to midnight. Self-parking in an underground garage costs $6 per day; valet parking is also available for $9. Since the hotel is within a few blocks of the Tarrant County Convention Center and I-30, it is easily accessible.

The Worthington Hotel
200 Main Street
Fort Worth, Texas 76102
817-870-1000
800-772-5977 in Texas
800-433-5677 in U.S.
Fax: 817-332-5679

General manager: Robert L. Jameson
Accommodations: 507 rooms and suites
Rates: $129–$169; double, $139–$179; suites, $300–$400
Added: 13% tax
Payment: Major credit cards
Children: Under 18 free in room with parents
Pets: Not allowed
Smoking: Nonsmoking rooms available
Open: Year-round

A hospitable staff, a good location, and an excellent fitness club make the Worthington a topnotch hotel. Built in 1981, it occupies three city blocks at one end of downtown Fort Worth. Its ultra-modern exterior makes an interesting contrast to Sundance Square, a turn-of-the-century shopping and entertainment area just across the street with fancy boutiques and restaurants. For a romantic tour of the city, you can climb into a horse-drawn carriage right at the hotel's doors. The city's attractions as well as many business addresses are a short drive away.

The Worthington's fitness club has an indoor pool, outdoor tennis courts, a sundeck, sauna, whirlpool, and exercise room with free weights, Lifecycles, and treadmills. The club is welcoming, from a sociable staff to such extras as a comfortable sitting area with magazines and newspapers, baskets of fruit, and a big-screen TV. The pool and whirlpool are free for hotel guests; the other facilities can be used for a daily fee.

Dining gets lots of attention at the Worthington: in addition to elegant Reflections and the casual Brasserie LaSalle, the hotel operates Winfield's '08 family restaurant and the Houston Street Bakery, both across the street, and Firehall Marketplace Deli, in Sundance Square. The room service menu is above average, featuring treats from the bakery as well as the hotel's own kitchen. Afternoon tea and lavish Sunday brunches are Worthington traditions.

The hotel has a distinctively contemporary design. Its marble lobby is softened by gentle waterfalls and lots of greenery. Redecorated in 1990 with contemporary furniture, rich mahogany, art deco lamps, and deep mauves and grays, the guest rooms are modern and sleek, with especially comfortable sitting areas. The prints in the rooms are from originals in Fort Worth museums. Terrace suites have expansive balconies overlooking the city, separate living and bed rooms, and lots of extra features.

Throughout the hotel, the staff is Texas-friendly, and a concierge is on duty for special requests. Valet parking costs $9; self-parking is $6.

Denver

The Brown Palace Hotel
321 17th Street
Denver, Colorado 80202
303-297-3111
800-228-2917 in Colorado
800-321-2599 in U.S.
Fax: 303-293-9204

General manager: Peter H. Aeby
Accommodations: 205 rooms, 25 suites
Rates: $149–$199; double, $159–$214; suites, $210–$625
Minimum stay: None
Added: 12% tax ·
Payment: Major credit cards
Children: Free under age 18
Pets: Prohibited
Smoking: 3 nonsmoking floors
Open: Year-round

Fashioned from Arizona sandstone and Colorado red granite, the Brown Palace juts up among Denver's reflective glass towers and aluminum shafts like some kind of rare, ancient tree in an ultramodern forest. The millionaire businessman Henry C. Brown had the brawny landmark built in 1892. He enlisted Colorado's leading architect, Frank E. Edbrooke, to design it, challenging him to conform its shape to a triangular plot at the edge of the downtown core. Edbrooke outdid himself, crafting a nine-story Italian Renaissance Victorian with an atrium lobby that soars past tiers of lacy balconies to a Victorian stained glass ceiling 80 feet above. In the afternoons, Denverites — who call it simply "the Brown" — gather there for tea, striding across the Mexican onyx floor into a more gracious and elegant century.

The refurbishing, which was done in preparation for the Brown's August 12, 1992, centennial, has the hotel looking better than it has in years. That includes the rooms, no two of which, it seems, are alike. They lean toward dark Edwardian furnishings and framed oil paintings with occasional forays into the red velvet and burled walnut of Old West baroque, or beveled mirrors and bright art deco colors. The suites give new meaning to the word "spacious"; those in the corners are especially desirable. President Eisenhower used the suite named for him as a summer White House; he even dented the molding in the fireplace while practicing his golf swing. Another suite is named for the Beatles.

Even before the centennial preparations, the Brown Palace reestablished its culinary credentials: the Palace Arms again ranks as one of Denver's foremost (and priciest) restaurants. Nineteenth century antiques, ornate mirrors, and rich Moroccan leather banquettes provide an Old World setting for the sumptuous cuisine that weaves together traditional American and classical French cooking with southwestern and new American influences. That translates into juicy rack of Colorado lamb with herbed goat cheese crust, veal chop with black Atlantic mussels, or applewood-smoked breast of duck with black coffee and Kahlua barbecue sauce. Some things haven't changed: the Ship's Tavern remains as relaxed, and nautical, as ever, down to its models of frigate ships and its crow's nest. The Brown's downtown location is convenient to the state capitol, which is five blocks away, the comedy and jazz clubs of Larimer Square, and the Denver Center for the Performing Arts.

The Burnsley Hotel
1000 Grant Street
Denver, Colorado 80203
303-830-1000
800-231-3915
Fax: 303-830-7676

General manager: Joy Burns
Accommodations: 82 suites
Rates: $95–$235
Included: Valet parking
Minimum stay: None
Added: 12% tax
Payment: Major credit cards
Children: Welcome
Pets: Allowed with prior approval
Smoking: Allowed
Open: Year-round

Originally a small apartment house, the 15-story Burnsley underwent an inspired $5 million remodeling to reemerge in 1985 as a handsome all-suite hotel. The lobby now resembles an opulent drawing room, with polished marble floors, shimmering brass, richly textured furnishings, and carpets in deep, sensuous colors. The ambience extends to a paneled lounge and an intimate, banquette-lined restaurant.

The suites, though not so lavish, still show a decorator's touch in their mauve, burgundy, and mint green color schemes. The smallest mimic hotel rooms with kitchenettes, but most have separate living rooms, bedrooms, and full kitchens (though pots, pans, and dishes are stocked only for long-term renters). All open onto private balconies.

Designed for business travelers, the Burnsley not only furnishes rooms with plush robes, color televisions, and phones, but also provides turndown service, a 24-hour concierge, excellent room service from the lobby restaurant, a small outdoor swimming pool, and complimentary valet parking. Overall, it emphasizes personal attention and has hired a professional staff eager to cater to guests. Among the Burnsley's other assets are live jazz in the lobby lounge from Thursday through Saturday, and moderately priced dinners of grilled salmon with hollandaise, chicken breast with wild mushrooms, or blackened Delmonico steak. The state capitol is only four blocks north, but the Burnsley basks in residential quiet.

Cambridge Hotel
1560 Sherman Street
Denver, Colorado 80203
303-831-1252
800-877-1252
Fax: 303-831-4724

General manager: Stan Cook
Accommodations: 27 suites
Rates: Midweek, $110–$210; weekends, $89
Included: Continental breakfast, limo service downtown
Minimum stay: None
Added: 12% tax
Payment: Major credit cards
Children: Free under age 18
Pets: Not allowed
Smoking: One nonsmoking floor
Open: Year-round

One of Denver's best-kept secrets is this jewel of a hotel on a tree-shaded street near downtown and half a block from the state capitol. Though tucked away in a nondescript 1940s building, the Cambridge has the intimacy and friendliness of a private club and pampers guests with all-suite spaciousness and grand-hotel services.

The elegant suites come in three types: parlor, one-bedroom, and two-bedroom. The task of choosing a room involves more than deciding on size, however. The design motif for each of the suites ranges over a broad spectrum, from English traditional to ultramodern. The Hunt Suite features antler chairs and floor-to-ceiling bookcases; the French Country Suite conjures up the Bordeaux wine country; and the Oriental Suite seems to have been imported from Hong Kong or Singapore. The common thread is a commitment to elegance and functional comfort, whether furnishings are antique or contemporary.

No matter what its theme, each suite has a butler kitchen with a coffeemaker (and complimentary supply of coffee and tea) and a refrigerator stocked with soft drinks, juices, and sparkling water. Suites also have terrycloth robes, hair dryers, phones, color televisions, and in some cases, trouser presses. Local phone calls are free; so are shoeshines. A Continental breakfast of orange juice, yogurt, and a choice of breads, pastry, or cereal is delivered to the rooms. At night, maids leave liqueurs and chocolates when they turn down the beds.

The staff could not be more attentive or friendly, arranging for anything from faxes to limos and helicopters. There's someone on duty 24 hours a day. Meanwhile, Le Profile, one of Denver's oldest Continental restaurants, is just off the lobby and provides room service. Legislators often gather in its lounge. The Cambridge enchants everyone who discovers it.

Castle Marne Bed & Breakfast

1572 Race Street
Denver, Colorado 80206
303-331-0621
800-92-MARNE
Fax: 303-331-0623

Innkeeper: Jim and Diane Peiker
Accommodations: 7 rooms, 2 suites, all with private bath
Rates: $70–$105; double, $80–$115; suites, $125–$150
Included: Full breakfast
Minimum stay: None
Added: 12% tax
Payment: Major credit cards
Children: Not suitable for children
Pets: Not allowed

Smoking: Prohibited
Open: Year-round

The imposing stone mansion called Castle Marne anchors a street of Victorian houses, 20 blocks east of downtown near City Park and the Denver Zoo. The silver baron Wilbur S. Raymond had the turreted and columned structure built in 1889. His architect, William Lang, is today best known for the Unsinkable Molly Brown House, but even then Lang had a reputation for ensuring that no two of his houses looked alike. And this Romanesque castle, constructed of rough-chiseled blocks of a rosy volcanic stone called rhyolite, has itself become a Denver landmark.

Sooner or later, Jim Peiker gets around to telling the story of Castle Marne and its series of owners to every guest who will listen. He saved the mansion from slow death as an apartment house. In order to restore it authentically, he delved into every nook and cranny of its history and ferreted out old photos that showed the original interiors and exteriors. In the end, he created not only a one-of-a-kind urban inn, but a Victorian period piece—or as Peiker puts it, "a step back in time."

He lavished attention on the accommodations, too. Though none of the original furnishings survived, Peiker and his family contributed their own lovely heirlooms, combed auctions and garage sales for authentic period antiques, and when all else failed, settled on high quality reproductions. Each of the nine rooms has its own personality and decor. The main floor Conservatory has a sunny bay window overlooking the garden, cabbage rose wallpaper, wicker furnishings, and a clawfoot tub. The quaint corner Balcony Room on the second floor, though small, features an antique iron and brass bed and opens to a large deck. The three-room Presidential Suite, a first choice with honeymooners, has a king-size tester bed, decorative fireplace, solarium with jetted tub, sitting room in the tower, and private balcony with a view of downtown Denver and the Rockies beyond.

A hand-carved oak staircase connects the floors, winding past the mansion's showpiece, a six-foot circular "peacock window" of stained glass. Guests pass it every morning on their way to breakfast in the cherry-paneled formal dining room where Peiker serves a gourmet feast of homemade muffins and fresh fruit, supplemented with fresh vegetable quiche, blueberry waffles, or whatever else he feels like preparing in what he laughingly calls "Denver's smallest commercial kitchen." In the late afternoon he sets out tea, scones, and shortbread in the living room, where there's always a puzzle to work on in the turreted alcove. He or some other member of the Peiker family is always on hand to give advice about restaurants or otherwise be of service, but Jim tells the best stories.

Merritt House
941 East 17th Avenue
Denver, Colorado 80218
303-861-5230
Fax: 303-832-3517

Innkeepers: Tom and Mary Touris
Accommodations: 10 rooms, all with private bath
Rates: $75–$95; double, $85–$105
Included: Full breakfast
Minimum stay: None
Added: 12% tax
Payment: Major credit cards
Children: Over age 12 welcome if well-behaved
Pets: Not allowed
Smoking: Prohibited
Open: Year-round

Lovers of Queen Anne Victorians can walk the streets of the Denver's Swallow Hill Historic District and see 29 examples of that architectural style, most of them built before the silver crash of 1893. That may be one reason some people choose to stay at Merritt House, a winsome 10-room inn at the edge of Swallow Hill. After all, it occupies the restored Queen Anne mansion Colorado Senator Elmer W. Merritt had built for himself and his family in 1889 from designs by architect Frank Edbrooke, who would later undertake Denver's fabled Brown Palace. There is, however, another compelling reason to bed down at Merritt House: breakfast.

To understand why that's so you have to go back to the mid 1980s when Mary and Tom Touris were still stripping a century's accumulation of paint off the oak-paneled ceilings, walls, and door trim. They'd begun thinking about opening a bed-and-breakfast five years earlier. The more they found out about the business, the more convinced they became that it would make sense also to be able to serve meals to the general public. Consequently, they endowed Merritt House not only with delightful, antique-appointed rooms but a restaurant kitchen as well. Thus their guests enjoy a pleasure rare to find at a B&B: the chance to order breakfast from a menu. The choices range from cereal and toast to berry pancakes and three-cheese omelettes.

Having Denverites stop in for breakfast on their way to work creates a certain amount of commercial bustle in the dining room every morning, and it recurs at midday when the restaurant serves lunch. But it never extends to the guest floors above. All of the guest rooms have been decorated in Victorian style, with four-poster or sleigh beds, armoires, wing chairs, ornate chandeliers, oriental carpets, and subdued floral wallpapers. But Tom also insisted on such modern amenities as remote control televisions, phones, air conditioning, and private baths —five of them with Jacuzzi tubs.

By midafternoon the activity downstairs subsides, and guests can sit undisturbed in the glassed-in sun porch or in the adjacent living room. Mary's always around, often in a Victorian dress, to make sure they have everything they need.

The Oxford Alexis Hotel

1600 17th Street
Denver, Colorado 80202
303-628-5400
800-628-5411 in Colorado
800-228-5838 in U.S.
Fax: 303-628-5413

General manager: Jill Johnson
Accommodations: 73 rooms, 8 suites
Rates: $115–$140; double, $125–$150; suites, single, $125–$275; double, $135–$275
Included: Limousine service downtown, shoeshines, gratuities
Minimum stay: None
Added: 12% tax
Payment: Major credit cards
Children: Welcome if well-behaved
Pets: Prohibited
Smoking: Allowed
Open: Year-round

The Oxford Alexis, Denver's oldest grand hotel, celebrated its centennial a year before the Brown Palace. Like the Brown, it was designed by renowned architect Frank C. Edbrooke. Unlike it, the five-story red brick structure took shape on the opposite side of downtown a scant block from Union Station.

From the moment it opened on October 3, 1891, it became a symbol of Gilded Age opulence. Its classically simple facade masked lavish interiors of marble, antiques, stained glass, frescoed walls, elegant carpets, and sterling silver chandeliers. There was even a "vertical railway"—or elevator—to whisk visitors to the upper stories for views of the mushrooming Denver metropolis, at the time the third largest city in the west.

The views from the upper floors have changed dramatically over the last century, but lower downtown is again a hub of activity following the successful rehabilitation of historic Larimer Square. And the Oxford, after closing for in 1979 to undergo a 4-year, $12 million restoration, is as grand and elegant as ever.

Now listed on the National Register of Historic Places, the classic hotel has 81 rooms. Antique dealers combed England and France in search of four-poster, brass, and canopy beds and the walnut desks, brass lamps, and curved armoires that go with them. Most of what they found was Victorian, but France produced enough special pieces to decorate a dozen rooms in classic art deco style. It fits because most of the bathrooms, while modernized in the 1980s, still retain art deco tiles and fixtures left over from refurbishing done in the 1930s. And art deco also reigns in the Cruise Room, a bar modeled after one on the Queen Mary, and amid the stained glass, rosy pillars, and little black tables of the Corner Room, a favorite for jazz.

The two-story lobby reverts to turn of the century, with its marble floors, oriental rugs, red plush sofas, wing-back chairs, and an ornate mahogany and marble fireplace. In the late afternoon, guests can stop by for complimentary glasses of sherry before heading off to dinner, perhaps in the adjoining McCormick's Fish House & Bar, where fresh seafood and steaks are dished out in an unpretentious oak-paneled room with marble floors and a stained glass ceiling.

Before of after, they can curl up in terrycloth robes, arrange a workout or massage at the adjacent fitness club and spa, walk to nearby Larimer Square or the Denver Center for the Performing Arts, or catch the complimentary limo for a trip downtown.

Queen Anne Inn
2147 Tremont Place
Denver, Colorado 80205
303-296-6666
800-432-INNS
Fax: 303-296-2151

Innkeepers: Charles and Ann Hillestad
Accommodations: 10 rooms, all with private bath
Rates: $54–$114; double, $64–$124
Included: Continental breakfast
Minimum stay: None

Added: 12% tax
Payment: Major credit cards
Children: Discouraged under age 15
Pets: Not allowed
Smoking: Prohibited
Open: Year-round

The lovable Queen Anne Inn waltzed into Denver's bed-and-breakfast scene in 1987, promptly took over the limelight, and has basked in the media's constant attention ever since, winning awards and adoring guests with equal ease. Its success can be traced directly to Charles and Ann Hillestad, the fortysomething couple behind it. Convinced that a great inn was somehow more than the sum of its antiques, they set out to invest the Queen Anne with an intangible spirit, to fill its rooms not only with lovely appointments but also with the promise of illusion and escape.

The beautifully restored 1879 Victorian fronts a park and fountain in a quiet historic district an easy four-block walk from downtown. Frank Edbrooke, who would later become Denver's most famous architect by drawing up plans for the Oxford and Brown Palace hotels, designed the three-story house, shingling the sides and hoisting a turret halfway back but leaving the front unornamented except for a porch. Though modest in appearance, it contains 6,000 square feet of floor space, more than enough for 10 antique-furnished guest rooms.

The Hillestads decorated each room differently. The lace-curtained Park Room, named for its views of the park across the street, mixes Laura Ashley prints with antique walnut twin beds (they can be made up as a king), armoire, and writing desk. The Fountain Room has a canopied queen bed, five windows, and a black sunken tub. In Columbine above the garden, stained glass windows soften the light that falls on a rare quarter-canopied tester bed and mirrored cherry armoire. While a hand-painted mural of an aspen grove in all its golden autumn splendor covers the curved walls and peaked ceiling at the top of the turret in the Aspen room.

All the rooms have private baths designed to fit with their individual decors, writing desks, and piped in stereo music. Many have sitting areas. Guests can help themselves to beverages stocked in a small refrigerator on the second floor, make full use of the abundant travel resource materials, magazines, games, and restaurant menus available in the cozy parlor, or curl up on its dark green velvet, Empire sofa with a glass of sherry. In the mornings, they come down to find a generous Continental breakfast of homemade breads, fresh fruit, rolls, and granola set out on the sideboard in the formal dining room (though breakfast in bed is also an option).

The Hillestads live next door and so are often around, though like them every member of the young, friendly 10-person staff is eager to help with anything from restaurant recommendations to ordering a horse-drawn carriage. It deserves its place in the limelight.

Victorian Oaks Inn
1575 Race Street
Denver, Colorado 80206
303-355-1818

Innkeepers: Clyde Stephens and Rick Boling
Accommodations: 9 rooms, 1 with private bath
Rates: $39–$69; double, $49–$79
Included: Continental breakfast
Minimum stay: None
Added: 12% tax
Payment: Major credit cards
Children: Welcome if well-behaved (no cribs available)
Pets: Allowed
Smoking: Allowed
Open: Year-round

Denver's first bed-and-breakfast inn winds through three floors of an 1896 Victorian mansion on a street of historic homes 20 blocks east of downtown and directly across from Castle Marne (see above). Shades of turn-of-the-century elegance survive in a dramatic hanging oak staircase, ornate brass chandeliers, leaded-glass windows, and tile fireplaces. In this case, however, elegance comes wrapped in a casual atmosphere at prices appealing to the budget-minded.

An eclectic collection of turn-of-the-century antiques gathered in Colorado, New Mexico, and Texas furnishes the nine rooms. Dust-ruffled beds with floral comforters stand out against walls painted vivid colors like teal blue. The molding is oak, as are the floors. The three rooms on the third floor, though small, snuggle beneath the gables. Eight of the nine share two baths with clawfoot tubs, marble vanities, and original porcelain tile. The one room with a private bath, in the former parlor just inside the entrance on the first floor, has a mahogany four-poster, oriental rugs, and a fireplace.

Clyde Stephens, who took over the inn from his family in 1989, encourages guests to use the living room, kitchen, and even laundry. In winter he keeps the fireplaces burning; at any time of the year he serves wine in the afternoons and a Continental breakfast of pastries, croissants, bagels, fresh fruit, and the morning paper at a large oak dining table beneath a crystal chandelier. Since he lives there, he's never far away when guests need advice about where to dine or what to see.

Detroit

The Blanche House Inn
506 Parkview
Detroit, Michigan 48214
313-822-7090

Innkeepers: Mary Jean and Sean Shannon
Accommodations: 7 rooms, 1 suite (all with private bath)
Rates: $60; double, $65–$115; suite, $115
Included: Full breakfast
Minimum stay: None
Added: 4% tax
Payment: Major credit cards
Children: Welcome
Pets: Not allowed
Smoking: Prohibited
Open: Year-round

Just east of downtown Detroit, in the neighborhood where the mayor resides, lies the Blanche House Inn. You may be disappointed when you pull up to the white picket fence of the 1905 Colonial Revival mansion; repainting the 20-foot tall columns and landscaping the tatty yard have remained low priorities. But the atmosphere changes immediately as you walk through the 10-foot-tall etched glass entrance door. The interior features, including elegant plastering, oak woodwork, and hardwood floors, mix with modern amenities such as televisions, telephones, and air-conditioning in each of the seven guest rooms.

The Lee Stanton Canal Room, named for the original owner, is dominated by an imposing brick Mayan fireplace, an 1880s queen-size bed, and a large porch with a swing. It overlooks the Stanton Canal, which flows into the Detroit River, less than a block away.

The spacious third-floor Snuggery is the most popular suite, with its hand-painted mural depicting pastoral scenes of the nearby river. The suite offers both a spacious hot tub in its own room and a bathroom with clawfoot tub, where the walls are painted with images of tall grass.

Breakfast, served in the Inn's elegant dining room, includes fresh fruit, homemade bran muffins, and pumpkin bread, followed by an egg dish.

Mother-and-son innkeepers Mary Jean and Sean Shannon also own the 1898 Gothic-style residence, the Castle, next door. While it takes overflow guests on busy nights, it is usually rented out completely for weekend weddings since its large downstairs easily accommodates parties of up to 50. The Inn also hosts murder mystery and spa nights.

The Dearborn Inn

20301 Oakwood Boulevard
Dearborn, Michigan 48124
313-271-2700
800-228-9290
Fax: 313-271-7464
Reservations: 800-228-2800

General manager: Peter Steger
Accommodations: 199 rooms, 23 suites in main building, motel units, and houses
Rates: $130; double, $145; suites, $145–$175, packages available
Included: All meals available
Minimum stay: None
Added: 11% tax
Payment: Major credit cards
Children: Welcome
Pets: By arrangement
Smoking: Nonsmoking rooms available
Open: Year-round

In 1929, Henry Ford was watching passengers arrive at the airport he had built across the street from his auto manufacturing headquarters in Dearborn, Michigan. Realizing that there was nowhere to eat or sleep closer than Detroit, 20 miles away, he decided to build a hotel. Opened in 1931 and renovated in 1989, the Dearborn Inn continues to welcome business travelers.

Working closely with Ford, the architect Albert Kahn designed the traditional Georgian structure with red brick and white trim. The lobby has elegant black and white marble floors and groupings of comfortable chairs and couches, with a portrait of Ford watching over the proceedings from above the fireplace. Adjacent is a small brick-lined sun porch with wicker furniture.

The detailing and furnishings in the recent addition blend seamlessly with the original rooms. You can hardly tell the difference, unless you notice the deep porcelain tubs found in the older units. The guest rooms fall into two basic categories, distinguished primarily by their wallpaper and color schemes —some in conservative stripes, others with a blue ribbon theme. The premium rooms on the second and third floors have their own gathering room with concierge service. The other rooms are across the street, in Colonial motel units added in 1960.

Offering bed-and-breakfast accommodations, five 18th-and 19th-century homes, all replicas of famous Americans' homesteads, form a semicircle behind the hotel. The largest of these, the Patrick Henry House, has six suites and two rooms decorated with bright floral wallpapers and antique prints. The white clapboard Poe Cottage can be rented as an individual unit, making it appealing to honeymooners.

Lunch and dinner can be enjoyed in the Early American Room, which has tall windows, crystal chandeliers, and an excellent menu that includes plank roasted salmon, prime rib, and veal scaloppine. Brunch is a Sunday tradition, enjoyed by both tourists and Detroit residents. Three meals are served daily at the Ten Eyck Tavern, which is rustic and informal, with dark wood Windsor chairs and tables surrounded by turn-of-the-century photographs. Tuesdays through Saturdays, a regular jazz combo plays at the Golden Eagle Lounge near the lobby, where guests can dance.

While business travelers fill the inn during the week, wedding groups are popular on Fridays and Saturdays. The formal, 3,444-square-foot Alexandria Ballroom features a cathedral

ceiling and period crystal chandeliers. It was inspired by similar ballrooms that Ford admired in Virginia.

You'll also find tennis courts and a swimming pool on the
inn's twenty-eight acres. The Dearborn Inn is just down the
street from the world-famous Henry Ford Museum and Green-
field Village.

River Place Inn

1000 Stroh River Place
Detroit, Michigan 48207
313-259-2500
800-999-1466
Fax: 313-259-1248
   Preferred Hotels and Resorts Worldwide
   800-323-7500

General manager: Ian Rumsey
Accommodations: 86 rooms, 22 suites
Rates: $150–$170; suites, $225–$350
   Weekend and corporate rates available
Minimum stay: None
Added: 9% tax
Payment: Major credit cards
Children: Welcome
Pets: Allowed
Smoking: Nonsmoking rooms available
Open: Year-round

Stroh River Place lies just one mile east of Detroit's central
business district. This oasis of apartments, shops, and restaurants is the Motor City's most ambitious redevelopment project
yet. It's also home to River Place Inn.

The building formerly served as the laboratories and admin-
istrative offices for the Parke-Davis pharmaceutical company,
which remained here until 1981. Many of the 108 rooms and
suites in the recently remodeled complex offer dramatic views
of the Canadian coastline or the bridge at Belle Isle. All have
high ceilings, polished wood furnishings, bold floral fabrics,
and marble-lined bathrooms with brass fixtures. The suites
include six multilevel penthouses.

Guests will find complimentary valet parking, personalized
check-in, same-day laundry and twice-daily maid service, free
newspaper, 24-hour room service and a helpful concierge.
Every room has several telephones, a refrigerator and mini-bar,
and remote control television. Free chauffeur service shuttles

guests to downtown appointments or to cultural events, just minutes away.

Aside from four fully equipped conference rooms, a tent can also be set up on the bank of the river for outdoor parties. Special dockage can be arranged for receptions and cruises aboard luxury yachts.

The River Place Athletic Club has a year-round pool, saunas, aerobics classes, fitness center, and outdoor tennis. Personal training, tanning, and massage services are available by appointment. This is one of the few hotels with its own championship-size croquet courts, and tournaments are scheduled seasonally. During the winter season, guests can play indoors on synthetic grass.

The River Room restaurant is a modern fish house with a stunning river view. The evening meal might include sea scallops Murat with cherry tomatoes, thyme, and artichokes or grilled mahi mahi with peppers, capers, and calamata olives. A brick-lined patio with wrought-iron tables is open for cocktails, lunch, and dinner; here, guests can watch the freighters as they pass by.

Food service for the restaurant and catered receptions is provided by the Rattlesnake Club, often considered the finest gourmet restaurant in the city. The Rattlesnake's own restaurant is also part of the 30-acre Stroh River Place complex. Just five minutes from River Place Inn are the elegantly restored Fox Theatre, Renaissance Center, Greektown, and Detroit Symphony Orchestra performances at Orchestra Hall.

The Townsend Hotel
100 Townsend Street
Birmingham, Michigan 48009
313-642-7900
800-548-4172
Fax: 313-645-9061
Telex: 798502
Reservations:
  Preferred Hotels Worldwide
  800-323-7500

General manager: Otto Haensler
Accommodations: 35 rooms, 51 suites
Rates: $179; double, $189; suites, single, $199; double, $209; executive suites, $479; packages available
Minimum stay: None
Added: 7.5% tax

Payment: Major credit cards
Children: Welcome
Pets: Not allowed
Smoking: Nonsmoking rooms available
Open: Year-round

The Townsend Hotel offers gracious accommodations in the upscale suburban community of Birmingham, 20 minutes northwest of downtown Detroit.

Floral patterned chairs and overstuffed couches grace both the wood-paneled lobby and the guest rooms. The color scheme throughout is a tasteful blend of blues, reds, and ivories. Marble-lined baths, terrycloth robes, French soaps, Belgian pillows, and fluffy down comforters are standard. The concierge speaks nine languages fluently, and room service is offered round-the-clock.

Three exclusive corner suites offer separate living and dining areas, butler pantries, and double balconies. Function rooms provide elegant facilities for gatherings of up to 400 and banquets for up to 200. Fine restaurants abound, including the hotel's Rugby Grill, which is a popular breakfast spot with locals.

Marley's Boutique, which sells travel items and clothing and gifts from Europe and Asia, is in the hotel. Set foot out the front door and you're in the center of one of the area's best shopping districts. Visit the Birmingham Theatre, which brings professional shows from New York to the suburbs each season. You will probably run into theater stars on the elevator at the Townsend, since this is where they often stay during the run. Not surprisingly, the Townsend offers theater packages.

The Westin Hotel

Renaissance Center
Detroit, Michigan 48243
313-568-8036
800-228-3000
Fax: 313-568-8666

General manager: Naveen Ahuja
Accommodations: 1400, including 52 suites
Rates: $125–$150; double, $145–$165; suites, $145–$195;
   packages available
Minimum stay: None
Added: 12% tax
Payment: Major credit cards
Children: Welcome

Pets: Small pets allowed
Smoking: Nonsmoking rooms available
Open: Year-round

The Westin Hotel is housed in the Renaissance Center, the trio of cylindrical glass towers that anchor downtown Detroit. A recent renovation has spruced up the spacious guest rooms, all with outstanding views of the Detroit or Windsor, Canada, skylines. Don't expect the height of luxury at the Westin, which functions primarily as a large-scale convention hotel.

With a combined area of more than 100,000 square feet, the hotel's thirty meeting rooms, including the fourth-floor Renaissance Ballroom, can accommodate groups ranging from five to 2,700 people. Four new executive levels for business travelers and executive lounges have recently been added.

The Westin's health club features a glassed-in pool, tanning capsules, a workout room with Nautilus equipment, free weights, exercise bikes, an aerobic dance studio and an outdoor half-mile jogging trail.

The Summit Restaurant, specializing in charbroiled steaks, is located on the hotel's 71st floor. The revolving bi-level restaurant offers a spectacular 360 degree view of Windsor and Detroit. Sunday brunch is popular here. Have a cocktail in the Summit Lounge, on the 73rd floor, and you'll be at the highest point in Detroit. Among the restaurants on the promenade level, River Bistro presents a sleek contemporary setting with meals like fresh Norwegian salmon and veal steak with morel mushrooms, rack of lamb and roasted baby chicken. Café Rio offers Tex-Mex southwestern fare.

The Renaissance Center, designed as a city within a city, is a concrete maze of offices, restaurants, and more than 80 shops. It is connected to the People Mover, an aboveground 2.9-mile transit system that links hotel guests with popular Motor City attractions such as Greektown, Joe Louis Arena and Cobo Center, and the theater district. Windsor, Canada, can be reached by tunnel or bridge.

Honolulu

Halekulani
2199 Kalia Road
Honolulu, Oahu, Hawaii 96815
808-923-2311
800-367-2343
Fax: 808-926-8004
Reservations: Contact the hotel directly.

Accommodations: 412 rooms and 44 suites
Rates:
   City/Palm court–view rooms: $245
   Palm court–view rooms: $275
   Ocean-view rooms: $325
   Prime ocean-view rooms: $365
   Diamond Head oceanfront rooms: $395
   Junior and master suites: $550–$1,100
   Presidential and royal suites: rates available on request
Payment: Major credit cards
Children: Under 14 free in room with parents; activity
   program during school holidays
Smoking: Nonsmoking rooms available
Open: Year-round
Recreation: Beach, swimming pool, fitness center, water sports

Halekulani means "house befitting heaven," a name that befits
the hotel perfectly in every aspect of its graceful operation.
There are certainly hotels in Hawaii on better beaches, and
even condominiums with more resort recreation, but very few
places can put a halo over your vacation as angelically as the
Halekulani.

It's the smooth, unerring execution of the basics that makes a
hotel a winner. You won't find a trace of flash or swagger at the
Halekulani, just genuine sophistication in all matters, however
mundane or minute. The staff address you by name at every
conceivable opportunity. Your laundry is returned in a wicker
basket. The elevators glide magically somewhere near the
speed of sound. You never feel that the hotel staff are trying to
awe you, and they don't miss a single detail in doing it.

The Halekulani hasn't always been so polished. Founded in 1907, it was overshadowed in the early Waikiki resort years first by the Moana and then by the Royal Hawaiian. As tourism burst the seams of dignity along this beach in the 1960s and 1970s, the Halekulani remained steadfastly old-fashioned. Finally the cottage-style accommodations here were the last low-rises on the beach, an oasis of tranquillity.

There were groans aplenty when the Halekulani Corporation, a subsidiary of Japan's Mitsui Real Estate Development Company, bought the property in 1981 and announced plans to demolish the bungalows and build a new structure rising sixteen stories. Similar changes and similar reactions abound in recent Hawaii history, but this is the only instance we know where the mourning period was momentary. The Halekulani Corporation achieved the miraculous, maintaining the spirit of the original inn, preserving the sense of serenity, and elevating standards to Elysian realms.

The architecture makes a significant contribution to the miracle. The main building of the old hotel, a two-story ocean-front cottage, was retained and elegantly restored. The plantation style, the roofline, and the openness of this structure were carried into the design of the four residential towers, which are stepped in height and separated from each other by peaceful courtyards. The lobby is a model of open-air subtlety, transporting guests from the street to the interior so dexterously that one doesn't feel the slightest jolt of passage.

The artistry of Halekulani service begins with the reception process. The bell desk passes your name to registration, where you are welcomed and then escorted to the privacy of your room to fill out the forms. A few other Hawaiian hotels attempt a similar reception, but nowhere else does it flow so evenly. Computers in the phone system allow the staff to greet you by name when you call anywhere on the property. This system also has been adopted at other Hawaiian hotels, but again, the staff at the Halekulani is much more adroit in using the mechanism to coddle guests.

The spacious rooms have an ingenious blend of contemporary convenience and opulent comfort. All of the 456 quarters, decorated in shades of white with blue accents, are constructed and furnished with the finest natural materials, right down to the premium cotton weave of the sheets. The rooms feature a large tiled lanai, comfy sitting area with love seat, wet bar, three telephones, and a business desk. Awaiting your arrival are lounging robes and a bowl of fresh fruit. The bathroom is one of the plushest in Hawaii, a place where you could pamper yourself all day. It's fitted with a deep soaking tub, separate glass and tile shower, a marble vanity, and mirrored closet doors that open into the bath as well as the sleeping space.

The main difference in the rooms is the view. The city and palm court quarters are a fine value because they overlook little or no water. The ocean-view rooms have an angled perspective on the Pacific, or face it directly from a distance of about a hundred feet. The best vistas are from the Diamond Head oceanfront rooms, close to the sea and scanning a long stretch of Waikiki beach.

If you can afford $800, upgrade to a Diamond Head Parlour Suite, a fantasy come true. Like most of the other suites, it features a wet bar, his-and-hers vanities in the bath, and two lanais—one off the bedroom and the other off the living room. Lottery winners might prefer the presidential or royal chambers, which rent for up to $3,000 a night. Both have a marble entry, full kitchen, study, one or two bedrooms, and an immense wraparound lanai.

The Halekulani's restaurants match the accommodations in magnificence. La Mer is the top French restaurant in Hawaii. Chef George Mavrothalassitis works wonders in the kitchen, combining fresh Hawaiian ingredients with authentic Gallic preparations. You begin your dinner as you would in one of the chef's former dining rooms in Marseilles and Cassis, with a flute of champagne and a luscious taste teaser, both included with the meal. An hors d'oeuvre might be oysters on the half shell with a horseradish and chive cream sauce—a briny, stimulating starter. The appetizers that follow are superb, the best course of the evening. Be sure to order the ravioli of escargot à la Diable, plump snails in fresh pasta with woodsy mushrooms and dill. Other tasty options include warm Norwegian salmon, smoked daily in the kitchen over kiawe embers, and sautéed scallops and prawns with a vanilla saffron sauce.

The entrée selections, delicacies of the sea, range broadly. The marinated baby lamb plays a medley on the tongue with thyme and garlic, the three dissolving together with hardly a bite. In the bouillabaisse, Mavrothalassitis adds lobster, nohu and hapuu, uncommon local fish that taste similar to the original Mediterranean ingredients. An even rarer catch, kumu, is served en papillote with basil, seaweed, and shiitake mushrooms. Some of the same dishes are available on five-and seven-course prix fixe menus, costing $75 and $98.

Orchids is also superior, rivaling the Hana-Maui dining room as the best all-day restaurant in the state. Open-air and seaside, like La Mer, it's larger than its sister and somewhat less expensive, particularly at lunch. The focus is on contemporary American cuisine, with dinner entrées ranging from shrimp jambalaya to a charbroiled filet with California pinot noir sauce.

Regardless of whether you stay at the Halekulani, if you are going to be in Honolulu on Sunday, make reservations for the Orchids brunch, a buffet feast of such fare as roast beef and turkey, duck l'orange, stir-fried vegetables, salads, sashimi, sushi, dim sum, and much more. You won't need to eat again for two days.

The Halekulani also serves a breakfast buffet and light lunches at the House Without a Key, immortalized in a 1925 Charlie Chan novel by Earl Derr Biggers, a frequent guest in the early years. The sunset cocktails here are another Waikiki must, regardless of where you lodge. Island music and hula dancing under an ancient kiawe tree have been a tradition since 1907, and today's rendition is as magnetically memorable as ever. Our favorite evenings are Mondays, Tuesdays, and Thursdays, when the dancer is the lithesome Kanoe Miller and the musicians are the Islanders.

The beach in front of the Halekulani is very small, though expansive sands are an easy walk in either direction and the hotel's oceanfront swimming pool is enormous for Waikiki. The beach center arranges golf and tennis off the property as well as water sports on the shore, while the fitness center provides state-of-the-art exercise equipment. Organized guest activities include aerobics classes, jogging sessions, and a children's program during summer, Christmas, and Easter vacations.

Everything offered at the Halekulani is unexcelled. Even the leader of the morning jog is a world-class runner. The vast majority of Hawaiian hotels, however grand, cut a corner somewhere or accept a condition less than ideal. Not the Halekulani. Easily the best urban resort in the state, probably the nation, it's always a heavenly experience.

Manoa Valley Inn
2001 Vancouver Drive
Honolulu, Oahu, Hawaii 96822
808-947-6019
800-634-5115
Fax: 808-946-6168
Reservations: Contact the inn directly.

Accommodations: 6 rooms, 1 cottage, 1 suite
Rates: rooms, $95–$120; cottage, $150; suite, $175

Included: Continental breakfast, afternoon fruit and cheese
Payment: Major credit cards
Children: Not appropriate
Smoking: No cigars
Open: Year-round

Intimate and elegant in a Victorian country style, the Manoa
Valley Inn (formerly the John Guild Inn) will shatter anyone's
stereotypes about Hawaii. Just two miles from both Waikiki
and downtown Honolulu, the inn looks and feels like it should
be thousands of miles and a century or so away from them.

The Manoa Valley Inn, built on this spot in 1915, was origi-
nally a home. Considerably enlarged by businessman John
Guild between 1919 and 1922, the building is on the National
Register of Historic Places. It deteriorated after Guild's death,
eventually becoming a student rooming house for the nearby
University of Hawaii.

In 1978, Rick Ralston, owner of Crazy Shirts, Inc., saved the
structure from the bulldozer and started a careful, expensive
restoration. Thirty-two different types of moldings, wainscoting, banisters, corbels, and other decorative elements had to be
refurbished or, in many cases, duplicated by local artisans with
custom millwork. Three-quarters of a million dollars later,
Ralston joked that his accountants were saying it would take 76
years and four months of 100 percent occupancy to break even.
Ralston is proud of his dedicated effort, however, and he should
be. He not only preserved one of the few historic structures
from this period left in Hawaii but also converted it into a
wonderful inn.

The guest rooms and cottage vary in size and furnishings, but
you can count on gracious and comfortable antiques, patterned

wallpaper, historical accuracy in the fixtures and hardware, lounging robes, and fresh tropical flowers. The bed will be delightful, whether it's a four-poster, antique iron, or other period piece. The least expensive rooms have a double bed and shared bath. The Dillingham room has two double beds and a shared bath. The Cooke room has a king-size bed and private bath, though the Baldwin and Moore rooms, which also have private baths, are very nice and a bit more economical. The John Guild suite has its own sitting area in addition to a bath and king-size bed. No more than two guests are permitted in the quarters except for the Dillingham room, where the maximum is three.

The complimentary Continental breakfast and afternoon cheese-and-fruit snack are usually enjoyed on the shady, wicker-furnished lanai overlooking the lawn and tropical garden. The parlor is a pleasant alternative, however, with its antique Victrola, nickelodeon, piano, and pool table.

For Victorian nobility the Manoa Valley Inn has few peers in Hawaii. When you want something different that's close enough to the action and also a world away, this is the place in Honolulu.

New Otani Kaimana Beach Hotel

2863 Kalakaua Avenue
Honolulu, Oahu, Hawaii 96815
808-923-1555
Fax: 808-922-9404
Reservations:
  New Otani
  800-421-8795 213-362-0639

Accommodations: 116 rooms and suites
Rates:
  Standard rooms: $99–$109
  Ocean-and Waikiki-view rooms: $120–$130
  Superior rooms: $145–$175
  Park-view studios: $140–$150
  Ocean studio superiors: $195
  Ocean studio deluxes: $210
  Garden apartments: $140–$190
  Junior suites: $165–$190
  Suites: $190–$550
Payment: Major credit cards
Children: Under 12 free in room with parents

Smoking: Allowed
Open: Year-round

When Robert Louis Stevenson wanted to escape the low-density development on Waikiki at the turn of the century, he sometimes walked the short distance to the peaceful Sans Souci Beach, not far from Diamond Head. He once penned a tribute to the spot, now occupied by the New Otani Kaimana Beach Hotel: "If anyone desires lovely scenery, pure air, clear sea water, good food, and heavenly sunsets . . . I recommend him cordially to the Sans Souci." Stevenson's idyllic beach is more crowded these days, but in comparison with Waikiki its winsomeness has grown.

Some of the credit for the allure today belongs to the New Otani, one of the most delightful small hotels in Hawaii. It has captured a balance between classy sophistication and casual naturalness that most places don't have the sense to seek. The guest list is full of experienced Honolulu visitors who want to be treated well but not suffocated with pretension or overwhelmed with superfluous flourishes.

Most of the stylish accommodations on three sides of the nine-story hotel are studios or junior suites. Though they are less spacious than most Waikiki quarters with those labels, they are also more affordable for their degree of luxury. Those called ocean studio superior are among the best values in Honolulu, with a wraparound lanai facing both the Pacific and the lights of Waikiki. The ocean studio deluxes, on the opposite seaside corner, also overlook the beach and are a little larger.

The junior suites have a separate sitting area, with double sofa bed, that can be closed off with sliding louvered doors. Some are oceanfront, between the two types of studios. The less expensive rooms are classified as Waikiki view—they have a panorama encompassing Diamond Head, the city, and the Pacific. From their wraparound lanai one can watch both the sunrise and the sunset. The same layout is available less expensively looking only at Diamond Head. A few grand suites on the top floor range upwards in size and price to two oceanfront gems.

The regular hotel rooms are barely large enough to hold their king-size beds. The standards have no view of note. The ocean-and Waikiki-view rooms have partial sights. Superior category quarters are larger and look either at Diamond Head or at the Pacific and the city. Their rate varies by $20 depending on the perspective. Superior ocean-view rooms are featured in a "Romance" package, which also gets you a convertible rental car and a bottle of champagne as a part of a specially discounted deal. The Diamond Head Wing, in a separate three-story building, has kitchenette facilities in studios and one-bedrooms. They are especially practical for long visits and rent more economically by the month.

Every room has air conditioning, a TV, a mini-bar, a lanai, and concierge service. The decor in the rooms is smartly fetching in a contemporary manner.

The New Otani's restaurants and lounge are the essence of Hawaii, which is probably why Tom Selleck liked them for location sets in Magnum, P.I. Just before the popular series called it quits, the TV crew filmed all day in the Hau Tree Lanai, one of the few remaining outdoor beachfront restaurants in the state, shaded by the ancient arbor that once sheltered Stevenson. Open for three meals a day, it usually excels in food quality as well as informal personality. In the evening, one can catch the sunset from the adjacent lounge and have a moderately priced dinner while watching Waikiki light up less than a mile away. The menu emphasizes seafood but provides plenty of other options.

The hotel's other option for dinner is Miyako, which provides a more traditional and satisfying Japanese experience than almost any of the fancier Asian restaurants up Kalakaua Avenue. It's one of the few places in the islands that serves authentic kaiseki dinners to guests who care enough to request them a couple of days in advance. The chef from the New Otani's Osaka hotel, a master of the artful, elaborate meals keyed to the season, spent a year in the Miyako's kitchen overseeing the local staff's training.

If you don't get your fill of fish at dinner, try the Hau Tree's Japanese breakfast, always a pleasant departure from bacon and eggs. All the American standards are also offered.

You may not even notice that the New Otani has no pool. Sans Souci Beach still provides fine swimming and a refreshing retreat from Waikiki congestion, as it has since the first tourists arrived in Honolulu. The New Otani allows you to get to the glitter on a moment's whim or — on a second thought — to survey it from your private perch a dreamy distance away.

Sheraton Moana Surfrider

2365 Kalakaua Avenue
Honolulu, Oahu, Hawaii 96815
808-922-3111
Fax: 808-923-0308
Reservations:
  Sheraton Reservations
  800-325-3535

Accommodations: 803 rooms and suites
Rates:
  City-view rooms: $195
  Tower partial ocean-view rooms: $250
  Moana ocean-view rooms: $270
  Tower ocean-view rooms: $300
  Suites: $525
Payment: Major credit cards
Children: Under 18 free in room with parents; summer
  activity program for children
Smoking: Nonsmoking rooms available
Open: Year-round

When the Moana Hotel opened in 1901, it was a stately establishment, known in the early years as the First Lady of Waikiki
Beach. At the time of construction a hotel seemed a risky prop-
osition in the quiet, residential area, then surrounded by rice
paddies and taro ponds. O. G. Traphagen, the architect, produced a striking design, adapting Colonial architecture to the
tropical climate and incorporating such innovations as bathrooms and telephones for every room.

The Moana inaugurated the Waikiki tourism industry and
became a symbol of Hawaii's romantic appeal. Robert Louis
Stevenson visited and wrote Pacific tales under the hotel's great
banyan tree. Edward, Prince of Wales, danced in the star-
lighted courtyard. The famous "Hawaii Calls" radio show,
which first stirred the American imagination about the islands,
broadcast from here to the mainland for several decades.

When Sheraton announced the 1987 decision to restore the
Moana to its original grandeur, it was the best news on Waikiki
since the reopening of the Halekulani in 1983. The hotel had
declined steadily for years into a tawdry caricature of its former
self. Tacky shops cluttered the lobby, the registration desk was
buried in a dark corner, the old ceilings and walls were covered
with synthetic surfaces, and outside, where Stevenson versed
and the Prince of Wales danced, Polynesian fire-eaters toasted
the South Seas fantasies of middle-brow tourists.

Now the Sheraton Moana Surfrider has become a symbol of a different sort—of Waikiki's renaissance. Following a careful, authentic rehabilitation, the hotel reopened in 1989, once again a distinguished destination and the most conspicuous statement yet of Waikiki's aspiration to retain world-class stature.

Sheraton officials and architects scoured basements and archives for old plans, photos, renderings, menus, even china. The most noticeable exterior additions are the aristocratic porte cochere and verandahs, modeled on the originals eliminated in an Eisenhower-era updating. The open-air lobby is once more lofty and gracious. The fire-eaters have been exiled to the other side of Kalakaua Avenue and the Banyan Court is again a spot to dream, write, and dance.

One of the most surprising successes of the project was the integration of the Moana's Ocean Lanai wing and the formerly separate Surfrider Hotel into the new operation. Built in 1952 and 1969 respectively, these structures never had the charm of the original. They flank the Colonial facade of the Moana, towering above it twenty-one stories in the case of the Surfrider, as wings of a single property that totals 803 rooms. While the modern buildings will never match their older sister in allure, the architects did a brilliant job of harmonizing the disparate facades.

The integration will be extended to room decor in a few years, but for the present accommodations in the newer structures—now called the Tower and Diamond wings—retain a fresh contemporary style. When they are eventually refurbished, these rooms will suggest, rather than duplicate, the elegance and period charm of the original Moana, now known as the Banyan wing.

Each of the five residential floors of the historic building is furnished in a different wood, as they were initially—oak, mahogany, maple, koa, and cherry. The style re-creates the mood of a century past, though the chambers are now cooled with air conditioning for the first time, and the handsome reproduction armoires hold a TV and mini-bar. Bathrooms are small by today's standards but are attractively outfitted with period-style detail.

The least expensive of the Banyan wing's rooms overlook the grand entrance and Waikiki traffic. The more desirable quarters are across the hallway, facing the ocean and the Banyan Court. For the choicest perspective, ask for a room on the third or fourth floor fronting the Pacific instead of angling toward it. The dozen or so premium perches have a moderate-size lanai furnished with wooden lounges rescued from a cruise ship.

Rooms in the two newer wings are generally larger, more likely to have a lanai, and in some cases get a broader vista of the sea. Our favorites of these are the corner rooms in the Diamond wing, where most of the accommodations are intimate with the beach. Rates vary only with the view, not the building, and everyone gets special amenities such as yukata lounging robes, in-room video message, and check-out service.

Moana means broad expanse of ocean, an apt name for the hotel. The beach in front of the grounds is wide and alluring. It does get crowded and clamorous, though early and late in the day the sands are glorious. In the peak hours you can escape to the swimming pool or one of the seaside restaurants.

W. C. Peacock and Company specializes in fresh fish and island ingredients in a comfortable oceanfront setting. The Ship's Tavern offers a Continental menu with a few Asian touches and an exhilarating panorama encompassing Diamond Head and the sunset. For breakfast try the peaceful, open-air Verandah, where tables are elegantly set with china replicating one of the Moana's original patterns. If you're a big morning eater, order the delicious eggs Volga, re-created from an early menu. The rich variation on eggs Benedict melds poached eggs, artichoke hearts, ham, and caviar with a silky béarnaise sauce on toast. Don't plan to swim for hours afterward.

Sheraton deserves plaudits for taking on the restoration of the Moana and carrying it out so effectively. It's still a little early to know if the historic hotel can regain her title of First Lady, but certainly she graces Waikiki Beach anew.

Waikiki Joy
320 Lewers Street
Honolulu, Oahu, Hawaii 96815
808-923-2300
800-733-5569
Fax: 808-377-1290
Reservations: Contact the hotel directly.

Accommodations: 101 rooms and suites
Rates: $120–$130; suites, $145–$255
Included: Continental breakfast
Payment: Major credit cards
Children: Under 14 free in room with parents

Smoking: Allowed
Open: Year-round

The name Waikiki Joy may sound a little cute, but it's apt. Opened in 1988, the small boutique hotel fills a void in an area bursting with expensive behemoths. A couple of blocks from the beach and its accompanying milieu, the Joy aims to provide affordable contemporary luxury and personal service with special appeal to the business travelers.

The hotel's sleek design incorporates art deco accents throughout the open-air, barrel-vaulted lobby, which also features marble floors, lots of greenery, and floral touches. A tile deck a few steps above the reception desk holds a small pool along with lounging and sitting areas. Guests gather here each morning for the complimentary Continental breakfast. Cappuccino's, just off the deck, serves two light meals daily, and scores of restaurants are an easy walk away.

Nearly all the guest rooms are in an 11-story tower, with suites in a separate eight-floor wing. Even the most basic room has a marble entry, carpeted floor, handsome contemporary pastel decor, lanai, phone, air conditioning, mini-fridge, and sophisticated JVC audio and video system with a cassette player and Bose speakers. Although the size of the bathroom varies with the rate, the Joy is the only Hawaii hotel with Jacuzzi bathtubs in every room and suite, and all have an additional American and European-style shower, ample vanity space, and good lighting. Rooms generally come with two extra-long double beds or a king-size bed, along with two overstuffed chairs or a couch in attractive wicker.

The club suites have wet bars and lanais big enough for a lounge chair. Executive king and queen suites are more expansive quarters with still larger lanais, a second phone in the bath, a bigger TV, and full kitchens with microwaves, bar, coffeemaker, and toaster.

Business travelers like the fax and modem telephone hookups in all quarters, the rental fax machines, and the conference room. The Joy accepts only small business groups, however, so vacationers don't have to endure conclaves of conventioneers.

Through special arrangement, health-minded guests can use the facilities of Gold's Gym for a nominal charge. The concierge and helpful reception staff will arrange tours and other activities.

The Joy is truly that for sophisticated, value-minded Waikiki travelers. On business or not, the level of attention to guests will elate you.

Waikiki Parc
2233 Helumoa Road
Honolulu, Oahu, Hawaii 96815
808-921-7272
800-422-0450
Fax: 808-923-1336
Reservations: Contact the hotel directly.

Accommodations: 298 rooms
Rates:
   Standard rooms: $135
   City/mountain–view rooms: $145
   Deluxe mountain-view rooms: $160
   Ocean-view rooms: $190
   Deluxe ocean-view rooms: $220
Payment: Major credit cards
Children: Under 14 free in room with parents
Smoking: Nonsmoking rooms available
Open: Year-round

The Waikiki Parc opened in late 1987 with a theme of "affordable luxury." Its rates, which are highly competitive, certainly demonstrate that commitment. Smaller and less splashy than most of the luxury hotels, more elegant despite being placed on top of a parking garage, the Waikiki Parc appeals to business as well as leisure travelers.

The hotel is owned and managed by the same company as the fabulous Halekulani, which is directly across the street. As you would expect from the parentage, the efficient staff provide individual, personalized service. Though you shouldn't expect the extraordinary standards of the Halekulani, you won't be paying for that either.

The 298 rooms in the 22-story building are all similar in size and appointments. Beautifully decorated, with understated elegance, they feature ceramic tile floors with plush inlaid carpeting, comfortable sitting areas, custom rattan furnishings, mini-bars, two telephones, and at least a small lanai. There is a choice of a king-size bed, two doubles, or two twins, and most of the rooms have a business desk.

Standard rooms on the lower floors face into the maze of Waikiki skyscrapers. Deluxe mountain-views and regular ocean-views are both good values for a bit of outside scenery. The highest rate, for a deluxe ocean-view, will place you on one of the top floors with a spacious lanai. Extremely competitive corporate rates, available on request to the business traveler, add a complimentary buffet breakfast and a host of business-related amenities at no additional charge.

An eighth-floor recreation deck, overlooking the ocean, has a moderate-size tiled pool, lounging area, and refreshment kiosk. For the beach, a hundred yards away across a slow street, the hotel provides a full array of services and rental equipment for sailing, canoeing, surfing, and snorkeling.

The Parc Café restaurant serves breakfast, lunch, dinner, and cocktails in an informal, indoor garden atmosphere. The à la carte menu offers Continental food and island specialties. The buffets also available at all three meals are probably the best quality for the price in Waikiki. They aren't lavish but do provide plenty of variety and healthy choices.

The lunch buffet includes lots of salads, a make-your-own sandwich bar, pasta, pizza, broiled chicken, a pair of tasty soups, and fresh fruit. Dessert temptations might include an ice cream sundae bar, macadamia nut cream pie, chocolate mousse, and coconut cake. Dinner buffets feature many of the same items, but also more substantial fare like leg of lamb, Peking duck salad, and steamed ulua perfumed with Asian spices.

Kacho, the sleek Japanese restaurant and sushi bar, is a more upscale, intimate dining space, open for the same meals. The fish is as fresh as any in town. If you need more dining options, you can sign for meals at the Halekulani's restaurants as well.

The Waikiki Parc incorporates many of the drawing cards that have made the Halekulani such an outstanding hotel, including a state-of-the-art computerized telephone system and a hospitality room with men's and women's baths for guests arriving early or leaving late. The newer hotel is no match for its sister across the street, but it affords a style of classy comfort rare in this price range.

Houston

Four Seasons Hotel Houston
1300 Lamar Street
Houston, Texas 77010
713-650-1300
800-332-3442
Fax: 713-650-8169

General manager: Francisco Gomez
Accommodations: 399 rooms and suites
Rates: $180; double, $205; suites, $435
Added: 15% tax
Payment: Major credit cards
Children: Under 12 free in room with parents, ages 12 to 18 half price
Pets: Allowed with leash
Smoking: Nonsmoking rooms available
Open: Year-round

For the traveler who values quality and aesthetics, the 30-story Four Seasons Houston is worth a special trip. Opened in 1982, it is truly grand—a combination of classic European style and Texas hospitality. The hotel occupies a city block in the downtown business district and is connected by a skywalk to the Park, a three-tier mall with boutiques and restaurants. The George R. Brown Convention Center, a state-of-the-art facility that opened in 1987, is two blocks away.

A grand staircase spirals up from the hotel's lobby, joining three floors of public space. On the fourth floor is a garden with one of the most attractive swimming pools in the city. A whirlpool, sauna, and game room are adjacent. Guests can also use the Houston Center Athletic Club (accessible by indoor walkway), which has racquet sports, jogging, and exercise equipment.

The guest rooms, decorated with custom furniture, have a residential feeling, and the bathrooms are stylish. All of the rooms are spacious and luxurious, especially the Four Seasons rooms, which feature a sleeping area in an alcove and a separate sitting area.

Service is cheerful and professional at the Four Seasons. Bed turndown, 24-hour room service, complimentary shoeshines, and one-hour pressing service are all standard. There's also free limousine service to downtown restaurants, businesses, and entertainment (even on weekends).

De Ville is an outstanding restaurant, headed by a bright young chef bursting with creativity. Dinner entrées, ranging from $13 to $18, may include smoked lamb nachos or sautéed Big Spring rattlesnake with anco linguine or lime cream and hickory-crisp duck with orzo–black bean salad. The Terrace Café serves lighter fare. The Lobby Lounge has buffet lunches and evening cocktails.

Valet parking costs $12 per day.

J. W. Marriott Hotel
By the Galleria
5150 Westheimer Road
Houston, Texas 77056
713-961-1500
800-228-9290
Fax: 713-961-5045

General manager: Bob Pittenger
Accommodations: 494 rooms and suites
Rates: $139–$159; double, $149–$169; suites, $500–$600; weekend rates available
Added: 15% tax
Payment: Major credit cards
Children: Free in room with parents
Pets: Small pets accepted with deposit
Smoking: Nonsmoking rooms available
Open: Year-round

Just across from the Galleria shopping mall, the 23-story J. W. Marriott is a sophisticated hotel. The lobby gleams with marble, polished paneling, brass, and crystal. A gift shop, hair salon, clothing boutique, and airline reservation desks line a side hallway. The Brasserie, with rare pre-Columbian artifacts, is the hotel's restaurant. The Lobby Lounge fills the air with the sound of live piano music.

The guest rooms are among the most tastefully decorated and comfortably appointed in the Southwest. The art was especially commissioned from Houston artists. The furniture is refined. There's a sitting area with a small couch, an armoire with a TV, and a convenient desk. The bathrooms have phones, small TVs, and built-in hair dryers. Terrycloth robes are a nice added touch.

The hotel's recreational facilities and health club are a real plus. The fifth-floor indoor-outdoor pool, although small, is a convivial gathering spot; a food service bar is next to the indoor portion. The health club has racquetball at $3 per hour. A coed sauna and steam room, and extensive workout equipment are available to hotel guests at no charge.

La Colombe D'Or
3410 Montrose Boulevard
Houston, Texas 77006
713-524-7999
Fax: 713-524-8923

Owner: Stephen N. Zimmerman
Accommodations: 6 suites
Rates: $175–$600
Included: Continental breakfast
Added: 15% tax
Payment: Major credit cards
Children: Free in room with parents
Pets: Not allowed
Smoking: Allowed
Open: Year-round

La Colombe d'Or combines the style of a country manor with the convenience of a city hotel. Small and intimate, it's also elegant and grand. Once it was the home of a wealthy family; today it welcomes guests from around the world. Here you are treated as a valued house guest, with an abundance of personal service. Expect a basket of fruit when you arrive. Enjoy a breakfast of fresh orange juice, croissants, and fruit served in your own dining room each morning.

The three-story yellow brick inn, built in 1923, has an attractively landscaped front yard with plants and sculptures, a welcoming front porch, a residential lobby decorated in treasures from Europe, a cozy bar named for the hedonistic wine god Bacchus, and a library where you can sip cognac. While some of the architectural elements have been added, the mahogany staircase and the decorated ceilings are original to the home. The second-floor hallway is lined with paintings, among them a work by Calder and watercolors of Houston landmarks.

Five guest suites, named after famous artists, are on the second floor. Each one is different—artfully decorated and unusual in its use of space. All have a king-size bed, sitting area, separate dining room, silk floral arrangements, telephone, clock radio, and bathrobes. Some have ceiling fans.

The Renoir Suite, although the smallest, is a favorite. Its dining area is separated from the bedroom by interior columns and draped fabric, yet the theme is Oriental, with Japanese prints, a carved screen for a headboard, Oriental rugs and a chest, and a glass-topped dining table. Its sunny dining room opens out onto a terrace. The Cézanne, once the master bedroom, is boldly decorated in green, rust, and blue. Playful paintings hang on the walls, while the floor is covered by a rich Oriental rug. The Degas suite, in rose pastel florals, looks like an Impressionist painting. Ivy vines grow along the ceiling of its airy dining room. Mauve and burgundy are the dominant colors in the Monet Suite, and there's a Bartlett print in the bath. Reminiscent of the artist's work, the Van Gogh Suite is more flamboyant, in ruddy browns and rusts.

The third-floor penthouse is even larger than the suites. Its antique furnishings are no surprise; the luxurious bathroom with an elevated whirlpool tub is.

The tempting aromas that waft upstairs are a constant reminder that just below there's a fine restaurant. Always popular with residents, it gained national attention during the Texas oil crash of the 1980s—the owner charged businessmen for lunch whatever the going rate was for a barrel of crude, so as not to deplete their almost empty wallets. His plan worked, and he's done a brisk business ever since.

Decorated in soft pinks and mauves, the restaurant is sophisticated and grand on a small scale. With an emphasis on regional products and fresh herbs, the cuisine is French Provençal. Entrées such as seafood Monaco, lamb Lyonnaise, and pasta Portofino keep guests from straying too far. The restaurant is open for lunch on weekdays and dinner every day but Sundays.

Plans are under way to add about 20 more suites on an adjoining lot. Currently, there is 24-hour concierge service; valet parking is free for guests.

La Colombe d'Or is about a 5-minute drive from downtown and within easy access of the Galleria, Texas Medical Center, Alley Theater, Wortham Center, and Jones Hall. The University of St. Thomas is a block away.

The Lancaster Hotel
701 Texas Avenue
Houston, Texas 77002
713-228-9500
800-231-0336
Fax: 713-223-4528

Managing director: Kim Nugent
Accommodations: 93 rooms
Rates: $145–$165; double, $170–$190; suites, $300–$800
Added: 15% tax
Payment: Major credit cards
Children: Under 16 free in room with parents
Pets: Small pets allowed with a $50 deposit
Smoking: Nonsmoking rooms available
Open: Year-round

In the midst of the downtown cultural district, the Lancaster is a small, elegant hotel with European style à la Texas and service spelled with a capital S. Its look is polished and refined. The lobby, like the rest of the hotel, is intimate, more like a parlor than a standard hotel lobby. Handsome elevators, with mirrors and polished wood, take guests to their rooms. There are no more than nine rooms on each floor.

In truth, the hotel hasn't always been so fine. Built in 1926 as the Auditorium Hotel, it has a colorful history. Gene Autry once rode his horse into the Stage Canteen in the basement. Symphony musicians, circus performers, wrestlers and ice skaters stayed here. So did the young Clark Gable, and rumor has it that he left his trunk as ransom until he could pay his bill.

In 1982 the building was transformed into a luxury hotel. The guest rooms have a British theme, with imported English tartan and chintz fabrics and wallpapers, prints of the English countryside, overstuffed chairs with stools, and carved two-poster beds. The bathrooms are sleek, in white marble and brass. Multiple two-line speaker phones, fully stocked refreshment centers, remote control TVs in armoires, terry robes, and such unexpected extras as umbrellas enhance the feeling of luxury. Expect a newspaper at your door in the morning and bed turndown at night.

The clublike Lancaster Grille, whose walls are covered with equestrian and hunt scenes, also has a British tone. The Grille, which serves all three meals and late night fare, is a popular dinner spot for theatergoers. For recreation and fitness, guests can use the Texas Club, a block and a half away. Facilities include a rooftop pool, Nautilus equipment, squash and racquetball courts, and a gym.

If you enjoy the performing arts, there's hardly a better place to stay in Houston. The Lancaster is next door to the Alley Theater, across the street from Jones Hall, a block from the Wortham Center, and within a few blocks of the Music Hall.

The hotel has a concierge, complimentary downtown limousine service, and 24-hour room service. Parking is $10 per day.

Omni Houston Hotel
Four Riverway
Houston, Texas 77056
713-871-8181
800-332-3442
Fax: 713-871-8116

General manager: Louis Martinelli
Accommodations: 381 rooms and suites
Rates: $190; double, $215; suites start at $300
Added: 15% tax
Payment: Major credit cards
Children: Under 17 free in room with parents
Pets: Not allowed
Smoking: Nonsmoking floors
Open: Year-round

A tranquil oasis in the bustling city, the Omni Houston Hotel is only a few minutes' drive from the Galleria and many businesses. Its parklike setting, among gleaming office towers, is unexpected. The wooded banks of Buffalo Bayou are on the eastern perimeter, and there's a reflection pond, the home of a family of swans, surrounded by weeping willows to the west.

Just inside, the Palm Court Lounge sets the tone. A lush tropical garden, it has a gentle waterfall, soft piano music, and views of the hotel's pools and fountains. The colors of the garden are repeated throughout, with a profusion of green marble in the lobby accented with Asian screens and modern paintings. Indeed, the entire hotel is like a garden, bringing the outdoors inside with lush plants while allowing expansive views of the landscaped grounds.

The guest rooms, with luxurious modern furnishings, look out on the grounds or the bayou. All the rooms have overstuffed chairs, remote control TVs, stocked mini-bars, hair dryers, and bath telephones. Terry robes add to the feeling of luxury.

A good choice for a weekend retreat as well as a business stop, the hotel is geared to recreation. It has two pools, four tennis courts, and bikes to rent, with trails in nearby Memorial Park. The health club has extensive exercise equipment and a whirlpool.

The dining choices are all good. Café on the Green, open from 6:30 A.M. to midnight, has a sumptuous Sunday brunch. La Réserve, the fine restaurant, serves French, American, and regional dishes. Entrées such as smoked chicken and eggplant salad served with a warm goat cheese torte range from $13 to $20. Afternoon tea, evening hors d'oeuvres, and Viennese desserts are all part of the Palm Court Lounge's bill of fare. Downstairs is the Black Swan, a pub named for the hotel's mascots. Offering more than 100 brands of beer, it serves light evening fare and has live entertainment, board games, darts, and dancing.

The hotel's mascots are two beautiful black swans that glide tranquilly across the reflecting pond. If you get too close, their docile nature disappears and you may find yourself running from an irate swan. Apparently the birds, who produce offspring prolifically, are suspicious of intruders, since fledgling swans are often given up for adoption.

The service is attentive, if somewhat slick. Self-parking is free, valet service costs from $10 to $15. Free limousine service is available to the Galleria and to a shuttle terminal, where you can catch a bus to either Intercontinental or Hobby Airport. Downtown Houston is about ten miles east of the hotel.

The Phoenix Fitness Resort

111 North Post Oak Lane
Houston, Texas 77024
713-685-6836
800-548-4701 in Texas
800-548-4700 in U.S.
Fax: 713-680-1657

Executive director: Sally Kerr-Lamkin
Accommodations: 5 rooms in-house, 297 at hotel
Rates: $1350–$1550 for 6 nights
Included: All meals and spa program
Added: 15% tax on hotel rooms
Payment: Major credit cards
Children: Not appropriate
Pets: Not allowed
Smoking: Prohibited
Open: Year-round, except for New Year's and Christmas weeks

The Phoenix is a top-rated luxury spa dedicated to one's overall health and well-being. Founded in 1980, it addresses physical fitness, nutrition, and the emotions. "Guests come for a new beginning," says a Phoenix representative. "Many want to get their lives in order." Weight loss may or may not be one of their goals.

The spa is in the Houstonian, a multifaceted facility comprising a hotel and conference center, health and fitness club, and a center for preventive medicine. Despite its urban location, the Houstonian is a wooded retreat, with winding paths and a wealth of fitness and recreational facilities. The program is primarily for women over 18, though occasional coed weeks are held.

Spa participants, limited to fifteen, have a choice of two programs. Both include fitness (stretching, toning, low-impact aerobics, advanced weight equipment, water exercise, brisk walks); nutrition (1,000-calorie-per-day menu, low in fat, sodium, and refined sugar); personal testing (body composition; strength, flexibility, and cardiovascular testing; personal fitness consultation); lectures (lifestyle management, fashion, healthy cooking, nutrition, eating disorders); and a beauty program (massages, facials, manicure and pedicure, hair styling).

The more expensive Ultimate Week has a broader beauty program than the Fitness Week Plus. Beauty services are at the

Christine Valmy salon, in the fitness club. When guests aren't involved in scheduled workouts, they can use the Houstonian Health and Fitness Club's racquetball and tennis courts, lap pool, outdoor and indoor tracks, whirlpools, saunas, and Swedish showers.

The Ambassador House, once a private home, is a nucleus for the Phoenix. Spa participants eat together in its private dining room, relax at its pool, and gather in the living room for lectures or socializing. Accommodations are on a separate floor of one hotel wing, accessible only to Phoenix guests. Aerobics classes are in a studio used by the Phoenix exclusively.

The staff members include a nutritionist, chef, psychologist, physiologist, and image consultant as well as a physical fitness team.

The atmosphere is casual at the Phoenix: there is no need to dress for dinner here. The schedule, while regimented, is flexible and can be modified for each person. Guests are encouraged to participate in the full program, but primarily, the staff "wants everyone to get out of the program what they came for," says a spokeswoman.

The Ritz-Carlton
1919 Briar Oaks Lane
Houston, Texas 77027
713-840-7600
800-241-3333
Fax: 713-840-0616

General manager: Luis Argoteg
Accommodations: 232 rooms and suites
Rates: $170–$285; double, $190–$295; suites, $450–$1,900
Added: 15% tax
Payment: Major credit cards
Children: Under 18 free in room with parents
Pets: With approval
Smoking: Nonsmoking rooms available
Open: Year-round

The Ritz-Carlton is a gleaming palace that combines sophistication with hospitality. Despite its size, it has a residential feeling. No large lobby yawns at its front door; instead, guests sign in at an unimposing hall desk. The public space is high on aesthetics — rotundas with skylights, alcoves with comfortable chairs, arched corridors with greenery.

Best of all, the hotel treats its guests as honored visitors. Personal preferences are noted and attended to, and staff members call guests by name. Valet parking ($12.50), 24-hour room service, and complimentary transportation to nearby shopping are all available.

The Lobby Lounge serves high tea to the strains of harp music, as well as light desserts, cordials, chocolate fondues, and champagne in the evenings. Nearby is the handsome bar, resembling an English men's club, with couches and a fireplace.

The guest rooms are comfortable and pleasing to the eye. The deluxe rooms are especially large, with bay windows and separate sitting areas. The baths are warmly decorated, with colored marble vanity tops. Suites have canopy beds, expansive wet bars with refrigerators, and large bathtubs with Jacuzzi jets. Terrycloth robes, a choice of down or synthetic pillows, three phones, and remote control TVs are appreciated. When you walk into your room you feel expected: the thermostat is set, the lights are on, and soft music is playing.

The second-floor pool is a tranquil hideaway. While the pool itself is small, the setting is like a garden, far removed from the city streets.

Dining is a stellar event. Choose from the formal Restaurant or the handsome Bar and Grill. The Restaurant's cuisine is new American, and the service is impeccable. Of special note on the menu are entrées designated as Fitness Cuisine. Lunch items such as grilled chicken with papaya al pesto ($12.50) and dinners such as venison medallions with crushed peppercorns in a lingonberry sauce ($26) and steamed salmon filet served in a dill vermouth sauce ($21) are completely satisfying, whether or not you're watching what you eat.

In Post Oak Park off Loop 610 West, the Ritz is a few blocks from the Galleria. It is easy to get to most business addresses, including those downtown.

Sara's Bed & Breakfast Inn

941 Heights Boulevard
Houston, Texas 77008
713-868-1130
  800-593-1130
  Fax: 713-868-1160

Innkeeper: Donna J. Arledge
Accommodations: 11 rooms (3 with private bath)
Rates: double, $50–$75; suite, $120
Added: 15% tax

Included: Breakfast
Payment: Major credit cards
Children: Accepted in only one unit; additional $10 per day
  per child
Pets: Not allowed
Smoking: In designated areas only
Open: Year-round

Downtown Houston is four miles away—you can see the sky-scrapers on the horizon. But here in the Heights, developed in the 1890s as one of Texas's first planned suburbs, you can relive the days of lemonade and cookies, almost forgetting that the glistening modern city exists. Here Victorian structures dominate; ninety of them are on the National Register. There's a central boulevard set with trees, a park with a lacy gazebo, and a public library that makes you want to curl up for hours.

Right on Heights Boulevard is Sara's, a wonderful two-story Victorian confection of gingerbread with a wraparound porch, a turret, and a widow's walk. In truth, the entire structure is not as old as its architecture suggests. The core of the house—a one-story cottage—was indeed built in 1898. But the flourishes were added in 1980.

In 1983 the Arledges bought the house and spent three years renovating it. Now the inn is fanciful and fun, offering lots of diversity. Sara's is a good place to start a visit to Texas, for each guest room in the main house is decorated to reflect one of its towns or cities. Get a quick tour of the state while choosing a room for the night. Dallas is sophisticated; Galveston has a nautical theme. Fredericksburg has Germanic hand stenciling; Paris, French furniture. Tyler, named for a city famed for its roses, is decorated in a rose motif. Austin, with its white iron and brass bed and a bay window, is the prettiest.

Jefferson, on the first floor, has a queen-size bed and is the only room in the main house with its own bath. The other baths have showers instead of tubs. On the second floor of a separate building, a balcony suite has two bedrooms, two baths, a kitchen (only light cooking allowed), and living area. Good for families, it is the only unit accommodating children, and a two-night stay is required.

Adjoining the main house is a large deck with a hot tub. Since most of the inn's interior is devoted to bedrooms, the deck is the primary gathering spot.

Breakfast is served in a small dining room. Donna's specialties are hot breads and creamy scrambled eggs with cheese.

The Westin Galleria and Westin Oaks

Westin Galleria: 5060 West Alabama
Houston, Texas 77056
713-960-8100
Westin Oaks: 5011 Westheimer
Houston, Texas 77056
713-623-4300
800-228-3000
Telex: 4990983
Fax: 713-960-6553

Managing director: Raymond Sylvester
Accommodations: Galleria, 489 rooms; Oaks, 406 rooms
Rates: $160–$190; double, $190–$220; suites, $300–$1,200
Added: 15% tax
Payment: Major credit cards
Children: Under 18 free in room with parents
Pets: Small ones accepted on leash
Smoking: Nonsmoking rooms available
Open: Year-round

Houston has two Westins, each offering luxury coupled with vivacity. Both are part of a "city under glass," the Galleria Mall, which was inspired by the Galleria Vittorio Emanuele in Milan, Italy. Houston's version has more than 300 shops and restaurants, an Olympic-size skating rink, and several cinemas as well as these two excellent hotels.

The 21-story Oaks, the first of the two, opened with the enclosed mall in 1971. The 24-story Galleria opened in 1977. About a 5-minute walk apart, the two complement each other in style and mood.

The guest rooms, furnished in contemporary decor, are large and well appointed. Each has a stocked bar and refrigerator, multiple phones, and balconies. Rooms have either one king-or two queen-size beds. Cable TV and movies are complimentary.

For dining and entertainment, there are six choices. (Guests at either hotel can charge services to their room at the other.) Delmonico's, at the Galleria, offers fine dining. Shucker's Sports Bar, at the Oaks, serves seafood and casual fare. Both hotels have an informal restaurant. Annabelle's, at the top of the Galleria, is the spot for dancing, and the Roof nightclub, at the Oaks, has live entertainment and happy hour buffets.

For recreation, you can swim at either hotel, play tennis at the Galleria, and jog at the Oaks. The Galleria also has a putting green. Guests can also use the University Club, in the mall, which has ten indoor tennis courts, a ball machine, whirlpools and saunas, and massage.

Hotel courtesies include a concierge, 24-hour room service, express check-in and check-out, and valet parking ($11.75). Self-parking is free.

The Wyndham Warwick

5701 Main Street
Houston, Texas 77005
713-526-1991
800-822-4200
Fax: 713-639-4545

General manager: Patrick Lupsha
Accommodations: 308 rooms and suites
Rates: $149–$169; double, $169–$209, suites start at $175; $20 extra person in room
Added: 15% tax
Payment: Major credit cards
Children: Under 17 free in room with parents
Pets: Not allowed
Smoking: Three nonsmoking floors
Open: Year-round

In a fast-paced city where change is the norm, the Warwick is a welcome link to the past. Not that the hotel itself is particularly old — the original structure was built in 1926. But its opulence only dates from 1964, when the hotel was totally renovated by the oilman John Mecom, Sr.

That refurbishment is the reason for the Warwick's historic character. The furnishings in the public areas are far from ordinary. A virtual museum of European treasures, they include ornate pilasters and exquisite paneling from the Murat palace in France, 18th-century statues from Italy, Baccarat crystal chandeliers (with over 5,000 pieces each), a 275-year-old Aubusson tapestry, and a profusion of art — all collected by the Mecoms.

John Mecom was a visionary, striking oil where others swore there could be none. He also had an eye for beauty. His business took him around the world, and wherever he went he added to his collection. While overseeing the renovation of the hotel (its purchase was sentimental as well as an investment, for Mecom had stayed in the hotel with his mother as a youth, and she had later taken an apartment there when he was a student at nearby Rice University), Mecom instructed his wife to use any color she wanted—as long as it was blue. Why blue? "Green is beautiful, too," he said. "But you look down at the grass to see green. You look up to see blue."

In Houston's museum district—a few blocks from the Museum of Fine Arts, the Cullen Sculpture Garden, the Contemporary Arts Museum, and the Museum of Natural Science—the Warwick is surrounded by beauty. Just outside its doors is one of Houston's favorite landmarks, the Mecom Fountains.

In recent years the hotel had gone from having a rich, mature look to being a little worn around the edges, in contrast to the burst of sparkling luxury hotels that opened in Houston in the early 1980s. So the Trammell Crow Company purchased the hotel, renovated it, and reopened the property as the Wyndham Warwick in 1989, maintaining its status as an elegant hotel. The list of notable people who have stayed at the hotel is truly impressive, including royalty, heads of state, and entertainment stars.

The guest rooms at the Warwick vary in size and decor. Most are furnished in the style of Louis XV, with custom furniture, marble-topped dressing tables, botanical prints, flowered bedspreads, and a choice of king-size or twin beds. The bathrooms have phones and blow dryers. Lanai rooms, in a separate wing, face the swimming pool and its terrace. Curved to allow maximum exposure to the outside view, their configuration adds interest as well as convenience. All have two baths and a balcony or patio, with easy access to the men's and women's saunas. One of the best room choices is a junior suite; some have refrigerators and microwave ovens. Most of the suites are one of a kind, and some have outstanding views of the city to the south (Bob Hope once labeled this view as the prettiest sight in the world).

The Hunt Room and Café Vienna are the Warwick's dining rooms. The Hunt Room, the more formal of the two, has rich woods and a fireside setting. Its menu has depth and excitement. Entrées, such as capon breasts with artichokes and rack of lamb, range from $17 to $25. The paneling in Café Vienna came from the Château la Motte au Bots, in northern France. There's a pasta bar at lunch, and dinner entrées range from $7 to $15.

Hotel services include valet parking and room service.

Indianapolis

The Canterbury Hotel
123 South Illinois
Indianapolis, Indiana 46225
317-634-3000
800-538-8186
Fax: 317-685-2519
Reservations: 800-323-7500

General manager: Letita Moscrip
Accommodations: 74 rooms, 25 suites
Rates: $125–$175; double, $150–$225; suites, $400–$750;
   packages available
Included: Continental breakfast; all meals available
Minimum stay: None
Added: 10% tax
Payment: Major credit cards
Children: Welcome
Pets: With prior approval
Smoking: Nonsmoking rooms available
Open: Year-round

Opened as the Lockerbie in 1928, this grand old hotel was refurbished in 1984, with the duke of Canterbury himself attending the opening. The English tradition of high tea is still practiced here from four to six in the afternoon, with scones, finger sandwiches, and elegant desserts served.

Small and luxurious, the hotel offers limousine, concierge, and 24-hour room service, weekday dry cleaning, and valet parking. There are no health facilities or pool on the property, but guests have access to two nearby clubs. Four conference rooms can serve up to 80 people.

Beaulieu, the hotel's restaurant, features salmon and lamb among the nightly specials. A newspaper accompanies the Continental breakfast each morning.

The spacious rooms have Chippendale furnishings and king- or queen-size beds. Two of the elegant Parlor Suites have whirlpool baths and marble-lined sinks. The downstairs lobby has dark green carpeting, accented by brass fixtures and hunting prints.

The usually splendid city views are currently obscured by noisy construction on a shopping center next door. But when the work is complete in 1994, the hotel will be linked directly to its excellent restaurants and shops.

Holiday Inn at Union Station
P.O. Box 2186
123 West Louisiana Street
Indianapolis, Indiana 46206
317-631-2221
Fax: 317-236-7474
Reservations: 800-HOLIDAY

Managing director: Bill Townsend
Accommodations: 243 rooms, 33 suites
Rates: $95–$98 ($10 per additional person); suites, $154–$184; train rooms, single, $124; double, $134; packages available
Included: All meals available
Minimum stay: None
Added: 10% tax
Payment: Major credit cards
Children: Welcome
Pets: Not allowed
Smoking: Nonsmoking rooms available
Open: Year-round

It's enough of a surprise to find yourself sleeping in authentic, beautifully decorated Pullman cars in a historic railroad station. But to realize that the fantasy has been pulled off by Holiday Inn, king of the cookie-cutter chain hotel—that's almost too much to bear.

During the renovation of Union Station in 1989, thirteen original 1920s Pullman sleepers were acquired to create twenty-six special guest accommodations. Brass, cherrywood, and marble were added to the rooms, which were named after personalities from the early part of the century. Sexy Jean Harlow mixes pink and green foil wallpaper with zebra–skin accents. Amelia Earhart gives the feeling of an early airplane cabin, with exposed mahogany and forest green touches. Paraphernalia relating to the celebrities include a New York Times article announcing Earhart's disappearance, a framed Louis Armstrong recording, and a showcard advertising a new film with Rudolph Valentino.

Cozy sitting areas here resemble old-fashioned parlors,

blending sofas and chairs with antique tables, lighting fixtures, wooden blinds, elaborate draperies, and lace curtains. Some say the rooms are so well decorated that they no longer have the utilitarian feeling of the old sleepers. But with the long, thin layout and the muffled rumblings of the active train station overhead, the illusion comes across loud and clear.

Another novelty room, the blue and white Indianapolis Colts Suite, has big-screen television, football helmet–shaped chairs, and a transparent table marked with yard lines. Although it can accommodate up to 30 fans, it's pretty tacky and only helps you appreciate the care that has gone into decorating the other rooms.

Standard guest rooms and suites can be found here, where the modern glass elevator, plant-filled atriums, and indoor pool and sauna blend attractively with the exposed steel girders of the old station.

The rest of the renovated station is worth exploring. Built in 1853, this was the first Union Station in the country. In 1888, the original structure was replaced by a brick Romanesque Revival headhouse, where 200 passenger trains steamed through daily. Thomas Edison once worked here as a telegraph operator, and Abraham Lincoln was known to travel these rails frequently.

Today, the station is a shopping, dining, and entertainment facility. Most weekend packages feature a carriage ride, which takes you on a scenic tour of downtown Indianapolis.

Omni Severin Hotel

40 West Jackson Place
Indianapolis, Indiana 46225
317-634-OMNI
Fax: 317-687-3619
Reservations:
  Omni Hotels
  1-800-THE-OMNI

General manager: Hans Strohmer
Accommodations: 423 rooms, including 38 suites
Rates: $140–$185; suites, $175–$375; packages available
Minimum stay: None
Added: 10% tax
Payment: Major credit cards
Children: Welcome
Pets: Not allowed
Smoking: Nonsmoking rooms available
Open: Year-round

The Hotel Severin, built in 1913, originally thrived on the 300 passenger trains that rolled daily into Indianapolis' Union Station across the street. Today, with the old station serving as a shopping, restaurant and entertainment complex, the Omni Severin Hotel has a new clientele.

Beneath a skylit lobby atrium, a 20-foot waterfall flows continuously into a marble pool. The contemporary look here is contrasted by the hotel's original 1913 furniture. Some of it can also be found in the guest rooms, though many are decidedly modern, with chrome and glass tables and tall thin lamps. Bi-level penthouse suites and plaza suites feature walkout balconies.

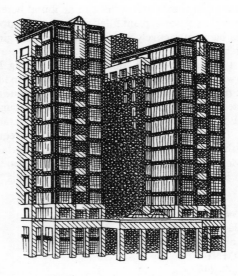

There are 17,000-square feet of meeting space, mostly broken up into smaller boardrooms. There are also two ballrooms, one quite ornate with crystal chandeliers.

An indoor swimming pool and exercise facility are accessed from men's and women's locker rooms. The hotel's restaurant, the Severin Bar and Grill, serves a lunch buffet and chef's specials including a French onion and apple soup. Drinks and appetizers are now served in the Lobby Café. You may opt instead for the wide variety of eateries and taverns at Union Station.

Kansas City

Doanleigh Wallagh
217 East 37th Street
Kansas City, Missouri 64111
816-753-2667

Innkeepers: Carolyn and Edward Litchfield
Accommodations: 5 rooms (all with private bath)
Rates: $80–$110
Included: Full breakfast
Minimum stay: 2 nights on weekends and some holidays
Added: 6.5% tax
Payment: Major credit cards
Children: By arrangement
Pets: Not allowed
Smoking: Downstairs only
Open: Year-round

The theatrical flair at Doanleigh Wallagh makes perfect sense when you learn that Ed Litchfield once worked at Twentieth Century Fox. Movie props, including a bust from The Agony and the Ecstasy and brass candlesticks from Desirée, highlight the common rooms. The big-screen television in the solarium has a VCR and a collection of more than 100 classic films. Ed and Carolyn proudly point out that Carol Channing rented this Georgian inn for a full week before performing in Kansas City.

The red leather wing chairs in front of the fireplace are from the Muehlbach Hotel, a Kansas City landmark. Before it was torn down, the Litchfields were able to purchase carpeting, beds, and other furnishings for their inn. The oak bookcase, meanwhile, came from a vicarage in England. There's also a grand piano and pump organ, used for small weddings.

A Mexican statue of St. Augustine greets you on the staircase leading to the guest rooms. The Hyde Park Room, originally the master bedroom, is the most lavish, with a woodburning fireplace, queen-size four-poster bed, a large armoire that holds a television, and a desk made from a 100-year-old grand piano.

There is a tiny fridge in the closet. The Westport Room, with its own porch, is also the only room with both tub and shower.

The breakfast menu has a similar taste of the dramatic, from French toast topped with honey and an orange glaze to eggs Benedict with fresh fruit to Russian pancakes with sausage and bacon. Guests can have breakfast in their own room or in the breakfast room. The innkeepers also keep a generous supply of cookies, candy bars, microwave popcorn, and soft drinks in the butler's pantry for guests.

The Raphael

Country Club Plaza
Kansas City, Missouri 64112
816-756-3800
800-821-5343
Fax: 816-756-3800, ext. 2199

General manager: Maxine Hill
Accommodations: 123 rooms and suites
Rates: $86–$98; double, $101–$125; suites, single, $104–$110; double, $119–$125
Included: Continental breakfast
Minimum stay: None
Added: 12% tax
Payment: Major credit cards
Children: Welcome
Pets: Not allowed
Smoking: Nonsmoking rooms available
Open: Year-round

Kansas City's Raphael successfully cultivates its image of a small private club rather than a big city hotel. Return guests are usually known by name. The European touch is noted in the tapestries and reproduction oil paintings that grace the wainscoted lobby walls, including the trademark image of Raphael's Count Castiglione. A Chopin étude plays gently in the background, quite a change from the busy comings and goings in the driveway outside.

Built in 1927 and having undergone several renovations, the Raphael retains some of its historic character. Some of the original deep bathtubs remain, while modern conveniences like 24-hour room service, nightly turndown, mini-bars and valet parking uphold the reputation for excellent service.

Most of the rooms here are suites, many overlooking the shopping, dining and entertainment district known as Country Club Plaza. The hotel restaurant keeps pace with the competition by providing a varied menu of beef, pasta, and seafood entrées.

The Ritz-Carlton Kansas City
401 Ward Parkway
Kansas City, Missouri 64112
816-756-1500
Fax: 816-756-1635
Reservations:
  Ritz-Carlton Hotels
  800-241-3333

General manager: Norm Howard
Accommodations: 373 rooms, including 28 suites
Rates: $139–$179; suites, $250–$1000; packages available
Minimum stay: None
Added: 11.975% tax
Payment: Major credit cards
Children: Welcome
Pets: Not allowed
Smoking: Nonsmoking rooms available
Open: Year-round

Kansas City's Ritz-Carlton is in the heart of the Country Club Plaza, Kansas City's prestigious and historic business, shopping, dining and entertainment district. The 14-story hotel, with its waterfalls, sculptures, and wrought-iron balconies, exquisitely reflects the Moorish influence of the Plaza.

Guest rooms are decorated in traditional style, with marble-lined bathrooms, hair dryers, remote control cable televisions, honor bars, twice-daily maid service, terry robes, three telephones, in-room safes, and fancy toiletries among the amenities. The Ritz-Carlton Club offers guest rooms on two floors with its own lounge and multilingual concierge staff, especially helpful when arranging airport transportation or securing restaurant reservations.

You may opt to dine in at the Ritz-Carlton's signature restaurant, The Grill, which serves a wonderful view of the Plaza along with its Continental and American cuisine. The Bar schedules live entertainment Wednesdays through Saturdays. The Café remains a popular spot for breakfast. The Ritz-Carlton offers more than 22,500 square feet of meeting and banquet space, including the Ballroom.

The hotel's fitness center provides state-of-the-art treadmills, stairmasters, and biocycle machines, as well as an outdoor pool. For joggers and tennis players, miles of trails and lighted tennis courts are just two blocks away.

Key to the Ritz-Carlton's success is its location amidst the courtyards, tree-lined walks, mosaics, sculptures and fountains of the Plaza. Brooks Brothers, Saks, Gucci, and Polo are just a few of the upscale shops. Make reservations early for two annual events—the Plaza Art Fair in September and the Plaza Lighting Ceremony at Thanksgiving.

Southmoreland on the Plaza
116 East 46th Street
Kansas City, Missouri 64112
816-531-7979
Fax: 816-531-2407

Innkeepers: Susan Moehl and Penni Johnson
Accommodations: 12 rooms (all with private bath)
Rates: $95–$125 ($10 per additional person)
Included: Full breakfast
Minimum stay: None
Added: 8% tax
Payment: Major credit cards
Children: 13 years and older
Pets: Not allowed
Smoking: On verandah only
Open: Year-round

Susan Moehl and Penni Johnson have worked hard to create an inn that's popular with business travelers while still providing warm hospitality to weekend guests. And while it is impossible to be all things to all people, these high-powered innkeepers come pretty close at Southmoreland on the Plaza.

To begin with, they have a superb location. The 1913 Greek Revival home is just two blocks from Country Club Plaza and its more than 300 stores, restaurants, and theaters. Sculptures and fountains decorate the Plaza, and horse-drawn carriages clop by in the evenings. The famed Nelson-Atkins Museum of Art and Henry Moore Sculpture Garden are also nearby.

The staid light gray exterior, more New England than Midwest, doesn't even hint at the often whimsical decoration inside. The innkeepers have amassed a fine collection of antiques from the Midwest and abroad. When restoring the house, they rebuilt the original staircase from blueprints; the addition that was required in order to have more guest rooms maintains the home's integrity.

Each room is named for a famous person from Kansas City. Romantics will love the Russell Stover Room, with its pink and blue decor, heart-shaped Jacuzzi, and complimentary box of Stover chocolates. The Leroy "Satchel" Paige Room, once a sleeping porch, now resembles a rustic log cabin with vintage baseball posters and miniature bats lining the walls. The picnic Victrola has Bessie Smith wailing on "Graveyard Dream Blues." Box seats for Kansas City Royals home games are included with this room.

Susan and Penni bend over backwards for business guests who check in after midnight or leave well before dawn. They send them on their way with at least a portion of their elegant breakfast, which includes baked apples with raisins, blueberry muffins, and fancy egg ramekins stuffed with bacon and Lorraine swiss. They even cater to vegetarian palettes by using artichoke hearts instead of meat. The morning paper waits at the table for each guest.

Afternoon wine and cheese are served in the white wicker solarium overlooking a croquet lawn shaded by century-old trees or in the dining room, with its woodburning fireplace. Have a question about theater tickets, dinner reservations, or museum hours? If Susan and Penni don't know the answer, they will find out in a snap.

Southmoreland on the Plaza is a beautiful place to visit, and the innkeepers want to keep it that way. So they recite a litany of house rules when you arrive, including instructions on how to use the plastic card key. Coasters, they remind you, should always be used when setting glasses down on a wood table. As a result, it may take sensitive guests a while to feel at home here.

Las Vegas

Alexis Park Resort

375 East Harmon Avenue
Las Vegas, Nevada 89109
702-796-330
800-582-2228
Fax: 702-796-0766

General manager: Stu Platt
Accommodations: 500 suites
Rates: $95–$535
Minimum stay: Two nights over New Year's
Added: 8% tax
Payment: Major credit cards
Children: Free under age 18
Pets: Subject to $50 minimum fee
Smoking: Nonsmoking rooms available
Open: Year-round

In a city animated by glitz and frenzy, the Alexis Park Resort stands out as an oasis of calm. This 19-acre enclave of low Spanish-style buildings and manicured lawns with waterfalls lies a mile from the neon of Las Vegas's main drag. It has no casino, diverting guests instead with a health club, tennis courts, swimming pools, a putting green, and a jogging track.

Tucked into sixteen U-shaped two-story buildings, its 500 two- and three-room suites have private outside entrances and views of a landscaped courtyard. All have been handsomely decorated in contemporary designer furnishings long on mauves, grays, and pastels. Even the smallest quarters have a separate narrow living room with a wet bar, coffeemaker, phone, television with in-room movies, and a bath with an oversize tub. The more deluxe suites add Jacuzzi tubs, fireplaces, and even lofts.

None of the rooms is far from one of the three strategically placed swimming pools, the largest of them an amoeba-shaped lagoon surrounded by sundeck and accented by a fountain. Off to one side is a complex of two lighted tennis courts and an aerobics fitness center. There's also a 9-hole putting green.

Alexis Park has two restaurants, among them Pegasus, which consistently ranks among the best in Las Vegas. Though pricey, it garners rave reviews for such international fare as medallions de veau Lucullus and lobster imperial. Tuxedoed waiters provide showy service inside beneath an art deco crystal chandelier or outside on the patio overlooking a waterfall and gardens. Afterwards, those looking for excitement are a short drive from the heart of the Strip; those who aren't are a short, calm walk from their room.

Caesars Palace
3570 Las Vegas Boulevard South
Las Vegas, Nevada 89109
702-731-7110
800-634-6661
Fax: 702-731-6636

Director of hotel operations: Michael Maggiore
Accommodations: 1,324 rooms, 194 suites
Rates: $95–$225; double $110–$240; suites, $270–$895
Minimum stay: None
Added: 8% tax
Payment: Major credit cards
Children: Free under age 18
Pets: Not allowed
Smoking: Two nonsmoking floors
Open: Year-round

Caesars Palace opened in 1966, and it still epitomizes Las Vegas glitz. Designed to imitate the grandeur of ancient Rome, Caesars lavished millions of dollars on marble statuary, temples, reflecting pools, fountains, and 50-foot Italian cypresses. It seems to be modeled, however, on the Rome from 1960s Hollywood movies rather than on anything from a history textbook. But never mind, it's the fantasy that counts.

The Rome of 2,000 years ago—complete with noisy revelers and a Caesar and Cleopatra—does appear in miniature inside the "World of Caesar," a $2.5 million exhibit using laser-powered sound and holography at the entrance to one of three people movers that shuttle pedestrians in from the Strip. The moving sidewalk ends inside one of three casinos that together cover a whopping 117,000 square feet.

The surprise of Caesars Palace is not the space devoted to slot machines and blackjack tables but the quality of the rooms. Fresh from a multimillion-dollar refurbishment (essential to keep pace with upstarts like the neighboring Mirage), Caesars

Palace has some of the best rooms in town. Even the most basic accommodations have burled wood armoires, dressing rooms, and marble baths with whirlpool tubs, plus such extras as remote control televisions, safes, round beds, and just enough ostentation—like marbled walls—to be fun without lapsing into bad taste. Most lavish of all are the $1.5 million Fantasy Suites, each with its own private dining room, servant's kitchen, audiovisual center, and simulated night sky on the parlor ceiling.

Also sprawled over its 86 acres are two landscaped swimming pools, a 28-foot Jacuzzi, tennis courts, a health spa, an Omnimax theater, and the Circus Maximus Showroom. Its nine restaurants range from the simplicity of the Food Court to the haute cuisine of the Palace Court to seven-course feasts in the Bacchanal. New in 1992 is the Forum, an indoor shopping arcade à la Rodeo Drive, expected to hold almost 100 shops and restaurants. Upstarts take note.

Desert Inn Hotel & Casino
3145 Las Vegas Boulevard South
Las Vegas, Nevada 89109
702-733-4444
800-634-6906

Vice president of hotel operations: Vince Matthews
Accommodations: 726 rooms, 95 suites
Rates: $75–$135; suites, $175–$1,500
Minimum stay: Some weekends and holidays
Added: 8% tax
Payment: Major credit cards
Children: Welcome
Pets: Prohibited
Smoking: 1 nonsmoking floor; nonsmoking tables in casino
Open: Year-round

Understated luxury is an endangered species in Las Vegas, since it withers when exposed to too much neon. One of the few places it thrives is the Desert Inn, an 800-room complex of two-story to 14-story buildings on the upper half of the Strip.

The Desert Inn, built in 1950, has the most tastefully appointed rooms of any hotel in Las Vegas, one of the city's best restaurants, La Vie en Rose, and 200 acres of parklike grounds containing an award-winning 18-hole golf course, tennis courts, and an elegant 18,000-square-foot spa and fitness center.

All that aside, guests cherish its peacefulness most. Apart from an animated casino and an intimate showroom for headline entertainment, the Desert Inn has little to attract crowds—

not even an all-you-can-eat buffet—and so remains an oasis of calm. It is actually possible to pass through the lobby or cross the casino without having to negotiate masses of humanity lured in from outside.

The newest and most alluring rooms are those in the 14-story Augusta Tower. Half of these spacious havens have bay windows overlooking the Strip; the other half have balconies and views of the swimming pool or golf course. Decorated in pastel green and blue, they have pickled-wood furnishings, wallpaper that simulates pale green marble, padded headboards, and remote control televisions. The bathroom is also appealing—it's two rooms actually, the first with two sinks in a peach granite vanity, the second with the bath, commode, and its own phone.

With its air of exclusivity, the Desert Inn gets more than its share of high-rollers and VIPs, yet its attraction goes beyond gambling. Its 18-hole golf course, which *Golf Digest* has ranked among the nation's top 75 resort courses, annually holds three PGA events, sending the pros out to tackle a narrow, accuracy-demanding course that plays 7,074 yards from the championship tees. Tennis players have access to ten hard courts and professional instruction, while the spa features a lengthy menu of pampering massages and beauty treatments, aerobics classes, a weight-training center, a heated pool, and an outdoor fitness track. The Desert Inn isn't only Las Vegas's most elegant hotel—it's also the most resortlike.

Excalibur Hotel & Casino

3850 Las Vegas Boulevard South
P.O. Box 96778
Las Vegas, Nevada 89193
702-597-7777
800-937-7777
Fax: 702-597-7040

Manager: Don Givens
Accommodations: 3,991 rooms, 41 suites
Rates: $39–$43; suites, $110
Minimum stay: None
Added: 8% tax
Payment: Major credit cards
Children: Free under age 13
Pets: Not allowed
Smoking: 400 nonsmoking rooms; nonsmoking areas in casino
Open: Year-round

Its elephantine size—4,032 rooms—and medieval castle–architecture guaranteed that Excalibur would achieve notoriety the moment it opened in June 1990. It instantly displaced the 3,079-room Las Vegas Hilton as the largest resort hotel in the world, earning a place in The Guinness Book of Records, 1991. It also became Las Vegas's newest tourist attraction.

Built at a cost of $290 million, the 28-story white castle, its turrets topped with red, blue, and gold spires, anchors a 117-acre site toward the southern end of the Strip. A moving walkway hustles pedestrians in from the sidewalk, carrying them along the battlements and across a moat and drawbridge into a cobblestone foyer and rock-walled atrium draped with velvet, satin, and heraldic flags, all illuminated by iron and gold chandeliers. Time lines cross as more than 2,600 slot machines and 100 gaming tables merge with Camelot.

Like other Circus Circus enterprises, Excalibur is part amusement park, part casino: although more than 100,000 square feet have been devoted to various games of chance, the fantasy castle also has diversions for those too young to gamble. That includes a medieval midway called Fantasy Faire, where barkers in Robin Hood outfits run games, knight races, and archery contests. Jugglers, magicians, madrigal singers, and puppeteers perform on the streets of the Medieval Village, lined with shops and restaurants with names like Lance-a-Lotta Pasta and Oktoberfest Hofbrau. Twice each evening, knights joust in a laser spectacular while spectators devour a medieval feast (without utensils) in the 900-seat amphitheater. Eerily true-to-life Magic Motion Machines recreate the thrills of a high-speed bobsled run or roller-coaster ride. Bathrooms are labeled "Sorcerer" and "Sorceress."

The castle motif extends to the average-size, utilitarian rooms, which feature medieval headboards, stone-patterned wallpaper, crimson or teal carpeting, and bathrooms with stall showers but no tubs. Even the suites—which are nothing more than a larger room with a Jacuzzi in the turreted corner—pale by Las Vegas standards. But then, Excalibur caters to the mainstream tourist rather than the high-roller and prices its accommodations accordingly.

The Golden Nugget Hotel and Casino
129 East Fremont Street
P.O. Box 610
Las Vegas, Nevada 89125
702-385-7111
800-634-3454
Fax: 702-386-8362

Vice president of hotel operations: Bob Sheldon
Accommodations: 1850 rooms, 90 suites
Rates: $58–$130; suites, $210–$750
Minimum stay: None
Added: 8% tax
Payment: Major credit cards
Children: Free under age 12
Pets: Prohibited
Smoking: 179 nonsmoking rooms
Open: Year-round

The Golden Nugget is the glamorous centerpiece of downtown Las Vegas. It spans two city blocks, yet it is not so much its size that sets it apart from its neighbors as its tasteful elegance. Inside, white marble, brass, and coffered ceilings with chandeliers like clusters of glass leaves lend it an almost antique splendor. Under Steve Wynn, who took control of the hotel in the 1970s, the once-faded casino acquired a touch of class.

The rooms he added, in two towers, have been decorated in more contemporary fashion than the public areas but with the same good taste. Spacious and cheerful, they have marble entryways, crown moldings, rose-covered fabrics, floral prints in brass frames, and marble-accented baths. And, in a further nod to comfort, the television has a remote control. Either tower provides easy access to the perpetually animated casino and its abundance of slot machines and gaming tables. But what would the Golden Nugget be without a few hunks of real gold? And since this is Las Vegas, nothing less than the largest in the world will do: in the casino, around the corner from the front desk, is a display case containing two huge gold nuggets, the larger of them weighing more than 61 pounds.

The casino aside, the Golden Nugget has the features you'd expect of a first-rate city hotel, including an amiable staff, a respectable Continental restaurant in Elaine's, a heated swimming pool, and a magnificent fitness center and beauty salon designed to resemble an Italian palazzo. It's worth the trip downtown.

The Mirage
3400 Las Vegas Boulevard South
P.O. Box 7777
Las Vegas, Nevada 89177
702-791-7444
800-627-6667
Fax: 702-791-7446

Vice president of hotel operations: Bill Hornbuckle
Accommodations: 2,775 rooms, 274 suites
Rates: $79–$225; suites, $375–$3,000
Minimum stay: None
Added: 8% tax
Payment: Major credit cards
Children: Free under age 12
Pets: Not allowed
Smoking: Four nonsmoking floors; 10% of casino is
  nonsmoking
Open: Year-round

Every half hour after dark, crowds gather in front of the Mirage
to watch its 54-foot volcano erupt. Smoke and fire spews 50 feet
into the air. Lights in the surrounding lagoons turn waterfalls
the color of flowing magma. Traffic slows to a creep.

Since it opened in 1990, the $630 million Mirage has given
neighboring Caesars Palace serious competition for the title of
Las Vegas's most fantastical casino hotel. A 20,000-gallon
aquarium with sharks, stingrays, and other sea animals fills an
entire wall in the registration area. A marble path bisects a
90-foot-high atrium lush with a rain forest of tropical plants
before continuing through a 100,000-square-foot casino. Beyond it, two rare white tigers, which perform nightly with illu-
sionists Siegfried and Roy, pose behind Plexiglas in a
Himalayan-like habitat created especially for them. Dolphins
cavort in another natural habitat behind a free-form pool of
interconnected lagoons, a waterfall, and lava rock outcroppings. Kids love it and so do parents, which is what Steve Wynn
(the man behind the Golden Nugget) intended, since his target
audience is families.

The centerpiece of this 100-acre tropical playground is three
hotel towers fused to form a Y. Eighteen-karat gold glazes the
windows of the 3,000 rooms, each with a view of the Strip,
mountains, or pool. What passes for tropical decor, however,
strikes many as garish, and the money lavished elsewhere on
the hotel seems to have been spared in the rooms—of reasonable size, they have cheap furnishings and small baths.

This is not the case in the suites. Located on the top five
floors and accessible only by special elevator, these one-and
two-bedroom sanctuaries have floor-to-ceiling windows, huge
marble baths, and elegant Caribbean or European decor. More
opulent still are six Lanai Bungalows, each with a private garden and pool, and eight palatial Villas, some with 5,000 square
feet of living space.

The suites and villas epitomize high-roller style, as do restaurants like Kokomo's, where steak and seafood are served in the atrium rain forest. There are seven other eateries, including a 60-item buffet and a pizza parlor. The Mirage also has a health spa and salon, an esplanade of shops, and the erupting volcano.

The Tropicana Resort and Casino
3801 Las Vegas Boulevard South
Las Vegas, Nevada 89109
702-739-2222
800-634-4000
Fax: 702-739-2469

General manager: John Chiero
Accommodations: 1,815 rooms, 93 suites
Rates: $65–$95
Minimum stay: None
Added: 8% tax
Payment: Major credit cards
Children: Free under age 18
Pets: Not allowed
Smoking: Five nonsmoking floors; nonsmoking blackjack and slot areas in casino
Open: Year-round

Two huge stone tikis at the southern end of the Las Vegas Strip guard the entrance to the Tropicana. As the name suggests, this Las Vegas landmark has an infatuation with the South Seas. It shows in the bamboo ceiling above much of the casino, which evokes a Polynesian hut, and in the resort's centerpiece just beyond—a glorious five-acre water park containing three swimming pools (one enclosed in winter), lagoons, waterfalls, several whirlpools, palm trees and other tropical foliage, water slides, bird shows, a Polynesian wedding chapel, a bar serving drinks and snacks, and a swim-up blackjack table. There's also a complete health club and spa nearby.

Built in 1986, the water park marked the Tropicana's shift from its original art nouveau decor—still evident in the spectacular 4,000-square-foot leaded glass dome above the casino's main pit—to something more festive and tropical. So it's not surprising that the newer Island Tower, on the far side of the water park, has the most appealing rooms. All of them have been done in Caribbean pastels, including the spectacular two-story suites with spiral staircases. Those in the original Paradise Tower seem subdued by comparison, with dark brown European furnishings, plaster rosettes, and chocolate-colored bathroom fixtures.

There is nothing reserved about Tropics, a three-tiered restaurant (one of seven at the resort) and lounge in the Island Tower overlooking the water park. The Comedy Stop books comedians from all over the country, and the Folies Bergère is one of Las Vegas's few remaining dinner shows. Though not the newest kid on the Strip, the Tropicana remains one of the most appealing.

Los Angeles

The Biltmore Hotel
506 South Grand Avenue
Los Angeles, California 90071
213-624-1011
800-245-8673
Fax: 213-612-1545

Manager: Randy Villereal
Accommodations: 700 rooms, 40 suites
Rates: $175–$245; double, $205–$275; $30 additional person,
  suites, $275–$1900; weekend packages available
Payment: Major credit cards
Children: Under 18 free in room with parents
Pets: Not allowed
Smoking: Allowed
Open: Year-round

When the Biltmore opened in 1923, it was the largest and most elaborate hotel west of Chicago. Constructed in Spanish-Italian Renaissance style with lavish interior ceilings and wall paintings by Italian artist Giovanni Smeraldi, the hotel was—and is—splendid. It has hosted presidents, kings, and Hollywood stars, as well as mere travelers, and along the way it has become a historic landmark.

It's been refurbished several times, most recently with a $40 million restoration that spruced up all the public spaces and guest rooms. Furnishings and bathrooms now reflect contemporary luxury, but the artistry that made the Biltmore famous in the 1920s may still be seen in the hand-oiled paneling, fine moldings and millwork, carvings, vivid frescoes, and stately columns and pilasters.

It's worth visiting the Biltmore just to see the wonderfully ornate Rendezvous Court, where you may take afternoon tea, cocktails, or dessert as you listen to the melodic strains of a piano.

Next to the Court is Bernard's, a classic, top-quality restaurant where the lighting is subdued and the meals are expensive. It features European and American regional cuisine. Each table is set with a single salmon rose, starched blue linens, crystal and silver. Much of the 1923 silver set, designed exclusively for the Biltmore, had never been used until it was discovered during the restoration.

Lighter and considerably less formal is the Court Café, serving pizza, pasta, and American cuisine. Service is generally slow, but you'll be entertained by the flourishes of the chef at the pasta bar as he prepares your order.

The Grand Avenue Bar, off the main lobby, is noted for its weekday lunch buffet, wines, and jazz, while the European-style Gallery Bar and Cognac Room features beer and liquors. Recent additions are a delicatessen, Smeraldi's, and Sai Sai, serving Japanese dishes. The hotel has sixteen grand banquet and meeting rooms.

The Biltmore's concierge desk will handle almost any request, for example, theater tickets, reservations, tours, laundry, and clothes pressing. Room service is available all day. Several languages are spoken by the staff—at this world crossroads, they're all needed.

The guest rooms are spacious and comfortable. They have modern or traditional French furniture, including writing tables, armoires that house television sets, and extending reading lamps. You can choose a king-or queen-size or two double beds. There are 26 room configurations, with three pastel color schemes that vary between pale yellow and gray, lilac, rose, and light green. Jim Dine's heart engravings hang on the walls. Each room has a mini-bar stocked with pricey snacks and drinks.

To attract the affluent business traveler, the Biltmore offers corporate packages that include special services and amenities. Deluxe Service features the hotel's most luxurious accommodations, express check-in and departure, daily newspaper, shoeshine, and twice-daily maid service.

If you reserve a suite or stay on the Biltmore Club Floor, you're provided access to the Club Lounge, where a concierge, copy machines, translators, and a small library are available. Complimentary cocktails and a Continental breakfast are served in the Club Lounge. All guests have free use of a private health club equipped with an indoor swimming pool, steam room, sauna, whirlpool, Nautilus equipment, and massage service.

The Biltmore represents opulence on the grand scale. It's a

fine old hotel that has fortunately been revived with style and a genuine sense of tradition.

Checkers Hotel Kempinski

535 South Grand Avenue
Los Angeles, California 90071
213-624-0000
800-426-3135
Fax: 213-626-9906

General manager: Volker Ulrich
Accommodations: 171 rooms, 17 suites
Rates: $175–$225, $20 additional person; suites, $400–$1000
Payment: Major credit cards
Children: Welcome
Pets: Allowed
Smoking: Nonsmoking rooms available
Open: Year-round

In the heart of downtown Los Angeles, this posh little hotel offers a tranquil and elegant retreat. If you value the finest in residential furnishings, antiques, artwork, accommodations, and service, you'll appreciate Checkers. Built as the Mayflower Hotel in 1927, the 14-story building underwent a $50 million restoration to be reborn as Checkers, which opened in 1989. Now it's part of Kempinski International, Inc.

The small, classic lobby is divided into three sections, each displaying beautiful pieces of contemporary and antique art. Among them are two 19th-century mother-of-pearl elephants, rare Japanese vases, a Chinese red lacquer screen, and a German armoire of ebony and rosewood that dates from 1725. On the mezzanine above are meeting rooms and a library/sitting room in soft gray, with more Oriental antiques. It's a favored gathering place for small groups, ideal when the lobby is too public and a guest room too private. All the guest rooms, furnished alike, are decorated in soothing, soft colors. They have clock radios, TVs with movie and sports channels, Belgian linens, mini-bars, writing tables, and phones with international signs on the buttons, in deference to the hotel's many foreign visitors. Attention to detail in appointments and service makes Checkers exceptional.

Orchids in the bathrooms, tub thermometers, makeup mirrors, I. Magnin toiletries, closets that light when the door opens, and padded satin hangers are a few of the special touches. The well-trained staff can respond to almost any need:

valet assistance, same-day laundry service, secretarial help, and 24-hour room service are routine. Guests receive complimentary limousine service to any downtown business area, as do dinner guests going to and from the Los Angeles Music Center.

A pleasant addition is the rooftop lap pool. There is also a well-equipped weight room and Jacuzzi; some guests like to exercise in the mornings, read the paper, and order a light breakfast here. Sweat suits and robes are provided.

Checkers Hotel's intimate restaurant is another serene, elegant gem in the same tradition and style as its sister hotel, the renowned Campton Place in San Francisco. The chef, Jerry Comfort, has earned an enviable reputation for his French-influenced contemporary cooking.

Next door is the remodeled public library. Pershing Square is a block away, and the Museum of Contemporary Art is nearby. Checkers also caters to the area's busy legal and business communities.

Disneyland Hotel
1150 West Cerritos Avenue
Anaheim, California 92802
714-778-6600

Manager: Hideo Amemiya
Accommodations: 1,131 rooms and suites
Rates: $115–$240 in summer, $109–$235 in winter; $15 additional adult; suites, $400–$1,250
Payment: Major credit cards
Children: Under 17 free in room with parents
Pets: Not allowed
Smoking: Nonsmoking rooms available
Open: Year-round

Here's a resort to thrill the young at heart. It not only has all kinds of entertainment, recreation, and restaurants, it's just a short monorail ride from the Magic Kingdom, every child's fantasy playground.

The hotel was built in 1955 by Jack Wrather, a Texas oilman who agreed with Walt Disney that the new theme park would draw enough visitors to merit a new hotel. So he acquired 60 acres adjoining Disneyland and built the official hotel of the Magic Kingdom.

It is a major attraction in its own right and an award-winning convention hotel. Most of the accommodations are in three towers, two of eleven stories and the other fourteen, surrounding Seaports of the Pacific, a marina playland and shopping and dining extravaganza.

The hotel is well laid out; despite its size, it is easy to find your way around, helped by signs and paths that cross the villagelike grounds. The property offers three swimming pools, ten tennis courts, and Papeete Beach, a pseudo-Polynesian stretch of sand complete with shipwreck decor. Around the Seaports of the Pacific lagoon are remote control boats, two-seat pedal boats, a miniature raceway with Baja Bugs operated by remote control, and a video game center.

Free entertainment adds to the hotel's considerable vacation value. Regular features are Dancing Waters, a twice-nightly display of fountains, lights, and music, and country and western music every night at the Wharf Bar.

The restaurants range from Mazie's, a sidewalk café serving garnish-your-own hamburgers and hot dogs, to Granville's Steak House, a dressy, candle lit place featuring steak, prime rib, and lobster. The children's favorite is Chef's Kitchen, with an all-you-can-eat buffet that takes second place to the Disney characters who join them for breakfast. Others include Shipyard Inn, on the marina, and Caffe Villa Verde, serving Italian food. Children's menus are available at all the hotel's restaurants.

Sgt. Preston's Yukon Saloon and Dancehall offers nightly dancing and entertainment, gold rush style. Here you can join in a rollicking, 1890s musical revue.

Hotel facilities include a barber and beauty shop, car rentals, foreign currency exchange, laundry and dry cleaning, a limousine, and interpreter services. Parents appreciate the portable cribs, babysitting referrals, and Mickey Mouse boosters and high chairs in the restaurants.

With all this, the guest rooms seem almost secondary. On the other hand, they're crucial to the hotel's appeal. A standard room is clean and comfortable and has a small stocked refrigerator, a TV with closed circuit channels and the Disney channel, and a narrow balcony overlooking the marina. On a clear day you can see from Bonita Tower to the beach.

A recent multimillion-dollar refurbishment upgraded all the guest rooms, giving them bolder colors and a fresher look. Each room has a reproduction of Disney artwork; the originals hang in the public spaces. The top three levels of the Sierra Tower are concierge floors, where guests receive extra attention. A few rooms are in Garden Villas and Oriental Gardens, two-story buildings located apart from the center of activity and entered through attractive gardens.

The landscaping and maintenance at Disneyland Hotel is extraordinary. A team of gardeners works continually to keep the floral color blazing, and the property is kept as immaculate as the clean streets of Disneyland. With an operation as carefully orchestrated as the famous theme park, it's not a surprise to learn that as many as four weddings a day have been held in the rose garden gazebo.

Eastlake Inn

1442 Kellam Avenue
Los Angeles, California 90026
213-250-1620

Innkeepers: Murray Burns and Planaria Price
Accommodations: 9 rooms (6 with private bath)
Rates: $49–$150, $15 additional person
Included: Expanded Continental breakfast
Minimum stay: 2 or 3 nights some weekends and holidays
Payment: Major credit cards
Children: Age 8 and older welcome
Pets: Not allowed
Smoking: Prohibited indoors
Open: Year-round

Angelino Heights is the most intact of Los Angeles's historic neighborhoods. Its well-preserved hilltop homes were, for the most part, built in the late 1800s when the district was a suburb. Now it's between Sunset Boulevard and the Hollywood freeway (Highway 101), within walking distance of Dodger Stadium, the Music Center, the Old Plaza, and downtown. Eastlake Inn, in the heart of the Historic Preservation Zone, is a gray-green Victorian with gingerbread detail in dark gray, green, eggplant, black, and off-white. The house was built in 1887 by two widows. Because each wanted her privacy, it has an unusual feature: two parallel staircases, each leading to one side of the second story.

The present owners have brought many years of experience to furnishing and decorating the Eastlake in authentic period style. Guests are entertained in the parlor by an old-fashioned stereopticon, jigsaw puzzles, games, and books. A collection of Victorian costumes and wallpapers adds to the 19th-century atmosphere. Rooms are furnished with antiques, and most contain examples of Murray's artistic talents—etched glass, painted fruits and flowers on a white fireplace, stenciled leaves on a stairwell.

If you stay in one of the two main floor "Champagne Suites," you'll be given champagne every night and, if you choose, breakfast in bed. The spacious Hummingbird Suite has a claw-foot tub in the bathroom, a library, and a view of the garden and feeder that draws flocks of iridescent hummingbirds. Skylight Suite, one very large room, features a Victorian parlor set and a leaded glass skylight.

The upstairs rooms are smaller but have their own appeal. Tucked into corners and just right for singles are Thumbelina, with a double bed and all-white decor, and Tom Thumb, which holds a twin bed, a well-loved bear, and an antique table and chair.

North Star and Moonrise are identical. Each has a queen-size bed and a private bath in an alcove. Sunset, its windows etched in constellation designs, can be combined with North Star as a suite. Sunrise is furnished in white wicker and has a double bed with a partial canopy.

Because these savvy innkeepers understand the demand for convenience as well as charm, Eastlake has phone jacks in several rooms, off-street parking, a morning newspaper delivered to the door, and a "Can't Miss List" of things to see and do. Baths are stocked with shampoos, razors, Alka-Seltzer, and even contact lens solution. Other special details include fresh flowers, baskets of fruit, and robes in the closets.

Murray and Planaria can arrange for restaurant and car rental discounts and will refer you to services such as dry cleaners or health clinics. Says Murray, "We've traveled a good deal and care about creating an environment where you don't have to worry about details." Perhaps for this reason, as well as the inn's location near the garment district and jewelry markets, business travelers make up a large portion of their clientele. Small meeting and conference facilities are available.

Eastlake offers several imaginative "Celebration Packages." They range from a Peanuts and Cracker Jacks Baseball Weekend to a Limousine Driven Tour of L.A.'s Best Ice Cream or Chocolate Palaces. Packages include three days and two nights at the inn, breakfasts, champagne on arrival, and a personal tour of two National Register homes on Carroll Avenue. On Halloween, you can attend a Ghoul's Banquet, go trick-or-treating, and get a guided cemetery tour. St. Patrick's Day features a seven-course Irish feast and a chauffeur-driven pub crawl.

One of the busy innkeepers is always on hand to greet guests, and the manager is just next door, but no one hovers. Unless you need something, you're on your own.

Hotel Bel-Air

701 Stone Canyon Road
Los Angeles, California 90077
213-472-1211
800-648-4097

Managing director: Frank Boling
Accommodations: 92 rooms and suites
Rates: $225–$395; double, $245–$435; suites, $480–$2,000
Payment: Major credit cards
Children: Welcome
Pets: Not allowed
Smoking: Allowed
Open: Year-round

In 1922, the oil magnate Alonzo E. Bell created a subdivision of estates in the foothills and canyons north of Sunset Boulevard, where palatial homes lie off winding, tree-shaded roads. Named Bel-Air, it became one of the most prestigious residential areas in Los Angeles.

Bell's planning and sales offices were in a mission-style building which was later converted to hotel accommodations —the centerpiece of the present Hotel Bel-Air. Now considerably expanded and renowned for its luxury, celebrated guests, and sequestered location, the hotel is also close to city shopping, restaurants, and offices.

The one-and two-story pink buildings are set on 11½ acres of towering ferns, palms, California sycamores, and native live oaks that shade fountain courtyards, a tumbling stream, and a tranquil pond. In the pond, beautiful (but cranky) swans float regally.

In season the gardens glow with yellow daffodils and tulips, pink camellias, and flowering fruit trees. Jasmine and gardenia scent the balmy air; red bougainvillea climbs to terra cotta tiled roofs. The lush and lovely grounds are tended by a team of ten gardeners. One of the plantings in their expert care is a 50-foot pink-flowering silk floss tree, the largest of its kind in California. It was planted by Alonzo Bell.

To enter the hotel from the attended parking lot, you walk beneath leafy branches to cross an arched bridge, past a waterfall and Swan Lake. The main building is crowned by a tower that is partly obscured by the brilliant red of flowering trumpet vines.

At the front desk, in a parlorlike lobby, you are asked which newspaper you'd like to have delivered to your door in the morning and then are escorted through the gardens to your room. Classical music plays softly on your radio when you arrive, and the lamps are lit.

Most of the rooms and suites are on the ground level, with glimpses of gardens through their rose-draped windows. They vary widely in size and decor; most have a patio or fireplace or both. Some are furnished in a French country style that is light, simple, and classic. Others are traditional American or have a California mission theme. The white tile baths have brass fixtures.

The best choices in the old section are the suites. For consistency in size and style, request a room in the newer section. Each is elegant in pastels and floral fabrics, and has its own fountain and whirlpool in a private patio. A few have small kitchens.

All guests receive tea service upon arrival and nightly turndown service. Some of the amenities are same-day laundry and dry cleaning, 24-hour room service, and a complimentary shoeshine.

The restaurant, at the end of a graceful arcade, is a soft, attractive room in peachy beige and green, with a prism chandelier glittering above an impressive floral display. Banquettes line the far wall, but most romantic are tables for two by the windows, which face tropical plantings and a terrace that is set for outdoor dining.

The award-winning executive chef, George Mahaffey, oversees the preparation of contemporary California cuisine. Fresh regional ingredients are used, with herbs from the hotel's gardens. Breakfasts are outstanding, and the presentation is stylish.

You may have breakfast, lunch, dinner, and afternoon tea in the restaurant or, for a change, eat lightly in the bar next door. With a pianist and vocalist performing nightly, the cozy bar is a favorite evening gathering place for Bel-Air residents as well as hotel guests.

There is a heated swimming pool, but few other recreational facilities, though tennis and golf are easily accessible. The Bel-Air is mostly a place to retreat and relax, and maybe take a romantic stroll through the quiet, sun-dappled gardens before dinner. But don't forget the shopping opportunities. You're close to Beverly Hills and Rodeo Drive, where glamorous boutiques and designer displays draw shoppers who can afford the best.

Hotel Shangri-La
1301 Ocean Avenue
Santa Monica, California 90401
310-394-2791

General manager: Dino Nanni
Accommodations: 55 rooms
Rates: $110–$450, for one to four people, $15 additional person
Included: Continental breakfast
Payment: Major credit cards
Children: Under 16 free in room with parents
Pets: Not allowed
Smoking: Allowed
Open: Year-round

Like the setting for a stylish Hollywood movie of the 1930s, the Shangri-La has an art deco motif that is beautifully accomplished. It's rare to find a theme carried through as well while keeping guests' comfort a priority.

The artfully curved seven-story hotel stands on a busy corner in Santa Monica, directly across the street from Palisades Park and the beach. Several fine restaurants are within walking distance and a major shopping mall is close by.

The small lobby contains soft green couches, torch lamps, and a large version of the hotel's signature design: stylized palm trees and a vast blue ocean, viewed from behind a pink balcony railing.

The rooms on the first six floors range from studios to two-bedroom, two-bath suites. The seventh floor is reserved for two penthouse suites with sundecks. All the rooms have television, phones, and movie posters that are reminders of the period the decor evokes. Most rooms, except for those on the fifth and sixth floors, come with equipped kitchens. The open-gallery design of the building, with exterior hallways, provides cross ventilation and ocean views.

One typical studio room contains curved chrome chairs and a painting of pink flamingos. There's a dressing area near the white-tile bath and a kitchen with a gas stove. At this location, and with this kind of style, $110 is not a bad price. And you get breakfast and afternoon tea, served in a pretty little breakfast room off the courtyard.

A one-bedroom suite on the sixth floor will have its own wraparound deck and sleek gray furniture striped with burgundy in the spacious living room and bedroom. All rooms on the sixth floor have private sundecks facing west. There is no restaurant at the Shangri-La and no recreational facilities. There's a tiled terrace with lounge chairs in the large courtyard in back, which has the only thing out of scale with the sophisticated charm of the hotel—a chunky, oversize gazebo.

For updated comfort with a touch of vintage L.A. in a light, bright setting by the beach, the Shangri-La is an excellent choice.

La Maida House
11159 La Maida Street
North Hollywood, California 91601
818-769-3857

Innkeeper: Megan Timothy
Accommodations: 11 rooms (7 in bungalows)
Rates: $80–$210; discounts for longer stays
Included: Expanded Continental breakfast
Minimum stay: 2 nights
Payment: MasterCard, Visa
Children: Not appropriate
Pets: Not allowed
Smoking: Prohibited
Open: Year-round

This Italianate villa, built in 1926 by Antonio La Maida, exudes romance and beauty from every corner. The inn is distinctive, thanks to the talents and personality of Megan Timothy. She has put her astounding energy and skills at decorating, cooking, painting, sewing, gardening, and carpentry—among others—into play to create an extraordinary retreat that is a few minutes' drive from the shopping, restaurants, and studios of Los Angeles and Hollywood.

Mediterranean in design, with white stucco walls, a red tile roof, and arched doorways and windows, the 25-room villa combines an Old World background with a fresh California outlook and Megan's inimitable style. On the main floor, off the entry hall, is a living room with two groups of chairs invitingly arranged beside the gold marble fireplace. A grand piano stands in one corner. Windows look toward the gardens and lily pond, which Megan designed and built. Also on the main floor are two dining areas, a den filled with books and soft cushions, and a solarium. Tropical plants grow luxuriantly in the glass-walled solarium, which opens to a back lawn with a splashing fountain and magnolia trees. The small dining room is where private dinners of culinary distinction are held. If you arrange it with Megan, she'll prepare a light supper before the theater or a four-course dinner with complimentary wine.

Walk up the curving mahogany staircase, past a brilliant red and gold peacock of stained glass (made by Megan, as are the other 96 stained glass creations throughout the inn), and you come to four bedrooms off halls displaying photographs from the innkeeper's world travels. The rooms all have phones, closets with luggage racks and robes, fresh flowers from the garden, clock radios, down comforters, and big tile bathrooms; some have whirlpool tubs. A thoughtful touch in each bath is the drawer full of toiletries—razors, toothpaste and toothbrush, Alka-Seltzer, and other extras often needed by travelers.

The Cipresso Suite, the largest, is an airy room overlooking the rose garden and tall cypress trees at the side of the house. It has a four-poster canopy bed and wicker chairs piled with pillows. The room named Vigna is dark and peaceful, with vine-green walls. From the window you see the grapevines that wind over the wall by the pond. The other two rooms are equally pleasant: Fontana, in crisp blue and white with twin beds, and Magnolia, furnished in handsome whitewashed pine.

Portable TVs and answering machines are available, and there is an executive conference room that accommodates twenty.

All the other guest rooms are in nearby cottages. The Streletzia Suite is the most luxurious, with a wood-burning fireplace, rattan furniture, stained glass accents, and a front porch that looks out on a Japanese fern garden with a goldfish pond.

Among La Maida's special features are the swimming pool behind one of the cottages, an exercise room, a complimentary morning newspaper, a library of travel guidebooks, fresh cookies at evening turndown, and breakfasts that are artistic feasts.

In a quiet residential area two blocks off busy Lankershim Boulevard, La Maida House is a great find. As several visitors have commented in the guest book, this is a magical place.

L'Ermitage Hotel
9291 Burton Way
Beverly Hills, California 90210
213-278-3344
800-424-4443
Fax: 213-278-8247

General manager: Jayne Levant
Accommodations: 112 suites
Rates: $285–$1,500; $25 additional person
Payment: Major credit cards
Children: Under 12 free in room with parents
Pets: Allowed
Smoking: Nonsmoking rooms available
Open: Year-round

When visiting celebrities want an elegant retreat, they often check in at L'Ermitage, where they can be assured of privacy, security, comfort, excellent service, and beautiful surroundings. From the lobby to the penthouse suite, fine art and furnishings create the atmosphere of a restful (and expensive) refuge.

There are no ballrooms or public restaurants; owner Severyn Ashkenazy decided to concentrate on private comforts when he opened the hotel in 1976. So all the accommodations are suites that have living rooms with fireplaces, dressing rooms, wet bars, balconies, remote control television, multi-line telephones, and kitchens. Cooking equipment is available upon request.

Marble bathrooms contain the hotel's own brand of toiletries (including a light and flowery cologne), as well as plush terry-cloth robes, slippers, and custom-milled soaps.

If it can be said to be a problem, the bi-level townhouse suites seem too large, lacking a cohesive plan. Rectangular rooms, upstairs and down, are lined with furniture and, despite the balconies, do not take full advantage of the view of broad Burton Way and its attractive green median. In one living room, a couch faces the underside of a staircase and the wet bar and built-in bookshelves are stuck behind a potted palm. The smaller suites have more appeal and a less sprawling design.

There's a full menu of breakfast choices in The Club. Recommended are the crunchy granola, thick French toast, and fresh orange juice. Next to the restaurant and divided from it by etched glass panels is a small lounge. Here a guitarist plays in the evenings and complimentary hors d'oeuvres of pâté and caviar are served on the pink granite bar.

Priding itself on service, L'Ermitage will fulfill almost any request. If you're traveling on business, you'll appreciate the typewriters, fax facilities, board room and salon (for groups of up to 80 people), 24-hour room service, and a staff that speaks several languages. As a vacationer you may wish to loll on the rooftop terrace beside the heated pool, enjoying the complimentary fruit and wine each suite receives. Or you may prefer to make use of the limousine service to nearby shops and attractions. The hotel is in a quiet residential area, close to the glittering shops of Rodeo Drive.

A daily newspaper is brought to your door each morning with the shoes you've had shined, and strawberries are delivered in the afternoon. For the kids, milk and cookies are provided in the evening, along with a teddy bear.

One guest privilege is rare indeed in the hotel world: those who stay at L'Ermitage may attend, at no charge, the highly acclaimed events of the Performing Arts Series presented by L'Ermitage Foundation. Programs featuring noted actors, musicians, and other artists take place at L'Ermitage or Bel Age Hotel, another of the eight boutique hotels in Ashkenazy's collection.

L'Ermitage is undergoing a $12 million refurbishment, designed to meet the needs of the business traveler of the 21st century. Foldout ironing boards, personal computer hook-ups, steam showers, and separate living and sleeping areas are among the features that will be standard in the suites.

Ma Maison Sofitel
8555 Beverly Boulevard
Los Angeles, California 90048
213-278-5444
800-221-4542
Fax: 213-657-2816

Manager: Richard Schilling
Accommodations: 311 rooms
Rates: $180–$200; double, $200–$220; suites, $250–$400
Payment: Major credit cards
Children: Under 18 free in room with parents
Pets: Allowed by prior arrangement

Smoking: Nonsmoking rooms available
Open: Year-round

This sleek ten-story hotel occupies a choice spot in West Los Angeles. It's close to the Pacific Design Center and Cedars Sinai Hospital and across the street from the famed shops of Beverly Center. It's also convenient to Beverly Hills, west-side offices, and Melrose Avenue boutiques.

Ma Maison Restaurant is a lovely dining spot on the corner, where well-prepared California cuisine is presented in a garden setting. Under a skylight, orange and grapefruit trees grow near vine-covered trellises and tables covered with pink linens. More casual is La Cajole, a bistro where you can dine outdoors if you prefer.

The hotel itself is functional and attractive, with a Mediterranean ambience. The lobby has tile floors, a sweeping staircase, textured walls, and Spanish furnishings. Colors are muted. It feels cool inside, as if it were an old building on the French Riviera.

The rooms, too, reflect a southern European style. The color schemes include flowered bedspreads and drapes and walls of soft brick or green with matching carpeting. Upper-floor rooms have French doors leading to outside terraces where one can sit and sip a drink or watch the world pass by below.

The hotel was designed primarily to serve business travelers with conveniences such as 24-hour room service, three phones per room, voice-activated message centers, mini-bars, and morning newspapers. Some rooms are on the small side and lack workable desk space.

If you plan to work during your visit, an Executive King room is a good choice. It has separate areas for sitting, sleeping, and dressing and includes a desk. The partial suite can be used as one large space or the areas can be separated by drapes for privacy.

The best rooms are on the north side, facing what residents call the Blue Whale (Pacific Design Center) and the Hollywood Hills beyond. The nighttime view, when it's clear, is spectacular. The closets are ample, but there are no bureaus for folded clothing. Some armoires have small drawers, but none is large enough for anyone planning a long stay or for a couple to share.

The hotel's conference facilities consist of seven rooms that vary in capacity, holding from 12 to 240 people. The Sofitel has a health club with Nautilus and a sauna, and massage services are available. There's an outdoor pool surrounded by a deck, lounge chairs, and umbrellaed tables—a popular spot in summer.

What sets Ma Maison Sofitel above many city hotels are its constant room service, babysitting, and same-day valet service. Also worth noting, if you're bored with airline food, is the box lunch—actually a fine meal—that the hotel especially prepares for air travelers. Packed in a Ma Maison Sofitel carry-on bag, it's available upon request at checkout. And everyone is given a French baguette to take along.

Rushed travelers appreciate the Three-Minute Breakfast, a selection of beverages, croissants, pastries, and seasonal fruit set up buffet-style in the lobby.

Marina del Rey Hotel
13534 Bali Way
Marina del Rey, California 90292
213-301-1000
800-8-MARINA in California
800-882-4000 in U.S.
Fax: 213-301-8167

General manager: Pierre R. Rouzier
Accommodations: 154 rooms, 6 suites
Rates: $125–$190; double, $145–$210; suites, $350–$400
Payment: Major credit cards
Children: Under 12 free in room with parents
Pets: Not allowed
Smoking: Nonsmoking rooms available
Open: Year-round

Sitting on your shaded balcony, watching the sun set over the Pacific and the yachts and sailboats come and and go, you can hardly believe that Los Angeles International Airport is just a 10-minute drive. But that's the beauty of this hotel. It's convenient to the freeway and the airport, yet it's a sunny retreat where you can fish from the piers, take a harbor cruise, stroll a sandy beach, watch windsurfers dart across the channel, or shop in a recreation of a New England fishing village.

The hotel provides 24-hour complimentary transportation to and from the airport, and cars are available to rent if you need to drive the ten miles to downtown Los Angeles or elsewhere.

Jaunty in white with blue awnings, the three-story hotel stands at the tip of one of the harbor's peninsulas, allowing for good views from most guest rooms (though some overlook the parking lot). Large windows and open spaces bring the outdoors in. Boats dock at the doorstep, here in the world's largest manmade yacht harbor. The location is this hotel's best feature.

Two restaurants and a cocktail lounge offer views of the harbor and sea from picture windows. Crystal Seahorse, a formal dining room specializing in seafood, serves crab and clams in dill sauce, and mussel soup with lime and saffron. Desserts are light, focusing on fresh fruits prepared in tempting ways. If you want to be even closer to the sound of the waves, you may dine outside on the terrace, which has seating for twenty. Dockside Café is much more casual and serves breakfast and lunch daily. The menu offers a variety of salads and sandwiches including the Del Rey salad, a house specialty involving julienned chicken, Chinese noodles, and a peanut butter dressing.

The rooms, emphasizing simplicity and comfort, are spacious and the colors cool and refreshing. A recent renovation considerably brightened the decor of the hotel, which was the first in Marina del Rey when it was built some thirty years ago.

The suites have king-size beds, contemporary couches, console TVs, dining areas and wet bars, and big closets with full mirrors. For the best view in the hotel, reserve Suite 3139. At times it seems that all the thousands of boats moored at Marina del Rey are sailing just below the balcony, which extends along two sides of the corner room. And the view of the sunset over the main channel is spellbinding.

The New Otani Hotel & Garden

120 South Los Angeles Street
Los Angeles, California 90012
213-629-1200
800-273-2294 in California
800-421-8795 in U.S. and Canada
Fax: 213-622-0980

General manager: Kenji Yoshimoto
Accommodations: 440 rooms
Rates: $135–$170; double, $160–$195; suites, $385–$750
Payment: Major credit cards
Children: Welcome
Pets: Allowed by prior arrangement
Smoking: Nonsmoking rooms available
Open: Year-round

When the New Otani opened in 1977, the management did not stress its Japanese heritage and connections. "We didn't want Americans to feel we were simply a Japanese hotel where they could not get by in English or find their eggs and bacon," says Kenji Yoshimoto. But it soon became clear that the touch of Japan was one of the hotel's main attractions. Now it's strongly emphasized, though all employees speak English—in fact, front desk personnel collectively speak nineteen languages.

East meets West in the 21-story hotel, where you may dine on New York steaks or yakitori, sleep on an American bed or a futon, and listen to cocktail piano music or a Koto player. You may encounter Japanese visitors in traditional kimonos, though up-to-date fashions and conservative suits are more common.

When you leave your car with the valet and enter the three-story lobby, you'll see a dramatic glass sculpture, and behind it the Rendezvous Lounge. In this raised, open area a pianist plays on weekdays. To the left is a shopping arcade; on the right a sweeping staircase winds up to a mezzanine and guest rooms above it.

Also on the lobby level is the Azalea Restaurant and Bar, where a contemporary interpretation of classic Continental cuisine is served. Upstairs, on the garden level, A Thousand Cranes features Japanese meals in a traditional setting at standard tables or in private tatami rooms. This is the place to try sushi, uni (fresh sea urchin), awabi (abalone cooked with sake wine), and tempura. The restaurant overlooks the "garden in the sky," a tranquil half-acre roof garden of pathways, ponds, and waterfalls bordered with azaleas.

Across the hall, beyond a bamboo and orchid floral arrangement, is Commodore Perry's, a restaurant with an American menu and the atmosphere of a 19th-century clipper ship. A harpist plays several days a week.

There are several types of guest rooms: Western standard, superior, suites, and Japanese suites. Each has a television, refrigerator, and desk in a lacquer red or pastel curved cabinet. Bedside tables match the dramatic red and gray or pastel decor. Shoji screens at the windows and a single flower or delicate piece of art complete the Oriental accent that complements the room full of traditionally Western luxuries. The bathrooms have phones, hand-held showers, and thick white towels with the hotel's name handsomely embroidered in red. Yukatas (Japanese kimonos) are available, as well as standard robes.

For the most interesting experience the New Otani offers, reserve one of the Japanese suites, the only ones in southern California. The parlor is Western, with modern couches and soft chairs, while the sleeping area behind sliding shoji doors is a large, elevated tatami room with a futon. The bath has a sunken tub, traditional in Japan.

At the Sanwa Health Spa, you may relax in a sauna or herb-scented Jacuzzi and enjoy a shiatsu massage, which involves pressure on strategic points and gentle slaps.

Other features are 24-hour room service, same-day cleaning, a beauty salon, and concierge services.

Special events and cultural programs exploring Japanese culture take place throughout the year. You can learn about the tea ceremony, take a calligraphy lesson, or study one of the many forms of ikebana (flower arranging). Traditional celebrations include Setsubun (the end of winter), the Hina Doll Festival, and Temari, a demonstration of a 1,400-year-old folk art in which colorful silk balls are created.

The New Otani, in Little Tokyo, is close to Los Angeles City Hall, the Music Center, city and county courthouses, and the Los Angeles Times building. Across the street is St. Vibiana Cathedral, one of Los Angeles's oldest.

The Regent Beverly Wilshire
9500 Wilshire Boulevard
Beverly Hills, California 90212
310-275-5200
800-421-4354
Fax: 310-275-5986

Manager: Alain Longatte
Accommodations: 155 rooms, 150 suites
Rates: $255–$365; $30 additional person; suites, $425–$4,000
Payment: Major credit cards
Children: Under 14 free
Pets: Allowed
Smoking: Allowed
Open: Year-round

The rococo facade of the Beverly Wilshire Hotel has been a famous landmark since 1928. It was glamorous then; now, after a $100 million renovation, it's given the word new meaning. The Regent Beverly Wilshire is one of the world's grand hotels.

Guest rooms are in two wings, the Beverly and the Wilshire, which are divided by a domed entrance road. In the lobby, marble columns, inlaid woods, massive bouquets, and tall palms whisper of elegance and good taste. The hotel spends thousands of dollars a month on flowers alone, employing six florists.

Socialites, business moguls, celebrities, and tourists mingle on the busy main floor, headed for brunch or a memorable dinner in the Dining Room, tea or cocktails in the Lobby Lounge, drinks in the clublike Bar, or hamburgers and milkshakes in the Café. The Regent Beverly Wilshire takes justifiable pride in all its eating spots, but the Dining Room is in a class by itself. Surrounded by French art, Regency furnishings, and parquet floors, you can order poached salmon with cucumbers and grapefruit in red currant sauce, Maine lobster with mango ginger chutney, venison medallions with black currants, and other imaginative dishes. The lengthy wine list offers a wide range of labels and prices. Remarkably, the foods are low in cholesterol, cooked without salt or butter. The skilled chef, Pierre Denis, changes the menu weekly.

The spacious, well-furnished guest rooms are decorated in sunny pastels. They have all the amenities expected in a modern luxury hotel, including three phones and the inescapable mini-TV in the bathroom. There are hair dryers, scales, robes, Nina Ricci toiletries, wonderfully fluffy pillows, and lots of pink marble. On each floor there's a room attendant who can be summoned with the push of a button. The attendant will mend a hem, pack your bags, produce an iron and ironing board, or bring in a basket of baby items and a crib. The service throughout the hotel is responsive but not obsequious.

The five-room, three-bath presidential suite retains the hotel's period flavor, down to the original pegwood floors and skylights. Other special suites are the cabana and verandah suites.

On the second floor of the Beverly Wing is a well-equipped fitness center. In addition to a room of weight machines there are saunas, hot tubs, a snack bar, and an outdoor pool (a replica of Sophia Loren's pool in Italy) surrounded by jardinieres of bougainvillea and creeping fig. Massage, facial, manicure and pedicure treatments are available.

Business travelers appreciate the secretarial, fax, telex, copying, computer, and delivery services. Shoppers revel in the hotel's location—it's directly across the street from Rodeo Drive, the famous street of designer shops. Other nearby streets have appealing boutiques, cafés, and art galleries, while major department stores are represented on Wilshire Boulevard.

The Ritz-Carlton, Huntington Hotel

1401 South Oak Knoll Avenue
Pasadena, California 91106
818-568-3900
800-241-3333
Telex: 549521
Fax: 818-568-3159

Manager: William Hall
Accommodations: 383 rooms and suites
Rates: $145–$240; suites, $350–$2,500
Payment: Major credit cards
Children: Under 18 free with parents
Pets: Not allowed
Smoking: Nonsmoking rooms available
Open: Year-round

Combining resort and hotel amenities, the Ritz-Carlton, Huntington offers tennis courts and a tennis pro, a swimming pool, and a fitness center with saunas and steam rooms. The complex is set on 23 acres at the base of the San Gabriel Mountains, a 15-minute drive from downtown Los Angeles.

The Ritz-Carlton opened in 1991, a reconstructed version of the Huntington, a famous, grand hotel built in 1906. The rebuilt hotel closely follows the original architecture, with its tile roof and imposing design. Two rooms were kept intact: the elegant Viennese Ballroom and the lovely restaurant, the Georgian Room.

The genteel ambience was also retained. Tasteful art objects are displayed and 18th-and 19th-century oil paintings hang on the walls. Overstuffed sofas, fresh flowers, and Oriental carpets add to the atmosphere of comfort and graciousness. Guests at the Ritz-Carlton recognize, appreciate, and can afford the finest.

A typical room has a king or two double beds, yellow damask walls, three phones, and an honor bar. The distinctive black and white marble bathroom has gray walls of shot silk and assorted toiletries. Guests receive twice-daily maid service, robes, evening turndown, and devoted attention from the staff.

Those who want even more amenities stay on the concierge floors and enjoy a private lounge and complimentary breakfast, afternoon tea, hors d'oeuvres, and cocktails. The hotel also has six cottages.

A major draw for business groups are the eight handsomely appointed meeting rooms, a large ballroom, and computer and secretarial facilities.

You can dine in style in the three restaurants. Try the elegant Georgian Room, with its Michelin-ranked chef; the clublike Grill, featuring steaks and chops; or, for casual fare, the Café and Terrace. Lunch and cocktails are available indoors and out at the Bar, and Continental breakfast, cocktails, and traditional afternoon tea are served in the Lobby Lounge.

The swimming pool is a restoration of California's first Olympic-size pool. A whirlpool has been added, and a pool lounge offering tropical drinks and light fare. To reach the Health Club, you cross the Picture Bridge, a part of the original hotel. Under its peaked roof are carefully restored triangular panels, each painted with a California scene.

Such reminders of its origins give the Ritz-Carlton a timeless atmosphere. Fostering this sense of continuity, the hotel participates in the annual Rose Parade with a float, as it has for 75 years.

Sunset Marquis Hotel and Villas
1200 N. Alta Loma Road
West Hollywood, California 90069
213-657-1333
800-858-9758

General manager: Jorge Plaza
Accommodations: 106 suites, 12 villas
Rates: suites, $215–$275; villas, $450–$1,200
Payment: Major credit cards
Children: Welcome
Pets: Not allowed
Smoking: Allowed
Open: Year-round

This lovely retreat is ideal if you're looking for quiet luxury in the heart of Hollywood's bustle. Just a half-block south of Sunset Boulevard and close to production studios, tourist attractions, and businesses, the Sunset Marquis seems a world away when one steps into the green-carpeted lobby. A few diners may be seated in the romantic little restaurant on the right, where soft music plays. A cordial staff member will show you to your room.

The three-story stucco hotel and its individual villas stand on two acres of cloistered gardens and hills. A fountain trickles in a patio, parakeets chirp in the trees, and rabbits can be seen hopping among the calla lilies and azaleas. White lounge chairs sit by the pool, each with its monogrammed pink towel.

You may lunch among the tropical plants at the poolside café or, if your villa is near the second pool, have your order delivered there by the butler.

Hotel rooms, most with pastel color schemes, are grouped around the pool and terrace. Each room has a television and VCR, two-line phones, a wet bar, and a bathroom with makeup mirror and hair dryer. In addition to the usual shampoos and soaps, sunscreen lotion is included.

If the rooms are attractive, the villas, with one or two bedrooms and baths, are stunning. All are light and spacious, with hanging plants, kitchens, and well-proportioned furniture. One unit has a baby grand piano. Some have private terraces overlooking the gardens and herringbone-brick walkways. Chocolates and wine await your arrival, and the butler will light your fireplace and bring in kitchen equipment if you need it.

The attentive service at Sunset Marquis equals the setting. Valet parking and shoeshines are available 24 hours a day, and a weather report is given to each guest at the evening turndown. If you place your breakfast order on your door, it will be delivered to your room in the morning. Limousine service is available. The concierge will arrange for theater tickets, tours, flowers, and appointments with hairdressers—all with a smile.

The Sunset Marquis is where many well-known names and faces go for privacy and relaxation. But whether famous or unknown, all receive the same courtesy. One British entertainer, a regular guest for years who now lives in Hollywood, still pops in for poolside lunches. "It doesn't matter how you look, the staff treats everyone well," he says, adding, "Me mum loves it. I put her here when she comes to visit."

Westwood Marquis Hotel and Gardens
930 Hilgard Avenue
Los Angeles, California 90024
213-208-8765
800-421-2317
Fax: 213-824-0355

Managing director: Jonathan Loeb
Accommodations: 258 suites
Rates: $220–$650
Payment: Major credit cards
Children: Welcome
Pets: Allowed
Smoking: Nonsmoking rooms available
Open: Year-round

In a typical California blend of urban elegance and unpretentious warmth, the Westwood Marquis strikes a fine balance that is less than grandeur but more than mere good taste. Behind its ivied walls are excellent restaurants, a plush little lobby, an unflappable concierge, a lounge where tea is served every day but Sunday, and sixteen floors of exquisite suites.

In a residential area near the trendy shops of Westwood Village and virtually next to UCLA, the hotel was built in 1969 as a dormitory for university students and later became a retirement home. But you'd never know it now. Since 1979 it has been an exclusive hotel, noted for its polished richness and personal service. Hollywood stars such as Dustin Hoffman, Lauren Bacall, Carol Burnett and Whitney Houston stay here when in Los Angeles, as do many top executives in the entertainment, financial and communications industries. Apparently they, like other discriminating travelers, seek integrity, top quality, and an atmosphere pleasing to the senses.

A valet will park your car. Then, from the sidewalk setting of luxuriant greenery, you step into a lobby of Persian rugs, tapestries, and marble. Light from wide windows sparkles on the prisms of glass chandeliers, and fresh flowers add color to every corner. The pastel colors are continued in the suites, which have one, two, or three bedrooms. The baths are in pink or beige marble and have oversize terrycloth robes and towels, hair dryers, two-line telephones, vanity tables, and a full array of toiletries.

In the living room you'll find another phone, a refrigerator, TV, writing table, and an attractive mix of Oriental art and impressionistic watercolors on the pale peach walls. All the suites have views of the San Gabriel Mountains or the pool and gardens.

If you're in one of the eighteen lavish penthouse suites, you'll have the services of a butler who's available all day to serve coffee or cocktails, bring in mail, and generally cater to your every whim.

A recent innovation is the opening of the Executive Business Suites, one-or two-bedroom suites which have speaker phones with data ports and voice mail, a fax machine, and assorted business publications. Another aspect of the hotel's effort to reach the international business traveler is Business with Breakfast. Portable phones, hand-held computers, and the Quotrek stock market reports will be brought to your breakfast table, so you won't waste a moment.

The gardens lend a touch of the country to this city hotel. A lawn rises up a slope from street level to a swimming pool surrounded by jacaranda, marigolds, and pots of geraniums. The scent of star jasmine fills the air. On one side of the pool are cabanas and changing rooms; on the other, a terrace for outdoor dining.

Café Perroquet, named for the wild parrots that fly through the gardens, offers open-air dining near the pool. Light fare is served here, grilled to order over an open fire.

There's another heated pool on the hotel's second level. Set in a shady courtyard bordered by Australian tree ferns, this pool is best for swimming laps. The hotel also has an exercise room, saunas, a Jacuzzi, and steam rooms.

Breakfast, lunch, and a sumptuous Sunday champagne breakfast are served in the Terrace, under white and green trellises and hanging ferns. Around the corner is the Erté Room, used for up to twenty-four guests' private dining. It was named for the noted artist and designer whose famous "Alphabet" lithographs adorn the red walls.

The more formal Dynasty Room has a regal setting of T'ang Dynasty porcelain artifacts, exotic plants, softly lit tables, and serpentine-shaped cushioned booths. Continental cuisine with a California flair is served.

Afternoon Tea in the Westwood Lounge is to be savored. To the delicate strains of a harp, you may enjoy sherry or a choice of Twining's teas. A trolley will be brought with sandwiches, golden caviar, scones, petits fours, and pastries that are baked daily by the hotel's pastry chef, Jean-Marc Polleveys.

You'll find few flaws in this lovely enclave. Traffic noise could be a problem but can be avoided by requesting a suite away from the street. You can hear the steady, annoying hum of a roof generator in some penthouse suites; again, it's avoidable by request. More pleasant are the church bells that ring nightly from across the street, a sound that only adds to the sense of harmony in this fine hotel.

Memphis

Embassy Suites Hotel
1022 S. Shady Grove Road
Memphis, Tennessee 38120
901-684-1777
800-EMBASSY
Fax: 901-685-8185

General manager: Jim Meeker
Accommodations: 220 suites (all with private baths, wet bars, and refrigerators)
Rates: $89–$109
Payment: All major credit cards
Children: Welcome
Pets: Small pets weighing under 20 pounds allowed
Smoking: Nonsmoking suites available
Open: Year-round

Though Embassy Suites is a chain, this hotel is not your typical cookie-cutter property. Every guest stays in a two-room suite, which includes a living room, bedroom, a dining/work space, wet bar and refrigerator. Some suites also feature sofa beds, ice makers, cooking facilities, microwaves, and exercise bicycles. Each room has a two-line telephone and a remote control color TV. The decor and colors used in the suites—rusts, greens, and browns—complement those in public areas.

All the suites are clustered around the atrium courtyard, filled with plants and fountains. Guests use this area for check-in, meeting other guests, and dining. A cooked-to-order breakfast is included in the tariff, as well as the two-hour cocktail reception each evening. Lunch and dinner at Frank Grisanti's Italian Restaurant are extra. Airport transportation, parking, and cable channels are also complimentary. The hotel also offers valet/laundry service, and express check-out.

Guests have the use of an indoor swimming pool, sauna, whirlpool, and exercise room. For an additional fee of $5, they may use the Sports Club nearby. There's also a billiards room where you can challenge your business partner in a game of pool. The hotel can accommodate small meetings.

Embassy Suites, off I-240 in East Memphis near the Regalia Shopping Center, is eleven miles from downtown.

French Quarter Suites Hotel
2144 Madison Avenue
Memphis, Tennessee 38104
901-728-4000
800-843-0353
Fax: 901-278-1262

General manager: Susan Esmonde
Accommodations: 69 two-room suites (all with private whirlpool baths and wet bars) and 36 maisonettes (all with private baths, wet bars, and refrigerators)
Rates: $92.50–$127
Payment: Major credit cards
Children: Welcome
Pets: Small pets allowed
Smoking: Nonsmoking rooms available
Open: Year-round

Though it's hundreds of miles up the Mississippi River from New Orleans, the owners of this unique hotel borrowed the name French Quarter and set out to create an experience similar to what you might find in that Louisiana city.

The four-story building, near Overton Square in midtown Memphis, about 5 minutes from downtown, has a French appearance. Faced in antique brick and stucco, it features French doors and wrought-iron balconies, from which hang several colorful flags. Guests step inside the interior courtyard lobby, surrounded on three sides with balconied guest rooms. Here guests check in, meet friends, enjoy cocktails, have informal meals, and often listen to live entertainment, including jazz on weekends, from 5:30 until 7:30 P.M.

Elegant dining is offered in Café Toulouse, featuring classic French and Cajun cuisine. For the enjoyment of guests, the hotel has an outdoor pool and exercise room. It also offers meeting space for small groups.

The guest rooms are ultra-private and quiet, designed to offer a home-away-from-home atmosphere—a luxury especially coveted by business travelers. The two-rooms suites are 500 square feet in area and include a living room with a wet bar; the 400-square-foot maisonettes, a refrigerator. All the suites and maisonettes have two television sets and two phones; some open onto balconies, some onto private patios. Classic 18th-and

19th-century Queen Anne reproductions and soft pastel colors have been used to create a warm ambience in each room.

The hotel offers room service 24 hours a day, complimentary newspapers, complimentary coffee in the room, and turndown service in the evening. The Continental buffet breakfast served in lobby each morning is on the house as well. The hotel provides complimentary limousine service to the airport.

The French Quarter offers romance, honeymoon, and wedding packages, including optional extras such as champagne, cheese and fruit, flowers, chocolates, and a candlelight dinner served in the room.

172 Kimbrough Place
Memphis, Tennessee 38174
901-726-5920

Management: Helen V. Denton, Bed & Breakfast/Corporate
Accommodations: 3 apartments (fully furnished and
   equipped, with private baths and kitchens)
Rates: weekly rentals, $72–$92 per night; monthly rentals,
   $34–$36 per night; optional $25-per-day housekeeping and
   $35-per-month private garage parking
Included: Cable TV, local phone, and fax machine
Payment: Mastercard, Visa
Children: Welcome
Pets: Not allowed
Smoking: Not encouraged
Open: Year-round

Bed & Breakfast Corporate, a division of Bed & Breakfast in Memphis, offers three luxury apartments near the Central Gardens residential area of midtown Memphis. A 10-minute trip from downtown, the properties are on the bus line and convenient to restaurants and museums. Located in a 1939 art deco building, the apartments overlook Central Gardens, a private, beautifully landscaped park. Apartment residents enjoy grilling out, playing croquet, or spending some quiet time here.

The properties are one-of-a-kind alternatives to hotels. They are ideal for business travelers or families who plan to be in Memphis a week or longer.

All three apartments have parquet floors, high ceilings, and come fully furnished in a classic, traditional style. All have cable TV, fax machines, and a VCR. Housekeeping and private garage parking are available for an additional charge.

The two-bedroom unit offers views of both the park and the city. Its most distinguishing feature is the double windows that frame the park view. It comes with a cable TV and a fax. The one-bedroom corner apartment has a living room, dining area, and a kitchen with a microwave. The king bed is an added luxury, as is the answering machine. The efficiency apartment is a spacious L-shaped unit with a sleeping alcove, kitchen, and bath.

Since the apartments are subject to availability and are often leased by the month, it's wise to try to book them at least two weeks in advance.

The Peabody

149 Union Avenue
Memphis, Tennessee 38103
901-529-4000
800-PEABODY

General manager: John Voegler
Accommodations: 438 rooms (all with private baths), and 16 suites (all with private baths, some with kitchens and fireplaces)
Rates: $130–$190; suites, $280–$795
Payment: All major credit cards
Children: Welcome
Pets: Check with management about arrangements
Smoking: Smoking and nonsmoking floors
Open: Year-round

Since the 1930s, the famous Peabody ducks have entertained guests at the South's Grand Hotel. Originally, the performance was a prank, but it was received so enthusiastically that it became a tradition at the hotel. Led by their trainer, the mallards leave their palatial penthouse on the Plantation Roof and ride the elevator to the lobby, where they make a grand entrance on a red carpet lined with camera-toting tourists and children sitting atop shoulders to get a better view. Flashbulbs pop as the ducks parade to the Travertine fountain in the middle of the lobby, where they do what most normal ducks do—splash in the water, clean themselves, and waddle around. At day's end, they assume their regal position and parade, single file, to the elevator to retire for the evening. A player piano contributes to the happy atmosphere. After three months of intensive performances, the flock retires to the farm and another takes its place. The world-famous ducks have been on tour to promote the hotel, and another group of performing mallards represents the sister hotel in Orlando, Florida. The Peabody ducks symbolize tradition, on which the hotel has built its excellent reputation and continues to thrive.

The Peabody has a wonderfully rich history. Built by Colonel R. C. Brinkley in 1869 and named for George Peabody, the hotel is synonymous with southern hospitality. The first structure was replaced by a finer building in 1925; it was completely refurbished and restored to its original grandeur by its present owners, the Belz family, in 1981. A National Historic Landmark, the 14-story hotel has hosted such notables as Presidents Andrew Jackson and William McKinley, General Robert E. Lee, writer William Faulkner, and aviator Charles Lindbergh. A piano that belonged to composer Francis Scott Key is displayed on the mezzanine. Writer David Cohn described the hotel aptly in 1935 when he said, "The Mississippi Delta begins in the lobby of the Peabody Hotel and ends on Catfish Row in Vicksburg. The Peabody is the Paris Ritz, the Cairo Shepheard's, the London Savoy . . ." Another story goes that Mississippians hope heaven will be like the lobby of the Peabody.

Guests at the hotel are pampered from the moment they enter the grand lobby, which is the center of activity, until they depart. Cordial bellmen, many of them old-timers at the Peabody, greet and escort guests to their rooms. Turndown service with chocolates is offered nightly, followed by a complimentary newspaper and orange juice the following morning. The hotel has five restaurants where guests congregate, including the informal Café Expresso in the Galleria and Chez Philippe, which serves classic haute cuisine and is considered one of the city's finest restaurants. Dux, known for its outstanding American cuisine, is also a favorite. Duck is not offered, for obvious reasons.

With 454 rooms, the Peabody is the largest hotel in the city. The spacious guest rooms are elegantly furnished and well stocked with amenities. Each of the Romeo and Juliet townhouse suites features a fireplace and marble staircase leading to a balcony overlooking the two-story living room and master bedroom—a great place for honeymoons and anniversaries. Guests enjoy the pool and spa. The Peabody Athletic Club has a full-time director. In addition to the meeting and banquet rooms, the third floor of the hotel is designated for meetings, with a person on duty to handle the needs of groups. The aristocratic Continental Ballroom remains a favorite spot for gatherings of Memphis elite. The Peabody has to have the finest room for ballroom dancing in the Southeast; the circular dance floor in the Skyway overlooking Memphis is so large that you can do grand sweeping waltzes and polkas without bumping into anyone. In addition, it's used for Sunday brunches. The Plantation Roof, also a great gathering spot, offers good views of the city.

The Peabody is a member of Preferred Hotels Worldwide. The downtown hotel is within walking distance of famous Beale Street, where the blues began, and the Mississippi River, where riverboats dock. It is also close to Cook Convention Center.

Miami

Bed and Breakfast Company: Tropical Florida
P.O. Box 430262
South Miami, Florida 33243
305-661-3270

Owner: Marcella Schaible
Accommodations: More than 100 (varying)
Rates: $27–$170
Included: Continental breakfast
Minimum stay: 3 nights; $5 surcharge if less than 3 nights
Taxes: Vary
Payment: Major credit cards
Children: Not allowed at some properties
Pets: Not allowed at some properties
Smoking: Not allowed at some properties

In a state where the term "B&B" can mean anything from a luxurious private guest house on an estate to a spare room in a modest housing development, Marcella Schaible takes all the guesswork out of finding the right B&B. An articulate, cultivated woman with a great respect for Florida's native beauty, Marcella has been in the business for many years. At one time, she listed properties only in the Gold Coast and the Keys. She now has B&Bs as far north as Jacksonville, along the Gulf coast, and in Orlando.

Marcella has an enormous variety of accommodations to choose from: an exquisitely furnished condo on Collins Avenue in Miami Beach, a quiet room in a B&B in the Old Town section of Key West, a riverfront apartment near St.Augustine, a place on a private island, a restored Gone with the Wind–style mansion outside Orlando, and dozens more. Many have pools and Jacuzzis. Some are unhosted: the owners leave you completely on your own. At hosted accommodations, the owners are very much in evidence, sharing sightseeing tips, breakfast in their kitchen, the living room TV, and—in a few cases—the bathroom.

Prices fluctuate as wildly as the types of accommodation.

Marcella is the sort of businesswoman who works hard to give you exactly what you want. In general, the more private and the larger the accommodation, the more expensive it will be. But be frank about what you want to pay: Marcella places a great many families on tight budgets in modest, reasonably priced homes near Florida's most expensive tourist attractions. If price is no problem, you can be honest about being picky. Marcella inspects every one of the accommodations she registers and can be counted on to give you a straightforward assessment.

One of the company's more restful properties is a guest house apartment on a horse farm in the countryside several miles outside Miami. It has rooms paneled in light wood, skylights in the high ceilings, and a beautiful new kitchen. Sliding glass doors lead onto a little deck overlooking pastureland. The main house, where the hosts live, has some budget-priced spare bedrooms. Also unusual is a Moorish guest house adjacent to a large home in Miami's Coconut Grove neighborhood. It has access to a large patio with a Mediterranean-style fountain, a swimming pool, and a tropical garden.

Colonnade Hotel

180 Aragon Avenue
Coral Gables, Florida 33134
305-441-2600
800-533-1337
Fax: 305-445-3929

General manager: Mario Abril
Accommodations: 140 rooms, 17 suites
Rates: $209–$255; suites, $189–$235; bi-level suites, $279–$295; lower weekend rates
Minimum stay: During special events and holidays
Added: 12½% tax
Payment: Major credit cards
Children: Under 16 free in room with parents
Smoking: Nonsmoking rooms available
Open: Year-round

Coral Gables was developed by a longtime Florida resident, George Merrick. The son of Solomon Merrick, the minister of the Congregational Church in Coconut Grove in the mid-to late-1800s, George Merrick developed Coral Gables during the Miami land boom of the early 1920s. But unlike many other developers, he did not simply put up flimsy homes and pave over cleared jungle. He designed a separate Mediterranean style town just adjacent to the Coconut Grove section of Miami that had broad boulevards and fountained rotaries and well-built houses tucked behind thick vegetation. During the 1926 hurricane that hit the city of Miami and surrounding areas twice in 24 hours, the only houses that dependably stayed in one piece had been built by Merrick's. Among them was the Colonnade, Merrick's office building. From here, Merrick sold 150 million dollars' worth of Coral Gables real estate. Merrick lost all his money in the Florida real estate crash of 1926 but both the Colonnade and Coral Gables survived. Lucky for us.

The original Colonnade building is a Greek Revival rotunda in pale pink stucco. Inside are fine coral and deep green marble floors, elaborate moldings, and white columns reaching up to a Greek revival atrium. The hotel was built in 1988 behind the original Colonnade. When one is inside, the shift from the original Colonnade and the hotel is nearly seamless, largely because the hotel developers were able to find a close match in the marble and have incorporated the columns and archways Merrick favored in the interior design of the hotel.

The first floor of the hotel includes several upscale boutiques and a marble rotunda, used for receptions, bar mitzvahs, and holiday parties. There are also two good restaurants—both the American bistro Doc Dammers Bar and Grill and the more formal Aragon Café have established excellent reputations in a short time in the restaurant-conscious South Miami/Coral Gables area.

The public rooms and individual accommodations display the same excellence. Even the hallways are attractive, with plaster friezes and brass and etched crystal light fixtures that hearken back to the 1920s. The marble and tile bathrooms have polished brass and ceramic fixtures, a wooden tray of toiletries, and a vase of fresh flowers. This is an expensive hotel even for Coral Gables, and most guests find the Superior and Deluxe rooms more than adequate. The double-bedded Superior rooms have plenty of space for a family. Mahogany furnishings include hand-tooled armoires that hide a remote control color TV. There are two phones and a mini-bar in every room.

Services include champagne on arrival, nightly turndown, and tea or coffee with a wake-up call. The staff are friendly but professional. There's a rooftop sundeck with a pool, Jacuzzi, and a fitness club. Nearby are boating and fishing, tennis and golf, museums, theater, and shopping in the Miracle Mile boutiques of Coral Gables, only 15 minutes from downtown Miami.

Grand Bay Hotel

2669 South Bayshore Drive
Coconut Grove
Miami, Florida 33133
305-858-9600
800-327-2788

Managing director: David Kurland
Accommodations: 181 rooms and suites
Rates: $195–$325; suite, $325–$750; penthouse, $1100;
  corporate rates and packages available
Minimum stay: With special packages
Added: 11% tax
Payment: Major credit cards
Children: Under 18 free in room with parents
Smoking: Nonsmoking available
Open: Year-round

The Grand Bay, the premier business hotel in Miami, is also a sophisticated vacation destination. The Grand Bay prides itself on mastering the details, with good reason. The prices are high, but so are the standards.

The hotel is on Bayshore Drive in Coconut Grove, just opposite the Grove's marina. Guests turn off this promenade into a circular brick drive and come upon a massive red sculpture of dramatic swirls. The Grand Bay looms like a Mayan temple, with brilliant purple bougainvillea spilling from concrete planters along the sloping side of the building.

European influence is evident everywhere. Guests register at inlaid Louis XIV desks in a quiet anteroom off the entrance: while doing so, they are served a glass of champagne or orange juice by the soft-spoken personnel. If the pianist is at the grand piano, it is worth staying a few moments. The lounge has Italian ceramic tile floors covered with fine Orientals, wood-mullioned floor-to-ceiling windows, large Oriental vases of potted palms, Moroccan leather sofas, and comfortable French country chairs. Philodendron plants cascade halfway to the floor from planters on the mezzanine. It is pleasant to unwind in the lounge after a long, hot Miami business day. Tea is served here each afternoon, with aperitifs, canapés, and scones.

The Grand Bay has the feeling of a small European hotel but offers 181 rooms, 49 of them suites, with high prices mitigated by a variety of special packages. The standard rooms come with a king-size bed, two doubles, or a Murphy bed, ideal for businesspeople who want to meet with associates in their rooms.

The junior suites are a bit larger, with a desk and generous work space. The penthouse and deluxe suites are spectacular, each decorated on an international theme: the Mandarin, the Gaucho, Italia, the Bristol, the Safari. Two are bi-level, with spiral staircases to the second-floor bedroom and bath. Standard rooms and small junior suites have balconies, while the more costly suites and penthouses have large private terraces.

All of the rooms and suites are better than average: the bathrooms have long marble countertops, a hair dryer and telephone, timed overhead heat lamps, a bidet, an array of expensive soaps and shampoos, and a small vase of fresh flowers next to the sink. Some of the suites have a Jacuzzi and a large living room with fine wood floors. Even rooms in the lowest price range have a spacious sitting area. Other amenities include mini-bars, remote control television, AM-FM clock radios, terrycloth robes, and twice-daily maid service, including evening turndown with mineral water. Services include same-day laundry and dry cleaning and shoeshine.

The range of services makes the Grand Bay popular for corporate retreats and small conventions and conferences. Business, telecommunications, and secretarial services are available. Meeting space includes the Continental Ballroom, which can be divided into three ballrooms for banquets, audiovisual presentations, and receptions, as well as meetings. In addition, there are three 450-square-foot meeting rooms. All the space is beautifully appointed, with antiques and good reproductions, original artwork, and spectacular arrangements of eucalyptus and exotic tropical flowers.

The hotel is owned by Compagnia Italiana Grandi Alberghi (CIGA), one of the finest hotel companies in Europe. The CIGA Bar is a meeting place for Miami executives and overnight business guests. This softly lit lounge is reminiscent of a men's club, with Moroccan leather club chairs, cubic tables of highly polished bird's-eye, large Oriental vases, and hunt scenes on the oak-paneled walls.

Regine's, the Grand Bay's famous nightclub and restaurant on the top floor, is open for dinner from eight o'clock till around midnight; the disco lounge, through a sliding glass wall, is open from 8:00P.M. until 5:00A.M.. Regine, a Frenchwoman renowned for providing sophisticated nighttime entertainment, has only two clubs in the United States—one in New York and this one in Miami. The views of the city's skyline are spectacular.

The Grand Café, overlooking an austere Italian garden, is an airy dining room with two floors. Decorated in art nouveau in plum and pink, it has pale terra cotta tile floors, large planters of flowers and greenery, ceiling fans, and small vases of spider mums on every pink-draped table. Food is nouvelle cuisine, with crisp vegetables and beautiful presentations.

The service at the Grand Bay is reminiscent of the best small hotels in New York and London. The staff are cordial, intelligent, dignified, and courteous, and may know your name by the second day of your visit. The doorman smiles and seems genuinely happy to see guests when they appear at the door. Bellmen act almost surprised when you tip them, as if you've paid them the highest of compliments. In a city where hoteliers have great difficulty hiring courteous workers, the Grand Bay maintains high standards.

The Grand Bay's private limousine will take you to the airport or anywhere in Coconut Grove within a few minutes' drive of the hotel. There is excellent shopping nearby at the Mayfair and, of course, the entire city for cultural and sporting events.

Outside there is a swimming pool and patio, screened by a tropical garden, and a small but well-equipped health club. Poolside services include a snack bar and a masseur. After a long day, this is a wonderful place to unwind. The pool is U-shaped, with a whirlpool at each end and a gentle waterfall flowing in a recessed grotto just a few steps away. Behind it rise the eleven floors of this Mayan palace, with their massive planters of cascading bougainvillea.

Hotel Inter-Continental Miami
100 Chopin Plaza
Miami, Florida 33131
305-577-1000
800-327-0200

General manager: Alvaro Diago
Accommodations: 645 rooms
Rates: $150–$210; suites, $300–$320; packages available
Minimum stay: None
Added: 12% tax
Payment: Major credit cards
Children: Under 14 free in room with parents
Smoking: Nonsmoking rooms available
Open: Year-round

The Hotel Inter-Continental Miami combines European elegance and big-city efficiency. Accessible by elevator to its architectural twin, the Miami Center office building, the Inter-Continental is one of the best business hotels in Florida. A tower of Italianate marble in the heart of the city, it stands austerely and majestically on the shores of Biscayne Bay and the Miami River. Nearby is the financial and business district and, just a few miles beyond, the upscale shops and residences of Coconut Grove.

There are thirty deluxe suites in the Inter-Continental, with an interesting mix of Oriental and art deco: Chinese-red ginger jar lamps, mahogany armoires, red lacquered chairs, sofas and easy chairs upholstered in tapestry, and chrome and black granite tables. Every suite has two luxury bathrooms, one with a Roman shower bath. At the windows are heavy brocade drapes with a wide embroidered trim. The neutral walls are decorated with fine prints and other artwork. Even the elevator is beautiful, with red mahogany paneling, chrome railings, and art deco embellishments. There are 645 rooms and suites on the thirty-one stories of this marble and glass tower.

A standard room has a king-size bed or two doubles, brass and mahogany campaign bureaus, an Oriental armoire hiding the television set, a mini-bar, and a large marble bath with toiletries in art deco bottles. Terrycloth robes hang in the mirrored closets and there are pretty flowers in a bud vase in the bathroom.

Convention space and services at the Inter-Continental are outstanding. A total of 55,000 square feet of meeting space includes the hotel's Grand Ballroom, which can accommodate up to 2,700 people for receptions and 1,350 for banquets. There are more than 20 smaller rooms for informal meetings, private dinner parties and receptions, and conferences. Facilities include a well-equipped business center with photocopying, fax, and telex machines.

A favorite lounge for guests attending conventions or conferences is the Oak Room, which has the air of a private club—which it is, frequented by Miami executives as well as hotel guests. This is a popular place at happy hour and during major sporting events. The room is paneled with dark-stained oak and has banquettes and chairs upholstered in a tapestry fabric of rich blue, red, and gold. The parquet floors are covered with deep-pile maroon carpets. The low bar has armchairs of rich leather.

The four-star restaurant at the Inter-Continental is the elegant Pavillion Grill, with gold carpets and dark blue walls accented with rich moldings. Serving American and regional gourmet cuisine, the restaurant has won a number of awards, and was recently rated by Miami/South Florida magazine as one of the top ten in the state.

The Royal Palm Court, just off the lobby, serves breakfast, lunch, and dinner, and resembles a large gazebo, with green latticework panels trimmed with pink molding. A charming ceiling mural of tropical birds and foliage is lit by recessed lighting behind a panel of burled wood. The three eating areas are sectioned off by latticework panels. The food is good and, though the service can be a bit slow, the waiters are friendly and polite. Although the restaurant is in the lobby, only fifty feet from the hotel entrance, it feels removed from the hustle and bustle.

A good place to take children for light meals and snacks is the Brasserie/Newmarket, which also sells gourmet breads, cheeses, and fresh produce. Although the Inter-Continental is a city business hotel, it is not a place where people traveling with children need feel uncomfortable. Deluxe suites are ideal for a family. Family packages are available.

The hotel sits on several acres of land, so there is room for a rooftop recreational wing with a swimming pool and a jogging trail landscaped with subtropical foliage. The view from the rooftop is nothing short of astounding with the exciting city spread out below and Biscayne Bay and the Miami River stretching out to Bay islands and the Atlantic beyond. Cruise ships are docked nearby, and many people stay here before embarking on one of them. As a result, the lobby is sometimes a little noisy with groups.

The high-ceilinged lobby on the first floor is a meeting place for a cosmopolitan clientele who chat at pleasant groupings of rattan lounge chairs. Green and pink woven rugs accent the marble floors. Cushioned wicker chairs and round bamboo tables with canvas umbrellas are placed informally throughout the lobby and lounge. Thirty-foot palm trees reach to an atrium ceiling paneled with tiger maple.

Dominating the center of the big room is a 70-ton marble sculpture by Henry Moore, surrounded by a hexagonal fountain with dozens of water jets. The sculpture is representative of the hotel itself: modern, distinctive, opulent.

Hotel Place St. Michel

162 Alcazar Avenue
Coral Gables, Florida 33134
305-444-1666
800-247-8526

Owner: Stuart Bornstein
Accommodations: 28 rooms and suites

Rates: $90–$105; suites, $125; $10 additional person
Included: Continental breakfast
Minimum stay: With some weekend packages
Added: 11% tax
Payment: Major credit cards
Children: Under 12 free in room with parents
Smoking: Nonsmoking available
Open: Year-round

The name recalls Paris, and well it should—the Hotel Place St. Michel is reminiscent of a fine Parisian hotel. The entrance sets the mood: a red canvas awning above an arched doorway with a coat of arms above. Inside are cool terrazzo tile floors, buff-colored stucco walls, and archways of rich ceramic tiles. French windows open to a bistro-style restaurant on one side of the hallway. A concierge presides at the ornately carved registry desk, with an Eastlake antique mirror and pigeonhole postal cases mounted on the wall behind. The floors in this lobby area are parquet, and French windows lead into a sitting/breakfast room of velvet settees.

A brass elevator takes guests up to rooms on the second and third floors of the building. Hallways are furnished with breakfronts and other period pieces. Above each room are stained glass transoms in art nouveau designs of green, mustard yellow, and cream. Guests can choose a room with two double beds, a queen-size bed, or a king.

Each room is different in shape, size, and decor, either with pretty wallpaper or painted a neutral color and then stenciled. The parquet floors are covered with fine old rugs; the furnishings are Victorian antiques. Rather than building closets for the extensive wardrobes of some visitors, owners Stuart Bornstein and Alan Potamkin furnished the rooms with large antique armoires. Televisions sit on old Singer sewing machine tables.

The tile bathrooms are modern, but blend in well with the old-fashioned bedrooms. They have freestanding basins, stenciling on the walls, and, in some cases, lovely floral tiles used as trim above the shower bath. Extras include herbal English soaps, lotions, and shampoo.

Two especially nice rooms are 306, with two corner windows, and 302, with its own Victorian-style sitting room. There are many special touches in all the guest rooms: vases of fresh flowers, gold and white French telephones, authentic-looking goosenecked lamps, carved bedsteads that must have taken many days of antiquing to find, bentwood armchairs upholstered in fine fabrics, and good paintings.

Guests may enjoy a Continental breakfast in their rooms

with a morning newspaper or downstairs in the sitting room. Breakfast features fresh croissants with jams and marmalade, juice, and tea or coffee. Other complimentary offerings are a fruit basket and cheese on arrival and Italian chocolates on the pillow with nightly turndown.

For lunch and dinner, there are a number of cafés and restaurants on Ponce de Leon Boulevard and elsewhere in Coral Gables, a separate municipality next door to the Coconut Grove section of South Miami. The Cuban section of Miami, on the Tamiami Trail, offers alternative dining options. Closer to home is the Restaurant St. Michel — it's a favorite dining spot for Miamians as well as hotel guests. The mood is European and so is the menu, with offerings such as escargot de Bourgogne, grilled swordfish with Mediterranean pepper relish, lobster sautéed in mushrooms and scallions, and crêpes for dessert.

The Hotel St. Michel was built in 1926 as the Hotel Sevilla and, from the outside, looks somewhat like a small European palazzo — the sort of place a lesser relative of the Medicis might reside in. Like many old Florida hotels, the Hotel St. Michel has had its ups and downs, and it's heartening that the management is preserving the beauty and dignity of such a worthy place.

Hyatt Regency Miami

City Center at Riverwalk
400 S.E. Second Avenue
Miami, Florida 33131-2197
305-358-1234
800-228-9000 in U.S.
Fax: 305-358-0529
Telex: 514316

Executive vice president: Bernard Guet
Accommodations: 615 rooms and suites
Rates: $150–$200; suites, $250–$550
Minimum stay: None
Added: 12% tax
Payment: Major credit cards
Children: Under 18 free in room with parents
Smoking: Nonsmoking available
Open: Year-round

Miami's Hyatt Regency is in a busy part of town — it's also surrounded by a number of hotels. What sets it apart from neighboring hostelries is its excellence as a convention hotel, its service, and its restful ambience in the midst of a stimulating environment. Miami is the "cruise ship capital of the world." The nearby Port of Miami welcomes millions of cruise ship passengers every year. Many of these passengers stay here before embarking on trips, including some teenage school groups, and they can be a little boisterous. But the international staff seem to take it in stride. The staff seem genuinely happy to be working here, and the hotel has one of the lowest turnover rates in the city.

Approximately sixty percent of this Hyatt's business is meetings and conventions. The hotel is adjacent to the Miami Convention Center and includes three floors of meeting space: an impressive ballroom, a concert hall, a 28,000-square-foot exhibit center, an auditorium that seats 444 with facilities to simultaneously translate up to six languages, and more than two dozen smaller function rooms. Much of the meeting space was redecorated recently. The walls are painted in soft colors or paneled in blond matchstick paneling, and the floors are carpeted or paved in a brick-colored tile. The higher you go in this Miami skyscraper, the better the view of the Miami River, Biscayne Bay, and the city.

Pleasant bellhops greet guests at the front entrance, which is reached by a semicircular drive. Inside is the sound of rushing water from coral fountains in the lobby. The lobby's centerpiece is an atrium sitting area dominated by a contemporary sculpture rising three floors. Throughout the day and evening, guests gather here on sofas and easy chairs to read or talk, the soothing sound of the fountains in the background.

Against the far walls are small shops and the informal Riverwalk Café and Currents lounge. Beyond these is the Esplanade Restaurant, open for lunch and dinner. Although this restaurant looks far more formal than the Riverwalk Café, with black lacquered Oriental chairs and dramatic black and gray place settings, the mood is informal. Many Miamians as well as hotel guests come here to relax and enjoy the American grill menu. In the winter, the restaurant's stone crabs are particularly popular.

An additional draw for the Esplanade Restaurant is its view of the Miami River, which could more accurately be called a canal. For a closer look at this interesting, busy waterway, guests can sit outside on the cut coral patio or take a walk along the Riverwalk. Sightseeing boats and a launch to Fisher Island tie up at the Hyatt's dock. Further along the palm-lined Riverwalk are a waterfront restaurant and the Bayside shopping center.

Another outdoor pleasure is provided by the Hyatt Regency's

recreational area. The heated swimming pool is accented by white planters of bougainvillea, which create a buffer between the city noise and the pool. A poolside bar is open on weekends and holidays and there are video games and vending machines inside.

To describe the recreational amenities and other features of the Hyatt is to say nothing about the rooms. Even the standard rooms are large and have a TV with pay movies, a comfortable sitting area, a small furnished balcony, French-milled and glycerine soaps, and a vase of flowers in the sitting area or the bath. The bathrooms are large and have three separate areas: a shower-tub and toilet; a sink and vanity with generous counter space; and a dressing area (which could use an overhead light).

Gold Passport and Regency rooms and suites are even better, with larger sitting areas and complimentary foods offered in special guest lounges overlooking the water. A varity of bed sizes are available in all three room types and there is also flexibility in making a standard room into a parlor suite. If you can afford it, request a room with a view.

Mayfair House

3000 Florida Avenue
Coconut Grove
Miami, Florida 33133
305-441-0000
800-341-0809 in Florida
800-433-4555 in U.S.

General manager: Herbert Spiegal
Accommodations: 181 suites
Rates: one-room suite, $250–$230; one-bedroom suite, $300–$400; two-bedroom suite, $500; $35 additional person
Minimum stay: With some packages
Add: 12½% tax
Payment: Major credit cards; personal check with major credit card
Children: Under 12 free in room with parents
Smoking: Nonsmoking available
Open: Year-round

The Mayfair House is part of World of Mayfair, an imaginative shopping complex in Coconut Grove on the southern edge of Miami. The shopping complex is one of the most beautiful on the east coast of Florida, with tropical greenery everywhere, waterfalls and fountains, sculpted planters that look as if they were rescued from a Mayan temple, and European and Mexican tile. The Mayfair Hotel is eclectic yet self-contained; there is a hushed gentility here.

The plaster walls of the public rooms and hallways are sculpted curves, with unexpected angles in the corners of the ceiling. Appointments in the lobby include art nouveau brass floor lamps in the shape of a serpent, cloisonne tables, large Oriental vases, and modern oil paintings. Many of the Honduran mahogany doors are hand-carved in intricate Oriental or art nouveau patterns. Visually, the Mayfair is an unusual place that startles one with its ingenuity in design.

Each of the 181 suites is different in shape, decor, and size. Some have room dividers of art nouveau etched glass or wood slats that have an Oriental look. Most of the artwork and appointments are new, but the designers also were able to find panels of original Tiffany stained glass, which they have incorporated into the hotel's design. Furniture includes hand carved bedsteads, and, in some of the suites, antique English pianos.

The suites share some wonderful characteristics. All have a Jacuzzi in the bedroom, living room, or on a trellised balcony. The furniture in each suite is custom-designed; the closets, also custom built, have heavy mahogany doors with built-in drawers and cabinets. A sofa, table, and chairs are in each bedroom and a TV and telephone are in the bathroom as well as the bedrooms. The baths are of marble and all have extra amenities such as a clothes hamper, hair dryer, and makeup mirror. The ceramic tile floors have mahogany detailing. At night, kimonos are left on the bed at turndown.

All luggage goes up to the guest room floors through a back service entrance. Guest bills are settled with the cashier behind the genteel reception desks. The staff are well-trained but sometimes a bit cold.

Limousine service is provided within a limited area. The hotel also has a rooftop pool and 24-hour room service, which includes in-suite catering for private dining. The hotel's restaurant, the Mayfair Grill, under new management, is excellent. Twenty-seven suites have separate dining rooms for formal board meetings and business entertaining. A separate executive conference center has various meeting rooms and a wide range of audiovisual equipment. The Mayfair Ballroom, with its striking use of copper and marble, is a distinctive space and also efficient. It can be subdivided into three areas and can accommodate up to 700 theater-style.

Hotel guests need never fear boredom. The hotel is an integral architectural unit of World of Mayfair, where there are restaurants, sidewalk cafés, bakeries, and more than a hundred shops and boutiques—one can spend hours strolling through the Mayfair complex and observing the architecture. Visitors also enjoy Coconut Grove day and nightlife, which has room for everyone—from latter-day hippies to blatant yuppies.

Milwaukee

The Marc Plaza Hotel
509 West Wisconsin Avenue
Milwaukee, Wisconsin 53203
414-271-7250
800-558-7708
Fax: 414-271-1039

General manager: Donald Raines
Accommodations: 468 rooms, 32 suites
Rates: $110–$125; double, $130–$145; suites, $150–$220;
   packages available
Minimum stay: None
Added: 12.5% tax
Payment: Major credit cards
Children: Welcome
Pets: Small pets allowed
Smoking: Nonsmoking rooms available
Open: Year-round

Though not as ornate as its sister hotel, the Pfister, the Marc Plaza holds its own as a classic hotel in the heart of Milwaukee's business district. The art deco image of the hotel (originally the Schroeder) has been compromised by years of use and renovations. Traces of that original grandeur can still be found in the main floor lobby, where exquisite carpeting, chandeliers, and flower arrangements are accented by the melodies of a grand piano.

The rooms are outfitted with floral bedspreads and traditional furnishings. Some have a more masculine feel as dark woods blend with deep burgundy sofas and chairs. The Marc Plaza Tower, a private five-floor section atop the hotel, offers such extras as nightly turndown service, complimentary newspaper, fancy toiletries, and concierge. All guests have access to the sunny indoor pool, with sauna and sundeck.

Benson's Milwaukee Grill recently took the place of the hotel's previous Le Bistro restaurant and regulars here say the change is a welcome one. The bi-level dining room is accented by marble topped tables and etched glass. The menu focuses on the restaurant's grill, and large salads are also popular. The Garden Café serves lighter fare while the Bombay Bicycle Club offers live entertainment on weekends.

Business guests will find eighteen meeting rooms, ranging from the intimate wood-paneled Churchill Room to the Regency Room, with its lavish imported crystal chandeliers.

The Pfister
424 East Wisconsin Avenue
Milwaukee, Wisconsin 53202
414-273-8222
800-472-4403 in Wisconsin
800-558-8222 in U.S.
Fax: 414-273-0747

General manager: Rosemary Steinfest
Accommodations: 250 rooms, 57 suites
Rates: $125–$155; double, $145–$170; suites, single, $150–$625; double, $170–$645
Included: All meals available
Minimum stay: None
Added: 12.5% tax
Payment: Major credit cards
Children: Welcome
Pets: Not allowed
Smoking: Nonsmoking rooms available
Open: Year-round

When Charles Pfister unveiled his namesake hotel in 1893, he wanted it to become the "Grand Hotel of the Midwest." He would be proud to know that his creation, recently polished to its original grandeur, has reestablished itself as Milwaukee's premier historic hotel. The lobby alone is worth a visit, with its marble-topped front desk, cherry paneling, and gold leaf. Bronze lions guard the grand stairway, which ascends to a series of brass-railed landings. Greetings on the wall read Salve, the Latin for "welcome."

The hotel comprises the main building and the 23-floor Tower, built in 1966. The top floor of the Tower houses a pool, a health club, and the Crown Room lounge, with a panoramic view of the city and Lake Michigan. Leslie Uggams, David Brenner, and Joan Rivers are among the entertainers who have performed here.

Though the accommodations aren't necessarily luxurious, they all have nice touches like live plants, wet bars, and hair dryers in modern, marble-lined bathrooms. The cabbage rose carpeting and paneled halls create a nostalgic atmosphere leading to the original Pfister rooms, which have Victorian wallpapers and flame-stitched chairs. Note the ornate doorknobs and knockers, also part of the restoration.

One of the country's most extensive wine cellars can be enjoyed through the English Room, the main dining room; the Café Rouge and the Greenery offer lighter fare. The massive parlor fireplace, originally a fixture in the lobby, now highlights the Café Olé lounge, a popular spot for Sunday brunch. The corridors and galleries here are lined with an impressive collection of 19th-century artwork.

You pay a high tariff for all these extras, from the concierge in high collar and tails to the shoeshine man with the cigar dangling out of his mouth, asleep in the corner. But it's worth it. As one employee proudly put it, anyone who's anyone still stays at the Pfister.

Wyndham Milwaukee Center Hotel
139 E. Kilbourn Street
Milwaukee, Wisconsin 53202
414-276-8686
Fax: 414-276-8689
Reservations:
  Wyndham Hotels and Resorts
  800-822-4200

General manager: Nicolas de Segonzac
Accommodations: 221 rooms
Rates: $139–$179; packages available
Minimum stay: None
Added: 12.5% tax
Payment: Major credit cards
Children: Welcome
Pets: Not allowed
Smoking: Nonsmoking rooms available
Open: Year-round

As the elegant cornerstone of a $100 million multi-use development, the Wyndham Milwaukee Center Hotel rises ten stories above the city's theater district. It's connected by a domed rotunda to the new Milwaukee Repertory Theatre, the Pabst Theatre, and a 28-story office complex. The granite and brick exterior overlooks the Milwaukee River and complements the nearby city hall and other prominent buildings.

The Flemish Renaissance-style interior offers touches like ornate millwork and marble both in the imposing lobby and the spacious guest rooms. All rooms have televisions, radio alarm clocks, shower massage, coffeemaker with complimentary coffee or tea, and fluffy down pillows. The 75 executive suites (actually large rooms) also have writing desks, sofas, and more telephones and televisions.

Meeting rooms range in size from an intimate executive boardroom to the 5,000-square-foot Grand Ballroom. For relaxing afterwards, the health club has a whirlpool, sauna, steam rooms, tanning beds, and exercise equipment.

Breakfast, lunch, and dinner are served daily in the Kilbourn Café, which specializes in Midwestern cuisine in an atmosphere of understated luxury. You are within 15 minutes of Bucks games at Bradley Center, the Milwaukee Art Museum, and the Milwaukee Zoo.

Minneapolis/ St. Paul

Chatsworth B&B
984 Ashland Avenue
St. Paul, Minnesota 55104
612-227-4288

Innkeeper: Donna Gustafson
Accommodations: 5 rooms (3 with private bath)
Rates: $55–$95; double, $60–$100
Included: Continental breakfast
Minimum stay: None
Added: 6.5% tax
Payment: Personal checks; cash
Children: With permission from innkeeper
Pets: Not allowed
Smoking: Prohibited
Open: Year-round

An international flair sets the Chatsworth B&B apart from the other bed-and-breakfasts popping up in the Twin Cities. The home, built circa 1900, is in a quiet St. Paul neighborhood. The rooms are cleverly decorated—the African/Asian Room has a bamboo bedstead and wicker chairs. Colorful hanging beads separate the bedroom from the bathroom and a private balcony overlooks the yard. The Scandinavian Room places simple antique pine furnishings on exposed maple floors. It shares a bath with the Oriental Room, which has a Chinese-made bed and linen curtains. Terrycloth robes come with every room, but this one offers kimonos.

A typical breakfast includes yogurt, fresh fruit and juice, granola, muffins, and fascinating conversation with innkeeper Donna Gustafson and her international guests. At last count, she had hosted travelers from more than fifteen countries. When she's not at home, Donna is herself a world traveler and holistic healing expert.

If globe-hopping guest rooms aren't to your taste, the inn offers more standard accommodations. Indeed, Donna admits that the Four Poster Room is her most most popular. It has a double whirlpool tub, marble sink decorated with a flower pattern, and a massive antique armoire. Her hidden sound system pipes music into the bedroom and bathroom. Among the books she leaves for guests is a soothing title called The Necessity of Open Places.

Donna admits she's stubborn when it comes to details. When she didn't like the color of the recently finished exterior, she had it repainted at great expense to its current green hue. The backyard is now serenaded by a small collection of wind chimes and hanging shells.

Chatsworth B&B is only 10 minutes from both Minneapolis and St. Paul. The neighborhood has its own ethnic restaurants and points of interest, especially the outstanding Victorian homes that line nearby Summit Avenue.

Nicollet Island Inn
on Nicollet Island
95 Merriam Street
Minneapolis, Minnesota 55401
612-331-1800
Fax: 612-331-6528

General manager: Royce Ring
Accommodations: 24 rooms (all with private bath)
Rates: $105–$125
Included: Continental breakfast Sundays only
Minimum stay: None
Added: 10% tax
Payment: Major credit cards
Children: Welcome
Pets: Allowed
Smoking: Nonsmoking rooms available
Open: Year-round

Though rooms on both sides offer views of the Mississippi, don't expect a secluded hideaway at this inn, for the teardrop-shaped island, reached by bridge, lies between downtown and northeast Minneapolis. The 1893 limestone building spent a good part of its life as Salvation Army headquarters before its transformation in 1982.

The guest rooms offer standard hotel amenities and Victorian touches in the decor. Reproduction four-poster and brass beds, armoires, wing chairs, fox and hound or flowered wallpapers, and exposed stone walls add to the appeal. Two rooms have Jacuzzis. All include morning coffee, juice, and a newspaper delivered to your room.

The Nicollet's steak, pasta, and seafood restaurant is open daily for all three meals. Guests may sit near the antique oak fireplace or on a glassed-in porch overlooking the Mississippi. Nick's Bar, on the lobby level, has a 30-foot counter decorated with carved figureheads, stained glass, and inlaid seashells. An outdoor patio can be enjoyed in the summer.

Business guests enjoy the hotel's location and its friendly, accommodating staff. You can walk to nearby restaurants, movie theaters, and night spots in the River Place entertainment and dining complex. And, unlike most lodgings in the Twin Cities, the Nicollet Island Inn offers free parking.

The St. Paul Hotel
350 Market Street
St. Paul, Minnesota 55102
800-292-9292
800-223-1588
Fax: 612-228-9506
Telex: 297008
Reservations:
   Historic Hotels of America
   800-678-8946

General manager: William Morrissey
Accommodations: 222 rooms, 32 suites
Rates: $110–$120; double, $125–$135; suites, $145–$595;
   weekends, $69–$79 per room; packages available
Minimum stay: None
Added: 11.5% tax
Payment: Major credit cards
Children: Welcome
Pets: Allowed
Smoking: Nonsmoking rooms available
Open: Year-round

Built in 1910 by the designers of New York's Grand Central Station, the St. Paul Hotel defines lodgings in this half of the Twin Cities. Elegant and simple, the St. Paul doesn't offer fancy fitness facilities or trendy room decor. But its old-fashioned service keeps it popular with no-nonsense business and vacation travelers.

Indiana limestone, glazed tile, white terra cotta, and Italianate cornices comprise the exterior. The lobby, done in a gray blue, salmon and beige color scheme with red upholstered chairs and couches, is subtly lit by four chandeliers, three of them originals from the grand ballroom. It usually has a massive flower arrangement as its centerpiece.

The floral theme extends into the bedrooms as well, on draperies, bedspreads, and dust ruffles. Suites offer private sitting rooms. With nightly turndown service comes a bottle of mineral water and a thoughtful card forecasting the weather. The concierge and chauffeur service prove extremely helpful.

There are two restaurants: the Café serves informal breakfast, lunch, and dinner, and the St. Paul Grill, offering a beautiful view of neighboring Rice Park, serves American fare from sizzling steaks to chicken pot pies. For breakfast, try the roast beef hash and eggs. Inquire about the inexpensive weekend packages, most of which include dinner. Seven banquet and meeting facilities can accommodate groups from 25 to 500.

St. Paul's skyway system links the St. Paul Hotel with other commercial, business, retail, and entertainment establishments. There are no fitness facilities in the Hotel, though guests can have bicycles and slant boards delivered to their rooms. They also have access to a nearby YMCA.

The University Club of St. Paul
420 Summit Avenue
St. Paul, Minnesota 55102
612-222-1751

Owner: John Rupp
Accommodations: 7 rooms, 1 suite (all with private bath)
Rates: $45–$85; suites, $85
Minimum stay: None
Added: 6.5% tax
Payment: Major credit cards
Children: Welcome
Pets: Allowed
Smoking: Prohibited
Open: Year-round

Built in 1912, the University Club was patterned after the prestigious Cambridge and Oxford clubs in London. The English Tudor manor, next to other stately homes on St. Paul's Summit Avenue, still exists as a private club, with some members in residence year-round. A handful of guest rooms are open to travelers seeking simple, reasonably priced accommodations with the added luxury of exercise facilities. Don't expect pampering or even attentive service. One employee calls the experience here "European style—to explain the occasional leaky faucet."

The extensive common rooms, including a library and lounge, have high ceilings. English antiques and landscape paintings grace the panelled walls. In the Grill Bar, F. Scott Fitzgerald's initials can be seen etched alongside those of other past members: the Roaring Twenties' writer was born just a couple of blocks away. One of his stories, "Winter Dreams," takes place at the University Club.

Owner John Rupp, an antiques collector, has furnished each room with an eclectic array of fine arts pieces, antique furniture, brass rubbings, and Persian carpets. All rooms have queen-size beds; the sole suite here has a bedroom and sitting room, as well as its own fireplace.

Active guests will be pleased to find that an overnight stay includes access to the University Club fitness center, outdoor swimming pool, and tennis court. An intimate dining establishment called The Ramsey Room is open for overnight guests and members only. A more casual dining room in the Club orders from the same menu.

The Whitney Hotel

150 Portland Avenue
Minneapolis, Minnesota 55401
612-339-9300
800-248-1879
Fax: 612-339-1333
Reservations: 800-323-7500

General manager: Brian Snell
Accommodations: 54 rooms, 43 bi-level suites, 3 penthouse suites
Rates: $95–$150; suites, $125–$250; packages available
Included: All meals available
Minimum stay: None
Added: 12% tax, $5 nightly parking charge
Payment: Major credit cards
Children: Welcome
Pets: Not allowed
Smoking: Nonsmoking rooms available
Open: Year-round

A sunny front desk clerk welcomes you by name. A concierge helps plan a trip to a museum while the hotel limousine waits to take you there. Room attendants leave fancy chocolates behind with evening turndown. In the morning, tea and coffee greet you in a shining silver service in the lobby. The Whitney Hotel in Minneapolis pulls these touches off with a special blend of midwestern sincerity and downtown panache that keeps its reputation solid and its guests coming back.

Built in 1878 as the Standard Flour Mill and renovated as a hotel in 1987, the Whitney's exterior retains its brick-lined prosaic quality. You may think wheat still gets ground here. Inside is another story entirely. The elegant European-style lobby boasts marble floors, crystal chandeliers, and a grand staircase winding up to meeting rooms and second-floor accommodations.

The guest rooms are furnished with Thomasville Queen Anne pieces and offer such amenities as terrycloth robes, bathroom telephones, Crabtree & Evelyn soaps, Neutrogena shampoos, and 24-hour room service. The ceilings are high (usually 12 to 14 feet), even in the standard rooms, while bi-level suites soar even higher, with loft bedrooms reached by spiral staircases. The penthouse, comprising three bedrooms and two living rooms, features a grand piano, fireplaces, whirlpools, and a deck with a spectacular view of the Mississippi River.

Five meeting rooms, richly appointed with polished mahogany tables and upholstered armchairs, can hold receptions or dinners of up to 200 people. Though the Whitney has the slightly sterile aura of a modern hotel, special decorating touches are found throughout, like the framed Victorian handbags, gloves, and lace collars that decorate some hallways.

The Whitney Grille, on the lower level, offers classic American cuisine. It feels like a private club with its paneled walls, intimate booths, and austere classical music just above hushed conversation. Entrées of lavender peppered shrimp or filet mignon are served on fine china with polished silver. In warmer weather, you can also dine on the more casual garden plaza.

Nashville

End o' the Bend Lodge & Landing

2527 Miami Avenue
Nashville, Tennessee 37214
615-883-0997
Fax: 615-889-7305

Innkeeper: Betty J. Holt
Accommodations: 2-bedroom log cabin (fully furnished and
   equipped, with two private baths)
Rates: $95–$150; weekly and monthly rates available
Included: Coffee
Payment: MasterCard, Visa; personal checks
Children: Not appropriate
Pets: Check with innkeeper
Smoking: Allowed on porches only
Open: Year-round

From the wicker-furnished screened porch of your own log
cabin, you can wave to the sightseers on the *General Jackson* as
it makes its way up the Cumberland River. You can enjoy a
picnic or a cookout on the lawn. You can sleep until noon under
a Laura Ashley or Bill Blass comforter. At night you can hold
hands on the porch swing or sit in front of a roaring fire. This is
seclusion and privacy at its best, even though it's located in the
city near the airport, interstates, and Opryland.

Don't ever think that this cabin is rustic, however, just because it's built of 150-year-old logs that were moved from another site and reconstructed here. The owner and innkeeper,
Betty J. Holt, has created a luxurious setting for her guests; she's
added all the modern conveniences and filled the house with
only the best—antiques, country French furniture, framed art
prints, plush carpeting, and expensive linens. The baths are
modern, the porches were added on, and the cathedral ceilings
create a feeling of spaciousness. Betty has been just as meticu-
lous on the outside, netting a Nashville Metro Beautification
Award for the landscaping. She has been in the music publish-
ing business for more than twenty years and lives just two doors
away.

Overnight guests have the cabin completely to themselves, except when Betty puts on her Beulah hat and tidies up the cabin. She can provide just about anything you might want, from a professional chef to hunting and fishing guides. The cabin is close to all of Nashville's attractions, including Opryland, which is only a mile away.

Opryland Hotel
2800 Opryland Drive
Nashville, Tennessee 37214
615-889-1000
Fax: 615-871-7741

General Manager: Jack Vaughan
Accommodations: 1,891 rooms and suites, including 4 presidential suites (all with private baths)
Rates: $149–$179
Payment: All major credit cards
Children: Welcome
Pets: Allowed for handicapped guests
Smoking: Allowed
Open: Year-round

From the balcony of Room 8496, you have a ringside seat for the Dancing Waters light, laser, water fountain, and music show, featuring harpist Lloyd Lindroth, who performs magic from his perch high over the two-acre European-style conservatory garden. Lights, lasers, and water fountains are orchestrated in perfect timing with the music, which Nashville's Liberace performs two times each evening. (He is one of many stars and entertainers from Opryland USA who perform in the hotel.)

You can also sleep with the windows open in the garden rooms and think you're in Hawaii, as the cascades and fountains lull you into dream world. Actually, the place has a Disney aura to it, but it is unique in every way.

The Opryland Hotel is itself something of a dream. It was designed by Earl Swensson to represent people architecture, a new form that encourages interaction between a building and its users. Built in 1977, the hotel has been enlarged twice—in 1983 and 1988. The Williamsburg-style hotel features a large central indoor garden around which are located shops, restaurants, the lobby, and guest rooms connected by ramps and walkways. Be sure to see the giant mural that depicts Nashville and its citizens at the turn of the century. Rooms are tastefully decorated with coordinating fabrics in draperies, bedspreads, and upholstered chairs and furnished in traditional mahogany. No amenity has been overlooked in the suites—down to Crabtree and Evelyn toiletries and dark green terrycloth robes. A part of Opryland USA, which also includes the Opryland showpark, the Grand Ole Opry, and the Nashville Network, it has received Mobil's four stars and AAA's four diamond awards.

Guests move freely in the spacious public areas, but don't be surprised if you get lost sometimes. Each building melds into another, so the hallways seem to go into infinity. Actually, it's not a bad idea to take a map along the first day or so. Everything you might need is contained within the hotel. (One departing guest said on leaving that he had not been outside the hotel in five days.) There are shops and more shops, many selling Opryland souvenirs, a revolving lounge, and several restaurants (Cascades, Rachel's Kitchen, the Veranda, Old Hickory, and Rhett's). The hotel has three swimming pools, tennis courts, and a golf course—the 18-hole Springhouse Golf Club. Tours of the Grand Ole Opry, Ryman Auditorium, and country music stars' homes leave from the hotel.

As the twelfth largest hotel in the nation and Nashville's largest convention hotel, Opryland can accommodate almost any trade show held in the United States. Ryman Exhibition Hall, named for Ryman Auditorium where the Grand Ole Opry played for years, is the nation's largest single-level, self-contained exhibition hotel facility, with 145,000 square feet.

As wonderful as all the trappings are, Opryland Hotel's biggest selling feature is its friendly, courteous staff. They also seem to have been properly trained in how to be hospitable without being phony. The smiles seem genuine and the hellos sincere. How can you not be impressed when everyone addresses you by name from the moment you check in until departure?

The hotel is located on the grounds of Opryland USA, a theme park built around the Grand Ole Opry and country music. If you happen to be in Nashville on Friday or Saturday, you can see Roy Acuff, Jean Shepherd, Hank Snow, George Hamilton IV, and other greats on the Grand Ole Opry, broadcast live over WSM radio (650), complete with spot commercials. Acquaintance with a performer or an Opry official may get you a seat on the stage right behind the spotlight. Since the Opry first went on the air in 1925 as the WSM Barn Dance, the show has never missed a Saturday night broadcast. The first show begins with a warm-up at 6:05 P.M. and stays on the air until 9:00 P.M.; the second show begins at 9:30 and ends at midnight. There's also a Saturday matinee. The stars are very accessible.

The theme park is worth several hours of your time. The grounds, beautifully landscaped with flowers and trees, are made up of eight different areas. Each has live entertainment, rides, games, shops, restaurants, and concessions. The *General Jackson Showboat* takes visitors on tours of the Cumberland River, which borders the park. The newest addition to the park is the Chevrolet/GEO Celebrity Theater, which features a nostalgic rock 'n' roll show.

Union Station

1001 Broadway
Nashville, Tennessee 37203
615-726-1001
800-331-2123
Fax: 615-248-3554

Owner: Grand Heritage Hotels
Accommodations: 112 rooms and 14 suites (all with private baths)
Rates: $75–$140
Payment: All major credit cards
Children: Welcome
Pets: Not allowed
Smoking: Allowed
Open: Year-round

Thousands of travelers have been reunited with friends and loved ones within the passages of this former railroad station, a

1900 Richardsonian Romanesque limestone building topped with gables and a clock tower and known for its magnificent vaulted stained glass ceiling. Restored beyond the beauty of its original grandeur, Union Station features 24-karat gold leaf on the decorative friezes of the lobby, original tile floors, mahogany and brass accents, and the time-treasured wall clock that passengers used to set their watches.

Guest rooms have been carved out of the vast space of the building, and some even look like showrooms through the big arched window enclosures. Privacy is guaranteed, however, by the use the heavy draperies. The hotel offers two outstanding restaurants—Greco's on Broadway, an Italian garden café, and Arthur's, a four-star gourmet restaurant featuring such delights as roast rack of spring lamb, pinwheels of salmon royale, and tournedos of beef. There's also a shop in the lobby where you can buy coffee, soft drinks, and mouth-watering chocolate chip cookies. A pianist often entertains in the grand lobby during cocktail hour. The hotel can accommodate small groups in rooms that still hold yesteryear's charms.

New Orleans

The Delta Queen
Robin Street Wharf
New Orleans, Louisiana 70130-1890
504-586-0631
800-543-1949
Fax: 504-585-0630

Owner: Delta Queen Steamboat Company
Accommodations: 88 rooms and 26 suites (all with private
  baths, 88 with showers)
Rates: $350–$1,150 per person for two nights; $1,950–$6,760
  per person for 12 nights
Included: Accommodations, five meals a day, and
  entertainment
Payment: All major credit cards
Children: Welcome
Pets: Not allowed
Smoking: Prohibited in guest rooms and dining room
Open: February–December

Everyone departing on the *Delta Queen* gets a big send-off from
the dock in New Orleans, complete with calliope music, Dixie-
land jazz, food, and drinks. It's all a preview of the good times
to be had during the three-night, seven-night, or twelve-night
journeys up the mighty Mississippi. The river trips have been
enjoyed since 1890, the year the line was founded by Captain
Gordon C. Greene and his wife, Mary. (The journey to Vicksburg takes a week.) The company also travels the Ohio, Cumberland, and Tennessee rivers.

The *Delta Queen* and her sister, the *Mississippi Queen,* are
the only two steam-powered paddlewheelers that offer overnight accommodations. Furthermore, the *Delta Queen,* which
dates to 1926, is the only authentic, fully restored overnight
steamboat in the world.

The nightly entertainment on board is sometimes heralded
under a particular theme, and there is riverboat gambling when
the vessel pulls into a port where it is allowed—just as in the

good old days. Gambling has been made legal recently in a number of states through which the boat passes. The wheel house is always open for tours. There are plenty of places for unwinding, a favorite being the Texas Bar, a paneled room overlooking the water.

Guest quarters are small but luxurious. Owned by the Delta Queen Steamboat Company, the boat has been completely refurbished in recent years. It features polished brass, hand-rubbed oak paneling, Tiffany stained glass, and soft velvet upholstery. Even the hardwood floors, made of Siamese bark, have been polished to their original luster. The boat was designated a National Historic Landmark in 1989.

The *Delta Queen* began its career as a shuttle between Sacramento and San Francisco. Following the end of World War II, it was towed more than 5,000 miles along the Pacific Coast, through the Panama Canal, and up the Gulf of Mexico to New Orleans and then on to Cincinnati, where it was disassembled for restoration in Pittsburgh. It has been traveling the inland waterways since 1948. You can sleep in rooms once occupied by world-famous figures. Room 340, noted for its oak paneling, is where President Jimmy Carter slept in 1979, while his daughter Amy occupied the adjoining room, number 338. The actress Helen Hayes slept in Room 103, and Princess Margaret occupied the Robert E. Lee Room, No. 119, which features a large bed, a clawfoot tub, and three windows (definitely a luxury). Five meals a day are served aboard the boat, with service like that on a cruise ship.

Hotel Maison de Ville and the Audubon Cottages
727 Rue Toulouse
New Orleans, Louisiana 70130
504-561-5858
800-634-1600
Fax: 504-561-5858

Owner: Lancaster Hotel Group
Managing Director: Alvin P. Danner
Accommodations: 16 rooms and 7 cottages (all with private baths)
Rates: $130–$385
Included: Continental breakfast; afternoon port, sherry, and tea; overnight shoeshine
Payment: All major credit cards
Children: 13 and older welcome

Pets: Not encouraged
Smoking: Nonsmoking rooms available
Open: Year-round

Playwright Tennessee Williams completed *A Streetcar Named Desire* while staying in Room 9 at the Hotel Maison de Ville. Dick Cavett, Cissy Spacek, and Jason Robards also slept here. Another claim to fame is the hotel's Bistro, voted the best bistro-style restaurant in the city by Zagat's restaurant guide and among the top ten restaurants by local critics. Parisian in style, with dark red interior and white tablecloths, it offers a variety of reasonably priced delicacies such as steamed mussels with basil cream and grilled rabbit pasta with white beans and tomato. Another distinction is the hotel's membership in Small Luxury Hotels of the World.

Several rooms have been renovated over the past year, and others are scheduled to get a facelift. Guests have a choice of accommodations—rooms in the main house, suites, and the Audubon Cottages, named for the American artist who occupied Cottage One while working on *Birds of America*. The rooms in the main house, which was built in 1743 by pharmacist Antoine Peychaud (inventor of the cocktail), are furnished with antiques, four-poster beds, and period paintings. The garçonnaire rooms in the former slave quarters are less formal. Rooms on Rue Toulouse tend to be a little noisy, but that's considered part of the atmosphere. A quieter choice is the Audubon Cottages, which date to 1788 and are located a block and a half away on Rue Dauphine. Each contains a living room, kitchenette (stocked with soft drinks and juice), bedroom, bath, and private courtyard.

Great attention is given to service at Maison de Ville. If you leave your shoes outside your door in the evening, you'll find them polished the next morning. A Continental breakfast is delivered on a silver tray to your room along with a newspaper, and later in the day the hotel provides complimentary tea, port, and sherry. The concierge will even arrange carriage rides and breakfast from Brennan's delivered to your door.

Hotel Villa Convento

616 Ursulines
New Orleans, Louisiana 70116
504-522-1793
Fax: 504-524-1902

Innkeepers: Warren, Lela, and Larry Campo
Accommodations: 23 rooms and 2 suites (all with private baths)
Rates: $54–$95, plus $10 for each additional person and $7 a
  day for parking
Included: Continental breakfast
Payment: All major credit cards
Children: 8 and older welcome
Pets: Not allowed
Smoking: Allowed
Open: Year-round

Built in 1840 of red brick, this three-story Creole townhouse,
with lacy wrought-iron railings in the heart of the Vieux Carré
is located on the original site of the Ursuline convent. The
Campos, who have been in the retail and wholesale music business for forty years in the city, restored it in 1982 to accommodate World's Fair visitors. The family members take time out
from their professions and many hobbies to share time with
guests. Warren, a professional musician who loves sailing, and
Lela, who judges flower shows, have traveled the continent in
their Air Stream trailer. Their son Larry, an accountant and
boating enthusiast, is also involved in the operation.

The Campos are always willing to share inside information
about the best restaurants and places to go in the city they love.
Guests may park their cars at a garage two blocks from the hotel
and then walk anywhere in the French Quarter. The Continental breakfast, served in the courtyard each day, features freshly
baked croissants and dark roasted coffee with a touch of
chicory.

The guest rooms, now being restored to expose their brick
walls, are furnished in Colonial-style hotel furniture; each has a
telephone and a television. The inn also offers two family suites
with queen-size beds as well as two lofts with twin beds.

Melrose Mansion

937 Esplanade Avenue
New Orleans, Louisiana 70116
504-944-2255
Fax: 504-945-1794

Innkeepers: Melvin and Rosemary Jones
Accommodations: 4 rooms (all with private baths) and 4
  suites (all with whirlpool baths)
Rates: $195–$395
Included: Full breakfast
Payment: Major credit cards; personal checks

Children: Limited
Pets: Not allowed
Smoking: Limited
Open: Year-round

The Melrose Mansion looks like something out of a movie—proudly standing on the corner of Esplanade and Burgundy, its three-story Gothic tower and side verandahs all gleaming with white paint, accented with dark green shutters, all brightly lit, ready and waiting to receive guests. Those who fly into the city will be met by the chauffeur-driven black limousine, distinguished by the license plate that reads Melrose. Others will not feel any less welcome, for the butler greets everyone at the front door and then offers a complimentary drink (a ritual practically any time of day in New Orleans).

Owners Mel and Rosemary Jones bought the house not knowing what they would do with it. But it wasn't long before they knew that the house had a special destiny—to be a bed-and-breakfast inn. They had always enjoyed entertaining at their home in northern Alabama, so innkeeping seemed the right thing to do in their retirement. It was their first experience with an old house, but Mel's many years spent working on new construction paid off. Built in 1884, the Gothic Victorian mansion had good design with unusual angles, 14-foot ceilings, bay windows, and heart pine flooring. The restoration took several months and was finally completed in 1989.

The Joneses have left no details to the imagination. Every room has been carefully designed to give it the optimum appearance and usage, and the result is nothing short of breathtaking. All the fabrics and furnishings were carefully chosen and coordinated by Rosemary, who bought all the antiques in the New Orleans area. Though there's not a bad room in the house, the one most often suggested for honeymooners and dignitaries is the Donecio Suite. (Mrs. Lady Bird Johnson was the inn's first guest and the first person to stay in the elegant room.) The suite features five windows draped in lacy curtains, which open out onto the balcony overlooking Esplanade. It also has a Jacuzzi.

Guests are served a full Creole breakfast in the formal dining room; they may have room service or eat outside. Featured items include fresh fruit, home-baked bread, and various hot entrees. Guests have use of the entire house, the tropical patio, and the swimming pool. The bar is always open, and drinks are complimentary. The inn is within easy walking distance to New Orleans' many fine restaurants and shops, and the Joneses are always happy to make suggestions, usually during the afternoon cocktail hour.

The Mississippi Queen
Robin Street Wharf
New Orleans, Louisiana 70130-1890
504-586-0631
800-543-1949
Fax: 504-585-0630

Owner: Delta Queen Steamboat Company
Accommodations: 195 rooms and 26 suites (all with private baths, 195 with showers)
Rates: $350–$1,150 per person for two nights; $1,950–$6,760 per person for 12 nights
Included: Accommodations, five meals a day, entertainment
Payment: All major credit cards
Children: Welcome
Pets: Not allowed
Smoking: Allowed
Open: February–December

Built in 1976 in the style of the old paddle wheelers, the *Mississippi Queen* is the sister boat to the *Delta Queen*. Both vessels travel the Mississippi, Cumberland, Tennessee, and Ohio rivers. Trips on the *Mississippi Queen,* lasting from two to twelve days, are fun from departure to disembarkation.

As on the *Delta Queen,* guests can enjoy nightly entertainment and gambling in ports where it is allowed. The *Mississippi Queen* is the largest steamboat ever built. It has seven decks, a calliope for send-offs, and a giant red paddle wheel. It is the largest, most luxurious steamboat on American rivers. The 382-foot-long, 68-foot-wide, seven-story vessel is decorated in a Victorian motif but has every modern convenience, including a gym, swimming pool, shuffleboard court, movie theater, library, and gift shop.

Guest rooms are very elegant, with great river views (especially in the suites), brass appointments, and amenities and service second to none. Cabins feature custom-made Victorian bedspreads and dust ruffles and framed prints of steamboat art. Staterooms have individual climate controls and telephones. The Grand Salon, where passengers congregate for conversation, is furnished in white wicker. Guests enjoy fine dining and piano music in the Dining Salon.

The Ponchartrain Hotel
2031 St. Charles Avenue
New Orleans, Louisiana 70140
504-524-0581
800-777-6193
Fax: 504-529-1165

Management: Grand Heritage Hotels
Accommodations: 60 rooms and 40 suites (all with private
    baths, some with Jacuzzis)
Rates: $125–$800
Payment: All major credit cards
Children: Welcome
Pets: Not allowed
Smoking: Smoking and nonsmoking rooms
Open: Year-round

2031 St. Charles Avenue is one of the most prestigious addresses
in New Orleans, and for many years it was the address for
permanent residents of the Ponchartrain Hotel, including one
of its builders, E. Lyle Aschaffenburg, who died in 1980.
Famous guests have included Beverly Sills and Richard Burton.
In recent years the Garden District property has become accessible to more people, having been transformed again into a
small luxury hotel in the style of elegant European hotels.

The hotel was built in 1927, on the eve of the Great Depression, and has offered continuous service to guests since then. It
was purchased from the Aschaffenburg family in 1987 by
David Burroughs and Associates and restored to its original
charm. Rooms and suites are extra large; some of the suites have
a parlor, large study, dining area, refrigerator, and wet bar. All
the furnishings are either antiques or fine reproductions. The
hotel's location on the St. Charles streetcar line adds to its
charm and makes it a five-minute trip to the French Quarter or
the central business district. (The streetcar runs from early
morning until late at night.)

The hotel's Caribbean Room is famous for its Creole Provençal cuisine, developed in the 1940s by Thelma Walker and
Nathanael Burton and continuing under chef Patrick Schellen-
berg, who hails from Lyons, France. Casual breakfasts and
lunches are offered in the Ponchartrain Café, known for its
homemade blueberry muffins. The walls of the Caribbean
Room and the Bayou bar feature paintings of the Louisiana
bayous.

With the acquisition and renovation of the adjacent Smith's

Drugstore, converted to a conference center, the Ponchartrain now caters to small groups.

Royal Sonesta Hotel
300 Bourbon Street
New Orleans, Louisiana 70140
504-586-0300
800-SONESTA
Fax: 504-586-0335

President/general manager: Hans W. Wandfluh
Accommodations: 468 rooms and 32 suites (all with private baths)
Rates: $135–$850
Payment: All major credit cards
Children: Under 18 free in room with parents
Pets: Boarding arrangements available
Smoking: Nonsmoking rooms available
Open: Year-round

Take your pick of fun-filled Bourbon Street or the inside court-yard at this New Orleans establishment in the heart of the French Quarter. Whatever side you choose, you'll be enter-tained, because you'll be in the midst of all the action. (You should catch lots of beads and doubloons during Mardi Gras.) The hotel isn't centuries old, having been built in 1967, but it's made to look that way. The service is based on tried-and-true traditions of hospitality, and if it seems a bit European, it proba-bly is. Hans Wandfluh, president and general manager, is a native of Spies, Switzerland, with many years' experience in the hotel industry in Europe. (The hotel is also affiliated with Son-esta International Hotels.)

The European influence is apparent in the elegant public rooms, the attentive service, and the cuisine. Guests enter the gleaming marble lobby, with its 19th-century fountain center-piece, polished brass fixtures, and splashes of pink shell and seafoam green. The guest rooms vary in decor but are consist-ent in the quality of wallcovers, carpeting, and furniture. In addition to the regular rooms are several types of suites — petit suites, split levels, a Honeymoon Suite, a Presidential Suite, and others. Guests have a choice of several dining experiences within the hotel — Begue's, which features Creole and French cuisine and serves three meals a day, and the Desire Oyster Bar and Bistro, a casual setting on Bourbon Street offering fresh seafood and poboys, a local specialty. (Of course, hundreds of wonderful restaurants are just a few steps away from the Royal

Sonesta.) There are several places of entertainment in the hotel —Can Can Cabaret (a live Parisian can can revue), Le Booze, the Daiquiri Shop, the Mystick Den Lounge, and the Quarter Deck Bar at the pool—in addition to all the Bourbon Street establishments.

The Royal Sonesta offers just about every kind of amenity you can imagine—from nightly turndowns to private concierge service to an outdoor pool. A fitness room, covered parking garage, valet service, room service, executive business center, and on-site travel agent are but a few of the other services available. The hotel is also an ideal place for meetings because of its location and amenities. Guests staying in the Tower get morning coffee and croissants, a daily newspaper, afternoon sherry and port, and sweets.

St. Charles Guest House Bed and Breakfast
1748 Prytania Street
New Orleans, Louisiana 70130
504-523-6556

Innkeepers: Dennis and Joanne Hilton
Accommodations: 36 rooms (22 with private baths, 14 with shared baths)
Rates: $25–$65
Included: Continental breakfast; beverages
Payment: American Express, MasterCard, Visa
Children: Welcome; rollaways available
Pets: Not allowed
Smoking: Allowed on decks and verandahs
Open: Year-round

Located in the Garden District just a block from the St. Charles streetcar line, this guest house is the best bargain in town. It's convenient, clean, and affordable, and the innkeepers and staff are friendly and hospitable. Granted, it's not in the same category as some of the four-and five-star properties in town, but the inn is definitely a great alternative. And the money you save on lodging you'll be able to spend on dinner at Commander's Place or breakfast at Brennan's. The St. Charles Guest House is about as close to a European guest house as you're ever going to get in this country.

New Orleans' first bed-and-breakfast inn, the St. Charles offers a number of rooms with private baths and some with shared baths (the less expensive ones share a bath). The decor is nothing to write home about, but it has a comfortable feeling—much like the experience you have at Aunt Belle's or

Grandma's. The backpacker rooms and Cajun cabins are a steal. Owners Dennis and Joanne Hilton call the decor "sweet and simple, not fancy, but cute." The rooms are in four contiguous buildings, constructed between 1850 and 1910, and the owners have access to homes that are ideal for families and are available for rent.

A Continental breakfast is served in the dining room, and you may enjoy it at your leisure. You may also help yourself to coffee and tea in the afternoon. When the humidity gets too high, you may cool off in the swimming pool or relax with a book on the deck under the banana tree. The inn has a well-stocked library.

Naturals at innkeeping, the Hiltons take a lot of pride in offering genuine southern hospitality. They'll gladly arrange swamp tours and picnics, line up a car, or make dinner reservations. They've even prepared a survival manual for getting around the city, complete with tips on city tours, places to eat, and riding the streetcar. The inn is only a 10-minute ride from the French Quarter. According to the Hiltons, the St. Charles Guest House is favored by writers, performers, academics, and seasoned travelers—they've all given it rave reviews in the guest register.

Soniat House

1133 Chartres Street
New Orleans, Louisiana 70116
504-522-0570
800-544-8808
Fax: 504-522-7208

Innkeepers: Rodney and Frances Smith
Accommodations: 18 rooms and 6 suites (all with private baths, 7 with Jacuzzis)
Rates: $110–$205
Included: Continental breakfast
Payment: Major credit cards
Children: Welcome
Pets: Not encouraged
Smoking: Allowed in designated areas
Open: Year-round

If you're looking for a small European-style hotel in the French Quarter that takes pride in offering service, you won't go wrong at Soniat House. It's historic, elegant, charming, convenient, personal, and service-oriented. In fact, you'll even forget it is a hotel because it is so much like a home.

Owners Rodney and Frances Smith, who formerly worked in fashion and retailing, want it that way. They've combined an 1830 Creole house and a turn-of-the-century boarding house into one of the city's finest hotels. You enter the older building through the shuttered doors on Chartres Street into the brick paved carriage way, which leads to the lush courtyard in the center. The Smiths won an award in 1983 for the restoration; the inn is a member of Historic Hotels of America.

To the left of the carriage way is the reception area, where you are greeted by the staff and offered a drink before being escorted to your room. The staff to guest ratio is one to one, so you'll never have to wait for anything. And Soniat House isn't the type of place that gets street traffic (it's open only to guests and their friends), so you'll feel perfectly safe. The hotel is only four blocks from Jackson Square, making it easy to walk to restaurants, shops, the river, and attractions.

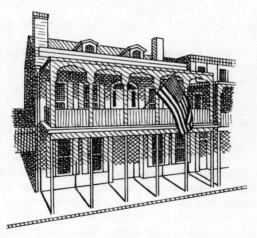

Guests are welcome to use the well-stocked honor bar at any time. Though the hotel doesn't operate a restaurant, it offers room service, as well as concierge service, 24 hours a day. Valet parking, cleaning and laundry, safe-deposit boxes, umbrellas, and evening turndown service are available.

The rooms at Soniat House are delightful (ask Paul Newman, who slept here). Some have balconies, and several open onto the courtyard. Three have fireplaces, and seven feature Jacuzzis. All are furnished in fine Louisiana, French, and English antiques, collected by the Smiths during their travels all over the world. The drapery and upholstery fabrics were custom-made in France, and the bed linens are of the finest quality. Original artwork by contemporary New Orleans artists complements the furnishings. All the guest rooms are equipped with telephones, radios, and televisions, plus extras such as goose down pillows and Crabtree and Evelyn amenities.

A Continental breakfast consisting of fresh, squeezed orange juice, hot biscuits with homemade strawberry preserves, and café au lait is served on a silver tray. It can be delivered to your room, your balcony, or the courtyard.

Windsor Court Hotel New Orleans

300 Gravier Street
New Orleans, Louisiana 70130-1035
504-523-6000
800-262-2662
Fax: 504-596-4513
Telex: 784060

Owner: Orient Express Hotels
Accommodations: 56 rooms and 254 suites (all with private baths)
Rates: $215–$750; summer and Christmas discounts available
Payment: Major credit cards
Children: Welcome
Pets: Not allowed
Smoking: Nonsmoking floors
Open: Year-round

One of the in things to do in New Orleans these days is to have tea at Windsor Court—British, of course, as the hotel name suggests. It's offered every afternoon in Le Salon, along with live chamber music, and you need an advance reservation. Afternoon tea isn't the only English experience offered in the European-style hotel; everything about it is English-inspired. The Grill Room, an award-winning restaurant, is similar to the Grill in London's Savoy. The Gallery, which actually is meeting space on the fourth floor, has a fine display of English seascapes, and works by 17th-, 18th-, and 19th-century masters—Reynolds, Gainsborough, Huysman, and others—are featured throughout the hotel. There's also a portrait of Edward VIII, Prince of Wales, in a foyer near the Polo Lounge. Two members of the royal family—Princesses Margaret and Anne—have already paid calls to the hotel, which opened in 1987.

Guest rooms (most are suites) are decorated in English sporting and floral themes. All the suites feature a separate living room, a small kitchen or wet bar, a European mini-bar, a bidet, and a dressing room adjoining the bedroom and bathroom.

Each evening guests receive turndown service with imported chocolates. All guests are provided with terrycloth robes and Crabtree and Evelyn toiletries.

Something of a contemporary castle surrounding a lush courtyard, the 23-story hexagonal hotel, in the heart of the New Orleans business district near the French Quarter, is built of rose-colored granite and bronze-tinted glass. Built in 1984, it was renovated in 1990–1991. The hotel has a fitness center and a 75-foot swimming pool with an underwater sound system, valet parking, massage service, 24-hour room service, valet, and concierge. With its multilingual staff, the hotel caters to groups with meeting space and secretarial and fax services.

Windsor Court, a member of Preferred Hotels Worldwide and Leading Hotels of the World, was purchased by Orient Express Hotels in the fall of 1991. In its short history, it has accumulated a mountain of awards from more than ten magazines and travel associations. In 1989 and 1990, *Condé Nast Traveler* rated it one of the top ten hotels in the world, and for three consecutive years (1989–1991) it was highly rated by the "Lifestyles of the Rich and Famous" television program. The hotel was built by James Coleman, Sr., a New Orleans developer, at the suggestion of his son, who spent two years studying in England.

New York

The Algonquin
59 West 44th Street
New York, New York 10036
212-840-6800
800-548-0345

Proprietors: Caesar Park Hotel America, Inc., Aoki
    Corporation
General Manager: Bodo Lemke
Accommodations: 165 rooms, including 23 suites
Rates: $170–$180; suites, $300; lower rates on weekends
Included: Weekend parking; welcome drink
Added: $25 each additional guest; 19.25% tax
Payment: Major credit cards
Children: Welcome
Pets: Not allowed
Smoking: 1 nonsmoking floor
Open: Year-round

In August 1991 the Algonquin completed a several-year $20 million restoration, its most thorough effort since it was built in 1902. The fame of this institution and of the Round Table commenced after the scalloped red brick and limestone building was purchased by Frank Case, a former employee, in 1907. (During his years as an employee, Case suggested changing the hotel's name from Puritan to Algonquin to denote strength and pioneerism.)

Case extended his hospitality and credit to his favorite patrons, writers and actors including Douglas Fairbanks, Sr., and H. L. Mencken. The group grew, and Case accommodated them at a round table in the Oak Room, providing celery and popovers as fodder to fuel the intellectual fires. By the mid-1920s, the Round Tablers comprised a group of about thirty literati, including such nobles as Dorothy Parker, George S. Kaufman, Edna Ferber, Ring Lardner, Robert Benchley, and Harold Ross, who went on to use the fruits of the Round Table discussions as editor of *The New Yorker*. Evidence of those days is found in Al Hirschfeld's drawings throughout the hotel and in copies of *The New Yorker,* supplied in every room.

The reverence displayed by Ben and Mary Bodne during their thirty years of ownership was respected by the new owners during the recent renovation, begun in 1987. The original oak woodwork of the Edwardian lobby, including the arched doorways, supporting beams, and Corinthian capitals, has been restored to its former luster, as have the plaster dentil moldings, the painted glass sconces, and even the furnishings. Today the lobby is a favorite place for afternoon tea, cocktails, and entertainment. The Rose Room, the feminine alternative for afternoon and evening dining, features rose-colored damask walls and banquettes, all under an Austrian crystal chandelier. Last, the Oak Room, with its clubby masculine feel and dark paneled walls, is the bastion of New York City hotel cabaret life, matched only at the Carlyle.

The twelve floors of rooms are intimately configured, decorated with original art depicting old New York, Round Tablers, and Algonquin legends. Because of the hotel's landmark status, it was allowed to retain the original open staircase that ascends the center of the building, of white wrought iron and marble. Accommodations are fresh and immaculate. While the standard rooms are quite small, and the smaller rooms cramped, the suites are a nice size and well worth the investment. Or try the standard center rooms with window seats below curved bay windows. Most of the Algonquin's original Edwardian furnishings have been either refinished or reproduced, set into schemes of peachy rose, mint green, or light blue, with solid colored walls, very high ceilings, and floral spreads matching structured drapes. The suites have striped paper in the bedrooms accenting the chintz. The baths are gleaming white, with prints of flowers, and offer Caswell and Massey amenities, a sewing kit, and a hair dryer.

The Box Tree
250 East 49th Street
New York, New York 10017
212-593-9810

Proprietor: Augustin V. Paege
General Manager: Nina Fuenmayor
Accommodations: 12 suites, all with private bath
Rates: $270–$300, including $100 credit toward dinner
Included: Continental breakfast
Minimum stay: None

Payment: American Express
Children: Allowed
Pets: Allowed
Smoking: Not allowed in rooms
Open: Year-round

Manhattanites have been preparing for the urban Box Tree for years. Its 20-year-old upstate relative in Purdys, 40 miles north, is a romantic guest house and culinary refuge. Since 1982, the Box Tree Restaurant has prepared wondrous dinners, but it began welcoming guests only in 1989. However much one readies for the Box Tree experience, it is nevertheless quite a stunning surprise: romantic, fantastic, whimsical. The brownstone on East 49th Street, between Second and Third Avenues, is marked by a verdigris marquee and a scripted sign adorned in gold leaves. Inside is an interior landscape created by Mr. Paege, the result of a lifetime of collecting and impeccable, eclectic, wondrous taste. Guests enter a patterned brick foyer. Among the curiosities are a Louis XIII tufted leather wing chair with a back that evolves into a hood. Two 18th-century Italian porcelain figures support a mantel designed specifically for the setting.

A series of intimate dining rooms on the lower two floors adds to the sense of evolution at the Box Tree, each scene capturing the imagination, proceeding quickly into another realm. The Music dining room has reproduction Louis XIII chairs covered in Aubusson muted tapestry, backlit by a turn-of-the-century stained glass window. Here, the magnificent fireplace mantel is supported by wide terra cotta columns inset with colored glass. Yet another dining room, the Marie Antoinette, looks lifted from Versailles, with lavish gilded millwork and molding, as well as candelabras and chandelier. Most masterful is the Gaudi-inspired staircase, sculpted by collaborator David Mills, which connects the two levels of dining rooms.

Each of the twelve suites on several floors above and in the adjacent brownstone is a private boudoir, a world unto itself, derivative of different countries, diminutive versions of palaces in China, Egypt, or France. The trompe l'oeil painted doors reflect their respective interior decor, painted by decorative artist Heinz Simon, who crafted much of the Purdys Box Tree. Each has a sitting area facing a working gas fireplace. The uppermost high-ceilinged suite has a malachite fireplace. The Chinese Suite has lacquered tables and chairs accented with Chinese porcelain filled with plants or atop tables. The Japanese Suite has Mackintosh English antiques. The King Boris of Bulgaria Room is filled with Louis XVI gilt. Horizontal gilded millwork decorates the walls in the Consulate Suite, with a green marble fireplace. The Irish linens have a 600-thread count. The amenities are by Guerlain.

Guests may either focus on the precious individual treasures and antiquities which decorate the inn or revel in the whirl-wind, atmospheric changes from room to room. It's a won-drous, magical place. Be sure to come back from shopping for high tea, a tradition seemingly invented for this setting, with fresh-baked delicacies made to be eaten in this lavish setting.

The Carlyle

Madison Avenue at 76th Street
New York, New York 10021
212-744-1600
800-227-5737
Fax: 212-717-4682

Proprietor: Carlyle Management Company
General Manager: Daniel Camp
Accommodations: 190 guest rooms and suites
Rates: $275–$350; suites, $500–$1,200
Added: $25 each additional guest; 19.25% tax
Payment: Major credit cards
Children: Welcome
Pets: Allowed
Smoking: Allowed
Open: Year-round

The Carlyle has consistently offered the highest level of over-night accommodations longer than any other New York City hotel. It was completed in 1931 by architects Bien & Prince, a square building culminating in a tall blanched-brick 35-story tower with a recognizable gilded crown, recipient of the Mobil Five Star award for more than twenty consecutive years. As established as it is in history, the Carlyle has kept up nicely with its modern competitors, with a new, gorgeous state-of-the-art fitness center, as well as constant refurbishment which redeco-rates the rooms every three years.

The Carlyle is just a block from Central Park and Museum Mile and Madison Avenue's finest galleries and boutiques. Inside, it is a world unto itself. One of its most wonderful fea-tures is Bemelmans Bar, a gallery of murals painted by Austrian artist Ludwig Bemelmans, author and illustrator of the Made-line books that have charmed generations of children. When he and his wife, Madeline, lived in the Carlyle in 1946–47, Bemelmans painted the murals, derived from his whimsical characters and memories of the monkeys in the Central Park Zoo.

Bemelmans spills into the Gallery, an intimate space like a genie's bottle, a plush re-creation of the Turkish Topkapi Palace where guests have tea and champagne suppers. The Café Carlyle is the forum for the much-loved music of Bobby Short, who has charmed audiences here for 26 years, as well as other cabaret entertainers, a lavish environment for the mural of French artist Vertes. The Carlyle Restaurant is a wondrously beautiful setting for its highly rated food. Banquettes, oil paintings, and a centerpiece five-foot floral arrangement contribute to the salon feel. In addition to renowned dining, the Carlyle wine cellar has an astounding 25,000 bottles.

Guests enter at 76th Street and descend to a lobby rich with Gobelin tapestries, black and white marble flooring, whose magnificent Aubusson antique carpets are lifted for a lighter look in warmer months. Discreet elevator operators politely take guests to their floor. The rooms are all unique in configuration and design. Dorothy Draper was the hotel's original decorator, and today Mark Hampton and his team follow in her footsteps. Uniquely, some rooms have original exposed wood flooring, covered with needlepoint and Oriental carpets. Audubon prints, architectural Piranesi engravings, hunt pictures, and English country scenes decorate the walls. The rooms have quite different looks: some in traditional chintz, others in bold oranges or hunter greens. The beds might have wood or upholstered headboards, the dressers may have antique marble tops supporting Chinese porcelain lamps—all extremely classic in the vein of the Carlyle's residential neighbors. All rooms have televisions, VCRs, stereos, and CD players. The marble baths include phones, and all have whirlpool tubs. As well, every room is equipped with its own fax.

The Carlyle's new fitness center is intimate, private, and beautifully appointed, with Lalique crystal doors, an atrium skylight, serene Canadian maple walls, French limestone, and English green slate tiles. In addition to cardiovascular equipment, there are saunas and steam rooms as well as private massage.

Despite its stature as perhaps the city's most famous grand old hotel, the Carlyle is a welcoming, nonstuffy place. Service is impeccable but approachable, understated without being cold, elegant but not pretentious.

Essex House

160 Central Park South
New York, New York 10019
212-247-0300
800-645-5687

Proprietor: Nikko Hotels International
General Manager: Wolf Walther
Accommodations: 591 rooms, including 61 suites
Rates: $265–$315; weekends, $185–$235; suites, $285–$850
Added: $25 each additional guest; 19.25% tax
Payment: Major credit cards
Children: Welcome, under 18 free
Pets: Not allowed
Smoking: Nonsmoking floors
Open: Year-round

Originally built in 1931 as the city's largest and tallest hotel, Sayville Towers, as the Essex House was called, opened with 1,286 rooms and such luxurious, modern amenities as a radio and private bath in every room. Over the years, the Essex sadly declined. Nikko Hotels bought the dowager in 1989 and undertook a $75 million renovation, completed in September 1991.

The Essex House was redesigned to evoke a nostalgia for the New York City of the thirties: the days of black and white balls, big bands, glamorous movie stars, and art deco extravagance. Even the location conjures up images of old New York, as the shoppers and hansom cabs whisk by on Central Park South.

There is a great deal of gilt at the Essex House: on the exterior and inside. Guests enter to a grand-scale lobby of brown and white parquet floors and coffered ceilings supported by heavy black pillars. To the left is Café Botanica, serving three meals and light California fare. The wonderful room has a terrace area facing Central Park South through floor-to-ceiling Palladian windows, with wicker and rattan chairs, chintz cushions, and verdigris sconces. In a tribute to its new owners, Ben Kay offers fabulous traditional Japanese breakfasts. Journeys is the Old World bar with the feel of an English club.

The high point of the public spaces is Les Célébrités, showcase for the French cuisine (with Japanese influences) of the chef Christian Delouvrier and a gallery for the artwork of well-known celebrities like Pierce Brosnan, James Dean, Gene Hackman, Elke Sommer, and Billy Dee Williams, among others. The paintings are proudly displayed on the walls, viewed from tapestried banquettes and comfortable chairs in a plush, patterned environment.

Guests proceed up to rooms on 41 floors via original etched brass elevator doors, which open to reveal a painted foyer on each floor. The decor is as traditional as the hotel is art deco, though the colors are bright and fresh, if predictable. Fine features are extremely large closets, pristine gray marble baths with large soaking tubs, phones, scales, eyelet curtains and tassel tiebacks. Chintz and stripes and bold carpets brighten the rooms, against a backdrop of traditional Chippendale furniture.

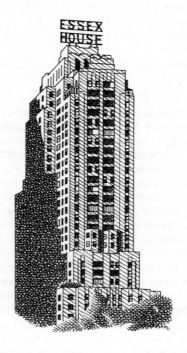

Nikko thought of its guests at work and at play. They designed a full business center, including computers and even a Japanese word processor. For play, the private health club and spa features a good amount of cardiovascular equipment and two types of massage overseen by a full staff.

The staff are extremely enthusiastic about their new place in New York and solicitous and respectful of the Japanese roots of the Nikko influence.

The Helmsley Palace
455 Madison Avenue
New York, New York 10022
212-888-7000
800-221-4982
Fax: 212-355-0820

Proprietor: The Helmsley Corporation
General Manager: Kevin Malloy
Accommodations: 1,060 rooms, including 160 suites
Rates: $255–$325; suites, $395–$2,500
Added: $40 each additional guest; 19.25% tax
Payment: Major credit cards
Children: Welcome
Pets: Not allowed
Smoking: 3 of 53 floors nonsmoking
Open: Year-round

The Helmsley Palace has some wonderful attributes—other than its notorious matriarch—that are relatively unappreciated. A marriage of old and new, the hotel houses one of New York's finest Old World mansions alongside an efficient glass and aluminum skyscraper. A block-long carpeted corridor connects the 50th and 51st Street entrances; or guests may also enter from Madison Avenue, behind St. Patrick's Cathedral, through wrought-iron gates, past the inlaid courtyard embraced by the palatial U-shaped five-story Villard mansion.

In 1882, financier Henry Villard commissioned the architectural firm McKim, Mead, and White to design a mansion for his family; the mansion was completed three years later in the manner of the Palazzo della Cancelleria in Rome. Bought by the Helmsleys, the Villard Mansion was magnificently restored over several years, starting in 1979 while the Tower was being built. Today it houses some of the city's loveliest public spaces: the Gold Room, for afternoon tea; the Madison Room, for hors d'oeuvres and cocktails, designed by Stanford White; and the Hunt Bar. With their marble pillars and fireplaces, gold leaf, hand-painted murals, inlaid flooring, mosaic groin vaulting, and marble pocket doors, these rooms defy description. Rather, guests should make plans for a tour with historian Rupert Rodriguez or request the Treasures of the Palace walking tour.

The rose marble foyer of the Villard Mansion is flanked by two staircases going up to the highly reputed Trianon Restaurant and the Hunt Room or descending to the block-long corridor. This marks the new hotel, designed by Emery Roth & Sons architects and, on the interior, by Tom Lee Ltd. Much effort has been made to replicate the wood, moldings, and marble of the Villard mansion in the new building. Harry's Bar is part of the new space, near the 51st Street entrance and several upscale shops.

The majority of guest rooms are in the main part of the hotel on floors 5–39. The Tower rooms and suites, above to the 54th floor, have their own private concierge, check-in, and extra amenities and services. All floors have a regal red and gold carpet and gold-painted millwork on the doors. The room design features the trademark gilded and upholstered headboards, matching spreads and drapery in a framed window, with Louis XV reproduction bergères, benches, desks, and marble-top dressers. The marble baths have terry and linen towels, scales, quite complete amenities including a sewing kit, and a stool by the oversized bath vanity. The suites have additional antiques, as well as bright yellow couches and some stocked kitchens. Compared with those in older hotels, the guest rooms are missing high ceilings and crown moldings— traded for 24-hour room service, full amenities, and triple-padded carpets in a soundproofed building.

The staff is letter-perfect in etiquette and service, and guests will surely forget that they are in a thousand-room hotel.

The Lowell
28 East 63rd Street
New York, New York 10021
212-838-1400
800-221-4444
Fax: 212-319-4230

General manager: Martin Hale
Accommodations: 61 rooms, including 48 suites
Rates: $320; suites, $420–$1,500
Minimum stay: None
Added: $20 each additional guest; 19.25% tax; $2 occupancy tax
Payment: Major credit cards
Children: Allowed
Pets: Check with manager
Smoking: Allowed
Open: Year-round

Though it was built in 1928 as a residence hotel, the Lowell was purchased by its present owners in 1984. They recently invested $25 million into its renovation, returning it to the glory days when Scott and Zelda Fitzgerald, Dorothy Parker, Eugene O'Neill, and Noel Coward were regular guests.

Extremely intimate, the Lowell is the only full-service New York City hotel with fewer than 100 rooms other than SoHo's new Hotel Mercer. Unusually, it has 33 working fireplaces in its suites. While others scramble to establish unique identities, the Lowell sits comfortably in its exclusivity. As a member of the elite Relais et Châteaux, the hotel is necessarily privately owned.

The 17-story art deco landmark in patterned brick sits on 63rd Street between Madison and Park avenues, its exterior so understated as to be mistaken for a private apartment building. Guests, laden with packages from Givenchy and Ungaro around the corner, enter the very formal lobby: faux marbling and Empire parlor sets are accented by Scalamadre window treatments and upholstery in regal gold silk. The concierge sits attentively behind his Edgar Brandt desk, adjacent to the modestly sized reception desk. Behind is a pediment-shaped bookcase, which is actually a door to offices. A neoclassic mural enlivens the setting.

Guests are escorted up black lacquer elevators to their rooms, a wide assortment of layouts and variety, though assuredly appointed in the height of good taste. Thirty-three suites have working wood-burning fireplaces, and 56 accommodations have kitchens stocked with china and silver. Ten suites have private terraces. In addition, the Gym Suite has a private exercise room with a treadmill, stairmaster, weights, and even a ballet bar with a wonderful view of the Upper East Side.

The rooms are as elegant as they are understated, with an overall relaxing feel amid precious antiques and furnishings. Appointed more in the vein of a Park Avenue pied-à-terre than a standard upscale hotel, the rooms are decorated with French and Oriental furnishings, leather chairs, ormolu mirrors, 18th- and 19th-century prints, and Chinese porcelain. The original mantels and fireplaces have been restored. Some spreads are heavy woven tapestries, others are done in quilted or in muted colors. Every room has its own library with leatherbound books. Umbrellas are provided for guest use. The baths are done in rich brown Italian marble with brass fixtures and exclusive Saks Fifth Avenue amenities including a loofah, terry robes, and fresh flowers. All rooms have mini-bars, televisions, and VCRs.

Service at the Lowell is hushed, discreet, and extremely personable, as if the staff is working for the guests rather than for the hotel.

The Mark

Madison Avenue at East 77th Street
New York, New York 10021
212-744-4300
800-843-6275
Fax: 212-744-2749

Proprietors: The Rafael Group, Georg Rafael and E. William
 Judson
General manager: Raymond N. Bickson
Accommodations: 180 rooms, including 60 suites
Rates: $265–$295; suites, $450–$1,800
Minimum stay: None
Added: $20 each additional guest; 19.25% tax
Payment: Major credit cards
Children: Welcome
Pets: Check with manager
Smoking: Allowed
Open: Year-round

The Mark is a welcome addition to the traditional row of elite
Upper East Side hotels, with unique neoclassic decor and a
highly regarded restaurant. Built in 1926 and known over the
years as the Hyde Park Residence and the Madison Avenue
Hotel, the building was bought by the Rafael Group, transformed for about $35 million, and opened in April 1989. The
Mark stands proudly as the American flagship property of the
Rafael Group, launched by hotelier Georg Rafael, who spent a
decade mastering the trade with Regent International Hotels.

The entrance sits on 77th Street, between Madison and Fifth
avenues. While the building is a classic Upper East Side brick
monolith, the brightly lit glass and brass doors at the Mark
promise something new. The intimate black and white marble
lobby is a transitional space with Beidermeier furnishings,
beckoning to a visitor to relax in the library setting of Mark's
Bar or to have tea or a lavish meal at the Mark's Restaurant.

The Restaurant is a wonderful gallery of tufted circular banquettes, gossipy sets of chairs around low tables under a backlit
greenhouse ceiling, separated from an upper dining tier by
tapestried screens and a wrought-iron rail under a faux skylight, in tones of teal, burgundy, and rose. The artistry of Nor-
mandy native Philippe Boulot is described as French-inspired
cuisine moderne and has been widely praised.

Architects Pennoyer Turino P. C. and designer Mimi Russell
are responsible for the neoclassic and Italian Renaissance elements of the interior spaces. Among the pieces that set the tone

are original Piranesi prints, Gundolt wool carpeting, and plentiful and neutral tones of Italian marble. The hallways are serene spaces with classic molding, in muted grays and whites, with classic sconces. The standard guest rooms have an odd, modernish scheme of rose lacquer, though all have mini-bars, VCRs, and televisions. The suites are highly worth the upgrade, unique in decor and configuration, with handsome furnishings in muted tones, and lovely neoclassic art on the walls. All rooms feature Frette top sheets and Belgian cotton linens and down pillows.

Most attractive at the Mark are the bathrooms, which accounted for about a quarter of the restoration's budget. Either done in geometric black and white ceramic tile or in several tones of Italian marble, they are quite deluxe, with Kohler soaking tubs and freestanding showers, crystal bath grains, Molton Brown amenities, fresh flowers, and potpourri. The suites feature marble baths with bidets.

With the Carlyle across the street, the Mark tries valiantly and gracefully to rise to its competition — an exciting and tasteful addition to the new New York hotels.

The Mayfair Hotel

610 Park Avenue at 65th Street
New York, New York 10021
212-288-0800
800-223-0542
Fax: 212-737-0538

Managing director: Dario Mariotto
Accommodations: 201 rooms, including 105 suites
Rates: Rooms, $275–$410; suites, $440–$1,700
Added: $30 each additional guest; 19.25% tax
Payment: Major credit cards
Children: Welcome
Pets: Allowed
Smoking: Allowed
Open: Year-round

The Mayfair Regent is one of the few city hotels with working wood-burning fireplaces, twenty-eight of them, mostly in suites. It has been the home of Le Cirque restaurant since 1974, one of the city's culinary treasures. Other unique touches include the Mayfair's Pillow Bank, offering guests twelve kinds of pillows in addition to the four down pillows in each room — neck rolls, water pillows, facial pillows, reading wedges, and so on; free local telephone calls; complimentary chicken soup to guests with colds; and a putting green in the new fitness center. Aside from these unusual offerings, the Mayfair is a picture of a traditional, classic hotel.

The Mayfair House opened in 1925 and evolved into a residential hotel over the years, until 1978, when Regent International Hotels assumed management. A $30 million renovation was completed in 1990, at which time the public and guest rooms were redecorated, and the stunning elevators were entirely restored—though still hand-operated by attendants.

Guests enter from 65th Street between Park and Madison avenues. The reception area is thoroughly elegant with a hint of Tudor influences, arched thresholds, Palladian windows, and mirrors under painted coffered wood ceilings. The Lobby Lounge is one of the better-known aspects of the Mayfair. It was a convivial gathering spot when the hotel opened, and this tradition continues today. Guests stroll the exterior or descend several steps to the sunken inner area with tufted couches, sitting areas, floral arrangements, in lemony, sunny colors, lifted by a series of arches and colonnades.

The rooms have very traditional decor in ecrus and pastels, quite plain, with reproduction Queen Anne furnishings, and some interesting prints on the walls. While the decor is not particularly inspired, the rooms are generously sized and bright, with VCRs and televisions. The baths are very pretty, with Neutrogena, Crabtree and Evelyn, and Vitabath amenities; among the usual features of robes, dryers, and phones are linen hand towels and fresh flowers. Umbrellas are placed in every room for guest use.

The two rooms of the fitness center have bright views of Park Avenue, cardiovascular equipment, and the professionally designed putting green.

Service at the Mayfair is friendly and eager, under the watchful gaze of active director Dario Mariotti. The staff is helpful and easily approachable.

Hotel Mercer

99 Prince Street
New York, New York 10012
212-478-7878
800-285-7800
Fax: 212-478-7888

Proprietors: André Balazs and Campion Platt
General manager: Klaus Ortlieb
Accommodations: 78 rooms and suites

Rates: $220–320; suites from $435
Included: Nightly turndown service
Minimum stay: None
Added: $25 additional guest, 19.25% tax and occupancy
Payment: Major credit cards
Children: Welcome
Pets: Not allowed
Smoking: Nonsmoking rooms available
Open: Year-round

New York City's latest adventure in hoteling is the Hotel Mercer, the only first-rate overnight property between midtown and Wall Street. While its chic SoHo location is enough to call it unique, there are many aspects of this newcomer that make it remarkable, progressive, and certainly worth a special visit.

On the corner of Prince and Mercer streets, the landmark Romanesque Revival red brick edifice was built in 1898 by John Jacob Astor. Late 1992 marked its opening, a $33-million reconstruction and restoration project that was two years in the making. The prominent owners of the property are Andre Balazs and Campion Platt, who wanted to complement their successful Los Angeles property Chateau Marmont with an East Coast correlative.

While design and clout may lead a visitor to expect another Ian Shrager-type creation of lobby socializing and the hotel-as-theater, the Hotel Mercer has an identity quite its own. Balazs and Platt have a new vision of overnighting, with clean lines and open spaces, where people prefer privacy to being seen, and where understatement is the hallmark of the future.

The building is a lovely sight, sturdy and graceful, the quintessence of a SoHo warehouse. The guidepost for the restoration was a 1904 picture of the building found by the owners. The lobby is a transitional place rather than the focal point, wide, airy, and functional. The cast-iron pillars reach two stories, set off by furnishings done in spare 1930s moderne, in simple earth tones. A restaurant and a neighborhood homeopathic pharmacy share the first floor space.

The six floors of guest rooms above line ell-shaped hallways, with about sixteen rooms per floor. The rooms are furnished in the spare, masculine furnishings of the lobby, designed by the owners with Serge Becker and Calvin Tsao in muted browns, taupes, and creams. Featuring double-paned glass, the windows stretch quite high, covered with elegant Roman shades and wood-slat blinds. Under the panoramic views is a long maple desk and an upholstered window seat, strewn with throw pillows. The centerpiece beds are fitted with a crepe spread, flanked by ample lighting. Each room features a TV and VCR, as well as a full stereo, CD and cassette player. An occasional reminder of the SoHo foundation may be a cast-iron pillar in the center of the room.

Discovering that hotel guests spend most of their time in the bathroom, the owners decided to devote 40 percent of the guest space to this purpose — the true highlight of a stay at the Hotel Mercer. The lavishness is summarized in the plush pair of Frette robes offered to guests. The bedroom opens through a sliding upholstered wall unit (an Asian feature) to the capacious bath, tiled in classic mosaic-size white squares, with bold silver fixtures, a freestanding marble sink, glass-enclosed shower, and a wonderful oversize tub encased in the classic tiling. Many have bidets, and all have fresh flowers, loofah sponges, and lovely amenities. Manager Klaus Ortlieb added the inventive touch of evening soap delivery, where guests may choose from a bountiful basket of a dozen or more savons. This is one of his many unique, personable touches which will make this a hotel of impeccable service.

SoHo, the historic neighborhood in lower Manhattan between Houston and Canal streets, has long been established as the working artistic hub of New York City, the center for art galleries, studios, art dealers, antiques, chic boutiques, and cafés. The architecture of sturdy turn-of-the-century warehouse buildings makes for wonderful walking. In 1992, the city will have completed a ten-block restoration effort: the streets will be re-cobblestoned (the first time since 1938) and 33 reproduction cast-iron lampposts will be installed. Across the street from the Mercer is the new branch of the Guggenheim Museum.

Hotel Millennium

55 Church Street
New York, New York 10007
212-693-2001
800-835-2220
Fax: 212-571-2317

Proprietors: H.J. Kalikow & Co., Inc.
Vice president and managing director: Susan G. Ricci
General manager: Michael P. Doyle
Accommodations: 561 rooms with 15 suites
Rates: $245–265; deluxe corner, $315; millennium room,

$325–345; suites from $395; special weekend packages
from $150

Included: Nightly turndown service
Minimum stay: None
Added: 19.25% plus city occupancy tax
Payment: Major credit cards
Children: Welcome
Pets: Allowed
Smoking: Nonsmoking floors
Open: Year-round

The Wall Street location of this brand new 58-story hotel is an
innovative draw in a city laden with midtown properties. When
magnate Peter Kalikow decided to build a hotel on this valuable spot of land adjacent to the magnificent old AT&T building, across from old St. Paul's churchyard, few could argue with
the idea. A hotel is a precious commodity in this business
mecca. Most visiting businesspeople waste valuable time shut-
tling from midtown in rush-hour limousines. Here, guests have
only to walk across Church Street to arrive at the World Trade
Center. The hotel opened its doors in June 1992, confident in its
role as the city's newest leading business hotel.

While New York is blossoming with beaux-arts revival
hotels, and Wall Street is a museum of Old World architecture,
The Millennium makes a striking modern statement: a commanding, stark 58-story black glass rectangular tower designed
by architect Brian Principe. Starting on the eighth floor and
soaring up to 55, the guest rooms offer nonpareil views of New
York—from all the rooms, not just the suites. The Millennium
takes advantage of the narrowness of the island at Wall Street
and offers panoramic reach-out-and-touch views of the Statue
of Liberty, the World Trade Towers, the East and Hudson
Rivers, the Brooklyn and Manhattan Bridges, and sweeping
views of the cityscape to the north.

Guests enter from Church Street to the long lobby which
stretches the length of the building, between Dey and Fulton
Streets. The dramatic lobby is a freestanding two story space
lined with gleaming rosewood and pink granite. The third
floor is home to The Grille and The Connoisseur Bar, and the
upscale Taliesin Restaurant, with Frank Lloyd Wright–inspired
decor and American food with Asian and Mediterranean influences. The fourth floor is devoted to extensive meeting
space. The fifth floor will be of interest to all guests, home to
the fitness room and the 20-by-40-foot pool, housed in a glass-

roofed atrium (joining the Millennium to the old AT&T building).

The guest rooms are contemporarily furnished in soothing, muted tones of taupe, beige, and peach—not at all like the generic chintz and Chippendale of most hotels. The furniture was custom-designed in teak and curly maple, with the beds encased in wood, platform-fashion. The corners of the entertainment cabinet, desk, headboard, and dressers are rounded, and the wood is light and smooth, lending a restful feel to the rooms. A round blond marble wall mirror complements a round blond marble table, and the chairs and sofas are also rounded and cushy. The clean bathrooms are done in black marble, with a phone, dryer, and two bathrobes. While all the rooms have quite stunning views, the corner rooms are even more stupendous, with two views meeting at a corner pillar, with floor-to-ceiling windows.

Quite an exciting property, the Millennium is striving to make an indelible mark in New York's upscale hotel market. The staff has been impecccably trained in service and friendliness.

Morgans

237 Madison Avenue
New York, New York 10016
212-686-0300
800-334-3408
Fax: 212-779-8352

General manager: David Baldwin
Accommodations: 113 rooms, including 29 suites
Rates: $205–$235; suites, $275–$400 (lower rates on weekends)
Included: Continental breakfast, morning newspaper
Minimum stay: None
Added: 19.25% tax
Payment: Major credit cards
Children: Welcome
Pets: Not allowed
Smoking: 3 nonsmoking floors
Open: Year-round

The first of Ian Schrager's three New York City hotel creations, Morgans is an ultracool, postmodern, high-tech place of supreme calm and style. Today, those who want to be seen go to the Royalton. Those who don't particularly want to be seen will go to Morgans.

The hotel, with a sophisticated three-column stone exterior with 20 floors of brickwork above, has a wonderful location on 38th and Madison, just a block north of the J. P. Morgan library and residence, for which the hotel was named. It was built in 1929 as the Duane Hotel, became the Executive Hotel, and was entirely redone in 1983 by Ian Schrager, Steve Rubell, and Phil Pilevsky.

There are few hotels in the low-key residential neighborhood of Murray Hill, despite the fact that Grand Central Station is only four blocks away. Guests might pass by the doorway of Morgans, marked subtly by bellhops who look like models on a break from a shoot, dressed in double-breasted black suits and white shirts. The lobby is striking and impersonal, marked by a trompe l'oeuil black and white parquet rug, with glass and bronze wall panels soaring two stories. It's not a comfortable place, but rather encourages guests to their rooms, reiterating the theme of privacy that prevails at the hotel.

Morgans created quite a stir when it opened as the city's first modern boutique hotel in 1984. French designer Andree Putman designed the interior: from the low-profile beds, to soothing window seats under wooden slat blinds, to the fabulous baths, with poured granite floors, stainless steel surgical sinks, and floor-to-ceiling glass-enclosed showers (made from bus stop enclosures), bordered in black and white parquet tiling. Robert Mapplethorpe was commissioned to do a series of black and white photographs for every room, justifiably the only artwork other than the fresh flowers.

With only about ten rooms per floor, each landing feels private and quiet. The halls are carpeted in soft gray, bordered in the ubiquitous black and white parquet. The rooms are carpeted in gray, with low beds covered in Oxford blue duvets from Brooks Brothers, topped by black and white wool blankets. The surfaces are stark, clean, and spare. A cassette player, VCR, and remote television sit in every room, attended to by 24-hour room service. Morgans has a library of more than 200 videos, any one of which may be brought up to one's room with hot popcorn. Unusually, most rooms have good sunlight and sometimes two exposures.

A special treat is Continental breakfast served in a sunny, cool breakfast room overlooking Madison Avenue and a chic bistro across the street. The staff is low-key, personal, and extremely attentive.

Paramount

235 West 46th Street
New York, New York 10019
212-764-5500
800-225-7474
Fax: 212-354-5237

Proprietors: Ian Shrager, Philip Pilevsky, and Arthur Cohen
General manager: David Miskit, managed by Morgans Hotel
   Company
Accommodations: 610 rooms, including 13 suites
Rates: $110–$170
Added: $20 each additional guest; 19.25% tax
Payment: Major credit cards
Children: Welcome
Pets: Not allowed
Smoking: 2 of 17 floors nonsmoking
Open: Year-round

In the heart of the theater district, Paramount is the stage and its guests are the players. This showcase of daring design was reborn in August 1990 after a three-year, $75 million investment. Predicting the recession, noting the abundance of unaffordable hotels in New York, owner Ian Shrager invented stylish overnighting on a shoestring.

The Century Paramount Hotel was designed by Thomas Lamb in 1927, architectural author of the Ziegfeld Theater and the Pierre Hotel, which fell into dowdiness over the years until Ian Shrager and partners bought it in 1986. While Mr. Shrager's Royalton is an example of the high art of hotel design, the Paramount is performance art with a sense of humor, designed by Philippe Starck.

The formidable exterior looks like the grandest of grand old hotels, its Carrara marble facade restored by Rockwell Newman, fresh from restoring Carnegie Hall and the Statue of Liberty. A marble breezeway is the transition where the fun begins. Like guests at a potluck dinner, Europe's best designers showcase their signature pieces: odd couches, a silver chair, weird lamps, and a ceiling inspired by Joan Miró, on a backdrop floor of gray Italian slate. Guests gaze up at framed duets of diners at the Mezzanine restaurant, which wraps entirely around the perimeter. From their second-floor balcony, they observe the lobby players, reached by a platinum leaf staircase.

Much is conceptual at the Paramount. The 18 floors of guest rooms are reached by elevators lit in primary colors. A wide weather mirror posts the day's climatic events on a stark wall along white hallways lined with rope rails, reminiscent of the ocean liners of the twenties and thirties.

All rooms have a black and white parquet low nap rug, a stark, Brancusi-style light/chandelier, clean-lined white cabinets for televisions and VCRs, and a brightly colored Starck armchair. Headboards in the single rooms are oversize replicas of Vermeer's masterpiece Lacemaker, with a maternal figure hovering over the bed, a restful platform smooth and white, with a long cylindrical pillow tied at both ends. The immaculate baths retain their Old World tiling with New Age charm, with Philippe Starck's trademark stainless steel sink and personalized amenities. Though the public spaces are playful galleries of design, the chic rooms were designed to be restful and welcoming.

Among the public spaces are a room derivative of PeeWee's Playhouse, done by the selfsame designer Gary Panter; a 24-hour exercise club; a sunny breakfast room off the Mezzanine; a Dean & DeLuca espresso/pastry bar; and an incredibly chic supper club that draws lines most evenings. If you can't stay overnight, a visit to the lobby restrooms will convey the playful, postmodern creativity of the Paramount.

Despite the overwhelming chicness of the Paramount, it is a very down-to-earth, friendly, accessible, affordable place. The theatrical staff literally auditioned for their respective roles as bellmen and concierges.

Parc Fifty-One

152 West 51st Street
New York, New York 10019
212-765-1900
800-338-1338

Proprietor: Park Lane Hotels International
General manager: Cary Turecamo
Accommodations: 178 rooms, including 52 suites
Rates: Rooms, $255–$325; suites, from $395
Included: Continental breakfast, morning newspaper
Added: $25 each additional guest; 19.25% tax
Payment: Major credit cards
Children: Welcome
Pets: Not allowed
Smoking: 1 of 7 floors nonsmoking
Open: Year-round

This elegant theater district hotel has the tony feel of an Upper East Side property, with one of the prettiest lobbies in midtown

Manhattan. Built in 1926 as the Taft Hotel, it enjoyed for nearly forty years a tradition of a bohemian, eclectic theater crowd. The property was closed for four years as it underwent a $100 million renovation, reopening to rave reviews in October 1987 as the Grand Bay Hotel at Equitable Center. The property transferred to the hands of Park Lane Hotels in 1990.

Guests enter on 51st Street on the corner of Seventh Avenue, a block from Radio City, through a well-lit portico. By the time they reach the reception desk at the lobby's far end, they have forgotten the blaring horns and madding crowds of this neighborhood. The marbled setting is lovely and serene, with floors a rosy pink hue and walls a cocoa brown. Oil paintings hang above the French antiques and bergères and gilded leg glass coffee tables. The main lobby reaches two stories upward, culminating in a gilded, pressed tin ceiling from which hangs a crystal chandelier. Huge floral arrangements dress polished antique tables. The original brass elevator doors were restored from the Roaring Twenties' days of the Taft.

Throughout five floors of guest rooms, the hallways are lined with plush neutral carpeting in gray, beige, and taupe, made residential by right-angled turns, antiques, and original art. Rooms have light-colored marble foyers and are unusually large with an average of 500 square feet. The doubles are done with geometric pastels and solids and traditional wood furniture with black and gold accents; the suites are done in French country and art deco. The French country rooms have beautiful pine furnishings, a king-size sleigh bed, and a large Empire sofa. Dividing the living from the sleeping room is a floor-to-ceiling armoire containing a swiveling television, stereo, and bookshelves (unusually, all rooms have several classic novels and books). The duvets, carpeting, and upholstery are done in neutral solids. The art deco rooms are surprisingly different, furnished in black lacquer and mauve accents. A unifying theme is the bottled mineral water offered in every room next to trademark green marble ice buckets.

All rooms, regardless of size, have magnificent baths, including five-foot tubs, cotton bath sheets, towels, and robes, hair dryers, televisions, and phones, amenities by Crabtree and Evelyn, and Neutrogena soaps. The floors and walls are done in blond marble, and the separate sinks and vanities are finished in green marble.

The Lobby Lounge near the reception area is a living room setting of muted tapestried chairs and plush down-filled sofas, featuring piano music and finger food in the afternoon and evening. Guests are served complimentary Continental breakfast in the hotel's restaurant, Bellini by Cipriani, an affiliate of the famous Harry's Bar in Venice, the hotel restaurant. Northern Italian lunch and dinner are served to the public in this light setting of leather chairs and verdigris sconces.

The Peninsula

700 Fifth Avenue at 55th Street
New York, New York 10019
212-247-2200
800-262-9467
Fax: 212-9034-3949

Proprietor: The Peninsula Group
General manager: Manfred Timmel
Accommodations: 250 rooms, including 30 suites
Rates: $275–$395; suites, $550–$1,100
Added: $20 each additional guest; 19.25% sales tax
Payment: Major credit cards
Children: Welcome
Pets: Not allowed
Smoking: 4 of 17 floors nonsmoking
Open: Year-round

This grand old property is actually quite a new property, the Peninsula Group's first American hotel. Built as the Gotham Hotel in 1905 by Hiss and Weekes for $2.25 million, the hotel was designed to complement its neighbor, the University Club. It sits across Fifth Avenue from the masterpiece St. Regis, completing quite an astounding trio of beaux-arts Italian Renaissance architecture, just below 57th Street.

The 23-story limestone structure lived a long life before a renovation was undertaken in 1979. However, plans were disrupted and the hotel sat boarded up for seven years. The property was bought in 1986 by the Pratt Corporation, renovated to its present grandeur, and opened in the spring of 1988 under the aegis of Maxim's de Paris. The Peninsula Group bought the hotel in October 1988 for $127 million.

While renovations have become as common as pillow mints in New York hotels, the Peninsula has two outstanding features that separate it from its cousins: a 35,000-square-foot state-of-the-art health club and spa and the wonderful PenTop Bar & Terrace, each with panoramic city views, wrap terraces peering over the copper cornice.

Guests enter from 55th Street to a transitional lobby with double-height ceilings, flanked by cozy parlors furnished with art nouveau antiques. A sweeping staircase of Italian classico marble ascends five steps and divides in either direction to Adrienne restaurant and Le Bistro d'Adrienne to the left and to the reception area and the Gotham Lounge for high tea and cocktails to the right. Immediately, a visitor is awestruck by the ornate plaster ceiling and faux pink marble under Corinthian capitals. The armoire on the landing was featured at the 1904 Exposition des Beaux-Arts in Paris. Other original pieces throughout the public spaces, including bergères, tables, and a sofa, were designed by art nouveau master Louis Marjorelle. The Palm Court features the astounding legerdemain of Ben Strauss, who painted the faux limestone walls.

The rooms are furnished with original art nouveau antiques and lighting fixtures, custom-designed furnishings, in masculine understated decor. The futuristic telephone consoles control temperature, lighting, and the television and offer assistance in seven languages. The baths have dignified brass fixtures, bidets, phones, and Lanvin amenities. Compared with the lavish public space, however, the rooms are muted, and a number have poor views of the interior air shaft.

The fabulous trilevel Spa hovers above the hotel on top floors, a blessed contribution of the Peninsula Group in April 1991. Guests enjoy the Cybex circuits and extensive cardiovascular machines in several windowed rooms with city views. Under an atrium roof is a 17-by-42-foot pool and whirlpool. The salon offers massages, facials, and beauty services. Guests enjoy a carpeted wraparound sundeck.

Chef Adam Odegard is a wonderful contribution to Adrienne, and his fine European cuisine is complimented in the restaurant's pretty salmon-colored setting. All is softspoken and understated at the Peninsula—the guests as well as the staff elegant and hushed in these grand-scale public spaces.

The Pierre

Fifth Avenue at 61st Street
New York, New York 10021
212-838-8000
800-332-3442

Proprietor: Four Seasons Hotels Limited
General manager: Herbert Pliessnig
Accommodations: 205 rooms, including 46 suites
Rates: Rooms, $310–$420; boudoir, $575; suites, $575–$900
Added: 19.25% tax
Payment: Major credit cards
Children: Welcome
Pets: Small pets allowed
Smoking: 10 nonsmoking floors
Open: Year-round

In April 1992, the Pierre completed a two-year renovation effort, resulting in the beautification of all its guest rooms and public spaces. The result is simply lovely, not an embellishment of an earlier Pierre, but an affirmation of how we have always thought of it—as one of New York's few and finest grandes dames, on the southeast corner of Central Park.

Charles Pierre, raised by a European hotelier, was invited into the fashionable set when he arrived in New York in 1904. After several years, he was able to open his own restaurant. By the 1920s, Pierre's Park Avenue was one of Manhattan's chic eateries. Through a venture with Wall Street magnates like Otto Kahn, E. F. Hutton, and Walter Chrysler, Pierre embarked on a dream of a grand hotel on Fifth Avenue. For $15 million, architects Schultze and Wener built a palatial Georgian monolith, its forty stories topped in copper. The Pierre Hotel took a year to build and opened in October 1930; but after only two years, the

Depression took hold of the hotel, Pierre filed for bankruptcy, and he tragically died in disappointment in 1934. The Four Seasons Hotels signed on to manage the Pierre in 1981, and the hotel has since reclaimed it upstanding place in New York's high society.

The perfection of the Pierre starts with its location. On 61st Street and Fifth Avenue, the Pierre has all the glamour and scenery of Central Park South without the tourism and horses. Guests enter from Fifth Avenue via a scenic and rather famous hallway, which playfully and elegantly toys with window shopping as art: well-known, upscale boutiques show off displays behind glass. Or guests can enter from the subtle 61st Street side, which brings them immediately to the reception area to the left, with a restful sitting area half a tier removed from the public space. The decor is formal and classic, with Edwardian antiques and glorious floral arrangements.

At ground level, to the immediate right of the 61st Street entrance is the Café Pierre, a quiet, rather undiscovered formal dining spot decorated in neoclassic grays and golds. Eventually, this route will lead to the magnificent Rotunda, a glorious feminine spot for afternoon tea and cocktails, a lounge underneath a French garden of murals. This is one of the Pierre's finest attributes, in an oval space of regal splendor. Intimate tables cluster on a brightly patterned carpet. Two wings of an ornately carved marble staircase ascend to a second floor, under the floor-to-ceiling murals with clouds painted overhead.

Upstairs, the guest rooms are wonderfully redone. In the blessed style of old hotels, the rooms at the Pierre often have surprising configurations and large closets. While the furnishings are nice but uninspired Chippendale or Queen Anne reproductions, the fabrics are lovely. In several schemes, the rooms are redecorated with bold colors and an unusual marriage of patterns. One room might be octagonal, with drapery and bedding in an oversized chintz on a bright yellow background, with a plaid bedskirt. Another room might have twin two-poster beds with fabulous blue toile spreads and drapery. Such unpredictability is refreshing in a large, traditional Old World hotel. The baths are glorious, some with wonderful wide old-fashioned sinks, others with plain pedestal sinks, all with terry towels and robes as well as linen towels. The walls and floors are black and white marble, and all have hair dryers, phones, and interesting amenities like Q-Tips and cotton balls in porcelain jars.

The staff seem extremely pleased in their updated classic environment. While professional and helpful, the Pierre staff don't go overboard with solicitousness—quite confident with their Old World stature.

Hôtel Plaza Athénée

37 East 64th Street
New York, New York 10021
212-734-9100
800-223-5843
Fax: 212-772-0958

Proprietor: Forte Hotels
General Manager: Bernard Lackner
Accommodations: 160 rooms, including 30 suites
Rates: Rooms, $310–$350; suites, $590–$900; single rates $35 less
Added: $30 each additional guest; 19.25% tax
Payment: Major credit cards
Children: Welcome
Pets: Not allowed
Smoking: 1 of 16 floors nonsmoking
Open: Year-round

With its bright red awnings flagging every window, the New York Hôtel Plaza Athénée pledges allegiance to its Paris inspiration, one of the world's finest hotels since it was built over a century ago. Despite its Old World appearance, the New York Plaza Athénée opened in September 1984, a transformation of the former 1927 Alrae Hotel with a redesign by architect John Carl Warnecke. It is surely the ritziest of the Madison Avenue boutique hotels and caters to an elegant European crowd.

Guests enter on 64th Street between Madison and Park avenues, under a portico draped with French and American flags, through polished brass doors, to a foyerlike lobby, with white marble inset with black squares, appointed in Italian marble and luxurious French antiques. Registration is at an 18th-century desk by the concierge, in a room of green silk-covered walls and antiques. Visitors may proceed down several steps at the center of the lobby to the restaurant Le Régence. The restaurant serves Continental food with a French flair by the hand of chef Jean Robert de Cavel in a very French setting, an ornate room with gold millwork, green walls, leather chairs, and crystal sconces and chandeliers under a cloud mural. The neighboring piano lounge is a clubby, intimate place for drinks and cocktails, under Brazilian mahogany millwork, with walls covered in dark green fabric and oil paintings.

The elevator banks in the lower lobby are surrounded by three walls of a lavish hand-painted mural of classical pastoral scenes. Guest rooms occupy 17 floors on intimate, hushed hallways appointed with Old World moldings. Irish Navan carpets quiet the step. Headboards are upholstered velvet. Two schemes of decor are a serene palette of muted aquas and beiges and a romantic setting of rusts. There is no chintz or clutter here, but classic silk and velvet in complementary colors or paisleys in handsome tones, with stretched valances above the windows. The furnishings were handmade for the hotel, from the Directoire night tables to the desks and television cabinets in dark wood. The bathrooms are beautiful, with stunning Portuguese Aurora Rose marble on the floors and walls. Lanvin amenities and Italian Frette terry robes add to the elegance. Eight suites have terraces or solariums. The rooms do not have mini-bars since the hotel places such emphasis on its full service.

The staff is reserved and solicitous, emphasizing the aura of formality that pervades the Plaza Athénée.

Rihga Royal Hotel
151 West 54th Street
New York, New York 10019
212-307-5000
800-937-5454

Proprietors: Rihga International U.S.A.
General manager: Frank Arthur Banks
Accommodations: 476 one-and two-bedroom suites,
   including 6 Grand Royal Suites
Rates: $260–$390; Grand Royal Suites from $425
Added: $25 each additional guest; 19.25% tax
Payment: Major credit cards
Children: Welcome
Pets: Not allowed
Smoking: 5 of 52 floors nonsmoking
Open: Year-round

Having opened in November 1990, the Rihga Royal initiated a challenge to all business-oriented New York City hotels. It runs like a clock and was planned very well by its Japanese-owned company. There are only 10 or 12 rooms per floor, creating an unusual amount of privacy and quiet for a 500-room property. The rooms are exceptionally large, averaging 572 square feet, with at least one bedroom set apart from a living room. The fitness facilities are extensive and brand new. The hotel offers a nice business center to guests, with a fax, a copier, a computer, and typewriter. And half the guest rooms have fairly good views of Central Park, others with views of the Hudson or East River.

The city's second tallest hotel—the tallest is the Millennium—stands 54 stories, designed by Frank Williams and Associates in the classic form of the soaring skyscrapers of the 1920s and 1930s. A tower of rose-beige brick and granite, the Rihga Royal teeters above 54th Street, narrowing toward its top. Porters flock to the revolving doors. The lobby is quite small for such a large hotel, decorated in two tones of polished marble two stories high. The elevator banks rest behind the lobby, extremely quick and efficient.

Guest rooms line the intimate hallways on either side, and again a visitor will be thankful for the tower structure, which permits more floors and fewer rooms per floor. Either one or two bedrooms, they are decorated similarly with white painted woodwork, in a peach or an aqua-teal color scheme. All guest rooms have sofabeds and bay windows in the living rooms, with remote cable televisions built into corner cupboards. Mirrored French doors close or open to the bedroom, most with a king-size bed. A bit lacking in warmth, the rooms are immaculate, colorful, and very utilitarian—some with wondrous views. The mini-bars have ice makers, the rooms have safes, and there are two televisions, one with a VCR. The baths are small but quite nice, with marble floors, a separate bath and shower, a telephone, amenities including Crabtree and Evelyn, a hair dryer, a lint brush, and a scale.

The Fitness Center, open 24 hours and staffed with a daytime personal trainer, has brand-new equipment in a large setting, including treadmills, Lifecycles, universal weights, and two saunas, with views to a small garden outdoors.

On the ground floor, to the right of the lobby is Halcyon, the Rihga's restaurant. The decor is classic, with forest green banquettes and Empire chairs under a lovely Italian mural. The sommelier is proud of the 140-wine list. Visitors have drinks and enjoy piano music in the living room setting of the Halcyon Lounge, open for light fare until 2 A.M. Halcyon also services the guests with 24-hour room service.

The Ritz-Carlton New York
112 Central Park South
New York, New York 10019
212-757-1900
800-241-3333
Fax: 212-757-9620

Proprietor: The Ritz-Carlton Hotel Company
General manager: Edward A. Mady
Accommodations: 228 rooms, including 23 suites and 5
    junior suites
Rates: $230–$380; suites, from $475
Included: Morning newspaper, morning limousine to Wall
    Street
Added: $30 each additional guest; 19.25% tax
Payment: Major credit cards
Children: Welcome
Pets: Not allowed
Smoking: Nonsmoking rooms available
Open: Year-round

The Navarro Hotel was built in 1928, and the Ritz-Carlton
Hotel moved into its shell in 1982. This New York property
embodies all the aspects of a Ritz-Carlton to a tee: the Old
World flavor of its Central Park South address and regal brick
facade convince a passerby or even a long-term guest that this is
one of New York's grand old hotels—especially in the understated elegance displayed by the solicitous staff and at the wonderful Jockey Club.

Guests enter from Central Park South through revolving
doors, descend several steps, and reach the parlorlike lobby.
The knotty pine paneling and oil paintings lend a living room
feel. Elevator banks rest beyond the lobby, and the Jockey Club
is through a threshold to the left. This is quite an institution, a
wonderful room lifted off the shores of Great Britain. The pine
walls are filled with oil paintings of equestrian and hunt themes
illuminated by lantern sconces, accented by corner shell cabinets, red leather banquettes adorned with brass. The room feels
like an English men's club, treated to the work of chef Tom Parlo
and an extensive wine list of about 175 bottles. After dinner,
guests will enjoy a nightcap at the Jockey Club Bar, presided
over by internationally known bartender Norman Bukofzer.

The guest rooms are gradually being transformed throughout 1992. While the older rooms have the gracious modest
elegance of a Park Avenue apartment, the new schemes are
highly decorated, with heavy drapery in Wedgwood blue laced

with gold thread, matching linens, and classic sofas. Televisions and mini-bars are fixed in lovely custom-designed armoires, wood with brass accents. While the rooms undergo redecoration, the baths are all in pristine condition, of light marble on the walls and floors, with classic fixtures, hair dryers, vanity mirrors, scales, phones, two robes, and an eyelet shower curtain, with extensive amenities. A nice touch is a Ritz-Carlton umbrella provided for guest use in every room. Be sure to request a park view.

Reliably, the service at the Ritz-Carlton is faultless, discreet, and extremely understated—a quiet refuge in the midst of Manhattan glitz.

The Royalton
44 West 44th Street
New York, New York 10036
212-869-4400
800-635-9013

Proprietor: Ian Shrager
General Manager: Terry Ford
Accommodations: 168 rooms, including 28 suites, 40 rooms
  with fireplace
Rates: $235–$350; suites, $370
Added: $25 each additional guest; 19.25% tax
Payment: Major credit cards
Children: Welcome
Pets: Not allowed
Smoking: Allowed
Open: Year-round

The Royalton is first a phenomenon, then a hotel. It looks like an art deco retrospective during the twenty-first century, like Alice in Wonderland in corporate America, as if the Algonquin's Round Table suddenly went elliptical under the hands of a space-suited Dorothy Parker.

Although it was built in 1898 as the Hotel Royalton, only the name remains remotely the same since its reintroduction to the New York chic elite in 1988 by the late Steve Rubell and Ian Shrager—a Hollywood-type producer of sophisticated Manhattan hotels. There is nothing to introduce the hotel from the street—no signs or flying flags—but the name modestly carved in stone on the pediment of the Greek Revival portico and the unearthly glow of the polished mahogany doors that signify importance.

Mr. Shrager and Mr. Rubell had this in mind: what nightclubs were to the seventies and restaurants were to the eighties, hotel lobbies will be to the nineties. The interior design of Philippe Starck immediately transports a guest into the Royalton world. A cobalt blue carpet, bordered on one side with a line of white dancing ghosts, stretches nearly the block-long distance of the hotel's granite floor. A gleaming bank of highly varnished mahogany doors lines one side of the corridor, topped by wall sconces with a peculiar horn shape repeated throughout the hotel. Lining the other side of the carpet are cylindrical gray pillars and dramatically lit spare furnishings. Asymmetrical muslin-covered chairs with broad backs of yellow, purple, green, or peach velvet contrast with generic white-slipcovered wing chairs, with dangerous-looking stainless steel legs.

Down several steps are dining and sociable tables, and decorating the walls are such oddities as four large glass bowls inhabited by fighting fish, a huge rectangular beveled mirror hung with two purple tassels, and exaggerated vases stuck with primary-colored tulips. Occasional lines of bright color emerge from the neutral backdrop of gray slate, stone, and carpet.

Visitors must be sure to visit the Round Bar for a drink. Its entirely round celery-colored tufted velvet walls give the feeling of being in a genie's bottle. Traditional black and white parquet floors are distorted in a dizzying round design. Like all things at the Royalton, the Round Bar has classic origins, designed after Ernest Hemingway's favorite bar, that of the Paris Ritz.

Whisked up in small mahogany elevators to one of 16 floors of guest rooms, a visitor is left off in a hallway as if dropped at sea at midnight. The halls are painted the same cobalt blue of the familiar specter carpet. The round room numbers glow eerily from the mahogany doors like portals from a ship's hull. The halls feel claustrophobic, and once inside the guest rooms, one feels an immediate sense of calm.

The palette is a simple one of slate gray, stainless steel, and white light from the lamps and bedding, the glow of mahogany, with the exception of a midnight blue velvet easy chair. Cool Vermont slate floors are covered in a thick-pile gray carpet. The low bedding is an oasis of creamy white brushed cotton down comforter with seven down pillows perfectly arranged. The upholstered headboard is covered in stretched cotton. Nightstands are inset portals cut into the mahogany wall on either side of the bed, with one fresh flower, a notepad, and a pencil. Tiny round stainless steel tables are placed just so. A candle is replaced at nightly turndown. Many of the rooms feature working fireplaces.

The spacious baths are the highest of high tech, a panoply of slate, steel, glass, and mirrors, warmed slightly by the plush white terry robes and towels. A stainless steel basin rests on one wall and a vanity mirror on another, with an amenity tray including potpourri, a fresh flower, and Royalton soap, shampoo, and cotton buds. The room may have either a five-foot-diameter tub or a tub with glassed-in shower, each with bath salts and a loofah sponge.

The rooms all contain mini-bars without liquor, pastries made by Dean and DeLuca in black lacquer boxes designed for the hotel. As well, all rooms have a television, VCR and stereo, with volumes of tapes available at the front desk which will be delivered to one's room with a bowl of warm popcorn.

The concierges are efficient and highly trained. Among other things, they will make reservations at the highly reputed 44, which serves a nouvelle Continental cuisine. Odd-hour diners will be glad for the Sushi Bar Without the Sushi, which serves light fare around the clock.

The St. Regis

Two East 55th Street at Fifth Avenue
New York, New York 10022
212-753-4500
800-759-7550

Proprietor: The ITT Sheraton Corporation
Managing director: Peter W. Tischmann
Accommodations: 359, including 49 suites
Rates: Rooms, $350–$450; suites, $550–$3,000
Added: 19.25% tax
Payment: Major credit cards
Children: Welcome
Pets: Not allowed
Smoking: 4 of 19 floors nonsmoking
Open: Year-round

When it was completed in 1905, the St. Regis was New York's tallest building, set conveniently on 5th Avenue in midtown. While it no longer holds that honor, it does bring to mind other superlatives as the city's most expensive and most upscale new hotel. After three years and $100 million of restoration and renovation, the St. Regis reopened in September 1991 to a glorious reception.

The 18-story building was constructed as a hotel for $5.5 million by Colonel John Jacob Astor IV, between 1902 and 1905, designed by Trowbridge and Livingston, who also designed the Hayden Planetarium and B. Altman's. The beaux-arts masterpiece was intended to be the world's finest hotel, with crystal chandeliers, antique tapestries, Oriental rugs, and antique Louis XV furnishings. While today's hotels boast of large video libraries for guest use, the original St. Regis had a 3,000-volume gold-tooled library of books for guests to check out. The restoration project was intended to replicate that turn-of-the-century majesty. Throughout the hotel are 600 crystal chandeliers, handmade in Czechoslovakia. Nearly 200 miles of wood molding and 23 miles of plaster molding were installed. The restoration involved the second largest gold leafing project ever undertaken in this country.

When Colonel Astor died on the Titanic in 1912, the St. Regis went to his busy son Vincent, who was forced to sell to the Duke family in 1927. One of the hotel's most noted treasures is the Maxfield Parrish mural King Cole, which was installed in the hotel in 1932. Three years later, Vincent Astor reclaimed the grande dame, and the hotel became the center of New York social life. When it opened in 1938, the Iridium Room was an immediate success for dining and dancing, with a skating rink that pulled out from under the stage. It was renamed the King Cole Grille in 1948 when the Parrish mural was hung here. The hotel was bought in 1966 by the Sheraton Corporation, which undertook the restoration in 1988.

The guest rooms on the upper floors were greatly enlarged during the renovation, their number reduced from 557 to 359, all with 12-foot ceilings and crown moldings. While furnished similarly, there are nearly 70 different room configurations given the old floor plan of the hotel. Decorated with reproduction Louis XV furnishings, the rooms are exquisitely done in soothing gray silks and damasks. These match stretched valances and heavy drapery, as well as chairs and sitting areas. The beds have upholstered headboards and featherbeds. The beautiful wood armoires with brass fittings were custom-designed to house the television and mini-bar, and the contents of the latter are complimentary to guests. The large baths are exquisite, with linen and terry towels, robes, Bijan amenities, in white marble, with large tubs and freestanding showers. Every floor has its own butler.

For mind and body, there is a full-service business center, as well as a fitness center on the lower level with ample cardiovascular equipment and saunas.

Guest will certainly want to enjoy high tea in the Astor

Court, with its hand-painted murals in a French, feminine setting. For a more masculine experience behind the Astor Court, the King Cole bar is a smoky, woody room featuring the romantic landscape of Maxfield Parrish. Lespinasse is the setting for formal French cuisine. Executive chef Michael Carrer and chef Gary Kunz received three stars from the New York Times shortly after the hotel opened. The china and flatware were designed specially for the St. Regis by Tiffany.

Expect solicitous service at every turn. The staff is exceptionally attentive at the St. Regis, as the hotel tries to live up to all the expectations prompted by the renovation.

The Waldorf Towers
100 East 50th Street
New York, New York 10022
212-872-4635
800-HILTONS
Fax: 212-872-4799

Executive director: Peter O. Wirth
Accommodations: 191 units, including 106 one-to four-
  bedroom suites
Rates: $350–$375; suites, $500–$4,000

The Waldorf-Astoria
50th Street and Park Avenue
New York, New York 10022
212-355-3000
800-HILTONS
Fax: 212-421-8103

General manager: Per Hellmann
Accommodations: 1,410 rooms, including 150 suites
Rates: $250–$325; suites, $375–$800
Added: $25 each additional guest; 19.25% tax
Payment: Major credit cards
Children: Welcome
Pets: Check with manager
Smoking: Nonsmoking floors in main hotel, not in Towers
Open: Year-round

There are two distinct properties within the massive walls of this New York landmark. The Waldorf-Astoria is an enormous hotel occupying floors 1–27; and the Towers are the intimate, luxury element, with a separate entrance and concierge, on floors 28–42. Certainly the more luxurious property is the Towers, offering perhaps the most elegant accommodations in the city. Yet, if you can't afford to stay there, you most certainly ought to try a stay at the Waldorf-Astoria, which has its own charm. There is an excitement about the Waldorf that encapsulates being in New York: the large, expansive common areas bustling with people, some of whom are probably famous; the grand old art deco architecture that so well represents much of the city; the feeling that something is going on that you're not a part of (certainly likely with the Waldorf's 25 meeting rooms); and that vague, exciting feeling of being lost, which often accompanies a visit to New York.

The Waldorf-Astoria and the Towers opened in 1931. Conrad Hilton acquired the management rights to the legendary hotel in 1947, and then the Hilton Corporation bought the hotel in 1977. An incredible $180 million renovation was completed in the late 1980s, which revived the mosaics, the bronze doors and elevators, the guest rooms, and all public spaces to their current awe-inspiring splendor.

Staying at the Waldorf Towers is like visiting a palace and staying in the king's quarters; in fact, it's likely that a king from some country or another will be a fellow guest. Guests have access to the public spaces and restaurants of the Waldorf-Astoria and can retreat to their privileged sanctuary where every possible wish is anticipated. Guests enter through the private side of the hotel, on 50th Street, to an impeccably restored lobby, with an intimate sitting area. They are escorted to their rooms on the original bronze and burlwood elevators, which have been brought up to futuristic standards. Every room is different and individually decorated in impeccable, classic taste. Every detail is flawless, from the antiques, to the beautiful and precious fabrics and linens, to the amenity-filled baths, with marble floor, linens and plush terry towels, and fresh flowers.

While the Towers are hushed and discreet, the Waldorf-Astoria is busy and grand-scale—though the magnitude should not imply lackluster service. The Waldorf-Astoria staff is savvy and professional, an attentive army matching guests on a one-to-one basis. In an ongoing refurbishment plan, 300 rooms are redecorated each year at the Waldorf, so be sure to ask for as new a room as possible. These will be assuredly nice, with lots of chintz, some pretty pieces like marble-top dressers, and quite nice baths: either gracefully Old World, similar to those in the Towers, with brown and black parquet in a large square room with arched molding and wide, old sinks and fixtures, or new and marbleized.

A wonderful new feature of the Waldorf-Astoria is the Plus-One Fitness Center, which opened in the spring of 1991, complimentary to Tower guests, available to regular guests for $15 (much less than the usual $25 for outside club use at city hotels). With terrific views looking north on Park Avenue, the club has an airy feel, appointed in beautiful light sycamore. Several staffers are available at once for fitness evaluations and personal training. Cardiovascular equipment is quite extensive, and treadmills and bikes are equipped with headphones and televisions. Five types of massage are available by appointment.

The lavish public spaces include all-day dining at Peacock Alley, with floral, feminine decor; clubby, elegant fare at the Bull & Bear; Oscar's coffee shop; and Inagiku, the country's first outpost of Japan's best restaurant, for lunch and dinner. After-dinner drinks can be had in a safari setting at Harry's Bar and Restaurant or at Cocktail Terrace overlooking the Park Avenue art deco lobby — also a perfect setting for afternoon tea.

Hotel Wales
1295 Madison Avenue
New York, New York 10128
212-876-6000

Proprietor and Manager: Henry Kallan
Accommodations: 92 rooms, including 50 suites and 1 penthouse suite
Rates: $145; suites, $175, $225; penthouse, $375
Included: Continental breakfast
Minimum stay: None
Added: 19.25% tax; $2 occupancy tax
Payment: Major credit cards
Children: Welcome
Pets: Not allowed
Smoking: Allowed
Open: Year-round

As daunting and impersonal as New York City can be for an out-of-towner, the Hotel Wales is just as comforting and friendly. This oasis on Manhattan's Upper East Side is as much a country inn as a city hotel, with refreshingly rural rates.

The Hotel Wales is located on Madison Avenue between 92nd and 93rd streets, a block from Central Park and far from the bustle of midtown. To know the area is to know the relative peacefulness of that part of town, which is referred to by New Yorkers as old-moneyed Carnegie Hill, named for the famed industrialist who built a modest home on Fifth Avenue and 89th Street (today, the fortresslike Cooper-Hewitt Museum). This high up on Madison Avenue, fashionable boutiques are outnumbered by posh private schools, as close as you'll get in Manhattan to suburbia.

The Wales was built in 1901 as a lovely brownstone hotel, designed as a leisurely place of respite for busy travelers who would stay for weeks at a time. Many of the suites have kitchenettes. The configuration is beneficial for nearly every room (except the smallest of singles): the suites are on the corners of the building, looking either southwest or west, but with a guaranteed view of glorious Central Park and the lakelike reservoir at 90th Street. Even if the pastoral setting is slightly obscured by the block between Madison and Fifth avenues, such obliqueness is a luxury: this is the highest-rent view in the city.

In early 1990, the hotel underwent a $6 million renovation that revealed ubiquitous oak woodwork: transoms, molding, trim, French doors, and mantels have been stripped of decades of paint and the original richness restored. The rooms are furnished with English antiques or credible reproductions in mahogany and oak, all excellent choices, often matched with original artwork. Each room is different, more in the style of a turn-of-the-century mansion than a hotel: a fine writing desk, a fireplace, or a canopy bed are pleasant surprises in some of the rooms. The bathrooms are nearly sparkling thanks to the renovation, with touches of marble here and there, and any native would say they are bigger than a city studio.

A word of advice: Make sure a crowded weekend does not leave you with one of the smaller singles, which are small even by city standards. Conversely, the penthouse is quite magnificent, a full one-bedroom apartment attached to 1,000 square feet of terrace overlooking Central Park.

Although there is no room service at the Hotel Wales, adjacent is handsome Busby's and one of the chic-elite brunch locales in the city, the immensely popular Sarabeth's Kitchen, which boasts a 45-minute wait on weekends without hope of reservations. Service at the hotel is hushed, reverent, and near to invisible. Continental breakfast is served in the recently finished salon, 1,600 square feet of grandeur, also the pleasant setting for Friday night classical concerts.

Westbury Hotel
69th Street at Madison Avenue
New York, New York 10021
212-535-2000
800-321-1569
Fax: 212-535-5058

Proprietor: Forte Hotels
General Manager: Stefan Simcovics
Accommodations: 180 rooms, including 51 suites
Rates: $270–$290; suites, $2,000–$2,200
Added: $30 each additional guest; 19.25% tax
Payment: Major credit cards
Children: Welcome
Pets: Allowed
Smoking: 1 of 16 floors nonsmoking
Open: Year-round

The Westbury was built in the Gatsbyesque days of 1926 by the family of an American polo player. It has been a hotel since, run today in the same privileged fashion by the gentle hand of the Forte Group since 1978. It represents a bastion of quiet Old World English elegance, housing the Polo Restaurant in a gallery of Ralph Lauren paisleys and equestrian prints amid intimate banquettes along street-front windows. With its Madison Avenue location, the Westbury, along with its relative, the Plaza Athénée and the Lowell, is in the heart of the country's finest and most exclusive boutiques.

The limestone entrance is on 69th Street between Fifth and Madison avenues, marked by an elaborate art nouveau portico and a modest set of highly polished brass revolving doors and trademark red awning valances on upper windows. As with most elite New York properties, the entrance is small, like a mansion's foyer, leading to a modest-sized double-height lobby overlooked by a second-floor balcony. A red-carpeted stairway leads to meeting space. The reception area is richly appointed with hanging tapestries, floral arrangements, and Oriental carpets on a marble floor. The elevators and the entrance to the Polo Lounge rest to the right of the diminutive reception desk.

The guest rooms rest above through 16 floors along a long, straight hall which parallels Madison Avenue. Though most rooms have a view of Madison Avenue, some have a quiet, blunt view of the back of another building. The rooms are extremely warm, having been recently redecorated in wonderful, busy schemes of boldly striped wallcovering and large-print chintz window treatments matching linens and throw pillow. The successful feeling is that of an English country home, with high ceilings and welcoming interior space. An upholstered bench rests at the end of the Chippendale Drexel reproduction headboard. Rooms or suites have several extremely comfortable club chairs or sofas with tasseled dust ruffles separated by tables with delft-type ginger jars or plants. Lovely prints and architectural drawings grace the walls, and Oriental scatter rugs enhance the low nap carpet. All rooms have televisions and VCRs and umbrellas for guest use; the suites have CD players. The pristine baths are clean, lined with marble and equipped with Caswell and Massey amenities; those in the smaller rooms are fit into cozy nooks, those in larger rooms have separate vanity areas.

The third-floor Fitness Center was a new addition in 1991, with views of Madison Avenue and ample cardiovascular equipment in a gray-carpeted room, with separate sauna and steam facilities.

The staff is letter-perfect at this long-standing property, gracious and softspoken.

Orlando

Courtyard at Lake Lucerne (The Norment-Parry Inn, I.W. Phillips House, The Wellborn)
211 N. Lucerne Circle East
Orlando, Florida 32801
407-648-5188
800-444-5289

Owner: Charles, Sam, and Paula Meiner
Accommodations: 6 rooms, 3 suites, 12 one-bedroom apartments
Rates: $65–$85; suites, $100–$150; apartments, $85–$150
Included: Continental breakfast and complimentary wine
Minimum stay: None
Added: 10% tax
Payment: Major credit cards; personal check
Children: Allowed with supervision
Smoking: Allowed
Open: Year-round

Orlando was once a sleepy southern town of turn-of-the-century mansions, wood-framed family homes, and veranda-hed bungalows. Ladies and gentlemen sat in wicker rockers on their grand porticoes or modest porches fanning themselves and gazing out at the lakes and ponds that fringed their quiet, residential neighborhoods. The casual visitor to this overdeveloped metropolis today might see this as a "once upon a time" story, but that's not quite the case. At the Courtyard at Lake Lucerne and a handful of other B&Bs in town, the southern grace and hospitality of an older Orlando survive.

The front verandah of the Norment-Parry, the first B&B to open of this cluster of three, certainly sets the mood. With gingerbread detail on the pillars and white wicker furniture, it overlooks Lake Lucerne and the Orlando skyline. Unfortunately, an exit ramp from the expressway obstructs some of the lake view. Still, the lake is beautiful, and so are the rooms at the inn.

The Norment-Parry Inn is the oldest house in the city and looks the part, with an exterior of buff-colored clapboard siding, white trim, and slate blue wooden shutters. With a history of more than one hundred years, this B&B has been the private home of a judge (Norment) and a tax collector (Parry), a rooming house, a Salvation Army dormitory, and a halfway house. Several years ago, it was bought by a local attorney, Charles Meiner, who gathered antiques for it on trips to England.

Meiner chose interior designers to decorate each of the guest rooms in the house and furnish them with Victorian appointments from his antique collection. Most of the rooms are named after their designers, and each is unique and elegant. The first-floor Crawford is a bedroom with blue and white wallpaper and a large sitting room with two daybeds, good for families. (Because of the antiques, families with young children are not encouraged at the Norment-Parry, though older children are welcome.)

The Honeymoon Suite has a bathroom big enough to accommodate a couple of curved-back antique chairs. It has an old clawfoot tub in one corner and a modern shower. The small Gena Ellis Suite is perhaps the cleverest in the house. Seeing that it had neither a bathroom nor the space to build one, the decorator simply created one right in the bedroom, indicating separateness with a change from carpeting to white ceramic tile.

All the rooms are furnished with Meiner's antiques and have deep-pile carpeting, vases of fresh flowers, Scottish soaps in the baths, and no TVs (except for the Crawford and Clippinger suites). The colors, furnishings, and fabrics in the guest rooms are baroquely sensual. Guests can revel in the Victorian plushness of it all.

A wonderful addition to the Norment-Parry is the I.W. Phillips house. Meiner had this old beach house moved a few hundred feet behind the Norment-Parry several years ago and set about transforming it into an elegant hostelry. He added French doors leading out to verandahs on both the first and second floors, which make the house look large and breezy. He spared no expense in the basic materials and fixtures he chose; he had stained glass windows that he'd saved for years installed in the house and had fine oak floors, staircases, and woodwork exposed, or, when necessary, installed new. As with the Norment-Parry, Meiner furnished the place from his storehouse of English and American antiques. The result is quite wonderful.

Individual rooms are named after colors, except for the Honeymoon Suite, which is spacious and elegant. It is decorated with pink and ivory balloon curtains at the large windows, a settee upholstered in rose-colored satin, a large Victorian wardrobe, and a queen bed. Two sets of French doors open onto a porch that overlooks the brick courtyard.

All of the bathrooms in the Phillips House are extraordinary, especially that in the Honeymoon Suite. There is a deep Roman tub with a stained glass window above, a shower, a modern toilet and bidette, and a sink and vanity in the dressing room area in addition to another sink in the the bathroom proper. The brilliant green and white ceramic tile and the porcelain and chrome fixtures are repeated in the bathrooms of most of the other suites. Heavy white terrycloth towels allow one to feel totally pampered after a long bath.

Each of the other rooms is lushly decorated with wardrobes of burled wood, rich satins and brocades on the sofas and easy chairs, marble-topped tables, and solid bedsteads. Suites have generous sitting areas and private verandahs.

The Wellborn, on the other hand, is done in art deco; it has its own sense of elegance and style. Meiner and his staff let their imaginations go wild. The Wellborn, built in the 1950s, was originally a small genteel apartment building. Today it is one of Orlando's best examples of art deco architecture, with both sharp and curved lines, a metal balustrade, and corner windows. Inside are thirteen one-bedroom suites, each with a small bedroom and bath, living/dining room, and a small but well-equipped kitchen. The decor is very 1950s, with a zebra-striped couch in one suite, black polka dot chairs in another, and tacky treasures from Thailand in another. The colors are red and black, black and white, banana, and off-white. Some of the wall sconces and a few pieces of furniture are originals.

The best room at the Wellborn is the Honeymoon suite, which has a bathroom big enough to live in; there are mirrors on all four walls and a wall of glass bricks above the double whirlpool bath. The rose and ivory suite is eclectic yet elegant; a 1930s Japanese safe inlaid with mother-of-pearl serves as a night table and a gorgeous rose and green Chinese rug is flung on the floor.

The bathrooms and kitchens in all the Wellborn suites are freshly tiled and painted. The rooms are airy and sunny, most with corner windows in the living rooms that have narrow venetian blinds. Guests can choose their bed size; there are doubles, twins, queens, and some kings. Many of the suites have pullout sofas in the living rooms—the largest suites can handle a family comfortably. Front rooms overlook the Orlando skyline, Lake Lucerne, and, unfortunately, the highway. Back rooms face the courtyard fountain and gardens, and first-floor suites have little paths to the courtyard.

The courtyard is one of the best reasons for staying here. By buying the Norment-Parry's neighbor, the Wellborn, and then moving the Phillips House behind the Norment-Parry, Meiner created a space of several hundred square feet to transform into a restful garden. There are curving brick pathways, urns of subtropical flowers, English park benches, palm and banana trees, and flowerbeds of azaleas, impatiens, and magnolias. Water splashes peacefully in the fountain. It is no wonder that dozens of weddings and receptions take place here.

The Courtyard at Lake Lucerne was recently named one of the top ten inns in Florida, and Meiner and his staff do all they can to maintain their enviable reputation. Upon arrival, all guests are offered a glass of sherry or cup of tea and given a complimentary bottle of French wine. The generous, complimentary Continental breakfast is served in the large drawing room of the Phillips House. Breakfast includes bagels or English muffins with whipped strawberry cream, a fresh fruit compote, orange juice, and coffee or tea. Guests eat breakfast leisurely on the sofa in the drawing room, out on the porch, or on one of the garden benches overlooking the fountain.

The Norment-Parry does not have a swimming pool or recreational activity for guests, but all of Orlando—including Church Street Station and the Historic District—is at the doorstep. There are also some lovely brick residential streets near Lucerne Circle that are ideal for a stroll. Delaney Street has a number of side streets extending from it that end at quiet Lake Avenue, which curves around a small lake, home to ducks and other wildlife. These streets, with their gracious homes and huge oak trees dripping with Spanish moss, offer lovely reminders of Old Orlando.

The Gold Key Inn
7100 S. Orange Blossom Trail (Highways 17/92 and 441)
Orlando, Florida 32809
407-855-0050

General manager: Carmen Robinson
Accommodations: 207 rooms
Rates: $56–$62; corporate rooms, $48
Minimum stay: None
Added: 10% tax; $6 extra person; $8 roll-away

Payment: Major credit cards
Children: Free in double rooms
Smoking: Allowed
Open: Year-round

Located on busy Highway 441, the Gold Key is a good place for business travelers. That there is a large corporate clientele here who could stay anywhere at the expense of their company might lead one to believe that this motel is expensive, but it is not. Though the northern end of Route 441, also called Orange Blossom Trail, is one of the ugliest highways in Florida, the Gold Key is on its southern end. The motel is near highways that lead to downtown Orlando and the Orlando International Airport, as well as Route 4 to Walt Disney World.

The Gold Key Inn is a modern, two-story white stucco building, modestly but attractively planted with greenery and some flowers. The lobby, painted and redecorated frequently, has a dark green rug, couches, and armchairs upholstered in a green and ivory Chinese floral pattern.

The rooms are modern and functional, sensible places to get a good night's rest after a hard day's work. Most of the clientele reserve a single room at the corporate rate on one of the corporate floors. A spouse can stay for an additional $6, and a child is free with parents who are paying the double rate. The rooms are quite attractive, with matching bedspreads and drapes and a room-darkening inner drape. Every room has a phone and a desk or table to work at. Guests are given a complimentary newspaper each morning.

The Gold Key Inn provides more than 8,000 square feet of banquet and meeting space. This is a good place for a convention or conference if you want to bring the family to Orlando; Disney World is only 20 minutes away.

Guests can unwind during the day in the exercise center or the Olympic-size pool outside, and there's entertainment and dancing every night in the Piccadilly Pub. The inn's Piccadilly Restaurant has a good reputation among visitors and residents for its British, Continental, and American fare. The red snapper soup and shrimp with ale are two seafood favorites. The popular steak Diane is flamed at tableside with flair.

Hyatt Orlando
6375 U.S. Route 192 West
Kissimmee, Florida 34746
407-396-1234
800-233-1234

Accommodations: 950 rooms
Rates: $109–$119; suites, $180–$470; packages available
Minimum stay: On some holidays
Added: 11% tax
Payment: Major credit cards
Children: Free in room with parents
Smoking: Allowed
Open: Year-round

While its Route 192 address makes the Hyatt Orlando sound as if it's on a busy highway, it is not. Guests drive, or are driven by the Hyatt's airport shuttle, into a tropical oasis several hundred feet off the road. Palms line the curved drive and a fountain by the entryway greets guests. The Hyatt Orlando is a wonderful hotel for conventions, particularly those organized by companies who want participants to bring their families. It's excellent for anyone who wants to spend a day or two at Disney World and enjoy a restful vacation as well.

Subtropical gardens covering the grounds create the ambience of a tropical oasis: native and imported, annual and perennial flowers and plants are used. Inside, large planters of greenery rest on the floors and tables and, in one of the restaurants, flowerbeds are built right into the floor.

Four restaurants serve good food—the al fresco Summerhouse and Limey Jim's are favorites. The Palm Terrace dining room, whose kitchens are overseen by the local Orthodox Union, is one of the few places in the area that serves kosher food. The Trellis lounge, serving evening drinks and light snacks, shows movies every night but Sunday.

Accommodations in this 950-room resort are in color-coded buildings spread over the lush acreage of the Hyatt. Rooms have wall-to-wall carpeting, attractive furniture, pretty bedspreads and drapes, and clean baths. Each of the four building clusters centers on a swimming pool, whirlpool, and children's playground. The hotel's three tennis courts, lighted for night play, are near the Hyatt's heliport. A jogging path meanders through the grounds.

Sea World, a few miles away, is one of the most interesting attractions in the area, with dolphin shows, whale shows, and lovely gardens. There are many other attractions within easy driving distance. The concierge can give you details—or you can listen to the clamoring of your children and go where they clamor loudest for.

Hyatt Regency Grand Cypress
One Grand Cypress Boulevard
Orlando, Florida 32809
407-239-1234
800-233-1234

General manager: Jack Hardy
Accommodations: 750 rooms, 72 suites, 48 villas
Rates: $200–$400; suites, $550–$600; villas, rates available
   upon request; cribs free; packages available
Minimum stay: Inquire in high season
Added: 10% tax
Payment: Major credit cards
Children: Under 18 free in room with parents
Smoking: Allowed
Open: Year-round

The Grand Cypress is not only close to Disney World, but also
one of the most exciting destination resorts in Florida. Outdoors, the recreational area is the centerpiece. Large swimming
pools with grottos, waterfalls, and lush greenery are all the rage
in Florida, and the Grand Cypress's vies with the best of them.
Guests walk out the back door to landscaped grounds and a
rope and wood slatted bridge across part of the pool. The area is
a little overdone with statuary, but kids and adults love this
aquatic playground. The pool twists around outcroppings of
volcanic rock and palms, several waterfalls, and an 80-foot
water slide.

Just beyond the pool is 21-acre Lake Windsong. On the walkway that runs along the lake are bicycles for rent, some with
infant carriers, which gives an idea of the family atmosphere
that prevails. The lake has a pretty beach and a small marina
with sailboats, canoes, and paddleboats for guests. Adjacent are
the tennis courts and racquetball and shuffleboard courts.
There's also a fitness center and several miles of jogging trails.
Golf is at a 45-hole course designed by Jack Nicklaus at the
Grand Cypress Golf Club. There's a pitch-and-putt course to
practice on as well. The Grand Cypress Equestrian Center
offers both Western and English riding, with expert instruction. There's also a day-care center and a children's program. So
there is enough to do—and time to do it— at the Grand Cypress to fill a month of activity.

There are four different restaurants, each appealing to a different palate and pocketbook. Hemingways, at the end of a
covered walkway on the grotto of the huge pool, has a Key West

decor and specializes in seafood. Children love the location and the menu appeals to the whole family. Cascades, the Grand Cypress's main dining room, is physically quite dramatic—a floor-to-ceiling mermaid fountain is along one wall, and the restaurant overlooks the lush grounds. Cascades serves Italian, American, and Oriental food and has outdoor and indoor service.

The Palm Café is extremely casual, serving pizza, salads, and sandwiches for lunch and a traditional menu for breakfast and dinner. More formal is La Coquina, an elegant restaurant serving nouvelle cuisine in a small dining room overlooking a lagoon. The Sunday champagne brunch may be the best in Florida. A huge buffet is spread out in the spotless kitchen. The first time through, guests choose from dozens of different salads, breads, cheeses, and whipped butter spreads; the second time they choose a variety of delicious brunch entrées; finally, they create their own grand finale with a tart, Key lime pie, fresh fruit, cheesecake, or chocolate torte. Ladies receive a lavender rose upon leaving.

Accommodations are comfortable, with pretty decor and Hyatt's standard bath amenities. The best rooms, particularly for conventioneers, are the executive-style Regency Club suites and deluxe rooms. Services include a concierge, a club lounge stocked with magazines, Continental breakfast and evening cocktails in the club, daily newspaper delivery, secretarial services, and extra amenities in the room.

However close it may be to Walt Disney World, the hotel itself is an attraction. It's a great place to stroll and people-watch. The lobby is one of the most impressive in any hotel in the region: large palm trees grow in beds set in the lobby's tile floor and a profusion of philodendron cascades from atrium planters several floors above. Orchids sprout from the trunks of the palm trees, colorful parrots jabber from their cages, and a little brook runs through it all. At one end of the lobby is an exquisitely carved Chinese jade ship in a museum case—a great draw for wide-eyed children. Elsewhere are other works of Oriental art and mammoth vases of birds of paradise and orchids.

Las Palmas Inn

6233 International Drive
Orlando, Florida 32819
407-351-3900
800-327-2114 in U.S.

General manager: Mario Barreio
Accommodations: 262 rooms, 4 suites
Rates: $50–$80; suites, $75–$125; packages available
Minimum stay: With some packages
Added: 10% tax; $10 roll-away
Payment: Major credit cards
Children: Free under 18 in room with parents
Smoking: Nonsmoking available
Open: Year-round

Las Palmas is a book one can judge by its cover. The grounds of this 260-room motor hotel have won awards in the past. There are often special touches, such as volcanic rock formations with flowers planted in their depressions. The landscaper has used imagination and heart. Though it may seem a petty detail, this matters in Florida, where so much time can be enjoyed out-doors—or not enjoyed, if the poolside is littered with cigarette butts or the flowerbeds are scraggly.

The same concern is evident in the hotel itself. The lobby is small and pleasant, with attractive Spanish tile at the check-in area and pretty flower arrangements. Rooms have functional motel furniture, but the coordinating bedspreads and drapes are attractive and fresh. There are only four floors to this stucco hotel; rooms overlooking the pool and grounds are the best. Despite its location on busy International Drive, with only the parking lot as a buffer, rooms are surprisingly quiet. The inn has convention facilities and, because it is relatively small, gives personal service. This is an ideal spot for combining business with family pleasure. Amenities include laundry facilities for guests.

The dining room is the casual Las Fiestas, which serves a mix of American and European cuisine, along with exotic drinks in Las Fiestas Lounge. The waiters and waitresses get along well with children. Walt Disney World is 15 minutes away, and many secondary attractions are nearby: Wet 'n Wild water park (directly across the street), Universal Studios, King Arthur's Feast, Flea World Zoo, Mardi Gras, and Mercado, a Mediterranean-style shopping center, to name a few. There are also a few outlet malls in the area.

Guests who have tramped through the Magic Kingdom or Sea World to the point of exhaustion will want to focus their attention on the pool — the L-shaped swimming pool is heated and can hold a big group of kids and adults. There are beige and white chaises longues and tables and chairs for enjoying a frosty drink from the poolside bar.

Las Palmas is clean and pretty, and the rates are extremely reasonable, with a number of economy rooms. Kids under 18 stay free with their parents, and group rates and vacation packages add to the savings. The hospitality of those who work here is the best bargain of all.

Omni International Hotel

400 W. Livingston Street
Orlando, Florida 32801
407-THE-OMNI (843-6664)
Fax: 407-648-5414
Reservations:
  Omni Reservations
  800-THE-OMNI

General manager: John Meunier
Accommodations: 309 rooms and suites
Rates: $114–$170; Omni Club rooms, $140–$185; packages available
Added: 10% tax
Minimum stay: With some packages
Payment: Major credit cards
Children: Under 18 free in room with parents
Open: Year-round

The Omni International is a modern hotel in every way. Just off I-4, it combines high style with high-tech business services. The hotel has more than 5,000 square feet of meeting space, including a large ballroom on the mezzanine floor and seven individual meeting rooms. Business services include access to a professional audiovisual service and the assistance of a trained convention staff. The Omni International adjoins Orlando's Expo Centre, which has additional meeting and exhibit space that totals 86,000 square feet. If you're planning a convention or meeting in Orlando, this is the place.

The hotel's restaurants include a good Italian restaurant, Petrones, the Livingston Street Café, serving three meals a day, and the vibrant Ozone Lounge. There are many restaurants and casual cafés in the Church Street Exchange, a shopping, dining, and entertainment complex by the old Church Street depot.

Although the Omni is primarily considered a hotel for businesspeople, many families come along with them and enjoy day trips to Walt Disney World, Epcot, and Sea World, which are only 30 minutes away. Across the street from the hotel is the Bob Carr Performing Arts Center, and next door is Orlando's Centroplex, a complex that offers a range of sporting activities. Centroplex facilities are available to all Omni guests and include lighted tennis courts. The hotel also has a recreation deck with a swimming pool and whirlpool.

Rooms at the Omni are businesslike and luxurious, with desks and chairs, eye-soothing fabrics in the drapes and bedspreads, and modern baths. The views are not always good— this is, after all, a city hotel, and one of the adjoining neighborhoods is a bit run-down. But if you request a room on a top floor, you'll see interesting cityscapes and perhaps one of Orlando's many lakes. The top two floors have the additional advantage of being Club floors with concierge services and various perks.

After work or sightseeing, it's pleasant to unwind in the Lobby Lounge, where tea as well as cocktails and snacks are offered. The sunken lounge has a number of small conversation groupings of chairs and sofas. Plaster and wood planters have flowers and plants, and a highly polished grand piano is against one wall. Above is an atrium that gives a feeling of airiness.

Peabody Orlando
9801 International Drive
Orlando, Florida 32819
407-352-4000
Reservations:
 800-PEABODY

General manager: Michael French
Accommodations: 891 rooms and suites
Rates: $165–$220; suites, $165–$1300

Minimum stay: With some packages
Added: 11% tax
Payment: Major credit cards
Children: Under 18 free in room with parents
Smoking: Nonsmoking rooms available
Open: Year-round

In an area with many hotels, the Peabody, with its stucco and glass exterior, doesn't seem like anything special when you first drive by. But the spectacular entrance, with lush plantings and the sound of rushing water from a pair of massive stone and tile fountains, will change your mind. The bellhops and valets, dressed in ivory polo shirts and beige slacks, efficiently help guests.

Inside, in the Mallard Lounge, several ducks spend their day in the fountain. At 11:00 every morning, a red carpet is laid out for the mallards — they walk along it to their lounge domain for a day of quacking, preening, and swimming. At five o'clock in the afternoon, they waddle back across the lobby and return to their home. This may sound bizarre, but it's just part of the fun at the Peabody.

The Peabody is also elegant; there is a feeling of tropical richness throughout the public rooms. Placed everywhere are interesting art and pottery and lovely arrangements of orchids and other exotic flowers. There are marble floors and deep-pile carpeting, beautifully furnished sitting areas, and enormous stucco baskets of flowers and palms.

Convention space includes 54,000 square feet of meeting and banquet space. And across the street is the 350,000-square-foot Orlando/Orange County Convention Center, the largest meeting facility in central Florida. The Peabody Orlando offers good deals for large groups, particularly during the off-season.

The food at the Peabody's several restaurants is uniformly good. Capriccio serves northern Italian cuisine in an elegant atmosphere, while Dux provides artistic nouvelle American. The Bee Line Diner, an interesting 1950s-style diner and deli open 24 hours, is excellent for a quick meal. The atrium Lobby Bar and the Mallard Lounge serve drinks, coffee, and pastries.

If all the culinary indulgence makes you feel guilty, plenty of recreation is offered. On the rooftop there are four lighted tennis courts, an outdoor whirlpool, a heated Olympic-size pool, and a large children's pool. Inside, the athletic club has fifteen Nautilus stations, a sauna, a steam room, a whirlpool, and rooms for facials and massages.

Next door to the athletic club is a "children's hotel," where kids can stay while parents work out, dine out, or go sightseeing. Staffed by professionals, the colorful room is set up like a nursery school.

Sooner or later, even conventioneers spend time at the EPCOT Center and Disney World, and the Peabody has service to and from both. After several hours of walking, it's pleasant to unwind in the luxurious guest rooms. The duplex presidential suites are the best accommodations, but the standard accommodations are not at all shabby: designer bedspreads and drapes, thick carpeting, ginger-jar lamps, comfortable easy chairs, remote control TV, turndown service, and the morning newspaper delivered to your door. The modern baths have imported soaps, a hair dryer, and mini-TVs, which kids love.

Sonesta Village Hotel Orlando
10000 Turkey Lake Road
Orlando, Florida 32819
407-352-8051
800-766-3782

General manager: Allan Sonnabend
Accommodations: 369 villas
Rates: one-bedroom single-level villas, $95–$140; one-bedroom bi-level villas, $110–$165; two-bedroom villas, $180–$260
Minimum stay: With some packages
Added: 10% tax
Payment: Major credit cards; personal check
Children: Free in room with parents
Smoking: Nonsmoking rooms available
Open: Year-round

The Sonesta Village Hotel is one of the nicest places to stay in Orlando for families tired of the crowded hotels closer to Walt Disney World. It's also an excellent convention hotel, making it difficult to put into any one category. It offers variety and excellence to everyone.

The complex has 369 one-and two-bedroom villas with fully equipped kitchenettes, living/dining rooms, separate bedrooms, daily maid service, and patios on the first floors, balconies on the upper floors. The villas are clustered, so guests don't feel overwhelmed; each cluster is grouped around a whirlpool spa. The older villas have recently been redecorated with cushiony carpets and pretty drapes and bedspreads. The two-bedroom villas are spacious and are ideal for those in the area for a week who want some room to spread out. They have one bedroom on the first floor along with a kitchen and dining and living room area. At the summit of an attractive curved stairway is a loft bedroom. The first-floor bedrooms have outside entrances, so older kids can run outside when parents upstairs are still sleeping or, conversely, parents can stay downstairs and come in late without waking their kids in the loft.

The one-bedroom bi-level villas also have a loft bedroom and are just as beautifully decorated. With a pullout couch in the sitting area, these accommodations are big enough for a family of four. This is where you can save money and still feel you are living a life of luxury. When you telephone for reservations, ask the clerk where to buy groceries on your way in so you can save by making breakfast, sandwiches, and snacks. The kitchens also make life much easier for families traveling with babies whose bottles of formula must be kept cool or teething rings frozen in the fridge.

The best value at the Sonesta Village Hotel is the single-level one-bedroom villa. These have all the amenities of the higher priced accommodations. For those who have small children and don't want to be going up and down stairs, the single-level villas are actually preferable.

When you're ready to treat yourself to dinner out, the Sonesta has the pretty Greenhouse restaurant, which also serves breakfast and lunch. The excellent and informal Terrace Café, overlooking the pool and grounds, serves great sandwiches and fresh fruits. For a special dessert or afternoon ice cream cone, kids love the Scoops Ice Cream Shop next to the pool. Both children and parents enjoy the Cabana Pool Bar and Grill, where barbecued hamburgers and hot dogs and cool drinks are available all day. In the evening, there's the Terrace Lounge for exotic cocktails, snacks, and live entertainment.

A tremendous range of activities is available on the Sonesta's 300 acres overlooking Sand Lake. There's a small beach area at the lake and a pier running out to a dock where you can rent jet skis and various types of boats. Waterskiing and jet skiing lessons are also available, and the staff can help you with whatever water sport you're interested in. Many types of waterfowl that are fun to watch from the pier enjoy preening and fishing here.

On dry land, you'll find a free-form swimming pool, a jogging path, health club, sauna, game room, and shuffleboard, as well as lighted tennis courts, a volleyball court, and bicycle rentals. For young children, there's a wooden jungle gym and a play area in an attractively planted setting. Throughout the property, the landscaping is beautiful and well-maintained.

There's a high level of service here, too, with a personal service manager on duty to help you rent tennis equipment or a car, hire a baby sitter, or give you information on how to get to the many attractions in the area. Sea World is just 5 minutes away and the Walt Disney World complex is 15 minutes away.

For those mixing business with pleasure, the Sonesta Village Hotel is ideal. The crush of people at conventions that is common at some Orlando hotels is not a worry here. There are plenty of conventions and corporate conferences held at the Sonesta; they're just handled quietly. The hotel has the impressive Oleander Ballroom for large groups and seven smaller function rooms overlooking Sand Lake. Businesspeople can get plenty of work done while their families enjoy the pool and the lake.

Philadelphia

Four Seasons Hotel
One Logan Square
Philadelphia, Pennsylvania 19103
215-963-1500
800-332-3442

Proprietor: Urban Investment Development Corporation
General manager: John Indrieri
Accommodations: 371 rooms, including 92 executive suites
  and 7 full suites
Rates:
  Rooms: $145–$195 weekends, $235–$285 weekdays
  Suites: $195–$285
Included: Complimentary shoeshine and morning paper
Added: $30 each additional guest; 12% tax
Payment: Major credit cards
Children: Welcome
Pets: Allowed
Smoking: 7 of 8 floors nonsmoking
Open: Year-round

Although the Four Seasons Philadelphia has a contemporary facade, it is one of the city's senior properties. Philadelphia's hotel boom occurred in the mid-1980s, foreshadowed by the opening of the Four Seasons in 1983. The majority of its rooms and the public spaces have a superb view of Logan Square's Swann Memorial Fountain, which was recently restored as a result of a $2 million fund-raising effort. The fountain was fashioned by Alexander Stirling Calder and installed in 1924. It is also referred to as Three Rivers, representing the Delaware, Schuylkill, and Wissahickon rivers.

This eight-story gray granite hotel, taking up an entire city block, was designed by Eugene Kohn. Guests enter at the well-trafficked corner of Ben Franklin Parkway and Race and 18th streets at a wide carport. The Four Seasons' trademark wide hallways are finished in polished rose marble, the walls a light anegre wood.

The finest aspects of the hotel are found in its rooms, in furniture copied by Henredon from original Philadelphia Federal pieces in the city's Museum of Art. The museum can be seen from most of the rooms. There are two color schemes in the rooms, historically appropriate: blue/cocoa and ivory/rust. The researched wallpapers are unusually patterned. While all rooms have stocked mini-bars, some have interesting pieces like an English wing chair in a toile print or perhaps an armoire with delicate inlay. The baths are furnished with a terry robe, a scale, a phone, and a hair dryer.

The popular Fountain Restaurant is a formal setting with tapestried chairs and blue, brown, and beige geometric carpeting, offering three meals under the supervision of chef Jean-Marie Lacroix. The Swann Lounge is the cushy, plush setting for afternoon tea, intimate conversations, and a Viennese dessert buffet on evening weekends, accompanied by the Tom Lawton jazz trio. The outdoor Courtyard Café, on the non–Logan Square side of the hotel, is a lovely alternative in warmer months, where visitors enjoy light-fare dining under umbrellas to the music of a cascading fountain on a backdrop of flowers and greenery.

The Health Spa features an indoor swimming pool, a Jacuzzi, a sauna, fitness classes, and an exercise room with universal equipment. Swedish, shiatsu, and sport massages are available.

Families are happy at the Four Seasons. Children are treated to milk and cookies upon arrival, child-size terry robes in rooms, special menus, Nintendo and children's movies, and the Swann Lounge brunch, with stuffed animals, toys, a train, and edibles like Jell-O squares, M&M cookies, chicken fingers, mini-pizzas, and bite-size hot dogs.

Hotel Atop the Bellevue
1415 Chancellor Court
Philadelphia, Pennsylvania 19102
215-893-1776
215-732-8518
800-221-0833

Proprietors: Cunard Hotels and Resorts
Managing director: Chris Van Der Baars
General manager: Ruedi Bertschinger
Accommodations: 173 rooms, including 28 deluxe and 50
 junior suites

Rates: $210–$250; suites, $275–$400; presidential suites, from
   $850
Included: Daily newspaper, shoeshine
Added: $20 each additional guest; 12% tax
Payment: Major credit cards
Children: Welcome
Pets: Not allowed
Smoking: Nonsmoking rooms available
Open: Year-round

The Bellevue rivals the finest property in any American city.
This architectural landmark, just three blocks from City Hall,
endured a $100-million, three-year renovation and opened to its
current grandeur in March 1989.

   The original Bellevue Hotel was owned by George Boldt in
1881 and sat across Walnut Street from its present locale. Boldt's
reputation as an unsurpassed hotelier prompted the Astor family to request his presence at their New York hotel in 1898. Four
years later, in 1902, Boldt returned to Philadelphia and built the
Bellevue-Stratford with $8 million. The massive French Ren-

aissance edifice opened in 1904, with unimaginable grandeur, immense curved stairways, lavish plaster crown moldings, and lighting fixtures designed by Thomas Alva Edison. Each of the 529 guest rooms was heated with its own fireplace. A rose garden was planted on the rooftop, transformed by flooding into a skating rink in winter.

While heeling faithfully to the original grande dame, the recent renovation effort proved quite interesting, especially in the hotel's configuration: the first eleven floors contain independent offices and luxury shops including Polo/Ralph Lauren, Gucci, Dunhill of London, Pierre Deux, and Tiffany. The guest rooms hover above, on floors 12–17, surrounding a seven-story indoor atrium and the informal Conservatory Restaurant.

In 1986, the interior design firm of Tom Lee, Ltd., headed by Sarah Tomerlin Lee, was hired to mastermind the decor. Since little remained of the original hotel but the Edison fixtures, Mrs. Lee created an imaginary period landscape. The decor of the nineteenth floor and reception areas is described as late Victorian, verging on Edwardian with Belle Époque playfulness. The guest rooms are done in American Empire. The side street entrance and lobby were inspired by the London Ritz.

The Conservatory atrium is an incredibly serene space, overlooked by half the guest rooms. The 3,600-square-foot piazza, in creamy white tones, feels warm in winter and cool in summer. The light wicker furniture, lush plantings, mummified 20-foot palm trees, green and white tiled floor, fountains, and glowing lanterns all rest under a 75-foot mural of clouds, supported by two pairs of columns.

The elevation of the Bellevue reveals two domes atop the building—the Barrymore Lounge and Founders Restaurant, with a small library tucked between. The Barrymore Lounge, introduced by a portrait of the eponymous actress, is the setting for afternoon high tea, evening cocktails, and hors d'oeuvres. The room looks like an inverted Wedgwood teacup, with seven shades of pale blue offset by white plaster molding, culminating in a ceiling mural 17 feet high, painted with coral, tassels, and swags on a background of stars—the theme echoed in the upholstery and the carpet.

Across the hall, Founders is the mirror image in masculine decor. The dining areas look more like parlor sets, observed by four cast-iron statues of influential Philadelphians from each corner of the room. American regional and Continental cuisine is served to the music of a trio, a preamble to Friday and Saturday night dancing. The Philadelphia Library Lounge rests between, where guests enjoy a fireside drink while browsing through a thousand books by or about Philadelphians.

The guest quarters are unusually large at the Bellevue, averaging 460 square feet, decorated with reproduction and antique American Empire furnishings and period wall coverings and borders. The highly sumptuous decor is done in a celery and rust theme or in several shades of blue. All have stocked mini-bars, rich cherry armoires with televisions, a VCR and stereo, executive desks, and three telephones. The marbled baths are luxurious, with a separate vanity area, hair dryer, makeup mirror, bidet, scale, Cunard amenities, a telephone and television, terry robes, and slippers. Upon full turndown, a kind reminder of tomorrow's weather is propped next to chocolates.

In the connecting building, accessible by fly bridge or a 10-foot walk from the concierge desk, is the Philadelphia Sporting Club. Though it has an outside membership, Bellevue guests have unlimited use of this 95,000-square-foot facility, which fills several floors in the height of utilitarian, neoclassic elegance. Among its features are 125 Nautilus machines, a jogging track, a five-lane junior Olympic indoor pool, and racquetball, handball, squash, and basketball courts. In addition, there are Jacuzzis, saunas, and steam rooms, a sports medicine center with cardiovascular conditioning, massage therapy, and a health bar and café.

For pampering after exercise, the luxurious Pierre and Carlo European Spa Salon is in the Bellevue Shops. Its experts are trained in massage, complex hydrotherapy, application of mineralized body masks, and facials including aromatherapy, body scrub, algae hand and foot treatments, and reflexology.

Service is to the Bellevue as beauty is to its setting: integral, quiet, classic, and elegant.

Independence Park Inn

235 Chestnut Street
Philadelphia, Pennsylvania 19106
215-922-4443
800-624-2988

Proprietors: Inns of Distinction
General manager: Thierry Bompard
Accommodations: 36 rooms, all with private bath
Rates: $120–$135; lower weekend and corporate rates
Included: Continental breakfast, afternoon tea
Minimum stay: None

Added: $5 each additional guest over age 6; 12% tax
Payment: Major credit cards
Children: Welcome
Pets: Not allowed
Smoking: 2 of 4 floors nonsmoking
Open: Year-round

Business travelers on a budget or who prefer an intimate, informal environment will adore the Independence Park Inn.
Weekend visitors will appreciate the personal service and
proximity to Philadelphia's Independence Mall.

The elegant granite building was built in 1856 as a dry goods
store for a wealthy merchant named John Elliott. It was designed by architect Joseph C. Hoxie to reflect the grandeur of
the owner's accomplishments. For decades during this century,
the building served as a baby furniture warehouse before it was
bought and restored in 1988 by the present owners, whose efforts put the building on the National Register of Historic
Places.

The exterior is five attenuated stories tall, with high and
narrow double-arched windows that span five across the front
of the building. The lobby is pretty, with three grand floor-to-
ceiling windows and tufted leather couches facing one another
in front of a working fireplace. Exposed wood floors are covered with a large Oriental rug. Guests are treated to quite a
lavish afternoon tea in this elegant setting. Toward the back of
the lobby is a long, narrow, sunny atrium between buildings
where guests have Continental breakfast.

There are nine rooms on each of the upper four floors, decorated slightly differently. Preferable are the front queen and
king parlor rooms, which have beautiful views of Independence Park through long three-quarter windows hung with traditional heavy striped curtains tucked behind round brass tiebacks. All rooms are furnished with two-poster beds and
reproduction Chippendale furniture. The rugs are bright green
and the walls are hung with historic Philadelphia prints. Televisions are hidden in large armoires, and two telephones are
provided in each room. The baths are nice, but not exceptional.
The smaller rooms that overlook the atrium are good for the
budget-minded and offer a fair sacrifice for the very friendly
service at the Independence Park Inn.

This is a friendly, casual place, pretty and sunny in an exceptional piece of architecture. While the innkeeper may be
dressed in a rather formal tie during the business week, the inn
relaxes quite nicely during the weekend to a leisurely pace.
Convenient to historic sites, the Independence Park has the

professional virtues of the many luxury hotels nearby on an intimate, friendly scale.

The Latham Hotel

135 South 17th Street at Walnut
Philadelphia, Pennsylvania 19103
215-563-7474
800-528-4261
Fax: 215-563-4034

Proprietor: LCP Hotels
General manager: Ronald C. Gilbert
Accommodations: 139 rooms with 3 suites
Rates: $150–$180; suites, $425; weekend packages available
Minimum stay: None
Added: $20 additional guest, 12% tax
Payment: Major credit cards
Children: Welcome
Pets: Not allowed
Smoking: 2 of 14 floors nonsmoking
Open: Year-round

This classic hotel was revived in 1990 for $1 million, and the commendable effort resulted in one of Philadelphia's finest values for business travelers. The Latham was built in 1923 on the northeast corner of Rittenhouse Square. Originally an apartment building, it opened as a hotel in 1970. The recent renovation lends comparisons to an intimate European hotel —this is the feel a visitor gets upon crossing the elegant beaux-arts limestone threshold under the awning and gilded portico.

The lobby is a wonderful place, exactly the proportions newer hotels try to approximate. Its small scale encourages privacy and feels like a mansion's foyer. The intimate space is narrow and high, brightened with brass and crystal chandeliers and sconces. The gilded coffered ceiling reaches to elegant Palladian arches at the top of its two-story height. Large planters, Oriental carpets, and traditional furnishings contribute to the Old World ambience.

The ground-floor eateries include the 17th Street Bistro, which has an elegant cork marble foyer and offers light fare, or Bogart's, serving new American cuisine. It's an enchanting place with a Casablanca theme, quite romantic, with banquettes, ceiling fans, and slatted ceilings. Chef Gerard Dougherty prepares such dishes as crisp roast duckling with black cherry sauce or baked trout with duxelle and crayfish sauce for $17 to $26.

The rooms are immaculate and bright, with traditional Chippendale reproduction furnishings decorated cheerfully with different schemes of soft chintz drapes and bedding; perhaps light floral wallcovering complementing carpeting and fabric in pastels of mint, peach or rose; or bold colors with accenting trellis patterns. Due to its origins as an apartment building, the rooms have interesting configurations, some with bay windows framed in floor to ceiling drapes. The baths are clean and bright, with gleaming white tiles, dryers, phones, and fine Scottish amenities. Unusual pieces may include marble top dressers and end tables, leather-top desks, or old European prints.

The staff is helpful, quite professional, and proud of the recent renovations.

Omni Hotel at Independence Park
Fourth and Chestnut Streets
Philadlephia, Pennsylvania 19106
215-925-0000
800-THE-OMNI
Fax: 215-925-1263

Proprietor: Omni Hotels
General manager: David J. Colella
Accommodations: 155 rooms on 12 floors
Rates: $205; special weekend rates
Minimum stay: None
Added: 12% tax, $20 additional guest
Payment: Major credit cards
Children: Welcome
Pets: Allowed
Smoking: 3 nonsmoking floors
Open: Year-round

In November 1990, Omni put a new face forward and introduced its first small European-style luxury hotel. The location is perfectly suited to Omni's new image: the hotel is outside the business center in the historic part of Philadelphia, directly across from Independence Park. The Omni is the only full-service hotel in this part of town, and its restaurant Azalea has gotten rave reviews for its American regional food.

The building nicely complements the historic structures of eastern Philadelphia. Its thirteen stories of brick, lightened with abundant windows, rest above two stories of a limestone base, constructed at a cost of about $25 million. Gabled peaks at the roofline have clerestory windows with classic overtones.

Guests enter under a brightly lit brass portico to the sweeping lobby, which has polished marble surfaces everywhere. The reception area is to the left. To the right are two large salons: a formally appointed area and a more contemporary space for socializing and music, including a jazz trio on weekends. Large windows permit ample light and views to Independence Park.

The second floor is home to Azalea, which has lovely treetop views of the park through floor-to-ceiling Palladian windows. The room, like the lobby below, is light and airy, softly furnished in pastel colors. The chefs are proud of their reliance on local farms for fresh herbs and vegetables, creating dishes like brook trout with cornmeal crust topped with smoked bacon, or smoked duck breast with honey and chestnut purée and walnut-stuffed figs.

There are about dozen rooms on each of the thirteen floors above—all facing Independence Park. While the color schemes of brown and beige are muted and dull, the rooms are spacious, with large windows and lovely marble baths.

Below ground is a lap pool with serene indirect lighting. The enthusiastic staff is helpful and enthusiastic about its new role in Philadelphia.

The Rittenhouse
210 West Rittenhouse Square
Philadelphia, Pennsylvania 19103
215-546-9000
800-635-1042

Proprietors: Amerimar Realty Co., General Electric Pension Trust
General manager: Paul E. Seligson
Accommodations: 98 rooms, including 12 suites
Rates:
  Rooms: $235–$260 weekdays; $130–$150 weekends
  Suites: $300–$350
Added: $25 each additional guest; 12% tax
Payment: Major credit cards
Children: Welcome
Pets: Small pets allowed
Smoking: Every other floor nonsmoking
Open: Year-round

Philadelphia is blessed with two entirely different, consummate luxury properties in the Hotel Atop the Bellevue and the Rittenhouse, which received its first five diamond award from AAA in 1992. This elegant, full-service property opened in

June 1989 as a result of a $120-million effort masterminded by developer David Marshall. In addition to housing 98 beautiful guest rooms on floors 5–9, the Rittenhouse has a deluxe Health Club and Spa, two highly rated restaurants, nonpareil views of Rittenhouse Square, and the exclusive Nan Duskin women's boutique.

The Rittenhouse is on the west side of the square that inspired its name, one of five of William Penn's original city squares. The 6.5-acre park is named for David Rittenhouse, born in Germantown in 1732, said to have invented America's first telescope. He served as Pennsylvania state treasurer from 1777 to 1789 and as the first director of the United States Mint in Philadelphia in 1792.

Despite its surrounding history, the Rittenhouse is a modern piece of architecture, a glass trapezoid that looks like a very wide staircase standing on its side. Interestingly, the Rittenhouse foundation was laid in 1973, but because the original developer went bankrupt, the 30-story shell stood empty for fourteen years before Mr. Marshall took the helm in 1987.

The lobby is a beautiful array of olive, taupe, teal, and cream, featuring ash wood molding and millwork, pine Louis XIV bergères, smooth round columns supporting a coffered ceiling with massive glowing ceiling sconces, and polished golden marble floors. The Cassatt Tea Room and Lounge is named for the family whose mansion graced this site. Alexander, the son, was the president of the Pennsylvania Railroad and married the niece of President James Buchanan; daughter Mary was the famous American Impressionist whose work graces some of the hotel's public spaces. The lounge is the setting for afternoon tea, cocktails, and piano music amid tapestried French chairs and huge potted trees. In warmer months, the arched French doorways open to a trellised garden café.

Rittenhouse accommodations are large and beautiful, reputed to have Philadelphia's finest baths. As a result of the building's jagged exterior, half of the guest rooms have not only wonderful views of Rittenhouse Square but interesting interiors with 90-degree alcoves. The staterooms are decorated in a country French theme, with masculine navy blues and beiges, striped bergères, Queen Anne chairs and writing desks, and border paper matching the striped drapes. Each room has three phones (one in the bath), two televisions (one in the bath), a VCR, and a mini-bar. The feminine suites are done in Laura Ashley pink chintz, with an upholstered king-size headboard under a gathered crown canopy. The beige and light brown marble baths have Neutrogena amenities, a hair dryer, and terry robes. Even the hallways are graced with original art, including several paintings by Joe Barker, who was discovered selling his work outside by Mr. Marshall.

Award-winning Restaurant 210 offers contemporary cuisine during lunch and dinner in a high-tech elegant setting overlooking the square. Neoclassic mahogany chairs and millwork, black and beige upholstery, black silk banquettes, and silver linen on the walls and columns make a muted backdrop for colorful abstract art. Executive chef Gary Coyle came from New York's La Côte Basque and prepares entrées, all above $20, like grilled magret of duck with smoked apple and jicama torte and green peppercorn sauce; preceded perhaps by Maine lobster medallions with tarragon roe quinoa and lobster dressing or leek and oyster pot pie with California chardonnay and mixed herb seasoning.

TreeTops is a floor below, a pleasant café that shares the view of Rittenhouse Square. It's decorated with rattan chairs, light yellow walls, and terra cotta floors. The jumbo lump crabcakes have been praised loudly around town. The woody Boathouse Row Bar is home to the Liz Ann scull which John B. Kelly, father of Grace, rowed toward a gold medal in the 1920 Olympics.

A grand feature of the Rittenhouse is Toppers Spa and Fitness Center, which opened in August 1990. The fitness facilities offer a pool, sauna, steam room, rowing and cycling machines, stair climbing machines, and Cybex exercise equipment. The

Esthetique Spa features massage, aromatherapy facials, seaweed body wraps, body scrubbing and polishing, and hydrotherapy baths.

The Ritz-Carlton

17th and Chestnut Streets at Liberty Place
Philadelphia, Pennsylvania 19103
215-563-1600
800-241-3333

Proprietors: Liberty Place Hotel Associates
General manager: Jim Beley, under the Ritz-Carlton Hotel
   Company
Accommodations: 290 rooms, including 16 suites
Rates: $195–$265; suites, from $425
Included: Five complimentary meal presentations on the
   Club level
Minimum stay: None
Added: $35 each addditional guest; 12% tax
Payment: Major credit cards
Children: Welcome
Pets: Not allowed
Smoking: Nonsmoking rooms available
Open: Year-round

While the majority of its properties are of entirely new construction, Ritz-Carlton hotels represent the finest in sophisticated Old World hospitality, inspired by the Ritz of London.
With rich wood paneling, classic moldings, extensive art col-
lections, lavish antiques, handwoven carpets, marble floors,
and elegant and comfortably furnished public spaces, the Ritz-
Carlton properties emulate stately mansions and English country manors.

The Philadelphia Ritz opened in November 1990. To get
here, look for the city's version of the Chrysler Building. Liberty Place is two twin glass skyscrapers, one of which pierces
the sky with its needle tip. A squat 15-story adjunct rests between them: the Shops at Liberty Place, with about 70 boutiques and specialty stores, and the Ritz-Carlton Philadelphia.

Guests enter a foyer on the ground floor and take an elevator
to reception, a floor above. Such is the Ritz-Carlton way, rid-
ding the lobby and reception area from the street's bustle and
creating an elite approach. When the elevators open, all is as it
should be: the trademark Italian marble floors gleam, handwoven carpets muffle one's step, 18th-and 19th-century oils are
kind to the eye, and the softspoken staff is eager to assist.

The common spaces on the reception floor are lovely and civilized. The Dining Room serves formal French cuisine under the direction of starred Michelin chef Philippe Reininger. In this American Federal room with light paint and bright white molding, guests dine under crystal chandeliers on bone china and the Ritz-Carlton trademark cobalt blue glasses. Waterford crystal oil lamps are placed on each table. The Grill and the Grill Bar serve light fare in a dark, clubby atmosphere with rich wood molding and ceilings and a green marble bar. The walls are covered in green damask, lit by a wood-burning French fireplace. The Lobby Lounge serves morning coffee, afternoon high tea, and cocktails in the evening, with a relaxing backdrop of live classical music or a jazz trio.

The guest rooms are lovely. The walls are damask gray and the furnishings are traditional. The baths are entirely marble, with two terry robes and ample Ritz-Carlton amenities. The top two floors are under the tutelage of the Ritz-Carlton Club —they have their own concierge and lounge and five complimentary meals are offered. The beautiful red Oriental hall carpet is modeled after the London Ritz.

The fourth-floor Fitness Center has a Nautilus and a rowing machine, two bikes, a dry sauna, Jacuzzi, and massage therapy upon request, all in a pristine marble setting.

Thomas Bond House

129 South Second Street
Philadelphia, Pennsylvnaia 19106
215-923-8523
800-845-2663

Proprietors: National Park Service
Innkeeper: Jerry Dunne
Accommodations: 12 rooms, all private baths
Rates: $80–150
Included: Full breakfast on weekends, Continental breakfast on weekdays, wine and cheese in the evening
Minimum stay: None
Added: 12% tax, $15 additional guest
Payment: Major credit cards except Discover
Children: Welcome
Pets: Not allowed
Smoking: Allowed
Open: Year-round

Visitors to Independence National Historic Park in Philadelphia can extend their time in the 18th century with a stay at the

Thomas Bond House. This bed-and-breakfast, uniquely restored by the National Park System, is on the National Register of Historic Places. The three-story brick brownstone, built around 1769, was the home of Dr. Thomas Bond, Ben Franklin's personal doctor. Additions were built in 1824 and 1840. Guests enjoy the proximity to the Visitors' Center Welcome Square, the Customs House, Penn's Landing, and Society Hill.

One walks past the narrow front of the building, three mullioned windows across, on South Second Street and enters at the wide side entrance, which is topped by a regal pediment. To the right of the foyer are two dining areas, the informal and the formal, with beautiful blue toile wallpaper above the chair rail. During the week, Continental breakfast is served, expanded to a full breakfast for weekend guests, who dine at Colonial tables made by a local artisan. To the left is the formal parlor, furnished with Williamsburg antiques, where guests enjoy wine and cheese in the early evening. Above the working fireplace hangs a portrait of Dr. Bond, father of another Dr. Bond who served as Surgeon General under President Van Buren.

There are four guest rooms on the second floor, six on the third floor, and two tucked into the pediment on the fourth floor. Decorated in Colonial simplicity, the rooms are comfortable and quite clean, filled with reproduction Williamsburg furniture. Twin, double or queen beds are covered with pretty white lace over blue duvets. Electric candles sit on windowsills, and old Philadelphia prints decorate the walls. Tiny sachets are hung on the bedposts. Each room has a television tucked in a highboy, and businesspeople will appreciate the desk and telephone. The baths were modernized during the restoration and have new brass fixtures and striped oxford skirts below the sinks.

In 1993, ten more rooms will be added in the nearby Bouvier brownstone, named after the family of the former first lady who lived here for years. Furnished in similar decor, the rooms in the Bouvier House are less expensive. Below the Thomas Bond House is the Key and Quill Shop, established in 1976, which sells reproductions of 18th-century Colonial furniture, accessories, and antique maps from around the world.

Phoenix/ Scottsdale

Arizona Biltmore
24th Street and Missouri
Phoenix, Arizona 85016
602-955-6600
800-528-3696
Fax: 602-954-2548

General manager: Bill Lucas
Accommodations: 502 rooms
Rates: single or double, $210–290; suites start at $600
Added: 10.25% tax
Payment: Major credit cards
Children: Under 18 free in room with parents
Pets: Small pets allowed with deposit
Smoking: Nonsmoking rooms available
Open: Year-round

Built in 1929, the Arizona Biltmore is the grande dame of Phoenix. Covering 200 acres, it offers many activities—two 18-hole championship golf courses, 17 tennis courts (16 lighted), three outdoor swimming pools, a putting green, lawn chess, shuffleboard, a health club, croquet lawns, bicycle paths, and jogging trails. Two of its restaurants, the Orangerie and the Gold Room, have won awards for cuisine and decor. Best of all, the hotel's staff works hard to please guests, offering a full range of services with professionalism and a smile.

Few hotels can claim such a distinctive look both inside and out. Frank Lloyd Wright was the consulting architect on the project, and his inspiration is evident throughout the hotel. Precast concrete blocks, molded on the site using Arizona sand, are the primary building material. The technique was developed by Wright, and the Biltmore was the first large structure to be constructed in this manner.

In the rooms, the colors are bright and the furniture has an individual flair. Mirrors, stained glass, and tile designs are generously used. The rooms are in one of five buildings or in cottages spread over the lush grounds. Called traditional, classic, and resort, they range from moderate size with a mini-bar to extra-large with a bedroom and sitting room, a mini-bar and refrigerator, a large bath with a separate shower and bath stall, and a private balcony or patio. All the rooms have views of the golf courses, mountains, or the beautiful gardens. In the gardens is an Olympic-size pool, evocative of an earlier era with private cabanas.

Dining is important at the Biltmore. The Gold Room (named for its gold-leaf ceiling) has always been the main dining room. The Orangerie is a fine restaurant where guests can expect meals such as pan-seared Chinook salmon with a three-pepper crust and champagne watercress butter ($17.50), roast rack of Colorado lamb with a guava mustard rosemary glaze served with braised Swiss chard and artichokes on Merlot peppercorn sauce ($22.50), and grilled escalar jack on mixed summer greens and plum tomato sorrel vinaigrette ($14.50). For lighter fare, there's the Café Sonora, serving American and Mexican dishes. There's also a snack bar by the pool, two cocktail lounges, and the Aztec Theatre, where plays are performed in a cabaret setting.

The hotel seems transported from an easier, more gracious time, and the extensive renovation in 1987 further enhanced the atmosphere. The Arizona Biltmore is now managed by Westin Hotels.

Self-parking at the resort is free. The exclusive shopping center, Biltmore Fashion Park (the hotel came first), is just down the road.

Hyatt Regency Scottsdale at Gainey Ranch

7500 East Doubletree Ranch Road
Scottsdale, Arizona 85258
602-991-3388
800-233-1234
Fax: 602-483-5550

Manager: Bill Edier Orley
Accommodations: 493 rooms
Rates: $115–$335; suites, $225–$2,200
Added: 10.25% tax
Payment: Major credit cards
Children: Welcome
Pets: Not allowed

Smoking: Allowed
Open: Year-round

The Hyatt Regency Scottsdale is a true oasis in the midst of the desert, with a water playground and beautiful setting that surpasses just about anything else in the Southwest. There are 27 holes of golf, a health and fitness center, eight tennis courts, lawn croquet, and jogging and cycling trails. The hotel opened in late 1986 as part of the Gainey Ranch complex, which includes residential and retail development. With hundreds of palm trees and other lush foliage, it's a beautiful resort. So special are the landscaping outside and the artwork inside that art and flora and fauna tours are given once a week.

The water playground is truly dazzling. Built on several levels, it has 28 fountains, 10 pools, and a 3-story waterslide—it's a water fantasy, a quasi-Roman-Grecian creation with a pure American sandy beach. Fort Kachina playground and Camp Hyatt Kachina provide many activities for kids, making the Hyatt especially appealing for families.

The lobby, decorated with international art, leads to three dining rooms. The Squash Blossom, offering southwestern cuisine, has all-day service with both indoor and outdoor dining. It is tastefully decorated, particularly for an informal restaurant, with touches such as hand-blown Mexican glassware. The more formal Golden Swan overlooks Koi Pond.

Sandolo offers the most intimate dining experience. The waiters sing as you enjoy Italian specialties, and the meal is followed by a romantic gondola ride on the pond, complete with a complimentary glass of wine. Sandolo's dinner entrées range from $8 to $12. Reservations are necessary.

The rooms are decorated in plums, mauves, and grays and have private balconies and stocked mini-bars. Cactus print robes are a refreshing change from the standard terrycloth. Regency Club rooms on the third floor include complimentary breakfast, afternoon hors d'oeuvres, and upgraded amenities. Several deluxe casitas (with a living room, two to four bedrooms, and stereo systems) are on the lake.

The resort's Regency Spa surpasses most fitness centers: in addition to sunny workout rooms, excellent exercise equipment, saunas, massage rooms, and herbal wraps, it has the Mollen Clinic, a physical fitness and medical facility that offers personal health evaluations and health programs.

Sample fees for the recreational facilities are $15 per court hour for tennis and $7 for exercise classes. Spa use is complimentary. Eighteen holes of golf, including cart rental, is $56 in the summer, $100 in winter.

John Gardiner's Tennis Ranch on Camelback
5700 East McDonald Drive
Scottsdale, Arizona 85253
602-948-2100
800-245-2051
Fax: 602-483-7314

General manager: Eleni Koliambas
Accommodations: 100 units; casitas and 4-and 5-bedroom
   casas (some with their own court)
Rates: $195–$325; 2-bedroom casitas (up to 4 people), $480–
   $540; weekend packages from $550 per person double
   occupancy; 1-week packages from $1,425 per person double
   occupancy
Included: Breakfast, lunch, and court time
Added: 9.05% tax and 15% service charge
Payment: Major credit cards
Children: During junior clinics only
Pets: Not allowed
Smoking: Allowed
Open: October through mid-May

If you want tennis combined with luxury, John Gardiner's
Tennis Ranch is the place for you. Here on Camelback Mountain, the rest of the world seems distant.

Tennis is king at this private club resort, which holds such
tournaments as the annual invitational U.S. Senators' Cup. Take
your choice of 24 championship courts. In keeping with tradition, players almost always wear white on the court. (The
ranch's official dress code states "predominately white.")
Weekly clinics offer 21 hours of instruction, 6 hours of optional
tournaments, complimentary court time, and two half-hour
massages—which you may need after all that tennis. (Weekend "tiebreaker" packages are also available.) More than thirty
pros provide instruction at a ratio of one pro to every four
guests. Workouts include computerized ball machines and vid-
eotape replay. In between sessions on the court, guests can relax
in three swimming pools, saunas, and whirlpools or have a
massage.

Lodging is in casitas or casas, all privately owned, scattered
over the resort's 50 acres. Casitas come in three sections, with a
living room in the middle and a bedroom on each side. You can
rent any part or the entire unit. Some have sun rooms and
private balconies. Most are decorated with a modern southwest
motif; all are luxuriously comfortable. The living rooms have
fireplaces and kitchenettes, and each section has a phone and

T.V. For the ultimate in tennis luxury, opt for a casa. Casa Rosewall (the home of Ken Rosewall) has a rooftop court and private pool.

Meals are served in the clubhouse, which by day is casual and at night is more formal—guests are asked to wear evening attire. One can eat indoors or outdoors, overlooking the valley below.

Marriott's Camelback Inn
5402 East Lincoln Drive
Scottsdale, Arizona 85253
602-948-1700
800-228-9290 or 800-24-CAMEL
Fax: 602-951-2152

General manager: Wynn Tyner
Accommodations: 423 units
Rates: $95–$290; suites (up to 5 people per unit), $160–$1,600
Added: 9.05% tax
Payment: Major credit cards
Children: Under 18 free in room with parents
Pets: Allowed
Smoking: Nonsmoking units available
Open: Year-round

The Camelback Inn was built in 1936 by Jack and Louise Stewart. With their hospitality and dedication, they wrote a romantic chapter in the story of American resorts. Their inn attracted noted guests from around the world, many of whom returned year after year to the popular desert resort. "In all the world, only one," was the Stewarts' guiding principle as they molded a lodging of rare charm, emphasizing attention to detail and personal service.

In 1967 the Stewarts sold the resort to the Marriotts, a family that had visited Camelback for 14 years. Today's resort is much larger than the one the Marriotts bought. But you don't have to look far to sense the tradition, which is a real treat in an area now crowded with posh new playgrounds.

"Where time stands still" is emblazoned on the inn's clock tower and at the entrance to the lobby. The message to guests is clear: forget about time and the outside world—relax and enjoy. Spread over 125 acres of desert terrain, numerous recreational facilities help "real world" cares slip away. Camelback has two highly acclaimed 18-hole championship golf courses (greens fees, including golf cart rental, range from $25 to $70, depending on the season), a driving range, putting green, ten tennis courts ($10 per hour), three pools, and five restaurants and lounges. The front lawn is an 825-yard executive golf course. Stables with horseback riding are nearby; free transportation to them is provided. Hiking trails lead up Mummy Mountain, at the resort's back door. There's a playground for kids, bikes to rent, shuffleboard, and lots of space to roam. Social programs during holiday seasons reflect the spirit of the Stewarts' resort.

Guests stay in low rooms scattered over the rolling grounds, which are studded with citrus, olive, and mesquite trees and more than 40 varieties of cactus. Lodgings include single rooms, rooms with an adjoining sundeck, and a variety of suites. There is a 4-bedroom manor house with a full kitchen, washer-dryer, and private pool. All the rooms have refrigerators and small cookstoves. Even the standard rooms are spacious, with extras such as two phones, a coffeemaker, ironing board, safe, stocked mini-bar, hair dryer, and remote control TV. The decor is southwestern.

The main lodge, small for a resort of this size, is decorated with an Indian theme; it has wonderful painted beams, Navajo rugs, and light fixtures made from arrows. The lobby is listed on the National Register of Historic Places.

Dining offers many choices, both in cuisine and price, and everyone, even finicky children, should be able to find something to suit their taste. Popular with guests and residents, Chaparral specializes in classic Continental cuisine. Entrées such as beef Wellington, steak Diane, rack of lamb, scampi flambé, and Dover sole range from $18 to $26. MAP, FAP, and CAP (Camelback American Plan, with breakfast and lunch) are available.

The Camelback also has its own spa, with state-of-the-art exercise equipment, a wellness center, revitalizing skin and body treatments, and a highly trained staff. Guests can use the facility for $18 per day ($10 after 5:00 P.M.). The outdoor massage rooms and 25-meter lap pool are especially pleasant, surrounded by terraced cacti and a glorious view of the city and the mountains. Sprouts, the spa's café, has a tempting menu even if you're not keeping track of calories, fat, and cholesterol. Above the spa, there's a mock Old West town where popular cookouts are held, and the Camelback has its own hiking trail up Mummy Mountain.

The Phoenician
6000 East Camelback Road
Scottsdale, Arizona 85251
602-941-8200
800-888-8234
Fax: 602-947-4311

General manager: Hans Turnovszky
Accommodations: 442 rooms, 107 casitas, 31 luxury suites
Rates: $270–$405; casitas for 2, $270–$405 (each extra
   person $50 per night); 1-bedroom suites, $750–$950; 2-
   bedroom suites, $1077–$1,275
Added: 10.25% tax
Payment: Major credit cards
Children: Under 12 free in room with parents
Pets: In the casitas only
Smoking: Nonsmoking rooms available
Open: Year-round

With the name of its lobby bar, the Thirsty Camel, and a sun inlaid in the marble floor as you enter the lobby, the Phoenician plays on its location in the Valley of the Sun. Developed by Charles Keating, the Phoenician opened in late 1988 as the newest and perhaps the most opulent resort in the area: $6.5 million was spent on art alone. Spread over 130 acres, the lushly landscaped property is dotted with lagoons and streams. The semicircular hotel rests against a hillside, with Camelback Mountain as a backdrop. Casitas, a spa, a clubhouse, and an 18-hole golf course comprise the lower half of the circle. Multilevel pools, one with mother-of-pearl tile, and fountains are in between, and the rooms fill the upper half.

The rooms, furnished with painted rattan furniture and soft pastel fabrics, are airy and spacious. The bathrooms are luxurious as well, with large oval tubs, separate showers, and marble floors. Robes are provided: terrycloth in the winter, cotton in summer. All the rooms have closet safes, hair dryers, ironing boards, scales, and telephones in the baths. The televisions are bigger than average, and VCRs are available upon request. Most rooms have balconies. Governors suites have two terraces, two rooms (the sitting room has a daybed), and two baths—one with a huge walk-in shower. The casitas have a more residential feeling; some have fireplaces and kitchenettes. For those who require even more space, two elaborate Presidential suites offer 3,300 square feet of pure luxury.

The Phoenician has several restaurants. The Terrace Restaurant serves Italian-American cuisine—entrées range from $15 to $25—and an elaborate Sunday brunch. For southwestern cuisine, try Windows on the Green, overlooking the golf course. The Thirsty Camel serves a fancy afternoon tea; the Oasis serves meals by the pool; and Mary Elaine's specializes in Mediterranean delicacies.

In addition to swimming and golf, there are 11 lighted tennis courts (one has an automated practice court) and a full-service health and fitness center for a daily charge of $10. Treatments such as massage and aromatherapy are charged at an hourly rate. Bicycles can be rented for $5 per hour or $20 per day. Supervised programs for children are also available. Interestingly enough for an active desert resort, there are no drinking fountains in the public areas, although the bartender will happily provide an ice cold glass of water in the Thirsty Camel.

The Pointe at Tapatio Cliffs
11111 North Seventh Street
Phoenix, Arizona 85020
602-997-6000
800-934-1000
Fax: 602-993-0276

General manager: Bob Brooks
Accommodations: 591 suites
Rates: $75–$260
Added: 10.25% tax
Payment: Major credit cards
Children: Welcome
Pets: Not allowed
Smoking: Nonsmoking suites available
Open: Year-round

The mood is festive at the Pointe. With pool parties and a host of special activities, it's like a giant cruise ship moored at an inland shore. Covering 400 acres, the Pointe is a sprawling, Mediterranean-style, cliffside resort village. It's a complete vacationland with 16 tennis courts, seven pools, four racquetball courts, horseback riding, hiking, mountain biking, three major restaurants, a spa, and an 18-hole golf course. A 2,700-acre preserve adjoins the resort.

The tennis courts are excellent, and extensive landscaping between them adds to their appeal. Horseback rides are charged by the hour or half-day; special rides include breakfast, lunch, and pony rides for children under seven.

The suites are arranged in buildings with arches, courtyards, and fountains. They have a sitting room with a wet bar and refrigerator, a bedroom with an armoire, a bath divided into sections, and a small balcony.

Pointe In Tyme restaurant was designed with a spirit of fun. Its interior is glitzy, and its menu, featuring dishes made famous at restaurants across the country, is enticing. There's pasta jambalaya from Mr. B's in New Orleans, veal Oscar from the Waldorf-Astoria in New York, and raisin rice pudding from the King's Arms in Williamsburg, Virginia, to name a few.

The crème de la crème is Étienne's Different Pointe of View, on top of the mountain. Étienne's bursts with energy, thanks to its innovative architecture, decor, and setting. Boasting a mile-long list of awards, it has one of the most impressive wine lists in the country — more than twenty pages of unusual bottles, including an extensive selection of California cabernets. Entrées range from $22 to $27.

Red Lion's La Posada
4949 East Lincoln Drive
Scottsdale, Arizona 85253
602-952-0420
800-547-8010
Fax: 602-840-8576

General manager: Derick MacDonald
Accommodations: 264 rooms
Rates: $65–$205; suites, $400–$1,050
Added: 9.05% tax
Payment: Major credit cards
Children: Under 18 free in room with parents
Pets: Allowed
Smoking: Nonsmoking rooms available
Open: Year-round

Red Lion's La Posada brings water to the desert and adds an extra dollop of glitz to Scottsdale's hotel row. The lobby, more like Las Vegas than the Southwest, has a profusion of fuchsia, gold, and sparkle. It's a lively place; the tone is upbeat and the staff greets you with a smile.

In back there's a half-acre swimming pool with a manmade boulder mountain, splashing waterfalls, and a partly hidden grotto bar. Directly behind the hotel is the area's most distinctive landmark—Camelback Mountain. The Garden Terrace Restaurant is a great place to eat while overlooking the pool and the mountain; the Sunday champagne brunch is a popular event, at $17.95. Like the lobby, it has a refreshingly energetic decor. The adjoining Terrace Lounge has live entertainment.

The guest rooms, spread over the resort's 32 acres, are in long stucco buildings with red tile roofs. Inside, brocades, formal furniture, and mirrors prevail. The smallest room is large by hotel standards—450 square feet. The cabanas are 759 square feet, the casitas, 950 square feet. All the rooms have small refrigerators, honor bars, TVs in armoires, and patios or balconies.

La Posada has six tennis courts, two racquetball courts, a volleyball court, fitness center, massage services, a putting green, table tennis, horseshoes, basketball, a sauna, and hot tubs. There's also a camp for children, concierge service, car rental, and airport transportation. A shopping plaza on the grounds has an Italian restaurant.

The Registry Resort

7171 North Scottsdale Road
Scottsdale, Arizona 85253
602-991-3800
800-247-9810
Fax: 602-948-9843

General manager: Manfred Braig
Accommodations: 318 rooms
Rates: $80–$210; suites, $285–$2,050
Added: 10.25% tax
Payment: Major credit cards
Children: Under 17 free in room with parents
Pets: Not allowed
Smoking: Nonsmoking rooms available
Open: Year-round

One of the resorts along Scottsdale Road, the Registry stands apart from its neighbors with its abundant tennis and golf. It is part of the McCormick Ranch development, comprising residential, office, and recreational facilities. The two golf courses, one next to the hotel, are 18-hole, par 72 championship courses. The 21 lighted tennis courts are exceptionally fine; court time is $15 per hour. The main swimming pool is one of the best in the area; not only is it large, it has a three-meter and one-meter diving board (rare for hotels these days) and a lifeguard on duty. Several smaller pools are also on the grounds.

The lobby is elegantly decorated with fine furnishings. The Registry's restaurant, Café Brioche, features southwestern cuisine and has outdoor seating by the pool. The Kachina Lounge has live entertainment nightly during the winter season, and the Phoenician Room, used for special functions, is opulent — a step back into supper club days, with a stage for live entertainment.

About a third of the guest rooms are attached to the main building. Casitas are spread over the grounds, interspersed with courtyards and flowering shrubs. Modern in decor, they have the expected amenities and are by far the most appealing accommodations. The resort also has room service, a health spa ($5 per day), and a putting green.

The Ritz-Carlton
2401 East Camelback Road
Phoenix, Arizona 85016
602-468-0700
800-241-3333
Telex: 543299
Fax: 602-468-0793

General manager: John Rolfs
Accommodations: 281 rooms
Rates: $90–$320; double, $90–$340; suites, $270–$695; $50 additional person
Added: 10.25% tax
Payment: Major credit cards
Children: Under 18 free in room with parents; roll-aways $20 per day
Pets: Not allowed; concierge can make boarding arrangements
Smoking: Nonsmoking rooms available
Open: Year-round

The modern pink exterior of the Ritz-Carlton is deceptive. When you walk into the lobby, you are greeted by gleaming Italian marble, Oriental rugs, and priceless antiques. The feeling of Old World elegance is remarkable for a new hotel.

Off to the side is the Lobby Lounge, the site where high tea is served every day from 2:00 to 4:30 P.M. The scones with Devonshire cream are a real treat. During the Christmas season, "Teddy Bear Tea" is served for children. The lounge is filled with Teddy bears, hot chocolate is served, and stories are read aloud to eager ears. On Friday and Saturday nights, couples dance to live entertainment.

Next door, the Grill has a men's club atmosphere. Original paintings of sporting and equestrian scenes, all predating the 1890s, hang on the paneled walls. The fireplace came from a castle in Germany. The Grill's specialties are prime aged meats, fresh fish, and pheasant, but if you don't see what you want, just ask; the chef will whip up something special for you. The Restaurant is formal and features beautifully presented Continental cuisine. The menu changes weekly to take advantage of whatever ingredients are in season.

The guest rooms are plush and attractive in gray and salmon. Marble baths, two telephones, hair dryers, robes, honor bars, safes, twice-daily maid service, and nightly turndown with chocolates are just a few of the many extras the Ritz offers. Guests on the keyed-access club level can take advantage of complimentary meals throughout the day, including Continental breakfast, midmorning snacks, evening hors d'oeuvres and cocktails, and late cordials and sweets.

Recreation has not been overlooked: in addition to the requisite pool, there's a fitness center, sundeck, and two tennis courts. Massages are available for $25 per half hour, $40 per hour. Tee times on the nearby Biltmore golf course can be arranged; transportation is free.

More than anything, attention to detail stands out at the Ritz. Even the public restrooms are marble, with fresh flowers and a supply of terry washcloths. The paneled elevators have marble floors covered with Persian rugs. The devoted staff is unequaled. The front desk keeps a record of guests' special requests for their next visit. The hotel also offers concierge, valet, and 24-hour room service. Shoeshines are complimentary; valet parking is $7 per day.

The Ritz has a convenient central location—it's about 15 minutes from the airport and near downtown Phoenix and Scottsdale's many golf courses. It is directly across the street from the Biltmore Fashion Park, which houses such fine stores as Saks Fifth Avenue and I. Magnin.

Scottsdale Princess

7575 East Princess Drive
Scottsdale, Arizona 85255
602-585-4848
800-223-1818
Fax: 602-585-0086

General manager: Stephen J. Ast
Accommodations: 600 rooms
Rates: $100–$300; suites for two, $225–$2,200; additional
   person $20 in summer, $30 in winter
Added: 10.25% tax
Payment: Major credit cards
Children: Under 16 free in room with parents
Pets: Not allowed
Smoking: Nonsmoking rooms available
Open: Year-round

Opened in 1987, the first Princess hotel in the United States is an estatelike resort, covering 450 acres several miles north of the other Scottsdale resorts. Hand your car keys to a parking attendant when you arrive. With all that this resort has to offer, including a capable staff to attend to your every need, there's really no reason to leave.

Built in a Mexican Colonial style, the main building is truly grand. There are majestic palms, fountain courts, and intimate nooks and crannies with wicker sofas. Two thirds of the guest rooms are in the sprawling main building; the casitas are clustered near the tennis courts, and the villas are next to the golf course.

Recreational opportunities abound. There are two 18-hole Tournament Players Club golf courses designed by Jay Morrish and Tom Weiskopf (the Phoenix Open is held here), nine tennis courts (including a 10,000-seat stadium court where the WCT Eagle Classic takes place in late February), three swimming pools, and a health club and spa with racquetball and squash courts, state-of-the-art exercise equipment, saunas, whirlpools, and health and beauty treatments. Club usage is $10 per day, which includes squash and racquetball court time. Next to the hotel, the city of Scottsdale has built a 400-acre horse park with nine equestrian arenas, two stadium arenas, a polo field, a grand prix field for jumping, and 500 stables.

The rooms are large and have interesting configurations, setting them apart from standard hotel rooms. They are attractively furnished in southwestern peaches, creams, and earth tones and have big terraces and wet bars. The extra-large bathrooms are luxurious, with separate tubs and showers, a telephone, robes, loofah sponges, and other top-of-the-line amenities. Casitas and villas are also available; casita suites have separate sitting rooms. All have balconies and fireplaces and share a common swimming pool. The villas are similar to the casitas but do not have fireplaces.

The Marquesa is the resort's fine restaurant, specializing in Catalan cuisine. For Mexican food, try La Hacienda. The casual Las Ventanas serves all three meals, and the Cabana Café serves food and frosty drinks by the pool. At the end of the day, you can head to Club Caballo Bayo for a night of dancing. The Grill at the TPC clubhouse is popular with the golfing set.

Stouffer Cottonwoods Resort

6160 North Scottsdale Road
Scottsdale, Arizona 85253
602-991-1414
800-HOTELS-1
Fax: 602-951-3350

General manager: Claudia Danks
Accommodations: 171 rooms
Rates: $85–$195; double, $95–$205; suites, $115–$265
Added: 9.05% tax
Payment: Major credit cards
Children: Discouraged
Pets: Under 25 pounds with a $50 refundable deposit
Smoking: Nonsmoking rooms available
Open: Year-round

Scottsdale Road is lined with glamour—a mix of resorts, boutiques, and restaurants. In the midst of it all, the Stouffer Cottonwoods offers the best of both worlds, providing a tranquil hideaway.

There is a residential, clublike feeling at this resort. One-story villa suites are scattered over its 25 acres of grounds, with flower-lined paths draped with cottonwoods. The pace is unhurried. Tucked among the villas and courtyards is a large swimming pool, inviting you to lounge. The sunken tennis courts, along grassy banks, have an intimate feeling. A jogging track with par exercise stations circles the grounds, passing desert landscapes. There's a putting green and croquet course on the property, and you can play golf at any of five nearby golf courses. Bicycles can be rented at the resort's gift shop.

The villas were designed for privacy, and each has a secluded patio. Decorated with a southwestern scheme, they have beamed ceilings and touches of regional art. The Flagstaff villas are the smallest, though somewhat larger than the average hotel room. They are furnished with one king-size or two double beds, a refrigerator, safe, and a vanity. Tucsons have a living room with a wet bar, oversize bedroom, and a private spa on the patio. The Phoenix villas are top-of-the-line, with a large living room and fireplace, a kitchen, a huge bath, a bedroom with a king-size bed, and an enclosed courtyard with a hot tub—truly a romantic setting.

The Moriah Restaurant is comfortably elegant and serves outstanding southwestern dishes. Tumbleweeds, the poolside bar and grill, is open daily. Scottsdale's cosmopolitan atmosphere is a few steps away—literally. The nearby Borgata Shopping Village, designed after an Italian hill town, has boutiques, galleries, and restaurants.

Wyndham Paradise Valley Resort
5401 North Scottsdale Road
Scottsdale, Arizona 85253
602-947-5400
800-822-4200
Fax: 602-946-1524

General manager: Randy Kwasnieski
Accommodations: 387 rooms and suites
Rates: Start at $69 in the off-season and $175 in high season for single or double; suites start at $400
Added: 9.05% tax
Payment: Major credit cards

Children: Under 18 free in room with parents
Pets: Not allowed
Smoking: Nonsmoking rooms available
Open: Year-round

The Wyndham Paradise Valley Resort has an unusual facade: it is built of angular cement blocks that mirror the bark patterns of the surrounding palm trees. At the entrance, there's a striking fountain with brass horses rising from the water.

The guest rooms surround landscaped courtyards, and colorful desert flora seem to be in bloom everywhere you look. The rooms themselves are pleasantly furnished with light woods and modern furniture with a southwestern air. Most have small sitting areas, terraces, and a vanity apart from the bath. All the rooms have mini-bars, coffeemakers, remote control TVs, and phones in the bath. The Presidential Suite is especially handsome, with large glass doors that open onto a terrace overlooking one of the main pool courtyards. Guests staying there will have no need to use that pool, however, since the suite has its own outdoor pool and Jacuzzi.

The resort has two swimming pools—one with a waterfall, the other with an adjacent hot tub and bar. Tennis is available on four outdoor clay courts and two indoor courts. The health club has two racquetball courts, steam rooms, saunas, and whirlpools. Golf can be arranged nearby.

Lunch and light meals are served in the Palm Pavilion. For dinner, Spazzizi's offers Italian and regional cuisine. Of course, a menu is also available for those who just want to lounge by the pool all day.

Pittsburgh

The Priory — A City Inn
614 Pressly Street
Pittsburgh, Pennsylvania 15212
412-231-3338

Proprietors: Maryann and Edward Graf
Innkeeper: Tracy Callison
Accommodations: 24 rooms, including 2 suites, all with
   private bath; $7 each additional person
Rates: $82–$135
Included: Continental breakfast
Minimum stay: None
Added: 11% tax; $10 for a roll-away
Payment: Major credit cards
Children: Welcome
Pets: Not allowed
Smoking: Allowed
Open: Year-round

Across the Ninth Street Bridge, which spans the Allegheny
River, a small hotel of supreme elegance and refinement overlooks the city of Pittsburgh from its half-mile distance. The
Priory was built in 1888, a refuge for Benedictine priests and
brothers serving the adjacent St. Mary's Parish. St. Mary's, built
in 1852 by Swiss and German Catholics, is one of the few examples of Italian classical architecture in Pittsburgh. Its luxurious
Austrian stained glass windows were added in 1912 once the
property was safe from anti-Catholic sentiments of a group
called the 'Know-Nothings.'

Less than a century later, in 1981, the Priory and St. Mary's
were threatened, this time for secular reasons, as the Transportation Department planned to traverse the site with a new part
of the interstate. At the last minute, however, the highway was
moved back 40 yards and the Priory was rescued and put up for
sale. The Graf family bought the church and the Priory and
completed a restoration effort of the latter in 1986. What stands
today is a monumental brick structure, with three stories of
attenuated arched windows and an air of otherworldly beauty.

Those interested in architecture will be fascinated with the elevation drawings on the walls of the Priory detailing its construction. The building centers on a stunning octagonal staircase, around which radiate common rooms and several guest rooms on the first floor and the more deluxe guest rooms of the second and third floors. Like the church's nave, a long wing stretches back from the center section, housing a beautiful marbled elevator and the large kitchen, breakfast rooms, and additional guest rooms on the upper floors. Mrs. Graf procured the sophisticated artwork and plates of Pittsburgh landmarks which adorn the walls of this European-style hotel.

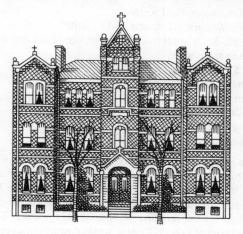

The rooms are furnished differently, but each has high, narrow windows trimmed simply in lace, original deep oak moldings, and stunning Victorian antiques and furnishings. All have a television, a private phone, and a brand-new bath with personalized amenities and fluffy towels. The rooms in the front of the Priory are quite grand, with tapestried Victorian chairs, precious writing desks, original faux marble mantels inset with fire screens, and antique brass, wood, or iron beds. The cozy rooms are just as nicely appointed on a small scale, adding to the breadth of the accommodations.

In the evening, guests are welcome to relax and enjoy a drink in one of two Victorian parlors, each with a working fireplace. The Continental breakfast is served in two informal breakfast rooms; muffins and coffee cake are baked in the Priory's beautiful original kitchen, exuding aromas as a wake-up call. There is also a wrought-iron courtyard at the back of the Priory where guests may gather in warmer months.

Most impressive is the warmth of the staff, who are friendly and helpful in this rather formal environment, happy to advise about dining, museums, and local events.

Pittsburgh Vista
1000 Penn Avenue
Pittsburgh, Pennsylvania 15222
412-281-3700
800-FOR-VISTA
Fax: 412-281-2687
Operated by Hilton International

General manager: Paul Kelly
Accommodations: 615 rooms and 42 suites
Rates: $162–$182; suites from $225; weekend packages from $85
Minimum stay: None
Added: $25 additional guest
Payment: Major credit cards
Children: Welcome
Pets: Allowed
Smoking: 4 nonsmoking floors
Open: Year-round

When a group of architects broke ground for Liberty Center in 1984, which would house the new Vista Hotel, they made sure not to compete with the wonderful landmark of the William Penn hotel. Instead, they built a gleaming glass tower which opened during the last days of 1986, for $137 million. The hotel is a small part of Liberty Center, which comprises an entire city block from 10th to 11th streets, from Penn and Liberty avenues. The striking landmark is one of the three points of the Golden Triangle, with B&O Railroad as the second point and Point State Park as the pinnacle.

The four-story atrium lobby is filled with greenery and sunlight, linking the interior to the groomed exterior landscape. Under the glass roof are smooth, clean surfaces: the floor is Greek marble and the carpeting is specially designed English Axminster. The interior throughout is lit with elaborate Venetian crystal chandeliers. The walnut furnishings are covered in contemporary tones of celedon, dark green, and mauve.

In addition to being a gathering spot, the lobby is a gallery for local artists. The five-foot terra cotta sculptures at the entrance were made by Jerry Kaplan; the centerpiece bronze sculpture was crafted by Ron Bennett; the four black and white paintings behind the desk are the work of Douglas Cooper. Other works include a wall-hanging textured in sand by Adrienne Heinrich and six commanding works in the Japanese style by artist Donna Bolgrem. Other Pittsburgh artists display works of pottery and ceramics in a stunning neoclassic cabinet by the elevators. Guests relax in the Atrium Lounge off the lobby for evening cocktails.

The Liberty Grill is Edwardian, with brass and glass sconces and chandeliers that reflect the richness of the leather and tapestried chairs. Local artist John Terzian was commissioned to do oil paintings for this space—the Impressionist style is in keeping with the Old World elegance. Guests eat in intimate settings on English china and Italian silver. As formal as is the Liberty Grill, the Orchard Café feels like an outdoor garden, with walls of yellow and cream and rattan furnishings. Artist Donna Groer contributed her Pennsylvania forest watercolors to the light setting. The Vista has its own nightclub, called Motions.

The V-shaped guest tower has about 30 rooms on each of its floors, the top three floors containing Executive rooms with special amenities. All the rooms are enlivened by the commissioned work of Pittsburgh artist Peter Contis, depicting scenes of the city. The decor is contemporary, with geometric and floral patterns in blues and greens for the drapes and bedding and solid tones for the love seats. The furnishings are mahogany with touches of burl oak. Notable are the views of the Pittsburgh and Allegheny rivers from nearly all the rooms, due to the shape of the building—try to request a corner room.

The Fitness Center on the fourth floor has a whirlpool, sauna and steam room, Keiser exercise equipment, a lap pool, and aerobics classes. Liberty Center is a thriving business world unto itself, and its flagship hotel runs efficiently.

Westin William Penn
530 William Penn Place
Pittsburgh, Pennsylvania 15219
412-281-7100
800-228-3000

Proprietors: Servico, managed by Westin Hotels and Resorts
General manager: Wayne Bodington
Accommodations: 595 rooms, including 47 suites
Rates: Weekends, $99–$115; weekdays, $150–$200; suites, from $275
Included: Continental breakfast, tea, valet parking on weekends
Minimum stay: None

Added: 11% tax; $20 each additional person
Payment: Major credit cards
Children: Welcome
Pets: Not allowed
Smoking: 1 of 9 floors nonsmoking
Open: Year-round

The Westin William Penn just celebrated its 75th anniversary. The Pittsburgh matriarch was built as a 1,000-room hotel for $6 million in 1916, a later work of the renowned architect Henry Clay Frick. Soaring a majestic twenty-three stories above the city, the E-shaped brick, terra cotta, and limestone building was renovated in 1984 for $34 million. It has lived through Pittsburgh's prosperity and poverty, the Depression and Prohibition, hosted twelve United States presidents, and was deemed a National Historic Landmark after the 1984 restoration.

The hotel was shockingly modern when it was built: every one of the thousand overnight rooms had a private bath with hot and cold running water, and the private telephones required the attention of 30 hotel operators. With the addition of an electric clock in every room, the William Penn contained the largest collection of timepieces in the world. Thirty miles of carpet lined the walnut paneled and green marbled corridors, done in Italian Renaissance style. The smallest room sold for $2.50 a night, and the fifteenth floor was reserved for bachelors. When the Grant Street annex added 600 more rooms in 1929, the William Penn became the second largest hotel in the world after the Chicago Conrad Hilton.

During its 1984 restoration, archives were consulted to find accurate period moldings, wall coverings, fixtures, and carpeting. The only original pieces remaining are the brass doorknobs. Visitors are awed by the Fontainebleau ceiling of the Georgian lobby. The grand piano, acquired in the mid-1980s for $29,000, belonged to André Previn while he led the Pittsburgh Symphony Orchestra. While having tea in the Palm Court under the coffered medallion ceiling, guests look through a panorama of elaborately carved two-story arches to an outer court. The Urban Room, designed in 1927 by Ziegfeld Follies Theater set designer Joseph Urban, is a good example of art deco style, with walls of black Carrara glass beneath a gold tree of life ceiling mural. The Grand Ballroom, on the top two floors of the hotel, shows off three crystal chandeliers—more than one hundred years old and crafted from 7,000 Baccarat crystals, they were purchased from a Cannes casino. The Terrace Room, in rich walnut paneling, is decorated with a mural of George Washington at Fort Pitt.

The suites are done in Colonial Williamsburg and Italian neoclassic styles. Standard guest rooms have classic mahogany furnishings, two-poster beds, striped bedding and drapes in light or rosy hues, and a desk and wing chair. The marble baths are clean and modern. Managed by the efficient Westin Hotels and Resorts, the hotel manifests no hint of the chaos that might accompany a 600-room property.

Portland

The Benson Hotel
309 Southwest Broadway
Portland, Oregon 97205
503-228-2000
800-426-0670
Fax: 503-226-4603

Managing director: Charles Indermuehle
Accommodations: 290 rooms and suites
Rates: $170–$180; double, $195–$205; $25 additional person; corporate rates available
Payment: Major credit cards
Children: Under 18 free with parents
Pets: Small pets allowed by prior arrangement
Smoking: Nonsmoking rooms available
Open: Year-round

The bronze drinking fountains that grace downtown Portland street corners were donated to the city by turn-of-the-century lumber baron Simon Benson, the man responsible for this distinguished, French baroque–style hotel and a number of other Oregon landmarks.

The hotel, built of brick in 1913 as the Oregon Hotel (doors to some guest rooms still bear the distinctive OH) and later changed to the Benson, was the grandest in Portland for decades. Newcomers challenged that status, but with a recent $20 million renovation, the Benson has regained its reputation for fine quality. It's a Northwest classic, with traditional furnishings and a gracious, clublike atmosphere.

The polished lobby with its high arched windows is still the Benson's best feature. Chandeliers hang above marble floors and Oriental carpets; walls are paneled in Circassian walnut that was shipped around Cape Horn from the forests of Russia. The silver-plated mirror at the head of the staircase dates from the 1880s, and the veined white Italian marble railing is cast iron. A blaze crackles in the fireplace in winter months.

The rooms have all been refurbished with fresh carpeting, gray and cream colors with touches of brass, queen-and king-size beds, and mahogany furniture. All rooms have desks. The Benson Rooms are the largest, and have comfortable sitting areas, similar to junior suites. There's a health club with fitness machines on the seventh floor.

The oak-paneled London Grill, below the lobby, has a lighter menu than in the past. Continental cuisine is served here and in the adjoining private dining room, Little London. For an even smaller party, the Wine Room is open for groups of eight to ten; here special dinners are designed around fine wines of the West.

Buffet luncheons, prepared in the London Grill, are served on weekdays in the Lobby Court, adjacent to the lobby. In the evenings, jazz lovers drop in for music and cocktails.

Also on the street level is Trader Vic's, with its South Seas ambience. With a smart remodeling it has the flavor of a tropical outpost.

The hotel's concierge is knowledgeable and helpful. He'll make dinner or tour reservations, order flowers, have luggage repaired, and recommend local picnic spots. Haircuts, manicures, and shoeshines are available, and there's a small gift shop by the Boyd's Coffee outlet off the lobby. The Benson, now a WestCoast hotel, has several meeting rooms and a ballroom.

Room service operates 24 hours a day; your wake-up call will be from a person rather than a computer, if you request it; and your bed linens are turned down at night. These personal touches, added to a full renovation, remind Portlanders of the days when the Benson meant the best.

The Heathman Hotel
Southwest Broadway at Salmon Street
Portland, Oregon 97205
503-241-4100
800-551-0011
Fax: 503-790-7110

General manager: Mary Arnstad
Accommodations: 152 rooms and suites
Rates: $135–$165; double, $155–$375; $20 additional person; suites, $265; 2-bedroom suites, $375; weekend rates and packages available
Payment: Major credit cards
Children: Free under age 6
Pets: Not allowed
Smoking: Nonsmoking rooms available
Open: Year-round

The original Heathman was Portland's grand Jazz Age hotel, but after it was converted to housing for soldiers and sailors during World War II, it lost its allure. Since reopening in 1984, however, some of the Heathman's earliest guests have returned to recall the weddings and proms they attended here and to express heartfelt gratitude at the gracious revival. Now the building is on the National Register of Historic Places.

The restored 1927 classical art deco exterior of terra cotta brick and sandstone remains unchanged, with the exception of a new white neon sign. The only original room is the tea court. Hand-rubbed eucalyptus-paneled walls, a curving stairway, arched windows, 18th-century oil paintings, and a Steinway grand piano create a sense of timelessness in this retreat from modernity. Only the fireplace was added during renovation.

If afternoon tea appeals to you, you'll enjoy the Heathman's ritual, complete with starched linen and silver tongs, received with great fanfare by Portlanders. Champagne and sherry are on the menu, along with scones and delectable pastries. Overflow seating is at mezzanine tables with a view of the court. Also on the mezzanine is a bar where light suppers and cocktails are served, a popular spot among theater-goers. The library here contains signed books from the many visiting authors who've stayed at the Heathman.

The restaurant across the lobby creates an entirely different ambience: three tiers of tables overlook Broadway through frosted, etched glass in an airy setting. Coffered ceilings and marble tables provide hints of the art deco style, and Andy Warhol's prints of endangered species enliven the walls. The menu is seasonal Northwest fare, meaning plenty of fresh seafood, with a nouvelle touch. Poached Northwest scallops with greens and citrus hollandaise, rack of Oregon lamb with wholegrain mustard and cracked black pepper, and Szechuan salmon with citrus beurre blanc are sample entrées from a recent winter menu. Lunch dishes include Oregon mussels steamed in white wine, shallots, and herbs, or a steamed chicken and bok choy salad served warm with ginger vinaigrette. Gelato is made on the premises.

Rooms, a third of them suites named for prominent Portland families, are reached by rosewood-paneled elevators from a small, elegant lobby of marble and Burmese teak. A residential atmosphere with touches of Oriental and contemporary decor characterizes the hotel's upper levels. English chintz bedspreads match Roman shades; headboards are rattan or hardwood, tables are travertine or brass, armoires are dark wood. Works of artists from the Northwest hang on the walls.

All television sets are concealed within cabinets, and an enormous selection of complimentary in-room movies — more than 200 — is available to guests. In the closet you'll find thick terrycloth robes, and in the bath, Portuguese black soap, bath gel, and other toiletries. Your bed will be turned down at night, and Jaciva chocolates placed nearby.

A runners' guide to the city is included in your room packet. If you'd like more extensive health facilities, you may visit a nearby health club for a fee. If you prefer, rowing and exercise machines will be delivered to your door free of charge.

The Heathman's style is represented by polished service and extra touches, such as fresh flower arrangements in public areas. Not only is the staff pleasant, greeting guests with smiles of welcome, it is endlessly resourceful. The concierge can handle almost any request, from car rentals to language intepreters.

In the heart of downtown Portland, the Heathman stands next to the city's Performing Arts Center and is just around the corner from the Portland Art Museum and Oregon Historical Society headquarters and museum. These institutions face the South Park Blocks, tree-shaded lawns that provide greenery and paths for pleasant city strolls. Portland State University is a few blocks to the south.

Heron Haus
2545 Northwest Westover
Portland, Oregon 97210
503-274-1846
Fax: 503-274-1846

Innkeeper: Julie Keppeler
Accommodations: 5 rooms
Rates: double, $85–$250
Included: Continental breakfast
Payment: Major credit cards
Children: Age 13 and older welcome
Pets: Not allowed
Smoking: Not allowed
Open: Year-round

This large, white turn-of-the-century house, built in 1904 for a prominent local family, looks as though it belongs on sorority row at an Ivy League campus. Indeed, layers of English ivy create a comfortably weathered covering along its west side. "I wanted to maintain the integrity of this lovely old house," says innkeeper Julie Keppeler. "The ivy gives a nostalgic feeling of permanence and stability."

Close to downtown Portland, Heron Haus is set against the northwest hills. It's surrounded by gracious old homes in a quiet residential district yet within walking distance of the restaurants and boutiques of one of Portland's liveliest neighborhoods. Also nearby are Portland's International Rose Test Gardens and Japanese Garden. These beautifully landscaped gardens in Washington Park, high in the southwest hills, offer wide views of the city, backed on the eastern horizon by majestic Mount Hood. For a taste of urban wilderness, walk the trails of Forest Park: it's one of the largest urban forests and arboretums in the United States.

Each guest room in the polished, immaculate inn has a Hawaiian name, reflecting the twenty-four years Julie spent in Hawaii raising four children. The spacious rooms have sitting areas, desks, and telephones, along with an abundance of magazines and books from Julie's library. In Kulia, an intimate room on the second floor with a queen-size bed and love seat, you may luxuriate in a raised whirlpool spa connected to a large, adjoining bath. An expanse of shuttered windows views the city lights at night. Ko (Hawaiian for sugar) is a large and airy junior suite with a garden view. Its original shower with seven spray spouts is still in place. Manu, a suite on the third floor, offers a secluded haven decorated in shades of blue.

Every morning the aroma of freshly brewed coffee wafts up the grand oak staircase, inviting guests to breakfast. Julie serves fresh fruits, croissants, and pastries from the city's finest bakeries, with gourmet jams and preserves. You may be served by the fireplace in the dining room or, on sunny days, in the enclosed porch overlooking the pool, the city, and Mount Hood.

Hotel Vintage Plaza
422 Southwest Broadway
Portland, Oregon 97205
503-228-1212
800-243-0555
Fax: 503-228-3598

General Manager: Craig Thompson
Accommodations: 107 rooms and suites
Rates: single, $125; double, $145; $20 additional person; suites, $165–$195
Payment: Major credit cards
Children: Under 16 free with parents
Pets: Not allowed

Smoking: Nonsmoking rooms available
Open: Year-round

When Kimco Hotels purchased and began renovating the historic Wells Building in 1990, Portlanders knew their city was about to gain a fine new hotel. The San Francisco–based firm is known for the quality of its accommodations in restored landmarks.

The Vintage Plaza, centrally located near Pioneer Square, the Center for Performing Arts, and downtown shopping, is a European style hotel which emphasizes personal service and attention to detail. An Oregon wine theme is reflected in the hotel's decor, and suites are named for Oregon wineries. In the 9 two-story Townhouse Suites, grape cluster patterns and rich wine damask fabrics carry the motif. The suites have granite-topped wet bars, VCRs, game tables, and soaking tubs with jets.

On the tenth (and top) floor are nine Starlight Rooms, featuring expanses of conservatory-style windows that overlook the city. The rooms have a clean, casual look, with rattan chairs and pale blue and green fabrics. Roman shades pull up from the bottom for privacy and to allow partial views of the stars.

All the other rooms and suites have custom-made cherry-wood furniture and granite and brass accessories. Each has an honor bar and refrigerator. Complimentary to guests are morning coffee and newspaper, shoeshines, and wine served by the dramatic marble fireplace in the lobby.

The lobby, set in a ten-story atrium, is a comfortable place to relax. It has inviting sofas, bookshelves, a piano lounge, and a picture window that looks into a wine-tasting room stocked with regional vintages. Adjacent to the hotel is Pazzo, an upbeat, San Francisco–style restaurant that has gained a devoted following for its innovative Italian cuisine.

Groups like the Vintage Plaza for its five conference rooms and full audiovisual services, while business travelers are pleased with the computer-compatible telephones and a business center that offers fax, computer, copier, and secretarial services.

Mallory Motor Hotel
729 Southwest 15th Avenue
Portland, Oregon 97205
503-223-6311
800-228-8657

Manager: Linda Anderson
Accommodations: 144 rooms
Rates: $45–$75 single, $50–$85 double, $5 additional person
Payment: Major credit cards
Children: Under age 12 free with parents
Pets: Allowed
Smoking: Allowed
Open: Year-round

The Mallory is a popular Portland hotel and a fine bargain. This well-maintained hostelry is a favorite among Oregonians who come from elsewhere in the state to visit their big city.

The 1912 buff brick exterior is just a bit run-down, but the bright and open lobby is a spiffy mix of crisp, off-white walls and dignified green wing chairs. Columns reach to a coffered ceiling with gilt rosettes, and small crystal chandeliers are elegantly reflected in a wall of mirrors that makes the space seem twice its size.

The dining room off the lobby continues the cream and green theme. It is a pleasant, open space with long white drapes at the tall windows. The Driftwood Room is a small, dark lounge on the other side of the lobby, a cozy, intimate spot for an after-theater nightcap (the Mallory is across the street from the city's oldest community drama center, Portland Civic Theater). Decor in the hotel's rooms is eclectic, with some rooms attractively appointed and others unexceptional. All have satellite TV, and corner rooms have refrigerators. The huge corner rooms are where the Mallory shines, and those on the upper floors view Mount Hood. Amenities in some rooms include a retractable clothesline in the bathtub (most rooms have both tub and shower) and an embroidered pincushion and sewing kit for guest use. Linen is perfectly clean and adequate, though you won't find extravagantly monogrammed towels here.

The Mallory doesn't pretend to be a luxury hotel. It provides serviceable, comfortable, and inexpensive lodgings with several extras. There is only one guest elevator, but you will enjoy friendly concierge and housekeeping services, soft drink and ice machines on each floor, free parking, and a lobby newsstand that carries the New York Times and Wall Street Journal, as well as Oregon papers.

The hotel is located across the freeway from downtown proper, a walk of a few blocks. Stop in at Powell's Travel Book Store in Pioneer Square for a good—and free—walking-tour map of downtown Portland.

Portland's White House
1914 N.E. 22nd Avenue
Portland, Oregon 97212
503-287-7131

Innkeepers: Larry and Mary Hough
Accommodations: 6 rooms (all with private baths)
Rates: double, $88–$104; $15 additional person
Included: Full breakfast
Payment: MasterCard, Visa
Children: Over age 12 welcome
Pets: Not allowed
Smoking: Not allowed
Open: Year-round

In the heart of a quiet, tree-filled neighborhood (but mere blocks from a large shopping center), stands one of Portland's most unusual homes: an ornate white mansion, complete with Greek columns, fountain, circular driveway, and broad verandah.

To enter the turn-of-the-century home, built by a wealthy lumber baron, is to step into the stately world of a bygone day. Entry hall walls are covered with landscape murals, floors are of polished oak and inlaid Honduran mahogany, and crystal chandeliers hang from the ceiling. The only sounds are the tick of a grandfather clock and the warbling of canaries.

A wide central staircase leads to a landing, where sunshine streams through the delicate pastels of antique stained glass windows. Upstairs, the rooms are furnished in a style befitting the period. A brass queen-size bed stands against one wall; lace curtains billow at the large windows; clawfoot bathtubs are commodious.

In the huge 1,650-square-foot basement ballroom, there is plenty of space for the banquets, receptions, and parties that are often held here. The Houghs' future plans include creating a TV room, game room, and sitting area in the ballroom.

In the graciously appointed dining room, you will join other guests in feasting on scones and jam, mushroom omelettes, porridge, and fruit. Mary Hough, born in Dublin and raised in Coventry, serves an English breakfast as she learned it at her mother's boarding house. Weather permitting, you may eat outside on the patio, and you also have the option of breakfasting in your room. Cookies and tea are provided in the afternoon, and sherry by the fire on cool evenings.

Every detail in this completely refurbished home, from Oriental carpets to brass doorknobs, is given loving attention. The resulting atmosphere combines an old-fashioned romantic elegance with warm hospitality.

RiverPlace Alexis Hotel
1510 Southwest Harbor Way
Portland, Oregon 97201
800-227-1333
503-228-3233

Manager: Richard Ransome
Accommodations: 74 rooms (all with private baths) and 10 condominium units
Rates: single, $150; double, $160; suites, $180–$500; weekend and corporate rates available
Included: Continental breakfast
Payment: Major credit cards
Children: Welcome
Pets: Not allowed
Smoking: Nonsmoking rooms available

Portland's splashy waterfront hotel has been described by its builders as evoking the feel of a turn-of-the-century resort, an English manor lodge, or a New England yacht club. The brick and wood exterior, three rooftop rotundas, window flower boxes, and the marina setting all contribute to an ambience of quiet luxury, yet the hotel also has an unmistakably regional and informal flavor.

Handcrafted rugs, oak wainscoting, tile and marble fireplaces, and sophisticated floral arrangements gracefully combine traditional with contemporary in the hotel's public areas and guest rooms.

A uniformed doorman escorts guests into the plush, carpeted lobby. At the east end of the lobby is the hotel's elegant restaurant, Esplanade, which features a Continental menu with fresh seafood. The Patio, open during the summer, serves meals on a terrace above the river; you may also eat outdoors on the verandah by the fireplace bar, a teak and slate lounge that is a nice spot for a light lunch or dessert.

Rooms are decorated in warm blues and yellows, their sleek lines softened by overstuffed furniture and flowers. Wet bars, whirlpool baths, and wood-burning fireplaces are some of the extras that grace RiverPlace Alexis suites. Views are of the city skyline, a landscaped courtyard, or the busy Willamette River. All rooms have movie channels, remote control television, and air conditioning, and four have facilities for the handicapped.

Sister to the Alexis Hotel in Seattle, RiverPlace Alexis features many of the same amenities: You'll be served complimentary sherry when you arrive and a Continental breakfast with your preferred newspaper in the morning, plush terrycloth robes hang in your closet, and the finest of toiletries are provided. Hotel-made chocolates are placed at your bedside, and if you request a down comforter or futon, that will be supplied too.

Service is exemplary, a point of pride at Alexis hotels. There is a strict no-tipping policy, except for food and beverage service. Whether you need a shoeshine, a shirt pressed, or assistance with tour or travel information, you will get it with a smile.

For exercise, you may choose between the waterfront jogging paths and the RiverPlace Athletic Club, available to guests for a nominal charge. The fitness center has a track, pool, weight room, and sauna and steam rooms.

RiverPlace Alexis stands on the west bank of the Willamette, just south of downtown Portland. It is at one end of an esplanade that is reminiscent of a European village, with small shops, quaint lampposts, and cobblestoned walkways. Pastel-colored condominium apartments rise six stories above the street, facing the 120-slip marina where yachts and sailboats dock. There are several restaurants in the RiverPlace community, including Newport Bay, which is right on the water, and Harborside above it. Both specialize in seafood.

Just north of the hotel is Tom McCall Waterfront Park, a greenbelt that is part of Portland's recent ambitious riverfront revival. Joggers and picnickers and strollers frequent the park, and festivals and community events are held here regularly. From the hotel you can walk beside the river to the downtown streets, a distance of about six blocks.

Sacramento

Aunt Abigail's
2120 G Street
Sacramento, California 95816
916-441-5007
800-858-1568

Innkeeper: Susanne Ventura
Accommodations: 5 rooms (all with private bath)
Rates: $70–$125; $35 additional person
Included: Full breakfast
Minimum stay: 2 nights on some holidays
Payment: Major credit cards
Children: Welcome by prior arrangement
Pets: Not allowed
Smoking: Prohibited indoors

Hospitality is the special attraction of this Colonial Revival mansion near downtown Sacramento. Built in 1912, the big white house with teal trim has large rooms and is nicely furnished with antiques. But it's Susanne Ventura's friendly, personal service that makes the inn truly distinctive.

Baskets of nuts and homegrown raisins are set out for snacking in the living room, and a thermos of hot water and tins of cocoa and tea are on the antique English sideboard upstairs. Robes hang in the armoires. Every room has a phone jack and each bathroom contains a cabinet filled with aspirin, shaving equipment, toothpaste, Tums, and other necessities. Susanne seems to have thought of everything a pampered bed-and-breakfast guest could want, including cats (Sabrina and Abigail) to accompany you up and down stairs.

Four of the guest rooms are on the second floor, and one is just off the landing. The morning sun floods through eleven windows in the Solarium Room. The Queen Anne, once a dark and forbidding room, has been given brighter colors and furnishings, including a two-door, mirrored armoire. The bath has its original herringbone tile.

The Uncle Albert Room looks as if it belongs to someone's kindly uncle, with books piled on the armoire, a wing chair, and a reproduction of an antique radio that holds a cassette deck. The pink tile bath has a shower and clawfoot tub.

Susanne serves a full breakfast of baked goods such as French toast or pancakes, fruit, and juice in the dining room. From this room, doors lead to a wraparound porch and fenced patio bright with flowers. The hot tub in the garden is available to guests.

One of Susanne's thoughtful touches is the bulletin board near the front door, where she posts notices of art gallery shows and other events in Sacramento. She and her husband, Ken, will recommend restaurants and make reservations for you. One highly recommended spot is Biba's, where classic northern Italian food is served in a cheerful, urban atmosphere.

The Driver Mansion Inn

2019 21st Street
Sacramento, California 95818
916-455-5243

Innkeepers: Sandi and Richard Kann
Accommodations: 9 rooms (all with private bath)
Rates: $85–$225
Included: Full breakfast
Payment: Major credit cards
Children: Welcome
Pets: Not allowed
Smoking: Prohibited indoors

Philip Driver was a native Californian, the son of a man who, lured by gold, came west in 1849. Driver became a prominent Sacramento attorney, active in civic affairs, and built an ornate mansion that remained in the Driver family until 1977.

The current owners, who are also part-owners of the luxurious Sterling Hotel, bought the mansion in 1984, renovated it, and opened the inn a year later. This is one of the classiest bed-and-breakfasts you'll encounter. Calico and teddy bears would definitely be out of place here. Stately antiques, thick carpeting, and fine art set the theme.

Pink, white, and red roses flank the pillared porch of the big house, which is set on a slope above a busy street. You may park on the street, and there are a few parking spaces in back. Traditional furniture faces a white brick fireplace in the parlor, where beverages are served in the afternoon. Musicians enjoy the grand piano. Breakfast is served at glass-topped tables in the dining room (or in your room, for a $15 fee). Fresh fruit, juice, and excellent coffee are prepared along with Belgian waffles, French toast, quiche, or other main dishes.

The six guest rooms in the main house all have antiques or reproductions, desks, private phones, and shirred white curtains at wide leaded glass windows. Each walk-in closet holds a portable television. The baths are in modern white tile, with glass and brass showers. The third floor penthouse includes a whirlpool tub.

The Carriage House, in a garden of brick walks edged with impatiens and shaded by oak, persimmon, and crape myrtle trees, has three rooms in a more contemporary style. Room 3 has a brass and white iron bed, soft violet walls, and wicker chairs. Good reading lamps, a clock, a Franklin stove, and individual climate controls are a few of the room's comforts. It has a big white bath with black marbled tile floor, pedestal sink, shower, and a jet hydrotherapy tub big enough for two.

The Sacramento Bee is supplied, and Sandi will recommend restaurants and suggest sightseeing attractions if requested. With intuitive tact, she knows when to leave people alone. "I try to be available, but not hover," she says. "We offer hotel-type accommodations, but with a warmer, more personal atmosphere."

Riverboat Delta King Hotel
1000 Front Street
Sacramento, California 95814
916-444-5464
800-825-5464
Fax 916-444-5314

General manager: Charlie Coyne
Accommodations: 44 staterooms and suites
Rates: staterooms, $95–$135; suites, $350–$400
Included: Continental breakfast
Payment: Major credit cards
Children: Welcome
Pets: Not allowed
Smoking: Allowed

If you yearn to return to the days when river travel reigned supreme, step aboard the historic Riverboat Delta King, an authentic 1926 sternwheel paddle steamer permanently moored along the waterfront of Old Sacramento. Preserved as a 28-acre historic district, Old Sacramento includes the Sacramento History Center, a State Railroad Museum (the largest of its kind), an 1860s railroad station, and shops and restaurants.

All are within easy walking distance of the gleaming white Delta King.

The five-story, 285-foot-long paddlewheeler was built during the peak of the steam navigation period in the Sacramento Delta. Like its twin, the Delta Queen (now on the Mississippi River), the King once plied the Sacramento from the capital to San Francisco. Although the riverboat was originally built for a then-staggering sum of $1 million, the meticulous restoration has cost more than $8 million.

Now in its original condition, the King gleams with polished brass fittings and the patina of paneling, window trim, doors and benches. A carpeted grand staircase sweeping up from the main deck to the saloon level is back in place. At the top of the stairs is the mahogany-paneled Delta Lounge, featuring an oyster bar and decorated with stained glass scenes of the Sacramento River of yesteryear. The lower deck lounge, the Paddlewheel Saloon, is a nightly disco and has live music on weekends. The gigantic revolving paddlewheel can be seen through the glass-walled stern.

Even more luxurious and spacious than the originals, the restored staterooms and suites are furnished in period antiques and decorated in teal blue and mauve or beige and sea green. Some of the baths have clawfoot tubs and pull-chain toilets. Other features such as air conditioning and tile showers have been added. The Captain's Quarters is a posh suite with a king-size bed, a wet bar, and a wheelhouse loft.

Morning fruit, juice, and pastry are served to overnight guests in the Pilothouse Restaurant, one of two restaurants that view the river. Both serve lunch, dinner, and Sunday brunch.

The 43,745-square-foot vessel contains a theater where guests can see musical revues and a show on the history of riverboating. Weddings can be performed on board, and an outdoor plank landing is next to the boat for receptions. Valet parking is free to guests.

The last of California's original steam paddlewheelers, the Riverboat Delta King has been placed on the National Register of Historic Places.

The Sterling Hotel
1300 H Street
Sacramento, California 95814
916-448-1300
800-365-7660

Proprietors: Richard and Sandi Kann
Accommodations: 12 rooms
Rates: $110–$225; $15 for roll-away
Payment: Major credit cards
Children: Welcome
Pets: Not allowed
Smoking: Prohibited

The Sterling is a small luxury hotel in the heart of Sacramento. Its amenities and convenient downtown location—near the capitol, convention center, and county courthouse—make it a favorite of business and government travelers, while its elegance and style draw discriminating vacationers.

The three-story, century-old Victorian structure was completely renovated in 1987, removing all vestiges of the apartment building it had been for fifty years. Now it has a gracious facade with a generous porch entry, a lobby with a marble floor, and a lounge where guests enjoy the morning newspapers and coffee by a black Italian marble fireplace. Japanese paintings, Chinese rugs, and a single vase of tall red ginger emphasize Oriental simplicity. More ornate are the lobby mirror framed in painted birds and flowers and the filigreed brass chandelier hanging from the open loft.

There are no ruffles or fringes in this contemporary hotel, but touches of its origins may be seen in the molding detail and lace curtains. The spacious guest rooms, on all three floors, have four-poster or canopy beds and Queen Anne furniture. The pink marble baths contain pedestal sinks with gleaming brass taps and oversize whirlpool tubs and showers enclosed by brass and glass.

On the hotel's lower level is an exquisite little restaurant, Chanterelle. It seats only forty people in three glass-partitioned rooms of restrained decor. The Continental cuisine is expensive but is considered some of the best in Sacramento. Fresh regional ingredients are used with traditional French techniques and California creativity. A specialty is veal with chanterelle mushrooms.

Next door, off a brick courtyard and behind a brick wall, is the Glass Garden, a conservatory imported from England. The 40-foot-long structure, with a glass roof in three graceful tiers, is used for receptions, parties, dances, and weddings.

Among Sacramento's attractions are the lovely capitol grounds and the oldest public art museum in the west, Crocker Art Museum. Old Sacramento has a railroad museum, a reconstruction of Sutter's Fort, and more than 250 shops and restaurants.

Salt Lake City

The Anton Boxrud Bed & Breakfast
57 South 600 East
Salt Lake City, Utah 84102
801-363-8035
800-524-5511

Hosts: Margaret and Ray Fuller
Accommodations: 6 rooms, 2 with private bath
Rates: $35–$55; double, $49–$59
Included: Full breakfast
Minimum stay: None
Added: 10.25% tax
Payment: MasterCard, Visa
Children: Welcome
Pets: Not allowed
Smoking: Prohibited
Open: Year-round

It's not often that owners who want to restore a turn-of-the-century home know in detail what it looked like at the time it was first constructed. However, when longtime Salt Lake City residents Ray and Margaret Fuller bought the historic Anton Boxrud House in 1988, they were able to find the original plans in the University of Utah library. Using them as a guide, they set about returning the Victorian house to something approximating its 1901 grandeur.

The front door opens into another era. The rich interiors of beveled glass, burled woodwork, pocket doors, oak wainscoting, and maple flooring largely recreate the appearance of the house when Anton and Minnie Boxrud moved in. Even some of the furnishings are original, for they'd been stored in the attic when the Boxruds passed away. The Fullers contributed pieces of their own, and a genteel little bed-and-breakfast was born.

Margaret Fuller encourages guests to make themselves at home. They have free run of the front parlor, which has a player piano and mission oak couch, and can curl up in the fireplaced den and in the sitting room beside an old RCA Victrola. All of the guest rooms are upstairs. They, too, have been furnished with many of the Boxrud's original chests and dressers. The largest of lot is the original master bedroom, whose queen-size bed faces a gorgeous stained glass window. It has a private bath. Of the others, the former maid's room, the smallest, bathes in sunlight because of its southern exposure. The others have been minimally decorated beyond the antiques, brass or oak beds, and lace curtains. Still, every one of them is immaculately clean.

Margaret serves wine and cheese in the afternoon and a full breakfast, which might be pancakes, quiche, or a homemade specialty like French toast with cranberry sauce. Downtown Salt Lake City is within walking distance.

Brigham Street Inn
1135 East South Temple
Salt Lake City, Utah 84102-1605
801-364-4461
Fax: 801-521-3201

Owners: John and Nancy Pace
Accommodations: 8 rooms, 1 suite, all with private bath
Rates: $75, double, $104; suite, $149
Included: Continental breakfast
Minimum stay: None
Added: 10.25% tax
Payment: Major credit cards
Children: Welcome over age 8
Pets: Not allowed
Smoking: Allowed
Open: Year-round

Most late-19th-century mansions make the transition to bed-and-breakfasts by becoming living museums of Victoriana, chock full of antiques and turn-of-the-century memorabilia. Not the delightful Brigham Street Inn—this two-and-a-half-story red brick house with deep green pillars hints at the Belle Époque in its high ceilings, rounded bay windows with leaded glass, pocket doors, and heavy-beamed staircase of quarter-sawn oak. Only one bedroom—and a single at that—contains Victorian antique furnishings. The rest are cheerfully contemporary and unique.

The transformation occurred in 1981 when John Pace, an architect, and his wife Nancy, now a city councilwoman, decided to buy the dilapidated 1898 mansion they'd fallen in love with and turn it into an inn. While undertaking the renovation, they lent the house, which was on the National Register of Historic Homes, to the Utah Heritage Foundation to use in its annual fund-raising Designers' Showcase. The Foundation brought in twelve interior designers to create a model bed-and-breakfast inn, assigning each a room to decorate and then opening the house to public tours. When it was over, the Paces bought the contents from the decorators and began innkeeping.

Unable to live there themselves, they hired young, personable managers to be on hand 24 hours a day, manning the desk and serving Continental breakfasts at a long oak table in the dining room. Attentive professionalism coupled with features like phones in the rooms and proximity to the University of Utah attracts both tourists and businesspeople. Guests gather on the comfortable sofas in the parlor, whose bird's-eye maple fireplace mantel is original, and compare notes about their rooms. Elegant Room 1 faces south through a bay window; the basement suite has contemporary Oriental style, a private outside entrance, brass bed, double Jacuzzi tub, and a kitchen with a microwave. Someone comes by each evening turn down the quilt, leaving a mint and fresh towels.

The Inn at Temple Square

71 West South Temple
Salt Lake City, Utah 84101
801-531-1000
800-843-4668
Fax: 801-537-7272

General manager: Marge Taylor
Accommodations: 75 rooms, 15 suites
Rates: Rooms, weekdays, $89–$115; weekends, $69–$89; suites, $130–$199
Included: Full breakfast
Minimum stay: None
Added: 10.25% tax
Payment: Major credit cards
Children: Free under age 18
Pets: Not allowed
Smoking: Prohibited and subject to fines
Open: Year-round

When the venerable Hotel Utah closed, Salt Lake City plunged into an accommodations dark age, no longer able to offer travelers a truly distinctive hotel in the heart of downtown. That changed in 1990 with the reopening of the Inn at Temple Square.

Though originally constructed in 1930 as a transient hotel, the seven-story red brick inn bears no resemblance to its Depression-era namesake except in its distinguished architecture. The doors open onto a European-style hotel, whose staff greets guests like friends. The intimate lobby rises two stories from its green marble floors to a coffered ceiling. Sunlight illuminates a hand-painted frieze of bluebells around the tops of the walls and reflects off brass chandeliers. On many afternoons, live piano music drifts down from the mezzanine library.

The rooms feature custom-made dark wood furniture and heavy Edwardian drapes, offset by light floral and bird print wallpapers. Even the smallish standard rooms, which face the back courtyard, have queen-size beds, down pillows, thick comforters, fine linens, armoires with remote control televisions, a small refrigerator with complimentary soft drinks, and phones with two incoming lines and a data port. The spacious king-bedded deluxe rooms look out on Temple Square, directly across the street. Businesspeople like the Parlor Suites, which have a completely separate room with a table, chairs, and half bath; honeymooners love the Bridal Suites for their four-poster beds and Jacuzzi tubs.

The price of the room includes a buffet breakfast of fresh fruit, pastry, eggs, pancakes, bacon, and more, served in the hotel's Carriage Court Restaurant amid Tiffany lamps and upholstered banquets. The restaurant also serves lunch and good, moderately priced dinners of seafood fettuccine, breast of chicken Oscar, and tournedos of beef. The hotel does not have a liquor license and is so adamant about its nonsmoking policy that guests risk eviction and fine for lighting up.

The Peery Hotel
110 West 300 South
Salt Lake City, Utah 84101
801-521-4300
800-331-0073
Fax: 801-575-5014

General manager: Ed Pilkerton
Accommodations: 71 rooms, 6 suites
Rates: $59–$84; suites, $99
Included: Continental breakfast
Minimum stay: None
Added: 10.25% tax
Payment: Major credit cards

Children: Free under age 16
Pets: Not allowed
Smoking: Permitted on the third floor
Open: Year-round

Listed on the National Register of Historic Places, the Peery Hotel evokes the era of train travel. Constructed in 1910, the three-story brick structure faced with gray sandstone stands halfway between the Rio Grande Railway Station and Temple Square. Its unprepossessing architecture suggests a history of transient guests, people who needed rooms for a night or two and cared more about cost than comfort.

But the Peery is much more. A half-moon of stained glass caps double birch doors that open onto a elegant lobby dominated by a grand staircase. The fine workmanship shows everywhere, from the dentil moldings on its high wooden ceiling to twin square pillars that anchor the staircase. Thick plum carpet covers the floor and stairs. Many of the lobby's furnishings are antiques, among them a monumental carved wood breakfront. More antiques create mini-parlors on the landings on the upper floors.

The rooms have high ceilings, decorative wood moldings, lavender and avocado color schemes, and tile baths. The layouts and decor vary. The inexpensive standard rooms, though small and without desks and tubs, occupy corner locations and thus have two windows. The deluxe rooms are roughly the size of a standard hotel room, while suites are really oversize rooms with sitting areas and perhaps a partial divider. The only disappointment is the bland furnishings and accessories, which seem more appropriate to a motel than a historic hotel.

But the depth of the Peery's amenities and services helps outweigh those shortcomings. All the rooms have remote control color televisions. Rates include a self-serve Continental breakfast, complimentary newspaper, free parking, free airport shuttle, and access to a tiny workout room and a hot tub. There are two restaurants off the lobby—one of them the very affordable Peery Pub & Café—both of which offer room service. There's even a liquor store and sundries shop.

The Pinecrest Bed & Breakfast Inn

6211 Emigration Canyon Road
Salt Lake City, Utah 84108
801-583-6663
800-359-6663

Owners: Phil and Donnetta Davis
Accommodations: 3 rooms, 1 suite, 1 guest house, 1 cabin, all
   with private bath
Rates: Rooms and suite, $65–$160; guest house, $135; cabin, $110
Included: Full breakfast
Minimum stay: None
Added: 9.25% tax
Payment: Major credit cards
Children: Welcome in suite, guest house, and cabin
Pets: Not allowed
Smoking: Prohibited
Open: Year-round

Pinecrest dates from 1915, when quarry owner W. S. Henderson
had it built as his home, using red and white stone from a quarry
nearby. He chose a location six miles up Emigration Canyon,
the historic Mormon route into the Salt Lake Valley, setting the
house alongside a gurgling trout stream on six acres wooded
with pines, cottonwoods, and river birch. His son, David, in-
herited the estate and added wrought-iron gates (which had
originally graced Paramount Studios in Hollywood) and formal gardens. The setting is so peaceful that it takes effort to
remember Salt Lake City is a mere 20-minute drive away.

Phil and Donnetta Davis purchased the house in 1986 and,
except for modernizing a couple of the baths, kept it much as
they found it. A huge living room and sitting area runs across
the main floor, with picture windows looking onto the gardens,
cherry-colored wainscoting on the walls and ceiling, Belgian
carpet on the floors, and a fireplace set in a wall of flat field-
stone.

There are three rooms and a suite in the inn proper, each with
a different decor and private bath. The original master bedroom, which takes up the entire upper floor, has become an
opulent Oriental Suite furnished with Ming silk couches, a
king-size bed, and a Chinese screen. It has views of the gardens,
its own rose-colored Jacuzzi tub, and a separate room with two
twin beds, making it ideal for families. Of the other rooms, the
smallest is done in Holland blue with white wicker, the largest
in a Jamaican decor complete with its own Mexican tile Jacuzzi
and a sauna. Also special is the two-story Stetson Guest House,
which has hardwood floors, a fireplace, kitchen, and Western
memorabilia. It holds a queen-size bed on the main level and
four bunk beds and a bath downstairs (Robert Redford stayed
here in the years before the Davises bought it). Tucked into the
pines near the Davises' own home a mile and a half away is a

1940s log cabin with its own fireplace, full kitchen, and two double beds in a loft.

Phil Davis prides himself on his sour cream banana pancakes; he serves them for breakfast on an antique dining table in the living room in winter or on a deck overlooking the gardens in summer. Beyond that, he is intermittently on hand to give advice and answer questions, leaving guests full run of the property. Guests can follow hiking trails into the woods, and the Davises can arrange horseback riding and dinner.

Saltair Bed & Breakfast

164 South 900 East
Salt Lake City, Utah 84102
801-533-8184
800-733-8184

Innkeepers: Jan Bartlett and Nancy Saxton
Accommodations: 5 rooms, 2 with private bath
Rates: $34; double, $49–$69
Included: Continental breakfast
Minimum stay: None
Added: 10.25% tax
Payment: Major credit cards (subject to 3%–5% surcharge); checks or cash preferred
Children: Welcome if well-behaved
Pets: Not allowed
Smoking: Prohibited
Open: Year-round

When Nancy Saxton and her husband Jan Bartlett wanted to open a bed-and-breakfast, they visited Saltair and immediately fell under its spell. "We believe in the spirit of homes," observes Nancy, "and this one feels very comfortable."

The Victorian house and its long, covered porch front a postage-stamp lawn on a residential street a mile from downtown. Though outwardly little different from its neighbors, it is listed on the National Register of Historic Places. Built in 1903 by an architect, it was sold in 1920 to the Italian vice consul Fortunato Anselmo. Among his overnight guests were the cardinal who later became Pope Pius XII, Mussolini's secretary (who was also Anselmo's mistress), and members of the Italian Olympic team. During Prohibition, Anselmo made wine in the cellar (authorities couldn't touch him since the house was regarded as occupying foreign soil).

Wine is no longer made in the cellar, but much of the house's fine interior detail survives. Beveled-glass snowflakes set in panes etched to resemble winter frost frame the oak front door. Inside, sunlight floods through large leaded glass windows into a living room and dining room rich with original oak millwork. Antiques abound, so do plants.

A polished oak staircase leads upstairs to the five main bedrooms, each furnished with antiques, family heirlooms, and fresh flowers. What they lack in size they make up for in cheerful comfort. Quilts or hand-crocheted bedspreads cover the brass and Shaker oak beds. Wall-to-warm carpet and new wallpaper add to the feeling of warmth and freshness. The most inviting of all are the Blue Crystal room, which has a sunny southern exposure, bay window, and queen-size brass bed (though its private bathroom is down the hall), and the Sweet Sage room, which has a queen-size brass bed and potbelly stove.

Healthy breakfasts, served family-style on a long oak table in the dining room, consist of fresh fruit, pastries, cereals, granola, fruit smoothies blended of various fruits and yogurt, coffee, and tea. Guests can have as much as they want. On winter afternoons, Nancy puts out hot cider and veggies, cookies, or popcorn. In summer, there is homemade ice cream and freshly made lemonade.

San Antonio

Bed and Breakfast Hosts of San Antonio
166 Rockhill
San Antonio, Texas 78209
512-824-8036

Operators: Lavern Campbell
Accommodations: About 30 in the San Antonio area
Rates: $45–$120; double, $60–$180
Included: Continental breakfast
Added: 13% tax within San Antonio city limits
Payment: Major credit cards
Children: Sometimes accepted
Pets: Sometimes allowed
Smoking: Not allowed
Open: Year-round

Lavern Campbell is known for her hospitable and efficient service, and her B&Bs range from families who welcome guests into their own home to inns run by a full-time staff. San Antonio is a popular city with lots of hotels, but B&B Hosts offers lodgings with intimacy. Some are near downtown, in the historic King William residential area; others are close to the Riverwalk, Sea World, Fort Sam Houston, and the airport.

In the King William area, a new guest house includes a downstairs bedroom with a double bed, a loft bedroom with twin beds, and a sofa bed in the living room. The adjacent hosts' home dates from 1871. Bikes are available for exploring the area.

Also available are several well-known lodgings. The Norton-Brackenridge House, which has won awards for its restoration, is a Victorian house with four guest rooms. Terrell Castle, near Fort Sam Houston, is fanciful and fun. Built in 1894 to resemble a mix of European castles and French châteaux, it's furnished with antiques. Nine guest rooms, all furnished differently, occupy the second and third floors; a loft-style room is on the fourth floor. The Colonial Room is hexagonal.

The Crockett Hotel

320 Bonham
San Antonio, Texas 78205
512-225-6500
800-292-1050 in Texas
800-531-5537 in U.S.
Fax: 512-225-7418

General manager: Kenny Gibson
Accommodations: 202 rooms and suites
Rates: $80–$160; suites, $125–$400
Added: 13% tax
Payment: Major credit cards
Children: Under 18 free in room with parents
Pets: Not allowed
Smoking: Nonsmoking rooms available
Open: Year-round

Built in 1909, the Crockett Hotel is on the National Register of Historic Places. Although it was completely refurbished in 1985, much care was taken to see that its original character was maintained. You are always aware of the building's age, and the Alamo's presence just across the street only adds to the ambience.

In keeping with the sense of the building, the hotel is simply decorated. The most striking elements in the lobby and adjoining enclosed atrium (once an outdoor courtyard) are the polished slate floors and mellowed brick walls—exposed in the lobby, softly painted in the atrium.

The guest rooms in the main building, called the Tower, are unpretentious, yet comfortable and spacious. Large windows keep them sunny and afford fine views of the city. "Courtyard" rooms are in a separate annex, added to the hotel in 1978. These rooms may lack the charm of the older building, but they are popular with families because they have more sleeping space and surround the hotel's tropical garden and swimming pool. Be sure to visit the Tower's rooftop hot tub and sundeck for a bird's-eye view of San Antonio.

The Crockett has two restaurants, Ernie's Bar & Grill and the Landmark Café. The Landmark's menu leans toward seafood and Texas steaks, and on weekend nights the waiters sing show tunes. Ernie's is more casual, serving burgers and other typical bar fare. Room service is also available.

Valet parking costs $7; self-parking in nearby lots is $4 per day. However, once the car is parked, you probably won't have much need for it; the Riverwalk and most city sights are a short walk from the hotel.

The Emily Morgan Hotel
705 East Houston
San Antonio, Texas 78205
512-225-8486
800-824-6674
Fax: 512-225-7227

General manager: Sandy Harper
Accommodations: 177 rooms
Rates: $80; double, $90; suites, $100–$175
Added: 13% tax
Payment: Major credit cards
Children: Under 12 free in room with parents
Pets: Under 20 pounds with deposit
Smoking: Nonsmoking rooms available
Open: Year-round

The Emily Morgan Hotel's Neo-Gothic tower with a flag on top catches the eye from almost every street corner in downtown San Antonio. This graceful hotel was built in 1926 as the Medical Arts Building, and you can still see medical symbols above some of the windows. Turned into a hotel in 1985, it is across the street from the Alamo.

Inside, the look is contemporary; attractive modern art hangs in the halls and guest rooms. The rooms are spare but have fine furnishings, such as curly maple dressers and wardrobes and wooden blinds. Large windows give the rooms an airy feeling. The bathrooms have scales, which may not be a plus in a city with so many fine restaurants. Many of the rooms have Jacuzzis and mini-refrigerators.

The hotel itself has one restaurant, open only for breakfast. Named the Yellow Rose Café after the woman who was said to have helped Sam Houston bring down Santa Ana, each table is set with fresh roses. Guests may wish to spend some time in the Emily Morgan Bar (Emily Morgan was the Yellow Rose of Texas), small pool, whirlpool, exercise room, or sauna.

Parking in nearby city lots is $6.50 per day.

The Fairmount Hotel
401 South Alamo Street
San Antonio, Texas 78205
512-224-8800
800-642-3363
Fax: 512-224-2767

Managing director: Linda Finger
Accommodations: 36 rooms and suites

Rates: $145–$185; double, $155–$195; suites, $225–$375
Added: 13% tax
Payment: Major credit cards
Children: Free in room with parents
Pets: Not allowed
Smoking: Nonsmoking rooms available
Open: Year-round

If you like class, pack your bags and head for the Fairmount. To call this wonderful hotel "service-oriented" is an understatement. From the moment you arrive until the moment you leave, you're pampered by a warm, friendly staff.

Built in 1906 in Italianate Victorian style, the hotel was in operation until the 1960s, when it was boarded up. In 1985 it made headlines when it was moved six blocks, becoming the largest building ever moved in one piece. The new owners transformed the building into a luxury hotel, building an addition that complements the original structure.

The Fairmount is next to San Antonio's La Villita Historic District, a picturesque assortment of shops and restaurants within a few steps of the famed Riverwalk. Across the street from the hotel are HemisFair Plaza and the city convention center.

Each room has a different decor. Common to all are high ceilings, reproduction antiques, bleached wood floors, and muted colors. The bathrooms have Italian marble and solid brass appointments. Luxury abounds: terry robes, bath telephones, makeup mirrors, oversize towels, remote-control TVs with VCRs and a complimentary film library to select from (including a tape of the Fairmount's move), twice-daily maid service, bed turn-down, and complimentary shoeshine.

Some rooms are designed for families, with two queen-size beds. (Children get milk and cookies.) The Veranda suites have separate living and sleeping areas, canopy beds, and stereos. The Master Suite is the largest, with all of the features of Veranda suites plus a whirlpool tub, wet bar, and separate dressing area.

Polo's, the Fairmount's restaurant, serves all three meals. Dinner entrées such as beef tenderloin stuffed with chorizo, spinach and mushrooms or oven roasted Szechuan duck in a Hoisin pear sauce range from $17.95 to $22.95. The appetizers are exotic; desserts are memorable. Breakfasts and lunches are sometimes served on the patio, and Polo's bar has live entertainment in the evening.

Hotel Menger

204 Alamo Plaza
San Antonio, Texas 78205
512-223-4361
800-345-9285
Fax: 512-228-0022

General manager: J. W. McMillin
Accommodations: 320 rooms
Rates: $78–$98; double, $98–$122; $10 additional person in
    room; suites, $152–$456; weekend packages available
Added: 13% tax
Payment: Major credit cards
Children: Under 18 free in room with parents
Pets: Not allowed
Smoking: Nonsmoking rooms available
Open: Year-round

The Menger claims to be the oldest continuously operating hotel west of the Mississippi. When William Menger, a German brewer, built it in 1859, he had a practical purpose in mind: the patrons of his brewery frequently needed a place to spend the night, and he was tired of converting bar tables into beds. San Antonio was still a frontier town (the Battle of the Alamo had taken place only 23 years earlier), and Menger added a strong dose of refinement, building a fine lodging with beautiful furnishings.

Over the years the Menger has played a part in Texas history. During the Spanish-American War, Teddy Roosevelt recruited his Rough Riders in the hotel's bar. The lodging was long popular with visiting cattlemen. Today, with its central location and moderate prices, it attracts families and other vacationers as well as business travelers.

The Menger continues to grow, sprawling out from its original design to include a motor inn. In early 1988, 33 rooms were added as part of a major refurbishment undertaken in conjunction with the creation of a new section of the city's Riverwalk, joining the Menger to the new Rivercenter Mall.

Care was taken to blend the additions as naturally as possible with the old hotel so that, despite their newness, there's a strong sense of history about the Menger. The Victorian rotunda in the original section is spectacular, with a stained glass ceiling and two oval mezzanine floors overlooking the lobby, filled with antiques.

To savor the history of the place, choose a one-of-a-kind suite such as the Devon Cattle or the King Suite. Each has a large carved bed with a canopy and a parlor with antique furnishings. The Roy Rogers Room was decorated to accommodate Roy and Dale when they visited HemisFair in 1968. All of the suites open onto the mezzanines. Other choices include the new guest rooms (top of the line, especially the palatial Presidential Suite), standard rooms (completely refurbished in 1987), and motel rooms (fairly ordinary). Rich greens, flowered drapes and spreads, and botanical prints dominate the courtyard rooms, reflecting the garden below. The rooms facing the Alamo have beige tones, mirroring the Alamo's honey-colored brick.

The hotel's pool, surrounded by lush landscaping, is especially attractive, as is the courtyard, with a fountain, used for dining in nice weather. The Colonial Room serves southwestern specialties for breakfast, lunch, dinner, and Sunday brunch. The Menger Bar, decorated with photos of Teddy Roosevelt and the hotel's early years, is well worth a visit.

Self-parking in a nearby lot is $3.95 per day. Valet parking is $7.95.

La Mansion del Rio
112 College Street
San Antonio, Texas 78205
512-225-2581
800-292-7300 in Texas
800-531-7208 in U.S.
Fax: 512-226-0389

General manager: Jan Leenders
Accommodations: 337 rooms
Rates: $130–$220; double, $150–$240; suites, $360–$1,500
Added: 13% tax
Payment: Major credit cards; no personal checks
Children: Under 18 free in room with parents
Pets: Not allowed

Smoking: Nonsmoking rooms available
Open: Year-round

At the heart of this popular tourist city is the Riverwalk, a gentle canallike river flanked by shops and restaurants. The most charming hotel near the water is La Mansion del Rio, a quiet retreat within a few steps of the Riverwalk's energy.

The Spanish colonial building dates from 1852, when it opened as St. Mary's Institute, a Catholic school that became a distinguished law school. A hotel since 1968, it is a composite of classical arches, wrought iron, and red tile. At its cedar-shaded Riverwalk entrance, a profusion of greenery cascades from stone walls, and an arched bridge spans the waterway. A rambling structure, due to sections being added during its years as a school, La Mansion has guest rooms spread over seven floors. Perhaps the most requested rooms are those overlooking the river, which have balconies ideal for watching the stream of people flow by on the Riverwalk below. Other rooms open onto two inner courtyards, one with an attractive swimming pool.

Spanish in decor, the rooms have beamed ceilings, luxuriant bedspreads, and plush carpets. While some rooms are rather small, all are attractive and comfortable. Every room has a dry bar with a refrigerator and a remote control TV in an armoire.

Restaurante Capistrano serves southwestern cuisine, with an emphasis on authentic Mexican dishes. The romantic Las Canarias restaurant overlooks the river and is known for its fine cuisine. Paella, grilled swordfish, blackened snapper, and veal scaloppine are typical entrées, ranging from $19 to $25. Las Canarias also holds a champagne brunch on Sundays for $19.95.

Hotel guests can use the facilities at two nearby health clubs. One has tennis courts, an indoor-outdoor pool, and exercise equipment (no fees); the second has racquetball, squash, handball, Nautilus equipment, and an indoor pool ($10 fee). Hotel services include a concierge, 24-hour room service, and valet parking ($7).

San Antonio is a romantic city with a Spanish heritage. La Mansion del Rio is the essence of the city, enveloping you in its charm.

Plaza San Antonio
555 South Alamo
San Antonio, Texas 78205
512-229-1000
800-421-1172
Fax: 512-223-6650

General manager: Rod Siler
Accommodations: 252 rooms and suites
Rates: $150–$190; double, $170–$210; suites, $250–$700
Added: 13% tax
Payment: Major credit cards
Children: Free in room with parents
Pets: Small pets allowed
Smoking: Allowed
Open: Year-round

The 6-story Plaza San Antonio is a hacienda hideaway only a few blocks from the Riverwalk, yet far removed in its tranquillity. Here you can get to a multitude of attractions within minutes, but retreat to the hotel's grounds in between sightseeing jaunts. A swimming pool surrounded by gardens, two tennis courts, a croquet lawn, and a health club are all on the premises.

The mood is Old Mexico — perfect for enjoying San Antonio and its missions, Mexican markets, and nearby La Villita Historic District. The entrance to the lobby is through a small Mexican tile courtyard with a fountain. Also on the grounds are remnants of early Texas. Three historic cottages, each representing a different style of architecture, serve a practical purpose as well as add character. Both the Alsace-Lorraine bungalow and the Victorian cottage are used for private groups. The restored Germanic house holds the health club, with a sauna and exercise facilities, and a front porch swing for lazy summer evenings. Next door to the main hotel is the 19th-century school built for the children of the German settlers. Today it's the hotel's conference center.

The guest rooms, in two connecting wings of the hotel, are spacious and attractively furnished in soft pastels and flowered fabrics. Extra pillows on the beds make them especially inviting. Many rooms have balconies overlooking the lush gardens. Junior suites have sitting areas with TVs and another TV in the bedroom. Bathrobes, bottled water, hair dryers, and cable TV with a movie channel are in every room.

Staffed by a concierge, the hotel has 24-hour room service and lots of special touches, from complimentary shoeshines, morning coffee and newspapers, and twice-daily housekeeping service to nightly turndown. Bicycles are available free of charge. There is a poolside bar and a small children's pool. Parking is $5 per day.

The Anaqua Restaurant, named for the stately trees that generously shade the grounds, has one of the most unique menus in town. A chef's station, featuring "hot rock" cooking (food is slow-cooked on granite slabs that come from the German Alps), opens out to the restaurant. "Bamboo Blue Plate" specials are Oriental dishes cooked in bamboo steamers, while Tex-Mex entrées are cooked on a wood-burning grill. Spanish tapas, homemade vinegars and breads, and exotic drinks such as kiwi margaritas and "Banana Boat Blue" (vanilla bean ice cream with blackberry brandy, fresh bananas, blue curaco, vodka, and cranberry juice) add to the restaurant's international flavor. For more informal dining and lighter fare, meals are served by the pool or in the Palm Terrace Restaurant and lobby bar.

St. Anthony

300 East Travis
San Antonio, Texas 78205
512-227-4392
800-338-1338
Fax: 512-227-0915

General manager: Nick Ghawi
Accommodations: 362 rooms and suites
Rates: $85–$109; double, $85–$129; suites, $135–$500
Added: 13% tax
Payment: Major credit cards; no personal checks
Children: Under 19 free in room with parents
Pets: With prior arrangement
Smoking: Nonsmoking rooms available
Open: Year-round

Designated a Texas and National Historic Landmark, the St. Anthony is a grand lady, reflecting the sumptuous grace of an earlier age. Built in 1909 by a prominent cattleman, B. L. Taylor, and a former San Antonio mayor, A. H. Jones, the hotel is European in design and decoration, pure Texan in tradition and hospitality.

Now a Park Lane Hotel, the St. Anthony was for many years owned by a wealthy railroad builder and rancher, R. W. Morrison, who turned it into a showcase for the art he collected in his travels. Today it's a treasure house of fine furnishings and paintings.

Venetian mosaic tile floors, Oriental rugs, leather sofas, bronze statues, 19th-century Chinese urns, and Empire chandeliers dripping with crystal grace the ornate lobby and public areas. Particularly beautiful is a rosewood and gold-leaf grand piano from the czarist embassy in Paris.

A quiet retreat from the flurry is Peacock Alley, which runs parallel to the main lounge and overlooks Travis Park—a spot of green in the midst of downtown. The Alley is actually a long hall with high ceilings interrupted by tall, arched windows, furnished with large bamboo chairs for intimate conversation; it has been a favorite San Antonio meeting place since the 1930s.

Do stop by the Anacacho Ballroom, where Prince Rainier and Princess Grace were once entertained. The Travis Room has a huge painting of cowboys on the range, again reflecting the St. Anthony's Texas soul.

The guest rooms have a sense of refinement with their traditional furniture, matching drapes and bedspreads, and brass accessories. No two are alike, and many have antiques and art objects. Doorbells add a nice touch.

Guests may dine all day at the informal Café, specializing in southwestern and Continental cuisine. For evening and live entertainment, Pete's Pub is the place to go. With its deep green interior and marble tables, it is remarkably elegant for a saloon. Pete's also serves lunch, snacks, and cocktails, and is open until 1:00 A.M.

Unusual for a hotel of its vintage, the St. Anthony has a heated rooftop pool and a large redwood sundeck with a view of downtown, as well as a small fitness room. Other features include room service (6:30 A.M.–11 P.M.) and valet parking ($8). Self-parking in an outdoor lot is also available ($5).

San Antonio Marriott Rivercenter

101 Bowie Street
San Antonio, Texas 78205
512-223-1000
800-648-4462
Fax: 512-223-4092

General manager: Ed Paradine
Accommodations: 1000 rooms and suites
Rates: $165; double, $185; suites, $250–$850
Added: 13% tax
Payment: Major credit cards
Children: Under 12 free in room with parents
Pets: Allowed
Smoking: Nonsmoking rooms available
Open: Year-round

The Rivercenter, with its many shops, restaurants, and theaters, has become the hub of activity for San Antonio's celebrated Riverwalk. The 38-story Marriott Rivercenter opened in 1988 to take full advantage of a prime location. Its busy glass-covered atrium lobby mirrors both the hustle and bustle and the glass architecture of the Rivercenter just outside.

The hotel has come up with just about every possible type of room a traveler could want. In the junior-king suites the bedroom is separated from the sitting area by French doors. Bed-sitting suites are two and a half times larger than a standard room. Two concierge floors serve complimentary breakfast in the morning, hors d'oeuvres in the evening, and late night desserts in the floors' private lounge. The rooms on the ladies' executive floor have special features such as razors, hair dryers, and satin hangers. The marquis floor has somewhat nicer furnishings than the traditional decor of the standard rooms, and includes extras such as shoe polishers and hot taps and instant coffee for making coffee in the room. Concert pianists won't have to miss a day's practice if they stay in one of the two presidential suites, equipped with baby grand pianos. Some rooms have Riverwalk views, and of course connecting rooms are available for families.

The Garden Café has a good salad bar and serves breakfast, lunch, and dinner buffets. Occasionally it runs special events, such as strawberry and seafood festivals, where the food of honor is spotlighted in a variety of dishes. The River Grill, featuring southwestern cuisine, offers elegant dining, with entrées ranging from $17 to $22. After dinner, guests can sample a wide range of liqueurs from the apéritif cart or move over to the Atrium Lounge, where a huge stuffed armadillo is perched at the keys of a player piano.

The hotel has a heated indoor-outdoor pool—the outdoor portion surrounded by an attractive sundeck. Guests without a bathing suit can purchase disposable ones at the pool office. A workout room, hot tub, and saunas are all next to the pool area.

The hotel maintains a business center for executives and a laundry room where guests can wash and dry clothes free of charge; a concierge is on duty in the lobby for 12 hours a day. Room service is available around the clock. Parking is $7 per night.

Sheraton Gunter Hotel
205 East Houston Street
San Antonio, Texas 78205
512-227-3241
800-222-4276
Fax: 512-227-9305

General manager: Lester Jonas
Accommodations: 325 rooms and suites
Rates: $89–$121; double, $99–$134; suites, $195–$490
Added: 13% tax
Payment: Major credit cards
Children: Under 18 free in room with parents
Pets: Small ones allowed with a $20 deposit
Smoking: Nonsmoking rooms available
Open: Year-round

The Gunter, built in 1909, is a classic, mirroring an earlier, grander era. Its expansive lobby is graced by columns, sparkling crystal chandeliers, and a molded ceiling. Throughout the 12-story hotel, marble floors and walnut paneling date from the time that the Gunter was the largest building in San Antonio. A montage of the hotel's history is displayed near the main elevators.

Newly decorated in 1990, the spacious yet intimate rooms have Queen Anne furniture and matching drapes and bedspreads. Four different color schemes have been used, so the rooms aren't carbon copies. There's a look of subdued plushness here accented with tradition — from high ceilings to heavy wooden doors.

Unlike some historic hotels, the Gunter is well aware of the modern bent toward recreation and fitness. The second-floor heated swimming pool and an exercise room with Nautilus equipment add just the right touch. For kids, there's a small video arcade in the hotel basement.

Just off the lobby and popular with theatergoers, Café Suisse serves European fare in a convivial setting of rich wood and soft lighting. Before your meal comes, one of the waiters keeps you entertained with his repertoire of magic tricks. Entrées such as lamb, duck, and prime rib range from $16 to $21. The dessert tray is tempting even after a filling meal. The pastries are prepared by the Swiss chef, who's also responsible for the luscious creations in the hotel's Pâtisserie Suisse Bake Shop. Café Suisse also serves a champagne brunch on Sundays.

Muldoon's, named for Padre Muldoon — an Irish priest who converted early Texans — is a bar on several levels next to an enclosed glass terrace. Lunch buffets are served upstairs during the week, and singalong happy hours usher in weekday evenings.

Service is important at the Gunter. A friendly staff, valet parking ($6), 24-hour room service, and bed turndown are all part of your stay. Two floors function as concierge levels. In addition to the not-to-be-missed pâtisserie, shops in the hotel include a barber shop and a fancy gift shop. Discount tickets to places such as Sea World are often available at the front desk.

The Gunter is in the heart of downtown, one block from the Riverwalk and five blocks from the Alamo. The Majestic Theater, which attracts top performers, is just across the street. Its ornate Moorish interior is so extraordinary, it's worth the price of a concert ticket just to see it. Special machines produce actual clouds that move across its seemingly starlit ceiling—making for a most memorable atmosphere and evening.

San Diego

Balboa Park Inn
3402 Park Boulevard
San Diego, California 92103
619-298-0823

General manager: Ed Wilcox
Accommodations: 25 suites (all with private bath)
Rates: $75–$175 1-4 people
Included: Continental breakfast
Payment: Major credit cards
Children: Welcome in family suites
Pets: Not allowed
Smoking: Allowed
Open: Year-round

Four pink stucco Spanish Colonial buildings on a corner near Balboa Park form this complex of suites, courtyards, gardens, and terraces. Luxurious and imaginatively furnished, each suite is a world of its own. They all have refrigerators, cable TV with HBO, phones (local calls are free), and daily maid service.

Each suite has a special theme. In Greystoke, for example, you'll sleep in the jungle beside a painting of Tarzan. In Nouveau Ritz, you'll enter the Hollywood glamour of the 1940s —it has curved black art deco couches backed by a glittery cityscape, and a bathroom in violet and black. Marianne's Southwest has a Hopi Indian motif, and Las Palmas is an exuberant splash of tropical color. Talmadge, on the ground floor, is a favorite of honeymooners. Off the inn's small lobby, it has white satin fabrics, a heart-shaped mirror behind the bed, a bar, a sizable kitchen with a gas stove, and a small bathroom in pink.

Tara is a roomy, tastefully furnished, residential-style apartment. It has an old-fashioned kitchen and a separate bedroom with a deep whirlpool tub. In the living room, a Gone With The Wind painting hangs on the wall. There's a wet bar, and a fire is laid in the fireplace. Tara is often used as a reception suite for groups of up to 25 people. It connects to the west courtyard and sun terrace. You can rent the suite alone or add the courtyard and terrace if you have a larger party.

The sun terrace is popular; it has lounge chairs and a bar overlooking a lower courtyard. The service here is exemplary, with a staff that's eager to be of assistance. You're escorted to your room and shown the laundry room that guests may use. In the morning, you're served a breakfast that includes huge muffins, bagels, fruit, and juice, along with the local paper. Parking is on the street, with no restrictions.

Optional services are breakfast in bed, picnics to go, and private dinners by candlelight.

The Bed & Breakfast Inn at La Jolla

7753 Draper Avenue
La Jolla, California 92037
619-456-2066

Innkeeper: Pierrette Timmerman
Accommodations: 16 rooms (15 with private bath)
Rates: $85–$225; $25 additional person
Included: Continental breakfast
Minimum stay: 2 nights on weekends
Payment: MasterCard, Visa
Children: Over age 12 welcome
Pets: Not allowed
Smoking: Allowed
Open: Year-round

La Jolla is a chic little town on the coast just north of San Diego. It's known for its scenic beaches and exclusive shops; it is also the home of the Salk Institute for Biological Studies, the Scripps Institution of Oceanography, and the La Jolla Museum of Contemporary Art.

Across the street from the museum, a few blocks from the sea, is the Bed & Breakfast Inn at La Jolla. Built in 1913, the boxy stucco inn is representative of the stripped-down style of the architect Irving Gill. Other examples of his influential Cubist work may be seen elsewhere in La Jolla.

It was a fine home when John Philip Sousa lived in it during the 1920s, but when Betty Albee bought the place, it had fallen into disrepair. Betty was determined to restore it as an inn yet keep the structure compatible with Gill's simple plan. "I could just see Irving Gill's design begging to be redone," she says. Working with a local architect and the city government, she accomplished her goal. Now the inn is on the San Diego Historical Registry.

The guest rooms are in the two-story main building and the annex behind it, off a courtyard garden. Bird Rock, a tiny room decorated in Laura Ashley blue and white pinstripes and flowered prints, shares a bath during the day with the inn's manager. It's one of five rooms on the ground level.

Upstairs, on a corner, Cove Room is furnished with a wicker table and rocker. A decanter of sherry sits on the table. A soft breeze blows through windows that open to a view of trumpet vines over the arbor next door. Until late in the evening, every quarter-hour you'll hear the gentle sound of chimes from a nearby church.

Across the hall is Ocean Breeze, a light room with white curtains and a lace comforter. It's small but cozy, with soft chairs, built-in bookshelves, a ceramic fruit basket on the night table, and a view of the courtyard and large podocarpus tree.

In the guests' sitting room there's a small refrigerator, a television, and a 12-minute videocassette explaining the inn's history and restoration. Shelves contain books, magazines, and games that include LaJollaopoly, in which players trade local properties instead of Park Place and Marvin Gardens.

Off the lounge are a rooftop sundeck and two guest rooms: the Shores, which has antique headboards on twin beds, and Peacock Salon, a brightly decorated room with a garden view.

The largest space is the Irving Gill Penthouse, at the top of the annex. It has a sitting room with a TV, and a small deck with a view. The most spectacular ocean view though, looking over rooftops two blocks to the cove, is from Pacific View. It's furnished with antiques in a nautical theme.

Breakfast is served in the dining room of the main house, near the foyer where information on local events is posted.

Catamaran Resort Hotel
3999 Mission Boulevard
San Diego, California 92109
619-488-1081
800-288-0770 in U.S.
800-233-8172 in Canada

General manager: George Harrington
Accommodations: 312 rooms
Rates: $105–$108 for 1–4 people, $15 additional person
Minimum stay: 2 nights on weekends
Payment: Major credit cards
Children: Under age 18 free in room with parents
Pets: Not allowed
Smoking: Nonsmoking rooms available
Open: Year-round

Polynesia comes to San Diego at the Catamaran, where the grounds are filled with palm trees, exotic birds, flowers, and streams. In the skylighted reception area, a waterfall cascades over stone into a pool of koi. A tapa cloth hangs behind the counter, and a full-size catamaran is suspended from the ceiling. The decor sets the mood for casual atmosphere at this seaside resort, which faces a long stretch of sandy beach.

The guest rooms are in a fourteen-story tower or in two-story motel units that surround a swimming pool or edge the beach. Each room in the tower has a balcony with a view—the higher the room the more expansive the view of Mission Bay and the San Diego skyline. One can see joggers and skaters on the path and the colorful sails of outriggers waiting by the pier on the beach below.

The tower rooms are furnished in a basic, contemporary style with no embellishments—nothing can compete with the glorious views. Even the penthouse suite is simple, though comfortable, with good reading lamps, textured tan walls and a crisp white bathroom. There's a kitchen suitable for cooking light meals. Drapes cover a wall of sliding glass doors that open to a balcony.

The rooms in lower buildings have balconies and patios, but their views are of the lush, well-tended gardens or the freeform pool. There's also a whirlpool spa and an equipped exercise room.

Water sports predominate. You can ride a pedal boat, take a sailboard or catamaran lesson, or rent a kayak. Two stern-wheelers cruise Mission Bay, available for private parties.

The Catamaran has several meeting rooms and is popular as a site for small conferences and seminars. You can eat well in the Atoll restaurant or on its patio, and enjoy drinks and dancing in the Cannibal Bar, one of San Diego's favorite night clubs. It has an oval bar of koa wood on one level and a large cabaret a few steps below. Complimentary hors d'oeuvres are served to hotel guests.

The Cottage

P.O. Box 3292
3829 Albatross Street
San Diego, California 92163
619-299-1564

Innkeepers: Carol and Bob Emerick
Accommodations: 1 room and 1 cottage (both with private bath)
Rates: $49–$65; $10 additional person

Included: Continental breakfast
Minimum stay: 2 nights
Payment: MasterCard, Visa
Children: Welcome
Pets: Not allowed
Smoking: Not allowed
Open: Year-round

The old homes and undeveloped canyons in the Hillcrest section of San Diego make it a quiet, unhurried part of the city. The Cottage, built in 1913 behind the Emericks' residence, fits well with the peaceful mood of a bygone day.

When you arrive, Carol greets you at the front door of the main house and guides you past the hibiscus hedge and black locust tree, under the rose-covered trellis to the cozy cottage in back.

A woodstove (wood is supplied), a sofa bed, and an oak pump organ stand in the living room. An Austrian carved breakfront by the rocker holds books along with menus of San Diego restaurants

The kitchen has a small gas stove and refrigerator, and a round oak table in the corner by the window. Wooden tea canisters line the yellow and black tile counter. Fresh coffee beans are in the refrigerator; Carol purchases them from Pannikin, known for its excellent coffee. You can grind the beans in a red electric grinder from the 1920s.

A king-size bed with a red quilt and white lacy pillows almost fills the paneled bedroom. Corner windows view a tiny, fenced garden of ferns, passion flower, and vines on a trellis. A television is hidden behind a woven blind in a wall niche; the room also has reading lamps, a phone, and clock radio. Travelers appreciate the padded hangers and the iron and ironing board in the closet. The immaculate blue and white bathroom, with vibrant touches of red, has both a tub and shower.

With the sofa bed, three people fit nicely in the cottage; any more would be crowding it.

Carol brings a hot breakfast from her kitchen in the mornings. Fresh bread, blueberry muffins, and apple cake are a few of her specialties that accompany coffee and juice or fresh fruit.

The Emericks have also opened a room in the main house to guests. The Garden Room has a private entrance and framed flower prints on deep teal walls. Some nice touches are the tie rack and light in the closet, the sliding mirror that covers a TV set into the wall, and a built-in refrigerator behind a louvered screen. The bath, a cheery yellow, has a tub and shower. If you stay in The Garden Room you'll have breakfast in the Emericks' pleasant, homey dining room. You're welcome to relax in the parlor, too, listening to the stereo and tape deck or looking through the books on opera. Other interesting items from the couple's collection include old bottles, a steropticon, and a working player organ that dates from 1875. Bob is an expert on piano and organ restoration; the pump organ in The Cottage is an example of his work.

Most of the furnishings here come from the owners' previous business as antique dealers. Now Bob teaches sociology at San Diego State College and, with their two daughters grown and gone, Carol manages the guest house.

Horton Grand Hotel

311 Island Avenue
San Diego, California 92101
619-544-1886
800-540-1886 in California
800-542-1886 in U.S.
Fax: 619-239-3823

Manager: Mark Briskin
Accommodations: 110 rooms and 24 suites
Rates: $109–$129, suites $159–$189
Included: Continental breakfast
Payment: Major credit cards
Children: Welcome
Pets: Not allowed
Smoking: Allowed
Open: Year-round

The Horton Grand is in San Diego's historic Gaslamp district, once a downtown core gone to seed but now prime urban property. The ornate hotel, two Victorian buildings joined by a courtyard and atrium, stands as a well-restored tribute to comforts past and present. While the transformation of the neighborhood is under way and land values are rocketing, it's not yet the showcase planners envision. But restaurants and nightspots have sprouted, there's a new convention center, and Horton Plaza, an open-air, multilevel complex of shops and theaters, draws hordes of curious visitors. It's lively and interesting, a cultural as well as a shopping experience.

When the site for Horton Plaza was announced in the late 1970s, a local developer and preservationist, Dan Pearson, realized that the oldest hotel in San Diego would be razed and he decided to save it. He moved the century-old Horton Grand to its present location two blocks from the Plaza. Then he heard that another historic hotel was doomed, so he bought that, too, moved it next door, and built an atrium to connect them.

Several years and $12 million later, the Horton Grand reopened in style. Now, when you drive up to the front door, energetic young valets whisk your car and luggage away and you step into a conservatory that turns out to be the lobby. Skylights, white wicker furniture, and a cage of chirping finches create a bright and cheerful atmosphere. The pleasant concierge, dressed in period costume, adds to the turn-of-the-century ambience.

On one side of the lobby there's a small museum and gift shop of Chinese antiques. On the other is the Palace Bar, a combination parlor and saloon with tapestries on the walls and rose and burgundy chairs at round marble tables. Renowned jazz artists play here on weekends. Next to the bar is the Ida Bailey restaurant, named for San Diego's most famous madam, whose house of ill repute was on this site during the bawdy, raucous land-boom days of the 1880s.

The brick courtyard is one of the hotel's most charming features. Four floors of guest rooms surround it, their balconies overlooking white garden furniture, birds that dart among the potted ficus, and vines climbing over lattices.

The rather small rooms are decorated individually, though they all have gas fireplaces and antique furniture. The best, and quietest, are the rooms overlooking the courtyard. The King Kalakana suite has a colorful Hawaiian theme, while the bridal suite has a full canopied antique bed. All have small sitting areas, rich Victorian draperies, lace curtains, and television sets nicely hidden in wall niches behind mirrors.

One room, 309, is supposedly haunted. Guests and chambermaids have felt an unusual presence there, and some speculate that it's the ghost of Roger Whitaker, who was killed in the hotel a hundred years ago by a gambling associate. The room has been booked solid since the phenomenon was investigated by psychics. "The ghost is harmless," they said. "He's really very nice." The Horton Grand offers several special packages, such as a Jazz Special, the Victorian Grand Tradition (including afternoon tea, breakfast in bed, and a sightseeing tour on San Diego's quaint trolley), and For Hopeless Romantics.

The hotel has recently opened a third building, which provides large, deluxe suites to corporate travelers on extended stays.

Hotel Del Coronado
1500 Orange Avenue
Coronado, California 92118
619-435-6611
800-468-3533
Fax: 619-522-8262

General manager: Dean Nelson
Accommodations: 691 rooms
Rates: $149–$345; $25 additional adult; $15 additional child
     under age 18; suites $375–$495
Minimum stay: 2 nights on weekends
Payment: Major credit cards
Children: Under 18 free in room with parents
Pets: Not allowed
Smoking: Nonsmoking rooms available
Open: Year-round

The Del, as it's affectionately called by frequent guests, is a living legend, a significant piece of southern California's history. More than that, it's a stunning hostelry that compares favorably with the finest of newer lodgings. In some ways it's a cut above them, for modern comforts have been added to the rich patina of past glories.

The Del Coronado opened in 1888, the result of the grand dreams of Elisha Babcock, who wanted to build a resort that would be "the talk of the Western World." The railroad tycoon and his partner, H. L. Story, began construction in 1887, using lumber from San Francisco and Chinese laborers who were trained on the job.

The hotel they built on a peninsula in San Diego Bay was the largest structure outside New York City to have electric lights. It's said that Thomas Edison supervised the installation of the incandescent lamps and that he pulled the switch for the hotel's first electrically lighted Christmas tree.

Quickly established as a cultural oasis in the sparsely settled West, the resplendent Del drew celebrities, dignitaries, royalty, and travelers from around the world. Twelve U. S. presidents stayed at the hotel during its first hundred years. Charles Lindbergh had a reception here following his solo flight across the Atlantic. Frank L. Baum wrote part of The Wizard of Oz on the premises and based the Emerald City on the towered Victorian structure. The Prince of Wales—later King Edward VIII and then the duke of Windsor—was honored at a dinner in 1920, when he reportedly met Wallis Simpson for the first time.

Numerous films and television shows have been made on the grounds. The most famous and most enduring was Some Like It Hot, filmed in 1958 with Marilyn Monroe, Jack Lemmon, and Tony Curtis.

All this history is on display in the hotel's lower level corridors, providing fascinating glimpses of change from 1888 to the present.

Nowadays, most people arrive at the hotel by driving across a high bridge that connects San Diego to Coronado. There's a sense of quaintnesss in the village, with its winding, tree-lined streets, small restaurants, and shops tucked away in courtyards. It also has a municipal golf course, several small hotels, and a Navy presence.

The original five-story, amply curved structure of the Del Coronado is still in use today, along with two newer sections closer to the beach. The guest rooms in the main building are grouped around the Garden Patio. Lawns, palm trees, and a latticed gazebo make this a favorite spot for weddings and quiet relaxation away from the hubbub of the lobby and arcades of shops. Between the courtyard and lobby is Palm Court, where you may purchase a Continental breakfast in the morning and order coffee all day.

In the richly carpeted lobby, clerks and a concierge staff work behind mahogany counters. An old-fashioned birdcage elevator, still operating, stands in a corner near the door to the Crown Room, the Del's majestic dining room. One of the largest support-free structures in the country, the redwood-paneled room has a 33-foot ceiling made of sugar pine, crafted without a single nail. Banquets and formal state dinners are held here, though the food is less spectacular than the atmosphere.

The more casual Ocean Terrace is open for breakfast on weekends and lunch and cocktails daily. It overlooks the gazebo bar, the Olympic-size swimming pool, tennis courts, and 2 miles of sandy beach. You can buy snacks in a cavelike basement deli, carved from the hotel's original stone cistern, and dine in intimate, elegant surroundings in the Prince of Wales restaurant.

A recent $15 million renovation took care of some much-needed updating. Rooms in the old section were improved both in comfort and style, retaining their period decor while meeting the expectations of today's travelers. The large rooms with private verandas facing the sea are the best. They have tall windows, comfortable couches, king- or queen-size beds, and roomy baths with showers. All the rooms have ceiling fans, television, phones, safes, and stocked mini-bars. Movies filmed at the hotel are shown nightly on one of the TV channels.

In Ocean Towers, the newer annex, seven floors contain 311 rooms, all redecorated. The guest rooms lack the Victorian ambience that gives the original Del its charm, but they're softer and lighter in decor and provide a retreat from the bustle across the way. The annex has its own triangular swimming pool. Most of the annex rooms have balconies, some facing the bay and others the ocean. All have air conditioning and king-size beds.

The service at the Del Coronado is outstanding. The award-winning staff is enthusiastic and eager to please, from the young est valets to those who've been loyal to the Del for forty years and more.

The hotel has meeting and conference rooms and a convention center that accommodates up to 1,500.

La Jolla Beach and Tennis Club
2000 Spindrift Drive
La Jolla, California 92037
619-454-7126
800-624-2582
Fax: 619-456-3805

General manager: Mac Brewer
Accommodations: 90 rooms and apartments
Rates: $60–$250; $15 additional person
Minimum stay: 2 weeks during some summer periods, 3
   nights some holidays
Payment: Major credit cards
Children: Welcome
Pets: Not allowed
Smoking: Allowed
Open: Year-round

Fifteen miles north of San Diego, the guest apartments at this private tennis club stretch along a quarter-mile of beautiful beach. About a thousand families in the well-heeled La Jolla area belong to the club, which is in a palm grove in a residential district. Visitors have full membership privileges.

With 12 championship tennis courts (four of them lighted), a pro instructor and pro shop, the club is a favorite with tennis players.

Around the 10-acre property's tropical lagoon is a 9-hole pitch-and-putt golf course, which guests may use for a nominal fee. A heated, Olympic-size swimming pool lies next to the patio, where lunch is served daily. You may also eat in the club dining room, facing the esplanade by the private beach.

Next door, to the south, is the Marine Room, a restaurant owned and managed by the tennis club. It's so close to the water that cresting waves, illuminated at night, sometimes splash against the windows. Live seahorses swim in the aquarium and skylights open to the sun or stars. A small orchestra plays for evening dancing.

The guest rooms and apartments are in low stucco buildings with red tile roofs. Most face the water, and some are just a step from the smooth sand that's white in summer and gray in winter. A typical room, decorated in a seaside motif, will have two double beds with rattan headboards, comfortable seating, and an equipped kitchenette. All the rooms are supplied with bottled water or piped purified water.

The club's seahorse logo is everywhere: at the bottom of a pool on a seaside terrace, in a tiled fountain in the central courtyard, on the bright yellow boards supplied as wind protection on the beach. The club also provides huge beach towels, chairs, and blue and white umbrellas for protection from the sun.

You may rent scuba and snorkeling gear, wet suits, and surfboards from a nearby surf shop. When snorkeling in La Jolla Cove, you'll see coral and other marine life among the wavy strands of kelp.

With apartments ranging from one to three bedrooms, this lodging appeals to families. It offers a variety of recreation and dining, from the snack bar by the pool to the dining room. Features include daily maid service, cable television, self-service laundromats, and a hair salon. Many guests have been coming here for years and book their rooms far in advance.

La Valencia Hotel
1132 Prospect Street
La Jolla, California 92037
619-454-0771
800-451-0772
Fax: 619-456-3921

Manager: Patrick Halcewicz
Accommodations: 105 rooms and suites
Rates: $135–$285; $10 additional person; suites, $300–$600
Payment: Major credit cards
Children: Welcome

Pets: Not allowed
Smoking: Allowed
Open: Year-round

In the heart of chic La Jolla, ten miles north of San Diego, this pink stucco hotel has been welcoming travelers and holding social events since 1926. The hotel and the town grew up together on the California Riviera, where palms sway in gentle breezes and the sun shines beneficently on sheltered La Jolla Cove.

On street level (which is also the fourth floor; three more stories descend a hillside toward the water, and several others rise above), you pass through a colonnade beside a palm-shaded patio to the lobby. Beyond the small, usually crowded registration area is a long parlor with colorful Spanish mosaics, a hand-painted ceiling, and, at the far end, a floor-to-ceiling window with a compelling view of the sea. From here you look down on tall palm trees, a green park flashing with Frisbees, a sandy shore, and the blue Pacific.

Double glass doors open to a balcony above a curved swimming pool and terraced gardens that descend to the road. Across the street is Ellen Browning Scripps Park and the shore.

La Valencia boasts three restaurants. Mediterranean Room, between the front tile courtyard and the gardens, glows with lights from its pale pink ceiling. Palms, pink and green linens, fresh flowers on every table, a superb view, and an acclaimed menu make it a popular spot for breakfast, lunch or dinner. The Tropical Patio, the outdoor section of the Mediterranean Room, is ideal for a leisurely lunch on a sunny day.

Café La Rue is next to the Whaling Bar, where a New England nautical decor sets the casual, charming theme. The bar contains authentic New Bedford harpoons and lanterns, ivory scrimshaw, and pewter candle holders. There's a model of a full-rigged sailing ship behind the leather booths, and the wall behind the bar has a mural depicting the old whaling days.

The romantic tenth-floor Sky Room, an elegant, intimate space, overlooks the ocean. The imaginative menu features such dishes as grilled scallops on tangerine tarragon sauce and magret of duck with sun-dried wild cherries and ginger. Lunch and dinner are available on weekdays, dinner only on Saturdays and Sundays, with both à la carte and prix fixe menus. The hotel has one elevator—it's the original, still manually operated. It's swift but is likely to be crowded at peak times.

The attractively furnished rooms have a traditional European flavor that combines stately lines with soft floral fabrics. Each has its own climate control, television, and queen- or king-size beds. A deluxe oceanfront room offers a panoramic view beyond double-glazed windows; furnishings include a brass chandelier in the living room, mint-green carpeting, soft gold walls, potted plants in a wicker holder, and a stocked mini-bar. The marble and black granite bathroom has an oval whirlpool tub.

The hotel has a small health spa and sauna. You can play table tennis or shuffleboard, lounge by the pool or on the beach, or join the vacationers shopping along Prospect Street. The La Jolla Museum of Contemporary Art is a few blocks from the hotel, and the underwater exhibitions at Scripps Institution of Oceanography are a short drive away.

San Diego's Old Town, Balboa Park, Sea World, and professional ball games are a few miles down the freeway. Tijuana, Mexico, with its markets, night clubs, shops, and sports events, is a 35-minute drive south.

Le Meridien San Diego at Coronado

2000 Second Street
Coronado, California 92118
619-435-3000
800-543-4300
Fax: 619-435-3032

Managing director: Sergio Mangini
Accommodations: 265 rooms, 7 executive suites, 28 villa studios and suites
Rates: $165–$225; suites, $475; villa studios and suites, $375–$625
Payment: Major credit cards
Children: Under age 12 free in room with parents
Pets: Not allowed
Smoking: Nonsmoking rooms available
Open: Year-round

The beauty of the surroundings and the southern California climate provided inspiration for the design of Le Meridien, a huge, elegant, beachfront resort with a light interior. Le Meridian sits on 16 acres at the northeast corner of Coronado Island, facing San Diego Bay, the bridge, and the city skyline.

In the lobby and public areas, limestone flooring and walls glazed in honey tones provide a backdrop to furnishings that range from oversize rattan settees to an antique armoire. A large flower arrangement is the centerpiece; crimson-flowering ginger and palms fill corner pots.

Marius, the dining room, is like a golden cave, softly lighted at night. The cuisine is Provençal. The less formal L'Escale serves meals in a bright setting; a wall of windows faces the terrace, the pool and the bay. In the cocktail lounge, La Provence, the San Diegans' passion for sailing is evident. Pictures of old schooners and of the sleek, 12-meter Stars and Stripes grace the walls.

The guest rooms, spread over three floors and outlying villas, have views of the bay, lagoon, or Tidelands Park, a 22-acre community park that borders Le Meridien. The standard rooms, with pale wood furniture and seafoam colors, are comfortable and generously sized. They have mini-bars, marble-topped vanities, deep tubs, hair dryers, and Lanvin toiletries. The corner executive suites have furnishings with darker tones and Laura Ashley designs.

The villas, named after Impressionist artists, are like private homes, each with its own terrace. The villa cluster has its own pool and whirlpool. Celebrities seeking seclusion and visitors on longer stays like these luxury lodgings with one or two bedrooms. They have wet bars, VCRs, built-in cupboards, double-headed showers, and oversize Jacuzzis, along with the more usual amenities. The resort has meeting and banquet space and a complete business center.

Le Meridien has drawn raves for the high quality of its service and accommodations since it opened in 1988, but its most striking feature is the landscaping. Tropical plantings and a pond with pink flamingoes set the tone at the entrance. Ducks, swans, and geese swim in a lagoon. As you walk the path that winds through the resort and along the waterfront, you'll see a koi pond, an aviary, fountains, and irises and lilies blooming along the water's edge.

At the dock, cruise vessels will take you on a cruise of the harbor or taxi you to Seaport Village, the convention center, and other stops. You can ride a trolley in San Diego and Coronado, take part in golf and tennis clinics, and bicycling, sailing, water skiing, and windsurfing can be arranged. The resort has six tennis courts, three pools, and a spa with a wide range of services. The spa packages range from a one-day rejuvenator (massage, facial, herbal wrap, lunch) to three days of body pampering treatments.

Prospect Park Inn
1110 Prospect Street
La Jolla, California 92037
619-454-0133
800-345-8577 in California
800-433-1609 in U.S.
Fax: 619-454-2056

Innkeeper: Jean Beazley
Accommodations: 20 rooms, 2 suites
Rates: $79–$109; double, $89–$119; $10 additional person; suites, $229–$259
Included: Continental breakfast
Payment: Major credit cards
Children: Welcome
Pets: Not allowed
Smoking: Not allowed
Open: Year-round

Like La Jolla ("The Jewel") itself, Prospect Park Inn is a jewel of a place. The small hotel has a perfect resort location, between chic, busy Prospect Street and the green parks, palm trees, and sandy beaches of La Jolla Cove.

It's easy to overlook the brick hotel, for its entrance is sandwiched between a corner shop and the pink La Valencia Hotel. But behind the gray and pink awnings and small, light lobby are three floors of charming rooms, all of them furnished in Mediterranean pastels, California style.

There's a minuscule library on the ground floor, with just enough room for a couch, two chairs, and a sideboard where you may help yourself to tea, coffee, chocolate, and cookies any time of day. There are a few shelves of books and magazines and a phone for guests' use. Coke and ice machines are down the hall.

All the rooms have a television. Studios and penthouses have kitchenettes with microwave and toaster ovens; the mini-suite has a full kitchen. Since the front door is locked and there's no desk clerk on duty after 11:00 P.M., your room key also opens a wrought-iron gate to a side entrance. Underground parking is available.

The Cove Suite is a penthouse that opens to a sundeck overlooking the shops and cafés on the corner of Jenner and Prospect, and the park and lovely cove to the west. Continental breakfast and afternoon tea are served on the deck.

The suite has one spacious bedroom behind double doors, a living area with a foldout queen-size bed, a self-contained kitchenette, and a large bath.

The Village Suite has similar features. The two penthouses share an entry foyer that may be closed off if a family or couples traveling together wish to share the hotel's upper story.

A few steps away are the famed attractions of La Jolla: beaches, art galleries, boutiques, and restaurants. Highly recommended for dinner is George's At The Cove.

For superb bird's-eye views of the coastline from Oceanside to Mexico, take the scenic drive up to the top of Mount Soledad. To get a close look at some of California's most exciting surfing action, go to Windansea Beach. Boomer Beach is also a favorite of experienced surfers.

San Diego Princess

1404 West Vacation Road
San Diego, California 92109
619-274-4630
800-542-6275
Fax: 619-581-5929

General manager: Tom Vincent
Accommodations: 354 rooms and 95 suites
Rates: $110–$130; double, $125–$145; $15 additional person, suites: $185–$900
Payment: Major credit cards
Children: Welcome
Pets: Allowed with permission
Smoking: Nonsmoking rooms available
Open: Year-round

In Mission Bay, north of San Diego Bay, is a 43-acre manmade island that was formed in 1962 from marshland and developed into Vacation Village Resort. The resort's one-level bungalows, surrounded by tropical plants and lagoons and the Mission Bay beachfront, along with numerous recreational facilities, made it a favored San Diego destination.

Now it's owned by Princess Cruises Resorts and Hotels, and has been renamed the San Diego Princess. Like its namesake cruise line, the hotel offers comfortable accommodations and vacation fun in the company of like-minded people.

More than half of the hotel's guests are leisure travelers, while the rest are visiting on business or staying with a group. It's an excellent choice for a group trip if you want to be near the water. The resort is a 10-minute drive from the airport and accessible by bridge from San Diego. It's convenient to the area's major attractions: Sea World, Balboa Park and the San Diego Zoo, and Old Town. Seventy golf courses are within easy driving distance.

From the contemporary white lobby, where rattan chairs and potted ferns provide a touch of the tropics, you and your luggage are taken by golf cart to one of the bungalows that lie along the property's curving roads (or you may drive; each unit has a parking space, in addition to the large main parking lot).

The spacious guest rooms, two to six to each white brick bungalow, have garden, lagoon, or bay views. Some have sliding glass doors to private patios or the sandy white beach that borders the island. Each room has a dressing area, refrigerator, stocked ServiBar, television with movie channel (a fee is charged for movies), clock radios, and air conditioning. Some contain kitchens. The rooms and baths are clean, but some of the furnishings are scuffed and faded and of lesser quality than you might expect at these prices.

The suites include eight Executive Suites with movable, soundproof walls, surrounding a garden suitable for outdoor meetings, a Governor's Suite, and a grand 4,500-square-foot Presidential Bay Suite. Meeting facilities are ample—20 rooms, covering 24,233 square feet. Full convention services are available, including audiovisual equipment.

There are eight tennis courts, five swimming pools, and a marina. You can play shuffleboard or table tennis, go bicycling, jog on paths or a mile of beach, and rent sailboats and motorboats.

The most expensive restaurant, Dockside Broiler, features steak and seafood and a view of Mission Bay. The Barefoot Bar & Grill has a casual, Caribbean flavor.

The service throughout the hotel is exemplary, with that special quality of sunny cheerfulness that seems to be a Southern California trademark. The most appealing aspect of San Diego Princess, the one that makes it different from other, similar resorts, is its beautifully landscaped grounds. Paths wind among tropical gardens lush with palm trees, ferns, pine trees, birds of paradise and banana trees. Many of the plantings are neatly labeled. Ducks paddle on a blue lagoon that is centered by a fountain and crossed by small, arching bridges. You can climb a high observation tower for a 360-degree view of the island, the waters around it, and the busy mainland on the other side of the bridge.

U.S. Grant Hotel
326 Broadway
San Diego, California 92101
619-232-3121
800-334-6957 in California
800-237-5029 in U.S.
Fax: 619-232-3626

Manager: R. Scott Lynch
Accommodations: 218 rooms, 62 suites

Rates: $135–$155; double, $155–$175; $20 additional person; suites, $245–$1000
Payment: Major credit cards
Children: Under 12 free with in room with parents
Pets: Allowed by prior arrangement
Smoking: Nonsmoking rooms available
Open: Year-round

In 1985, the historic U.S. Grant Hotel underwent a four-year, $80 million restoration. The hotel had become run-down and then closed for nine years, a far cry from its illustrious beginnings in 1910, when it was built by Ulysses S. Grant, Jr., in honor of his father. It had been a San Diego landmark for decades, before it fell into disrepair.

The expensive restoration returned the hotel to classic grandeur, with a soaring lobby marked by Palladian columns, 18th-century reproduction furnishings, Dutch and Venetian oil paintings, and Chinese porcelains. The project also created severe financial problems, but by early 1989 the hotel was on an even keel again, under the ownership of Sybedon, Inc., with Home Federal Bank taking an active management role.

The U.S. Grant takes up a full block in the heart of San Diego's renewed downtown district, across from Horton Plaza, a multilevel shopping center. However, when you drive up to the hotel you don't enter at this front door, but at the parking lot entrance to the lobby, where a valet will take your car to the hotel garage.

In the large lobby, a concierge is on duty, prepared to obtain tickets for any cultural, theatrical, or recreational event or to arrange for secretarial and other business services. A wide marble staircase leads to the meeting rooms on the mezzanine. The guest rooms, though small, are well furnished with Queen Anne mahogany two-poster beds, armoires, and wingback chairs. Each has television with cable and movies are available. Baths of travertine marble and ceramic tile have hand-milled soaps and terrycloth robes.

The suites feature decorative fireplaces and built-in bars. Their decor is comfortably traditional, if uninspired, and their casement windows open to views of the city and downtown redevelopment. There are few complaints about the service at U.S. Grant. Not only is it prompt and courteous, it is given with genuine warmth.

The cocktail lounge is a congenial room with polished paneling and a fireplace. Next door is the Grant Grill, which has a classic La Broche rotisserie kitchen. Grilled entrées are served in an atmosphere of rich wood and brass, with fresh flowers on crisp linens.

The Village Inn
1017 Park Place
Coronado, California 92118
619-435-9318

Proprietors: Betsy and Peter Bogh
Accommodations: 14 rooms (all with private bath)
Rates: $50–$70, 2 to 4 people
Included: Continental breakfast
Payment: Major credit cards
Children: Welcome
Pets: Not allowed
Smoking: Allowed
Open: Year-round

Coronado is an exclusive and charming beach community on a peninsula across the bay from San Diego. It has historic mansions, an 18-hole championship golf course, dozens of specialty shops, restaurants, tennis courts, and a yacht marina. While it does not offer much in the way of budget lodgings, the Village Inn is a nice exception.

The little white stucco hotel with a red tile roof is on a quiet residential street, away from the crowds at the famed Hotel del Coronado, yet less than two blocks from a sandy beach with clean water and good swimming. The Village Inn is popular with Europeans who know the value of a casual, simple, clean hotel that meets travelers' needs without the expense of added frills.

The hotel, built in the 1920s, was recently updated with new furnishings and remodeled baths, but its bargain rates remain. Two people may book a small room with double bed for $50. Four people can sleep in a room with two double beds for $70. If you stay a week in winter, you get the seventh night free. Rollaway beds are available.

All the rooms are on the second and third floors, reached by an elevator with grillwork doors. The rooms have rattan and pine furnishings, ceiling fans, and windows that open outward to catch the cool ocean breezes. (Directly on the Pacific, Coronado is usually about 10 degrees cooler than San Diego.) Four rooms have pine beds with canopies.

The Boghs provide homey touches not often found in budget hotels — fresh greenery in the rooms, lacy pillows, alarm clocks and an iron to lend. There are ironing boards in some closets.

The "coffee kitchen," with a stove and microwave oven, is handy for fixing tea, light snacks, and lunches. A breakfast of muffins, fruit, juice, and coffee is set out in the morning.

Up the street from the inn is an excellent wine shop and deli, Park Place Deli. It's a good place to fill a picnic cooler. Take your cooler to the beach with the hotel's $5 rental "beach pack" (umbrella, chair, and big towel), and you'll enjoy the pleasures of Coronado at a small fraction of the prices most tourists pay.

San Francisco

The Archbishops Mansion
1000 Fulton Street
San Francisco, California 94117
415-563-7872

Owners: Jonathan Shannon and Jeffrey Ross
Manager: Kathleen Austin
Accommodations: 15 rooms (all with private bath)
Rates: $115–$285
Included: Continental breakfast
Minimum stay: 2 nights on weekends
Payment: Major credit cards
Children: Welcome
Pets: Not allowed
Smoking: Not allowed in public spaces
Open: Year-round

If you want lodgings in San Francisco that remind you of home, don't stay at this inn unless you live in an opera set. The opulence of the Archbishops Mansion is best enjoyed by those who revel in the lavish, the lush, and the extravagant—all carried off with great taste and a sense of humor.

The inn, across the street from Alamo Square, is eight blocks from Golden Gate Park and six blocks from the Civic Center, Davies Symphony Hall, the Opera House, and the Museum of Modern Art. The Alamo Square area, its streets lined with lovely Victorians, has been designated a City Historic District, thanks in large part to the efforts of Jeffrey Ross and Jonathan Shannon. In 1980, they began the painstaking task of restoring every inch of their time-battered mansion.

The three-story home, built in 1904 as a residence for Archbishop Patrick Riordan, was based on Second Empire French styling; the new owners gathered furniture from around the world to reflect that period. When they were through, they had created a Belle Époque French château and, because it is grand and so close to the Opera House, named the rooms after romantic 19th-century operas.

The rooms are furnished with flair. The smallest is La Bohème, which has a partial canopy treatment above a bed that is as elaborate as the tent of a fabled sheik. Romeo and Juliet is another elegant little room, with flowers and garlands. Cosi Fan Tutte is a suite with antique lace, gilded molding, and French pine doors separating the bed and sitting areas. Don Giovanni is an expansive suite with cherubs carved in the four-poster bed. There's a dramatic fireplace (one of several in the inn), and in the bath a seven-headed shower.

La Traviata, on the main floor, features a sitting room with a glazed tile fireplace, head-high wainscoting, and a gilded chandelier hanging from a high, coffered ceiling. In the white tile bathroom, which nicely combines the old and the new, are robes, a shower, a pedestal sink, and a lighted makeup mirror. All the rooms have impressive antiques or reproductions.

Breakfast, brought to your room in a picnic basket, includes juice, croissants, granola, eggs, and tea or coffee. You may have breakfast in the formal dining room at the end of the main hall if you prefer.

The hall is another stunning example of the owners' unerring sense of atmosphere. It has chairs inlaid with mother of pearl, a gilt-framed pier mirror from Abraham Lincoln's home in Illinois, and columns of polished redwood and mahogany. At one end is a grand piano—playable, but also computerized, so you may hear a tune without a piano player. A pair of 17th-century Venetian blackamoor statues guard the wide staircase; above the stairs is a 16-foot stained glass dome.

Early coffee is served in the front parlor, along with complimentary newspapers. The parlor has been exquisitely restored and has a stenciled ceiling in French Renaissance style, upholstered French chairs, and a crystal chandelier.

The refined decor has not made the mansion intimidating or stuffy. The owners have been careful to encourage a lively, friendly ambience. The innkeepers will make restaurant reservations and help with tour ideas, and they'll arrange for a taxi if you need transportation; you probably won't want to walk or take the bus at night. Parking is available in a tiny area beside the house, but it's less than convenient, as cars must stack up and then be moved.

The Archbishops Mansion is a member of Romantik Hotels, an elite international organization of top-quality lodgings.

Campton Place Kempinski

340 Stockton Street
San Francisco, California 94108
415-781-5555
800-647-4007
Fax: 415-955-8536

General manager: Peter Koehler
Accommodations: 110 rooms, 10 suites
Rates: $185–$320; suites, $395–$800
Payment: Major credit cards
Children: Welcome
Pets: Allowed
Smoking: Nonsmoking floors available
Open: Year-round

Campton Place is a jewel. Around the corner from Union Square, in busy downtown San Francisco, it offers extraordinary luxury, superb service, and a fine restaurant.

When you arrive, uniformed doormen usher you into a marble lobby with a theme both French and Oriental. Carved Buddhas, antique jars, and a 16th-century Japanese sumi screen accent the graceful curves of French furniture. An antique Swedish chandelier hangs above a glass table supported by four swans. Off the lobby is a sunken lounge, divided from the dining room by a curving sweep of glass etched with a swan, the hotel's emblem.

Since the restaurant opened in 1983, it has consistently received rave reviews. Those who mourned the departure of executive chef Bradley Ogden have discovered that his sous chef, Jan Birnbaum, has maintained the same standards. He uses the best fresh ingredients to create wonderfully complex flavors and a unique and outstanding (and expensive) cuisine.

In a pastel setting of peach and apricot walls, white Wedgwood china, and Swiss linens, with a Sonia rose on each table, diners feast on foods presented as works of art. The seafood sausage with caviar, lemon, and chive sauce is extraordinary. So is the fruit-laced brioche soaked in raspberry sauce and served in a luscious pool of lemon sauce. Both California and European wines are available.

Service throughout the hotel is cheerful, personal, and efficient. There are no VIP floors or differing levels of attention. A valet will unpack your luggage and, when you leave, repack it in tissue paper. The valet will run your bath at just the right temperature (each tub has a thermometer) and assist you with tours, or, if you prefer, set up your entire visit.

Other routine services include a choice among four complimentary morning newspapers, overnight shoeshine, immediate pressing, same-day laundry and dry cleaning (if you spot your jacket during lunch it will be cleaned and returned to you before the bill for your meal arrives), twice-daily housekeeping, and a full concierge service. Valet parking is available.

The guest rooms have a residential ambiance, with custom contemporary and traditional furnishings. There are oversize beds with comforters, Henredon armoires housing remote control television sets, Louis XVI writing tables, and limited edition art on the pastel walls. Double-glazed windows keep street noise at a distance, but they open if you prefer the city's sea breezes to air conditioning. Marble baths contain vanities, scales, phones, hair dryers, and terrycloth robes. Luxurious French milled soaps and shampoos and gels by I. Magnin are among the toiletries provided.

The hotel is actually two buildings, one of sixteen stories and the other, seven. On the lower rooftop is a garden with potted petunias and citrus trees and a view of Union Square. This is a pleasant little oasis for enjoying the morning sun, despite the noise from machinery hidden behind a lattice.

Campton Place used to be the Drake-Wiltshire Hotel, dating from the early 1900s. Changed and remodeled several times, it lapsed into decline until 1981, when Ayala International acquired and rebuilt the property. Most recently it was purchased by Kempinski, owners of fine hotels worldwide.

The Fairmont Hotel

950 Mason Street
San Francisco, California 94106
415-772-5000
800-527-4727
Fax: 415-781-3929

General manager: John Ceriale
Accommodations: 535 rooms and 65 suites
Rates: $165–$285; $30 additional person; suites, $475–$6,000
Payment: Major credit cards
Children: Welcome
Pets: Not allowed
Smoking: Nonsmoking rooms available
Open: Year-round

Opulence on the grand scale in a historic building at the top of one of the world's great cities—that's the Fairmont. When it opened in 1907 (after a delay caused by the 1906 earthquake and fire), the community was impressed by its resemblance to a European royal palace. It's still impressing locals and visitors alike with its ornate facade, magnificent lobby, fine accommodations, and panoramic views of the city and San Francisco Bay.

In recent years the Fairmont, long known for its luxury and upper-income clientele, has achieved wider fame as the location of the popular television series Hotel. Television and film celebrities show up regularly, both as guests and performers. Guests have been entertained in the darkly rich Venetian Room from 1947 until 1989, when Tony Bennett sang "I Left My Heart In San Francisco" for the last time in that room and the supper club closed. Now it's used for private banquets. The New Orleans Room fills the gap with cocktails and lively entertainment.

The Fairmont has several restaurants. The plush Squire features seafood and an extensive wine list; at Masons you may order meats grilled over Hawaiian kiawe wood.

The Fairmont Crown, reached by a glass-enclosed elevator, is as noted for its stunning views as its lavish buffets. In Bella Voce, you'll hear operatic arias as you dine on pizza, pasta, and seafood. From Chinese food in the Polynesian-style Tonga to chocolate sundaes in Sweet Corner, you can find just about anything your tastebuds yearn for within the hotel's walls.

If it's people-watching you want, just sit in the lobby for awhile. Fascinating crowds come and go between the marble pillars that soar to a gilded, ornamented ceiling.

Ten of the hotel's suites overlook the rooftop garden and terrace, a green oasis of palm trees and flowers. There is no pool, but a fitness center with weight machines, sauna, whirlpool, steam room, and massage service is available.

The guest rooms feature simple, elegant furnishings. Down pillows, 200-count cotton sheets, a TV with a movie channel, electric shoe buffers, and daily maid and turn-down service are some of their luxuries. To assist the corporate traveler, multi-line, modem phones are in each room. Voice mail and a business center are available.

The rooms in the main building vary, but in general they are larger and have more spacious baths and closets than those in the adjoining 23-story tower. The architecture of the tower, which went up in 1963, is outlandishly inappropriate to the imposing original building, but there's no denying the beauty of the views from the inside out. Some suites feature balconies that overlook the garden or downtown to the Financial District.

The suites vary in decor. You may see a classical Roman theme, with off-white colors and low tables made to resemble temple columns, or a more traditional look with dark woods and antique reproductions.

For the ultimate in luxury, reserve the penthouse, the most expensive hotel suite in the nation and possibly the world. The eighth floor, eight-room suite, reached by a private elevator, rents for $6,000 a night, which includes an around-the-clock butler, maid, and limousine to and from the airport.

Four Seasons Clift Hotel
495 Geary Street
San Francisco, California 94102
415-775-4700
800-332-3442
Fax: 415-441-4621

Manager: Paul Pusateri
Accommodations: 329 rooms and suites
Rates: $195–$305; double; $190–$335; suites, $350–$1,000
Payment: Major credit cards
Children: Welcome
Pets: Small dogs allowed
Smoking: Nonsmoking rooms available
Open: Year-round

When you want the very best city lodgings—accommodations that are absolutely top quality in every regard—check in at the Four Seasons Clift, two blocks from Union Square. Its atmosphere, furnishings, amenities, and above all its service make the updated Clift one of California's finest hotels.

The 1915 Clift has always been a luxury hotel of dignity that attracted the celebrated and the elite. But it didn't keep up with the times, and by the early 1970s the grand old place seemed a relic of a bygone era. Then Four Seasons, the wizard of modern hospitality, took over.

Millions of dollars later, the re-named Four Seasons Clift had surpassed its initial luster and was on its way to becoming the jewel it is today. Its sense of history and elegance remained, while its facilities were modernized.

From the buff brick exterior and snazzy glass and brass entry, you step into a wood-paneled lobby with crystal chandeliers, hanging ivy, and great bouquets of lilies. Not imposing or grand, it's a gracious, welcoming place where businesspeople with briefcases and kids with lollipops are equally at home.

One of the main attractions of the Four Seasons Clift, and of San Francisco, is the Redwood Room. Built in 1934, it is an art deco masterpiece that shouldn't be missed, whether you stay at the hotel or not. The walls of the lounge, reaching 22 feet to a ceiling of pressed metal, are paneled in aged "curly" redwood, taken from toppled giants that had lain in Northern California stream beds and gullies for years. The inner wood from these ancient tree trunks, when polished, takes on a deep patina of bronze and topaz. (When the room was rejuvenated in the mid-1980s, 43 layers of dulled varnish were removed to expose the panels' original brilliance.) Frosted glass sconces, pyramid chandeliers, and black Italian marble tables continue the art deco motif. But the most striking element, other than the redwood itself, is the mural above the 75-foot bar, a stylized woodland scene of inlaid woods.

In the evenings, Ricardo Scales dons his tuxedo and plays jazz and classical selections on the lounge's black grand piano. At 6:00 P.M., the French Room opens to diners looking for fine Continental cuisine featuring regional foods—seafoods from California waters, produce from valley farms. California labels dominate the award-winning wine list, which also offers European vintages.

In addition to its classic menu, the French Room offers Alternative Cuisine, a program of flavorful low-calorie meals overseen by executive chef Kelly Mills.

The guest rooms in the 16-story hotel are large and luxurious. Request a room on one of the higher floors to avoid traffic noise. They all have numerous amenities: mini-bars, two-line phones, remote control TV, hairdryers in marble bathrooms, and tiny booklights for bedtime reading. A Petite Suite has a sitting room with Henredon furniture, window drapes in sophisticated gray and white stripes accented with peach, pearly gray walls, and windows that view Nob Hill on one side and Twin Peaks on the other.

A typical Designer Suite, set on a corner, has plush rose carpeting, mauve and plum couches by a glass coffee table, and a dining table for eight, lighted from above by a teardrop chandelier. Original artwork hangs on pale green walls. There are potted palms, soft robes, an array of toiletries in a white ceramic basket, and a dressing room bigger than many San Francisco apartments.

The Clift offers unmitigated luxury, but it's the service that draws the most admiration. Under the management of perfectionist Paul Pusateri, the staff provides unobtrusive, impeccable attention to every guest. They will remember your name, see you quickly through check-in and check-out, provide near-instant 24-hour room service, polish your shoes, bring in a computer, launder your jeans, and place a flower on your pillow at night. There's no hint of obsequiousness or snobbery in all this pampering; each person seems genuinely glad to be of help.

Children ("Clift dwellers") receive equally happy treatment. The hotel provides supplies for infants, games, comic books, balloons, and treats, as well as babysitting services and a whole program of activities.

Several function rooms provide space for meetings, receptions, and parties of eight to 800. Many a bride and groom have chosen to be married at the Clift before slipping upstairs to celebrate with champagne for two in a sybaritic honeymoon retreat.

The hotel is within walking distance of the shops near Union Square, fine restaurants, Theater Row, museums, and art galleries; and it's just a cable car ride away from other San Francisco attractions.

The Four Seasons matchbook cover says it all, with a quote from Baudelaire: "There, everything is order and beauty, richness, quiet and pleasure."

Galleria Park Hotel

191 Sutter Street
San Francisco, California 94104
415-781-3060
800-792-9855 in California
800-792-9639 in U.S.
Fax: 415-433-4409

General manager: John Brocklehurst
Accommodations: 177 rooms and suites
Rates: $135; suites, $165–$375; weekend and corporate rates available
Payment: Major credit cards
Children: Welcome
Pets: Not allowed
Smoking: Nonsmoking rooms available
Open: Year-round

Urbane and sophisticated, the eight-story Galleria Park is just one block from the financial district and two blocks from Union Square. One of the Kimco boutique hotels, it offers incentives designed for the business traveler.

There are conference and reception rooms, a full array of support equipment for meetings, and a catering service. A full-time program coordinator will handle arrangements with professional care. Parlor suites are suitable for small and informal meetings.

The hotel offers same-day laundry and valet service and a parking garage. Runners appreciate the track on the rooftop terrace. Each room has soundproofed windows, well-lighted writing desks, direct-dial telephones with long cords, television, and digital clock radios.

Both leisure and business travelers (along with a good many San Franciscans) like Bentley's, the oyster bar and restaurant off the lobby and through etched glass doors. On the street side, windows etched in shell and lobster designs fill the wall. With tiled flooring, a zinc bar, and brasserie tables, the mood is of a classic oyster bar—always crowded and usually noisy. A jazz pianist plays most evenings.

Up on the carpeted mezzanine, overlooking the curved bar where delectable oysters nestle in their shells on ice, the atmosphere is softer. Bentley's seafood menu has received superlative reviews, especially for its shellfish. Other highlights are grilled yellowfin tuna and salmon, blackened rock cod with garlic lemon sauce, and egg and spinach fettuccini with bay scallops.

The hotel's small lobby has a distinctive Art Nouveau decor. Beyond the glass and marble entrance are padded green fabric walls and soft couches underneath a skylight. The wall fixtures are opaque glass in tulip shapes; in a corner there's a curving, hand-sculpted white fireplace. Complimentary wine is served by the fire on Friday and Saturday evenings.

The guest room configurations vary, because a restoration in 1988 worked within the existing spaces. The Galleria Park is an extensive remake of the Sutter Hotel, which was built on the site in 1911.

There are seven junior suites and seven hospitality suites, plus the popular two-bedroom Grand Suite, with a fireplace and a whirlpool tub. A typical suite has a sitting room with a large TV (making it a good gathering place for a small group wanting to watch a ball game together) and a white brick fireplace on a raised hearth. In the bedroom are a king-size bed and small television.

The suite's comfortable furniture and assortment of potted plants and flowers create the ambience of a city apartment.As in most Kimco suites, the space is in the sitting area.

The Galleria Park offers several packages and special rates. Ask for the Romantic Rendezvous and you'll stay in a junior suite and receive champagne, Godiva chocolates, and a rose, as well as Continental breakfast in bed.

The hotel is next to Crocker Galleria, three levels of shops and restaurants under a spectacular vaulted glass dome. Within the airy streetscape are some of the world's best retailers and specialty shops. Two rooftop parks in the shopping center have benches and greenery, pleasant sites for a picnic lunch or rest.

Golden Gate Hotel

775 Bush Street
San Francisco, California 94108
415-392-3702
800-835-1118

Innkeepers: John and Renate Kenaston
Accommodations: 23 rooms (some with shared bath)
Rates: $55–$89
Included: Continental breakfast
Payment: Major credit cards
Children: Welcome
Pets: Allowed with permission
Smoking: Allowed
Open: Year-round

In the heart of downtown San Francisco just north of Union Square, this hotel is more than a terrific bargain. It has several extras you wouldn't expect at these prices.

The tall, narrow, white Edwardian building trimmed in pink and blue was built in 1913 and has been carefully maintained by the Kenastons, who manage it with warmth and enthusiasm. Half their guests are experienced travelers from abroad, and many are return visitors.

Bright geraniums bloom at bay windows in front, where an awning marks the marble entrance. In the little parlor with windows overlooking the rush of Bush Street traffic, coffee (the city's strongest, Renate claims), tea, and croissants are served in the mornings. Afternoon tea and cookies are also offered, at seats near the fireplace. It's a relaxing spot to read, chat, and listen to classical music.

An old-fashioned birdcage elevator, operated by the original drums and relays, connects four floors of guest rooms. The more expensive rooms have private baths; the others have washbasins but share bathrooms down the hall. All the rooms have television and several have phones. Renate sees that each has fresh flowers. Though some accommodations are quite small, they're clean, nicely furnished with antiques and wicker, and have a European charm.

The friendly, multilingual (German, Chinese, French, and Spanish) hosts are delighted to help with sightseeing tours. The hotel is within walking distance of the city's great shops, many of its best restaurants, and Chinatown. The cable car stops at the corner and follows Powell Street to Fisherman's Wharf and North Beach.

Parking garages are available at $11 and $14 for 24 hours.

Golden Gate Hotel is not a luxury establishment, but it offers excellent quality for the price. It's a good San Francisco find.

Hotel Griffon

155 Steuart Street
San Francisco, California 94105
415-495-2100
800-321-2201
Fax: 415-495-3522

Manager: Kathryn Houskeeper
Accommodations: 59 rooms, 4 suites
Rates: $130–$140 single or double, suites $170–$190
Included: Continental breakfast
Payment: Major credit cards
Children: Under 18 free
Pets: Allowed
Smoking: Allowed
Open: Year-round

With the dismantling of the Embarcadero Freeway, the view from the back of this small hotel near the waterfront has improved dramatically. Now you can see boats scudding across the water and the Bay Bridge stretching to the East Bay. The front of the hotel faces San Francisco's busy financial district.

As you enter the Griffon, which was refurbished and opened in 1989, you'll notice its namesake, a papier-mâché griffin standing beside the fireplace in the small lobby. This is a busy spot, separated by a glass partition from one of the city's popular bistros, Rôti. Light jazz plays in the bistro, where country French cuisine is prepared on the rotisserie and grill. Hotel guests partake of a buffet breakfast here between 6:00 A.M. and 10:00 A.M.

Upstairs, the fresh, light rooms have custom-carved bedsteads and marble baths. Most suites have a sleeping and sitting area in one room, rather than separate spaces. Lots of style went into appointing these rooms. Rough brick behind the beds contrasts with the smooth white walls and high ceilings, tapestry-covered pillows and window seats. Among the items in the stocked mini-bars are bottles of Sonoma Valley chardonnay with the hotel's own label. The fifth-floor suites have private decks with a sitting area.

The Griffon has become a favorite with business travelers and tourists for its atmosphere, service, and convenient location. It's close to the BART system and the Bay Bridge, and is a few steps from Embarcadero Center, and cable car and ferry service. Parking is available, with 24-hour in-and-out privileges.

While you're exploring San Francisco, don't miss one of its most talked-about, interesting restaurants, the Cypress Club. The atmosphere is lively and the interior highly unusual, with sculptured walls, mounded copper, overstuffed bar stools, and a massive mural. The food is imaginative, the desserts sublime.

Hotel Juliana

590 Bush Street
San Francisco, California 94108
415-392-2540
800-372-8800 in California
800-382-8800 in U.S.
Fax: 415-391-8447

Manager: Jan Misch
Accommodations: 107 rooms, 28 suites
Rates: $114; suites, $140–$150
Payment: Major credit cards
Children: Welcome
Pets: Not allowed
Smoking: Nonsmoking rooms available
Open: Year-round

During the past several years, a number of affordable little first-class hotels have opened in San Francisco, filling a niche between small economy and big luxury hotels. Bill Kimpton, founder of Kimco Hotels, has opened several such European-style hostelries since 1981; one of the best is the charming Juliana.

The nine-story beige brick building with burgundy and blue trim is on a busy corner on the Nob Hill side of Union Square. Built in 1903, it has been completely renovated and boasts modern comforts with the atmosphere of a Continental pensione.

The strains of taped viola music play as you enter the small lobby, cheerful and fresh in shades of peach, teal, and green. Soft chairs and couches are grouped by the pink marble fireplace. Against one wall is a table with hot coffee, tea, and a tray of fresh fruit. Complimentary wines are served every evening. On the walls here and throughout the hotel hang artworks provided by local galleries. The rotating collection showcases contemporary pieces that are available for purchase.

The guest rooms have three pastel color schemes (peach, robin's egg blue, and green) coordinated with flowered drapes and bedspreads. The atmosphere is that of a nicely furnished private apartment with a French flair, befitting this tradition-ally French area. The Juliana is across the street from Notre Dame de Victoire, where mass is still spoken in French.

All the rooms have direct-dial telephones, well-lighted desks, honor bars, large baths, and television with HBO. VCRs and movies are available.

Complimentary limousine service is provided to the finan-cial district in the mornings. These and other services, such as same-day laundry and valet service, put the Juliana in the cate-gory of the city's better hotels, while its budget-minded aspects (room service is available only part of the day; the bellman doubles as concierge) keep it affordable.

Next door to the hotel is Vinoteca, which serves Italian food. Hotel guests have the option of sitting at a family-style table — a chance to get acquainted with others while you're traveling.

Hotel Nikko

222 Mason Street
San Francisco, California 94102
415-394-1111
800-NIKKO US
Fax: 415-394-1156

General manager: W. Andrews Kirmse
Accommodations: 522 rooms and 33 suites
Rates: $205–$285; $20 additional person; suites, $375–$1,300
Payment: Major credit cards
Children: Under 16 free in room with parents
Pets: Not allowed
Smoking: Nonsmoking rooms available
Open: Year-round

In angular simplicity, the Nikko rises 300 feet above Mason and O'Farrell streets, two blocks from Union Square and four blocks from the Moscone Center. With its exterior of white Italian granite and glass corner panels and a wide lobby in smooth white marble, the hotel seems sleekly modern. Yet the atmo-sphere is not cold or sterile. Cascading water, conversation areas bounded by gray leather couches and low pink armchairs, re-cessed lighting, and elegant floral arrangements create a sooth-ing effect and welcoming atmosphere in the busy lobby area.

Prosperous-looking business travelers, many of them Japa-nese, patronize the Nikko, which Japan Air Lines opened in

1987. Business and leisure travelers alike receive the best of care, from a computerized key system for security to a fitness center where you can relax under a Shiatsu massage.

Off the lobby is the Fountain, a lounge with television and nightly entertainment. The Fountain also offers cocktails, Continental breakfast, or a quick lunch.

Café 222 is a restaurant on the mezzanine level, overlooking the lobby. Regional cuisine is served in white marble surroundings enlivened with vibrantly striped red, yellow, and blue china. Appetizers include smoked lamb and pistachio sausage with roasted garlic sauce; typical entrées are fresh Dungeness crab cakes and sauteed Pacific salmon. During your meal you may hear show tunes played on the piano in the lobby below.

High on the 25th floor, reached by smooth and silent Mitsubishi elevators, is Benkay, an authentic Japanese restaurant. It offers a sushi bar, traditional Western seating, and private tatami rooms that accommodate from 2 to 16 guests. In the tatami rooms you may order a nine-course Japanese dinner, served by waitresses in kimonos, or choose from the Benkay menu. You might start with an appetizer of shrimp on green tea noodles and continue with thin slices of beef cooked in the traditional shabu shabu pan and served with the restaurant's original sauces.

The guest rooms and suites, serene in shades of gray, are furnished in a contemporary style. All state-of-the-art conveniences are included: a stocked refrigerator that automatically charges your bill when an item is dispensed, a switch by the king-size bed that turns on all room lights, speedy in-room television checkout.

If you're traveling on business you may prefer one of the four business suites on the sixth floor; they have meeting rooms and the latest audiovisual equipment. Other conference rooms are available—the Nikko offers 18,000 square feet of meeting space.

The top three floors, called Nikko Floors, feature additional services such as a Continental breakfast, hors d'oeuvres, and cocktails served in the split-level Nikko Lounge.

On the fifth floor there's a health facility with an inviting glass-enclosed swimming pool, whirlpool tub, tanning machine, saunas, massage service, and exercise equipment. The locker rooms are cramped and showers (at least in the women's section) are so limited as to seem an afterthought, without space to hang a wet swimsuit. Otherwise the center is attractive and useful—and the shiatsu massage refreshing. Outside, on the rooftop, there's a sunning area with lounge chairs.

To lure vacationers, the Nikko offers special weekend packages that include deluxe accommodations, use of the fitness center, and free valet parking.

Hotel Vintage Court
650 Bush Street
San Francisco, California 94108
415-392-4666
800-654-7266 in California
800-654-1100 in U.S.
Fax: 415-392-4666

Manager: Jan Misch
Accommodations: 106 rooms, 1 suite
Rates: $114; suite, $225
Payment: Major credit cards
Children: Welcome
Pets: Not allowed
Smoking: Nonsmoking rooms available
Open: Year-round

A restful environment, reasonable rates, and one of the city's best French restaurants draw increasing numbers of travelers to this attractive downtown hostelry. The Vintage Court is a part of the collection of boutique hotels that have provided a new lodging option in San Francisco in recent years. Bill Kimpton, with his highly successful Kimco Hotels, is a leading figure in the move to renovate old buildings and turn them into distinctive, stylish hotels with rooms at comparatively low prices.

The Vintage Court opened in 1983, built in an eight-story hotel originally constructed in 1913. Its wine theme is carried out in the decor, with rooms named for California wineries, fabrics in muted grape cluster patterns, and impressionistic paintings of vineyard scenes.

Complimentary wines are served every evening in the lobby, near the marble fireplace; classical music plays in the background. A rack of brochures and a Coke machine are tucked away in a corner.

One rather slow elevator takes you up to the guest rooms. The color schemes are periwinkle blue and light green, or peach with dusty rose and green. Cabinets house the stocked refrigerators. Additional comforts, many geared to the business traveler, are padded headboards, writing tables with good lighting, direct-dial phones, and digital clock radios. A single corner suite on the eighth floor has a separate living room with working fireplace, views of the city skyline, and an original 1913 stained glass skylight.

Complimentary morning limousine service to the financial district is provided, coffee and tea are served on each floor, and same-day laundry service and express check-out are available. A modestly priced breakfast buffet is set up in the restaurant, Masa's, for hotel guests.

Masa's is mentioned in tones of hushed reverence by San Francisco gastronomes. Exquisite food is served in the small, flawless restaurant. Under a coved ceiling with moldings of polished oak, etched mirrors reflect tables set with crisp burgundy and white linens, Christofle silver and fresh flowers. Exuberant bouquets spring from brass planters; the lighting is subdued and the music soft. It's a fitting environment for the remarkable meals served Tuesday through Saturday nights.

Chef Julian Serrano, from Spain, follows the tradition established by the late Masataka Kobayashi, the restaurant's founder. He combines fresh ingredients with classic sauces to create dishes that are works of art. Highlights are the seafood and game specialties: grilled Maine lobster with herbed butter and shrimp quenelles, roast breast of pheasant with morels, and quail stuffed with wild rice.

The wine list, with more than 500 fine French and California selections, is extraordinary. Desserts include a silky lemon charlotte with raspberry sauce, feather-light puff pastries, thick wedges of chocolate with hazelnuts, and fruity mango sorbet in a praline cone.

Predictably, reservations at Masa's can be difficult to come by — Tuesday or Wednesday nights are your best chances of getting a table in the dining room, which seats 100.

The Huntington Hotel
1075 California Street
San Francisco, California 94108
415-474-5400
800-652-1539 in California
800-227-4683 in U.S.
Fax: 415-474-6227

General manager: Micarl T. Hill
Accommodations: 100 rooms and 40 suites
Rates: $160–$210; double, $180–$230; suites, $245–$635
Payment: Major credit cards
Children: Welcome (infants free)
Pets: Not allowed
Smoking: Allowed
Open: Year-round

This dignified 12-story red brick hotel at the top of Nob Hill thrives on tradition and a reputation for excellence. Almost since the day it opened in 1924 as an apartment building, it has been owned by the same family. John Cope, president of the ownership company, is the great-grandson of the developer who bought the property the year it was built. Many on the staff have been with the Huntington for years. Whether you're a repeat guest or a newcomer, you are greeted by name, and the concierge always calls to be sure you're comfortably settled in.

Understated elegance, unobtrusive service, and assurance of privacy make this San Francisco landmark a romantic retreat and a favorite with a demanding clientele that has included Luciano Pavarotti, Margaret Thatcher, Robert Redford, Andres Segovia, and Princess Grace, among other well-known names.

Little changes at the Huntington, though the lobby has been recently remodeled and expanded and the rooms are occasionally refurbished.

Off the gracious lobby is the hotel's dining room, the Big Four. It's named for the early San Francisco railroad tycoons Collis P. Huntington, Leland Stanford, Charles Crocker, and Mark Hopkins, and displays a collection of railroad memorabilia. The impressive room has dark woods, etched mirrors, and reflective walls. The menu, under the skilled direction of Gloria Ciccarone-Nehls, offers innovative American and Continental dishes with seafood and game specials. The chef's spectacular chocolate creations give new meaning to dessert. Wines are California and French vintages. A pianist performs nightly in the Big Four's lounge.

The guest rooms and suites are all larger than average, a legacy from their former years as residential apartments. Each was individually decorated by Anthony Hail, Lee Radziwill, Elizabeth Bernhardt, and Charles Gruwell, using differing color schemes and furnishings that include a generous smattering of antiques and original art. Suites have refrigerators and wet bars, and some contain kitchens.

Every room has large windows that open to gorgeous views of San Francisco Bay, the city, or Huntington Park and stately Grace Cathedral. Accouterments include fluffy down cushions, Neutrogena toiletries, hair dryers, plush bath towels, and linen hand towels. Twice-daily housekeeping, overnight laundry service, valet parking, and delivery of your choice among three daily newspapers are some of the services provided. The Nob Hill Club fitness center, which guests may use, is two blocks away.

The hotel has several handsome meeting rooms suitable for board meetings and receptions. The concierge is on duty all day and will arrange for tours, theater and restaurant bookings, secretarial services, and babysitters. A Cadillac limousine will take you to the financial district and Union Square at no charge on weekdays. And the cable car stops at the hotel's front door.

If you'd like to dine in traditional elegance and cosmopolitan style, try 1001 Nob Hill, a short walk from the Huntington. It has a piano lounge, imaginative art, superlative service, and a fine Continental menu. The crab cakes and duck confit are especially commendable.

Inn at the Opera

333 Fulton Street
San Francisco, California 94102
415-863-8400
800-423-9610 in California
800-325-2708 in U.S.
Fax: 415-861-0821

Managing director: Tom Noonan
Accommodations: 30 rooms and 18 suites
Rates: $130–$155; double, $140–$220; suites, $165–$205, additional person $10
Included: Continental breakfast
Payment: Major credit cards
Children: Under 16 free in room with parents
Pets: Allowed by prior arrangement
Smoking: Nonsmoking rooms available
Open: Year-round

Although San Francisco's Civic Center has long been the cultural and governmental focus of the city, with the Opera House, Davies Music Hall, San Francisco Ballet School, Civic Auditorium, Museum of Modern Art, and City Hall grouped closely together, the area has lacked a first-class hotel. With the restoration of the 16-story Inn at the Opera, it gained a gem.

The hotel was built in 1927 as the Alden, to house visiting opera performers. Over time it fell into disrepair and was eventually purchased in 1983; after a $7 million renovation it reopened in 1985, again hosting internationally acclaimed singers and conductors as well as patrons and tourists. Here is where you may see such luminaries of the performing world as Mikhail Baryshnikov and Placido Domingo at the breakfast table.

Entering the inn is like stepping into the parlor of a gracious private home. Classical music flows around French armchairs in silk and damask, past tall mullioned windows, potted palms, and porcelain jardinieres painted with curling dragons. At the end of a short hallway lined with Paul Renouard sketches of Paris Opera Ballet dancers is the focal point of the hotel: Act IV.

Act IV, an intimate lounge and restaurant, is rich in texture and color. Its dark woods, muted jewel tones, subdued lighting, and exotic fabric wallcoverings patterned with jungle birds create a sensuous, elegant mood. Green velvet sofas, facing a fireplace in the bar, are favored seats for enjoying post-performance liqueurs or steaming espresso. A pianist plays every night.

The menu, which changes regularly, features Mediterranean foods and California wines. Act IV is one of the city's few restaurants offering after-theater dinner. Until 1½ hours after the performance, you may order light fare such as salads, soufflés, and antipasti.

You may choose to have breakfast delivered to your room or eat in the restaurant, where orchids grace tables with white linens. Fresh fruit, yogurt, cereals, muffins, quiche, and a cheese tray make this a generous morning repast.

There's just one elevator, but it takes you swiftly to guest rooms in the boutique hotel. Accommodations include six junior suites, six one-bedroom suites, and six two-bedroom/two-bath suites. All rooms and suites, which were recently redone, have half-canopy queen-size beds, microwave ovens, stocked mini-bars, and oversize baths. They're furnished with dark mahogany antiques or reproductions and color schemes of blue, green, and peach that exude a soft and welcoming warmth.

The least expensive and smallest are Regular rooms; Superiors are larger, but all have the same amenities—a basket of apples, plenty of pillows, fresh flowers, and evening turndown. You'll find a different sweet treat (chocolate truffles, strawberries dipped in chocolate, almond marzipan cakes) in your room each night. In the distance the steady rumble of the freeway never stops, but to light sleepers it's less disturbing than the horns and squealing brakes of downtown traffic.

You may park on the street, but it's not recommended in this urban neighborhood. Valet parking is available.

Jackson Court
2198 Jackson Street
San Francisco, California 94115
415-929-7670

Manager: Pat Cremer
Accommodations: 10 rooms (all with private bath)
Rates: Rooms, weekdays, $88–$98; weekends, $95–$108;
   suites, $125–$140
Included: Expanded Continental breakfast
Minimum stay: 2 nights on weekends
Payment: Major credit cards
Children: Not appropriate
Pets: Not allowed
Smoking: Allowed in designated areas
Open: Year-round

A mining engineer who made his fortune in Australia at the turn of the century built this solid mansion in fashionable Pacific Heights. It withstood the 1906 earthquake and fire and now offers lodging to San Francisco visitors who prefer a quiet but convenient retreat away from the downtown bustle.

Parking is easy in this hilly neighborhood of lovely old residences. You can leave your car on the street or in a garage two blocks away.

Marble stairs under a curved arch of red stone lead to a courtyard with greenery and a skylight at the entrance to Jackson Court. Inside, there's an intimate parlor furnished like a fine residential salon. Velvet couches sit on an Oriental carpet beside the fireplace, which is carved with cherubs, their mouths pursed as if to blow on the hearth. Ceiling beams and wainscoting are of dark woods. Fresh flowers are arranged on the coffee table, an encyclopedia is handy, and game boards are set for dominoes and backgammon. Sherry is served by the fire in the late afternoon.

The two suites are just off the parlor. The Executive Suite has a brass bed and a large sitting area with a marble fireplace and built-in bookcases. The Garden Suite, originally the dining room, features handcrafted paneling, a bed with a curved brass headboard, a black marble fireplace, and a private patio filled with flowers.

The other rooms are on the second and third floors. Beautifully furnished, they convey the ambience of a well-appointed apartment. A few have working fireplaces. Room 1, once the library, is a big favorite for its quiet atmosphere, brass bed, and gray marble fireplace.

All the rooms have television and private phones. There's no charge for local calls.

Just off the wide landing is a breakfast nook where fruit, croissants, and various cereals are available in the mornings.

Guests are welcome to use the cooking facilities here, a convenience if you're staying for any length of time.

Jackson Court is more like a home than a hotel because its accommodations are all time-share studios. They're managed by the capable Pat Cremer, who will recommend good restaurants, give you a map and the morning newspaper, and answer questions about the city. "It's very informal here," she says. "This is a casual place. No one ever wants to leave."

Kensington Park Hotel
450 Post Street
San Francisco, California 94102
415-788-6400
800-553-1900
Fax: 415-399-9484

Manager: Steven J. Montez
Accommodations: 86 rooms, 1 suite
Rates: $115; suite, $160–$350
Included: Continental breakfast
Payment: Major credit cards
Children: Under 12 free in room with parents
Pets: Not allowed
Smoking: Nonsmoking rooms available
Open: Year-round

Kensington Park is a good example of the small, service-oriented boutique hotels that are sprouting up all over San Francisco. It has a prime location half a block from Union Square, competitive prices, comfortable accommodations, and individual character.

The 12-story hotel, built in 1924, is a remodeled Elks Club. Its classic design was retained, with contemporary comforts and safety features added. A marble lobby with a baby grand piano, European furnishings, and handpainted beamed ceilings and ornamentation give the hotel unusual style. It's a conservative, quiet place, though there are a theater and modeling agency in the building, and the Elks still meet here.

The guest rooms, decorated in rose and blue, contain mahogany furnishings, writing tables, telephones, and television. They all have the same format; twelfth-floor accommodations feature extras such as terrycloth bathrobes and English toiletries. English prints adorn the white walls and rose damask curtains hang at windows with views up Nob Hill to the Mark Hopkins' fluttering flag.

The burgundy Royal Suite, the most luxurious and expensive

in the hotel, has a dining table that seats twelve. There is a four-poster canopy bed, a carved Oriental coffee table, an immense television set, and a two-sided gas fireplace. The marble bath features brass fixtures and a whirlpool tub.

Most rooms are average in size and, despite the elaborate antique armoires, basically simple. Fluorescent lighting gives the bathrooms a ghostly look, but they're immaculate.

The hotel's service is outstanding. Coffee, tea and croissants are served on every floor in the mornings. Afternoon sherry, tea, and cookies are offered in the lobby, along with piano serenades. Other services include complimentary limousine service to the financial district, same-day laundry service, overnight shoe shine, and valet parking. Meeting rooms can hold up to 50 people, and audiovisual equipment is available. The concierge will arrange sightseeing tours and theater tickets.

Kensington Park is one of five small San Francisco hotels in the family-owned Hotel Group of America. The hotels cater mainly to a business clientele looking for a convenient location and reasonable rates.

The Majestic

1500 Sutter Street
San Francisco, California 94109
415-441-1100
800-869-8966
Fax: 415-673-7331

General manager: Barry Stover
Accommodations: 50 rooms and 9 suites
Rates: $135–$250; $15 additional person
Payment: Major credit cards
Children: Welcome (no charge for use of a crib)
Pets: Not allowed
Smoking: Nonsmoking rooms available
Open: Year-round

San Francisco's turn-of-the-century golden era is brought to life at the Majestic, a beautifully restored five-story Edwardian structure. It's just outside the bustling downtown area, about six blocks from Union Square.

Entering the glass-paned double doors of the hotel takes you even farther from the modern rush and city noise. Wide stairs of green marble lead to a carpeted lobby where a chandelier with torch globes gives a warm glow to the antique-filled room. A fire burns in the fireplace and Oriental vases hold sprays of golden lilies. Fringed lampshades and cushions, lace curtains at narrow windows, and glass-fronted bookshelves add to the old-fashioned, homey atmosphere.

To the left of the lobby are the Café Majestic and bar, the latter a clubby spot with a 19th-century mahogany bar from France. The café—actually a full-scale dining room with a pleasantly French ambience—is noted for its combination of classic San Francisco dishes with California nouvelle cuisine. Among the memorable desserts are orange creme brulee and chocolate cake with jalape164&o chiles.

Some of the guest rooms have four-poster canopy beds, boudoir chairs, and velvet or plush couches. It's easy to imagine yourself in an old San Francisco residence—an updated one, however, with TVs, clock radios, and direct-dial telephones. Several rooms have gas fireplaces. Despite their furnishings and atmosphere, the accommodations don't match the promise of the delightful entrance area and restaurant. There is limited space to hang clothes, and some fabrics are frayed and worn.

If you can overlook these minor flaws and you'd like to step into a long-gone era, you'll enjoy the Majestic's charm. Soak in the clawfoot tub or sit at your desk in the bay window overlooking the trees and strollers on Sutter Street, and you might be a guest visiting in 1902, when the hotel was built. Recently it was fully restored, receiving state recognition for historic and architectural preservation.

More of today's services include valet parking, complimentary limousine service to the financial district and Union Square, afternoon sherry in the library, and nightly turndown service. The concierge will arrange for restaurant reservations and wine country tours.

The Mansions
2220 Sacramento Street
San Francisco, California 94115
415-929-9444
800-826-9398

Owner: Robert C. Pritikin
Accommodations: 29 rooms
Rates: $74–$150; double, $89–$200; $15 additional person; suites, $200–$225
Included: Full breakfast
Payment: Major credit cards
Children: Welcome (under age 12 free)

Pets: Allowed
Smoking: Allowed
Open: Year-round

Two long-time San Francisco hotels, side by side in a neighborhood of apartments, homes, and a medical center, have recently joined to form an unlikely combination. The Mansion Hotel, a twin-towered Queen Anne structure, is known for its sense of fun and eclectic mixture of whimsy and Victoriana. The Hermitage House is a serene, urban refuge. Connected now by a hallway, they are The Mansions.

Robert Pritikin is a hotelier of boundless energy and many interests. He writes books (Christ Was an Ad Man), collects sculpture (he has a major Benjamin Bufano collection), keeps a macaw in the hotel parlor, and plays the musical.

A few of his original hotel's features are a "hauntress" named Claudia who plays the piano, a billiards room with a wall-size mural of pigs, caged white doves, and priceless Joseph Turner and Joshua Reynolds paintings.

One of the world's largest examples of stained glass stands in the dining room. The colorful mural, first created for a villa in Spain, is nine feet high and stretches the length of the room. Prix fixe dinners are served nightly (except Sunday) in the dining room.

The grand home was built in 1887 by a senator from Utah, Charles Chambers, who earned a fortune in silver mines and moved to San Francisco. It's a historic landmark now, filled with museum-quality art and antiques.

Accommodations, divided among three floors, are sumptuous, with four-poster beds, potted palms, and elaborately trimmed wardrobes. They have piped-in classical music, fresh flowers and candy, velvet quilts, and red carpets. The Lillie Coit Room, up in a third-floor corner, is a cozy hideaway. It has a queen-size brass bed, a phone on a ceramic elephant table, and windows that look out on the Golden Gate Bridge and Mount Tamalpais.

Breakfast is served in the country kitchen or brought to your room with the morning paper: fresh coffee ground in an antique grinder, cereal, fruit, crumpets, eggs, English sausage, and potatoes are on the wide-ranging menu.

With all its trappings, the hotel has a lighthearted atmosphere. Even the ghost seems to have a good time, concluding her evening concerts with a rousing march or ragtime tune, while bubbles float to the ceiling.

The west wing (formerly Hermitage House) has a different flavor. Tasteful Laura Ashley prints and fabrics grace most rooms with a French country decor. High coffered ceilings, mullioned windows, antiques, and flowers give this side of the hotel a European flavor. Most rooms have fireplaces.

A room on the top floor, once the original owner's study, retains its library atmosphere with shelves full of books. The room also boasts a mahogany and oak-inlaid floor, redwood shake paneling, and a fine city view.

The Mark Hopkins Intercontinental
999 California Street
Number One Nob Hill
San Francisco, California 94108
415-392-3434
800-327-0200
Fax: 415-421-3302

General manager: Sandor J. Stangl
Accommodations: 361 rooms, 30 suites
Rates: $180–$275; double, $200–$305; suites, $375–$1,000
Payment: Major credit cards
Children: Under 14 free in room with parents
Pets: Not allowed
Smoking: Nonsmoking rooms available
Open: Year-round

In the devastating earthquake and fire of 1906, the fabulous Mark Hopkins mansion at the top of Nob Hill burned to the ground. The more modest structure that followed was moved in 1925 by a mining engineer, George D. Smith, who then began building the luxury hotel that stands today.

The nineteen-story Mark Hopkins, a combination of French château and Spanish Renaissance architecture, has been a world-famed city landmark since it opened in 1926 and was proclaimed "perfect, flawless." Ownership has changed several times (most recently in early 1989, when it was acquired by a Japanese firm), but its traditional style and quality of service remain. In 1988 and 1989, a $10 million major renovation updated the tired lobby, restaurant, and all the guest rooms and suites.

Because the hotel comprises a central tower and two wings, every room has a view of San Francisco Bay and the city skyline. Even the lowest rooms, on the second floor, overlook machinery-screening flower boxes to the city below. The public spaces are grand and gilded, befitting a hotel of such prestige. Only its neighbor, the Fairmont, vies with the Mark Hopkins for compelling views and an air of festivity and excitement.

Limousines crowd the brick driveway at the impressive entrance. The lobby is rich with Oriental screens, lush floral displays, ornate chandeliers, and rococo standing candelabra. Off the lobby is the Lower Bar, where cocktails, high tea, and light meals are served on crisp white linens under a Tiffany-style skylight. Each table bears a single rose in a silver bud vase.

In the Nob Hill Restaurant, creative Continental cuisine is served, with dishes such as sauteed escalope of foie gras with lentils, apple puree and olive oil and roast loin of lamb in a fresh herb coulis. The herbs come from what is probably the most expensive herb garden in the world: a little plot of land the hotel owns on nearby Mason Street, valued at $4,000 a square foot. The wine list includes labels from 34 of 41 wine-producing states.

The Top of the Mark is obligatory on every San Francisco tourist's must-see list. As a result, the rooftop lounge is crammed every night with imbibers trying to catch a glimpse of the breathtaking views. Everyone seems in a celebratory, holiday mood.

The guest rooms have been redone in a neoclassic style, with color schemes of gray or khaki and gold. The quilted chintz bedspreads, thick carpeting, and damask wallcoverings were all designed for the hotel. The nightstands have tortuma tops made with crushed South American gourds in black resin. Televisions and mini-bars are encased in cherrywood armoires.

The best of the preferred accommodations are the corner terrace suites. Each features an enclosed solarium with a closeup of the hotel's elaborate architectural ornamentation and the spectacular panorama beyond. The living rooms are comfortably furnished (though the carpets show frayed edges). Each suite has three phones, a desk, and a white marble bath with pedestal sink, a built-in hair dryer, oversize towels, robes, and assorted toiletries.

The service at the Mark Hopkins is excellent, and the presence of groups (the hotel has a conference capacity of 600) does not seem to detract from it for the individual traveler. The concierge will handle most requests. An additional level of service, Guest Relations, provides for special needs—foreign-language interpreters, VIPs, group assistance.

Several packages and special rates are offered. For a weekend bargain, ask about the $145 package for two.

The Pan Pacific Hotel

500 Post Street
San Francisco, California 94102
415-771-8600
800-533-6465
Fax: 415-398-0267

Manager: Bob Schrader
Accommodations: 311 rooms, 19 suites
Rates: $185–$335; suites, $550–$1,500
Payment: Major credit cards
Children: Under 18 free in room with parents
Pets: Allowed
Smoking: 7 nonsmoking floors
Open: Year-round

The Pan Pacific, formerly the Portman Hotel, rises 21 stories above the corner of Post and Mason streets, a block west of Union Square. Famed for its elegant, contemporary style, the hotel was designed by architect John Portman, who is known for introducing the open atrium to large convention hotels. This is a smaller, more opulent version of the Portman trademark.

In the porte cochere, you are met by a white-gloved attendant who welcomes you effusively and whisks your car away. Inside, on the third-floor lobby level, a seventeen-story glass and brass atrium soars above a dazzling array of lights and an Elbert Weinberg sculpture, Joie de Danse.

At one side of the large, open lobby is an attractive lounge with Oriental carpets and potted palms. Near it the Pacific Grill menu offers Asian-influenced California cuisine. Room service features dishes on the restaurant's menu.

The floor below has a large ballroom and an executive conference center, the only one like it in downtown San Francisco. It comprises four conference suites, a dining room, and one large suite and has audiovisual equipment.

The hotel is noted for its impeccable service, a continuation of the tradition established by the Portman Hotel when it opened in 1987. Each floor has three valets who are responsible for the comfort of the guests on that floor. Your valet will unpack luggage, deliver newspapers, press clothing, shine shoes, and tidy your room every time you leave. He knows when the room is empty, because he's placed a broom bristle against the door; if it has fallen, he'll come in to empty ashtrays, straighten the bed, and re-stock your refrigerator.

The guest rooms include sixteen Pacific Suites and three

specialty suites: the Penthouse, the Olympic, and the California. The Penthouse occupies 3,000 square feet on the 21st floor. It has two bedrooms with canopy beds, two baths (and a huge whirlpool tub), powder room, living room with working fireplace, dining room, study, access to an open-air terrace, valet's room, and pantry.

The rooms have television, phones with call waiting and voice mail features, Swiss-milled soaps, and terry robes in lavish bathrooms of Portuguese marble (though counter space is lacking). Decorated in gray on gray with accents of pale mauve, the rooms are reminders of the seafog that swirls through this coastal city's streets.

There are no fitness facilities, but you can arrange to use nearby clubs and the valet will deliver an exercise bicycle to your room if you ask. The check-out system is flexible, and the hotel will provide airport and in-city transportation in a Rolls Royce. Semicircular windows, lavish lighting, Oriental art objects, and an extensive use of rosewood and glass create intense visual interest in this unusual hotel. They don't soften the cool, corporate tone, however. If you like a clean-edged, high-tech look, you will enjoy the Pan Pacific.

Petite Auberge
863 Bush Street
San Francisco, California 94108
415-928-6000

Manager: Rich Revaz
Accommodations: 25 rooms, 1 suite
Rates: $105–$155; $15 additional person; suite, $215
Included: Full breakfast
Payment: Major credit cards
Children: Under 5 free in room with parents
Pets: Not allowed
Smoking: Not allowed in public spaces
Open: Year-round

A French country inn in the heart of San Francisco, between Nob Hill and Union Square, Petite Auberge offers the best of both romantic worlds. It has flower-filled window boxes on every floor, and French and American flags fly over a green awning.

Inside the narrow, five-story hotel, light and breezy pastels, floral fabrics, comfortable antiques, and French landscape paintings set the tone. The registration desk is just inside the front beveled glass doors, but the gathering place for guests is belowstairs, where couches are pulled up to the fireplace, daily newspapers lie on the tables, and afternoon tea is served.

Just beyond the lower lounge is a quiet breakfast area. Guests have their juice, cereals, egg dish, croissants and coffee at round tables, viewing a little garden full of well-tended shrubs and delicate ferns.

The guest rooms line pale cream halls with paneled wainscoting. The rooms on the first floor tend to be dark; those on the upper floors are more attractive. They vary in size and are decorated individually, but all carry through the French country theme with striped and flowered wallpapers, pastel comforters, muslin curtains, handmade pillows, and fresh flowers and fruit.

Most of the rooms have gas fireplaces. Linens are changed daily, and each bed has three pristine sheets, one folded to protect you from touching the blanket. Robes are provided, along with baskets of shampoos and lotions.

Every room has a teddy bear, one of the signature touches in all Four Sisters Inns. The company, which owns a collection of inns, was begun by Roger and Sally Post in Pacific Grove, when they opened their own 19th-century home to guests. The Posts' four daughters helped make it a family venture and gave the new innkeeping company its name. The sisters are still involved in the operation of the inns. Sally Post, who decorates with flair, worked with other designers to create inns modeled on those in Europe.

Each inn has bits of whimsy. At Petite Auberge they include an antique carousel horse by the front door, floppy-eared ceramic rabbits, and the ubiquitous bears, which may be purchased.

The staff at Petite Auberge is helpful in arranging for dinner reservations or tickets to the symphony or other events. Valet parking is available.

If you're looking for flowery charm, downtown convenience, and warm hospitality, this little inn is an excellent choice.

Prescott Hotel
545 Post Street
San Francisco, California 94102
415-563-0303
800-283-7322

Manager: Patrick Sampson
Accommodations: 167 rooms, 34 suites

Rates: Rooms, $155; suites, $205; penthouse, $525; Club Level rooms, $175, Club Level suites, $225
Included: Continental breakfast on Club Level
Payment: Major credit cards
Children: Welcome
Pets: Not allowed
Smoking: Nonsmoking rooms available
Open: Year-round

Here's another boutique hotel with the winning Kimco Group combination: small but attractive rooms, reasonable rates, and a top-quality restaurant. Bill Kimpton's collection of old buildings, restored and given new luster, fill an important niche for city visitors.

Curved copper awnings mark the entrance to the Prescott, which is close to Union Square. Inside you'll find a quiet sitting area with couches and wingback chairs in the lobby, and curving staircases leading to the mezzanine's meeting rooms and guest rooms above.

The smartly appointed rooms, more elaborate than the other Kimco hotels, have hair dryers and robes in the modern, well-lighted baths. The compact suites make efficient use of space and are more like urban apartments than hotel lodgings. On the Club Level (the fourth through seventh floors), guests have their own concierge and lounge where appetizers—catered by the Prescott's restaurant, Postrio—are served in the evenings. A complimentary buffet breakfast is provided, along with the morning papers.

When the hotel opened in 1990, Postrio earned immediate raves. Lavish bouquets, Robert Rauschenberg paintings, and hand-blown glass light fixtures hung with copper spirals create a bright and whimsical setting for the outstanding California cuisine. Pizza is a specialty, but you won't go wrong ordering anything on the menu. Reserve a table when you make your room reservation; Postrio is usually booked weeks in advance, but a few tables are held for hotel guests.

The Ritz-Carlton, San Francisco
600 Stockton Street
San Francisco, California 94108
415-296-7465
Fax: 415-296-8559

General manager: Marcos Bekhit
Accommodations: 292 rooms, 44 suites

Rates: $185–$325; junior suites, $300–$400; suites, $450–
$2,700
Payment: Major credit cards
Children: Welcome
Pets: Not allowed
Smoking: Nonsmoking rooms available
Open: Year-round

One of the city's best examples of neoclassical architecture has
joined the Ritz-Carlton group of luxury hotels. Built in 1909 for
the Metropolitan Life Insurance Company, the stately, historic
structure on Nob Hill was restored and opened in 1991. Like the
other Ritz-Carlton hotels, it offers sumptuous accommodations in a conservative setting. The staff dresses in sober navy or
black and white and the walls are adorned with museum-
quality 18th- and 19th-century paintings. Art from this period is
used because, says Horst Schulze, president of the Ritz-Carlton
Hotel Company, "its timeless themes portray a quality of life
and attention to detail that exemplifies the Ritz-Carlton's phi-
losophy."

However, this being San Francisco, there's a light-hearted
quality that keeps pretension at bay. Heavy, dark woods have
been kept to a minimum. One of the most appealing places in
the imposing hotel is its sunny outdoor terrace, with its fountain
and umbrella tables. Part of the Restaurant, the terrace offers
courtyard seating for breakfast, lunch, and dinner, the only
hotel restaurant in the city to do so. The food is first-rate. You
may also dine in the intimate, elegant Dining Room, where
Continental cuisine is served and the wine list is lengthy.

The hotel bustles with activity, as many social functions take
place here, but the halls, padded in gray damask, are quiet.
Guest rooms are handsomely furnished in classic residential
style, with dashes of color here and there. The marble bathrooms are lovely, down to the orchids on the counter, but you
may notice minor flaws, like no shelf in the oversize shower,
and only a single hook on the door.

Rooms and suites on the 8th and 9th floors are designated
the Ritz-Carlton Club. Guests have the use of a concierge, a
private lounge with a subdued atmosphere, and complimentary
snacks and cocktails. All rooms have numerous useful features:
remote control TVs (VCRs and a video library are available),
stocked honor bars, plush robes, clock radios, safes. Some have
bay views, but if you prefer a quiet room, follow the example of
frequent San Francisco visitors and request one on the courtyard side.

Services by the eager multilingual staff include twice-daily maid service, valet parking, a 24-hour concierge, child care, and newspaper delivery. Disposable sweatsuits and swim wear are available in the fitness center, where you'll find a swimming pool, whirlpool, sauna, and weight machines.

Sheraton Palace Hotel

2 New Montgomery Street
San Francisco, California 94105
415-392-8600
800-325-3535
Fax: 415-543-0671

General manager: Donald N. Timbie
Accommodations: 500 rooms, 51 suites
Rates: $195–$295; double, $215–$315; suites, $400–$500; $20 additional person
Payment: Major credit cards
Children: Under 18 free
Pets: Not allowed
Smoking: Nonsmoking rooms available
Open: Year-round

After a 27-month, $150 million restoration, the historic Palace opened again in April 1991. The grand hotel that was built in 1875 as the first hotel west of the Mississippi, and rebuilt after burning in the 1906 earthquake and fire, has been returned to its former glory—with a few additions. Now there is a conference area and business center, a health spa, and a skylighted swimming pool. When it was the largest, most luxurious hotel in the world, the Palace hosted royalty, presidents, and celebrities; no doubt more will follow, along with other world travelers.

The glamour has returned, with the lovely Garden Court as its centerpiece. A magnificent stained glass dome covers the famous restaurant, where ten sparkling chandeliers hang above the potted palms, gilded marble columns, and linen-covered tables. This is a beloved lunch, tea, and Sunday brunch spot for San Franciscans who remember the old days, as well as for awed newcomers. Breakfast service can be slow, however.

Another restaurant, Maxfield's, features grilled and light fare. It, too, has a stained glass ceiling, uncovered during the hotel's restoration. Maxfield's was named for Maxfield Parrish, the artist commissioned to paint the mural that adorns the hotel's Pied Piper Bar (once chosen as "one of the world's seven greatest bars" by Esquire magazine). Valued at $2.5 million, the mural depicts the story of Robert Browning's Pied Piper of Hamelin. Kyo-Ya is the Sheraton Palace's third restaurant. Named for the company that now owns the hotel, it offers Japanese cuisine for lunch and dinner.

Acres of marble, high ceilings, polished woods, and numerous amenities characterize the guest rooms and suites. There are hair dryers and magnifying mirrors in the baths, refrigerators, movies, robes, and hook-ups for personal computers. Overnight valet service, nightly turndown, and 24-hour room service are offered. Business travelers like the telephones with custom message, conference call, voice mail, and call waiting features.

The hotel's location is convenient for both business and pleasure; it's adjacent to the financial district and within walking distance of Moscone Center and Embarcadero Center, and the theaters and the shops of Union Square are nearby.

The Sherman House

2160 Green Street
San Francisco, California 94123
415-563-3600

Owners: Manouchehr and Vesta Mobedshahi
General manager: Gerard Lespinette
Accommodations: 14 rooms
Rates: $200–$750
Payment: Major credit cards
Children: Not appropriate
Pets: Not allowed
Smoking: Allowed in designated areas
Open: Year-round

This intimate, exclusive hostelry in one of the city's most fashionable districts is an 1876 French-Italianate mansion. Once the home of Leander Sherman, founder of the Sherman Clay Music Company, it is now a princely enclave catering to a discriminating clientele. The rich and famous find it a haven, as do those looking for service far above the ordinary.

Manou Mobedshahi, an Iranian economist turned San Francisco entrepreneur, bought the historic landmark in 1981 and, with his wife, an art preservationist, carefully restored the house and its formal gardens. In 1983 the Sherman House opened to guests in all its 19th-century elegance.

Behind its black iron railings and white exterior lies a salon, the Music Room, where finches trill in a bird cage that is a miniature of Château Chenonceau in France. With classical music in the background, it's easy to imagine Paderewski playing the grand piano in the corner, as he did in years past. Wine is served in the afternoon, and occasionally there's a special wine tasting or a music recital.

The gallery above the Music Room provides a pleasant sitting room, with cushioned seats at five bay windows, a fireplace, and French provincial armchairs and sofa.

The guest rooms are in the main house and carriage house, which was remodeled to contain three suites. One of the suites has its own garden with a deck and arbor. Furnishings in all rooms are antique or custom-made. Hand-loomed carpets, Coromandel screens, Belgian tapestries, marble fireplaces, brass fixtures, crystal chandeliers, and original art fill the interiors, planned by the late great designer William Gaylord. Most rooms adhere to a French Second Empire theme, popular in Leander Sherman's day, with a few in a Biedermeier or Jacobean motif. All have a sense of solidity and permanence.

Some rooms have sweeping views of the bay, Golden Gate Bridge, and Alcatraz. The Garden Suite, set among the multilevel lawns and cobblestoned pathways, is the largest. It has a spacious living room with freestanding fireplace, lattice walls, and wide windows overlooking shrubs and flowers, a gazebo and a pond. The polished brown floors are of slate from Beijing, and part of the bathroom is finished in teak. Hollow core rattan wraps the four-poster bed. The suites upstairs in the carriage house are equally light and bright. The top-floor suite features a sunken living room with French doors to a balcony overlooking the bay.

Canopied and draped beds have down comforters. Each elegant black marble bath has a small TV and second telephone, thick white towels and robes, and imported toiletries.

Three meals a day are served in the intimate dining room, which is open to the public for special events. French cuisine with California accents is served, under the direction of Donia Bijan.

Needless to say, the service and attention to detail at this hotel are impeccable. Whether it's room service at any hour, immediate shoe repairs, secretarial services, a tour of the Napa Valley, or a ride to the airport in a vintage automobile, Sherman House will oblige. This is a lodging of polish, privilege, and ease.

The Villa Florence Hotel
225 Powell Street
San Francisco, California 94102
415-397-7700
800-553-4411
Fax: 415-397-1006

General manager: Jim Dowling
Accommodations: 177 rooms, 36 suites
Rates: $119; suites, $139–$189
Payment: Major credit cards
Children: Welcome
Pets: Not allowed
Smoking: Nonsmoking rooms available
Open: Year-round

The Villa Florence is one of the city's distinctive small hotels offering stylish lodgings in a historic building to cost-conscious travelers. Bill Kimpton helped to lead the way for these boutique hotels when he saw a niche to be filled and began renovating a few of San Francisco's rundown but usable structures.

Formerly the Manx Hotel, built in 1916, the Villa Florence was remodeled with an Italian Renaissance theme and opened as one of the Kimco Hotels in 1986. In the busy lobby are a marble fireplace and a gauzy mural depicting 16th-century Florence. A rare antique velvet tapestry hangs on one wall. Indirect lighting on the marble columns highlights the ceiling details in the ivory, cream and burgundy room.

Separated from the lobby by etched glass walls is Kuleto's Restaurant. Its head chef, Robert Helstrom, continues its reputation for Italian food with a California perspective. Highlights are the pastas, innovative salads, and grilled fish and meats. A specialty is the excellent antipasto bar. The small portions can be ordered as hors d'oeuvres or combined as a main course. Baked goods and desserts such as pumpkin tarts and rich chocolate decadence on raspberry sauce are made daily on the premises.

The restaurant's ambience combines an aura of old San Francisco with Italian vitality. Dark wood, warm lighting, and strings of peppers, herbs, sausages and garlic hanging above the bar add to the atmosphere. Ficus trees grow to the ceiling under three stained glass skylights in the light and airy dining section.

The guest rooms, which include junior and deluxe suites, have a pleasant pastel decor, with flowered fabrics and pale furniture. All include honor bars, concealed televisions, direct-dial phones with long cords, and soundproofed walls and windows. Even if the ice machine is just outside your room, you won't hear it when the door is closed. Desk space is on the skimpy side—adequate for writing postcards.

Some bathrooms are very small. Much roomier are those in the junior suites, which also have sitting areas, though not divided rooms. The deluxe suites have two rooms.

The hotel offers morning and evening room service, complimentary limousine service to the financial district, and same-day laundry and valet service. There are three meeting rooms and a full range of audiovisual equipment. Room keys are coded for security.

Villa Florence is just south of Union Square on the main cable car line, not a poor location but highly touristed, with many trinket shops and hordes of people. With new developments such as the snazzy shops of San Francisco Centre, the tenor of the neighborhood may change.

The White Swan Inn
845 Bush Street
San Francisco, California 94108
415-775-1755

General manager: Rich Revaz
Accommodations: 25 rooms, 1 suite
Rates: $145–$160; suite, $250; $15 additional person
Included: Full breakfast
Payment: Major credit cards
Children: Under 5 free in room with parents
Pets: Not allowed
Smoking: Not allowed in public areas
Open: Year-round

Once this four-story hotel with a marble facade and bay windows was the Hotel Louise, built after the great earthquake of 1906. Fully renovated in 1986, it reopened as one of the Four Sisters Inns, a collection of hotels owned or managed by Roger and Sally Post and their four daughters.

The White Swan, between Nob Hill and Union Square in downtown San Francisco, has an English garden theme, providing a tranquil retreat from the busy city. This is one of the more expensive of the Four Sisters inns and has the most amenities.

Its heavy, beveled glass doors open to a large reception area with granite floors, an antique carousel horse, and English art. Downstairs is the guests' lounge, where breakfast and a full afternoon tea, with scones, cheeses, fondues or other hearty snacks, are served. Parquet floors, dark green woodwork, and richly colored wallpaper provide contrast to the neighboring alcove and garden court.

Here, too, are the parlor and library, with inviting chairs before the granite fireplace, shelves full of books, colors of burgundy and hunter green, and a standing world globe — a peaceful setting with an English manor house motif.

The terrace outside, shaded by a large avocado tree, is next to a conference room that can accommodate up to thirty people. The White Swan also does catering upon request. A few of the hotel's special services are one-day laundry and pressing, complimentary cookies and fruit all day, business equipment, and complimentary wine and roses in every guest room.

All rooms have wet bars, a television, fireplaces, and phones. The hotel's suite has two fireplaces. Four-posters, antique reproductions, and books in the rooms lend a residential ambience. The baths are modern, with basins set in granite counters, but contain some original tiles.

Valet parking is available, and the front desk provides concierge services, booking restaurant tables and tickets to events.

Several fine restaurants are close to the hotel. Recommended are Fleur de Lys, Rue L'Epic, and Café Mozart. Kuleto's and Trattoria Contadina serve excellent northern Italian cuisine, and I Fratelli is noted for its dishes of southern Italy.

Santa Fe

The Bishop's Lodge

Box 2367
Santa Fe, New Mexico 87504
505-983-6377
800-732-2240
Fax: 505-989-8739

Innkeepers: Jim and Lore Thorpe
Accommodations: 74 rooms
Rates: $120–$180; double, $160–$315; suites, $205–$345
Added: 8.75% tax
Payment: Personal checks or cash; no credit cards
Children: Welcome
Pets: Not allowed
Smoking: Allowed
Open: April to January 2

Downtown Santa Fe is only 5 minutes away, but at the Bishop's Lodge, which occupies 1,000 acres in the foothills of the Sangre de Cristo Mountains, guests find peace and quiet far from the crowds.

Retreating to these juniper-studded foothills at the head of the Tesuque Valley is not without precedent. In fact, at the heart of the lodge's charm—its gentleness and hospitality—is the memory of the man for whom it is named. Archbishop Lamy of Santa Fe (the model for the main character in Willa Cather's *Death Comes for the Archbishop*) came to this very spot about a century ago for rest and eventually retirement. Over time he planted an orchard, supplementing the fruit trees planted by the Franciscan Fathers during the early 17th century. Remnants of the orchard are still sprinkled over the grounds.

Next to his adobe home the archbishop built a private chapel —a simple structure with vaulted ceilings and painted glass windows that simulate the stained glass of the cathedrals in his native France. The tiny chapel, now on the National Register of Historic Places, still stands, creating an atmosphere of warmth, peacefulness, and history.

Only a few steps away, down a path lined with flowers, is the main lobby, where guests can sign up for activities, eat in the central dining room, and enjoy spectacular sunsets from the terrace bar. Life is casual here; while men are asked to wear jackets at dinner and women are requested to "dress accordingly," there's an informal air throughout the resort. Breakfast and lunch are served buffet style. Cocktails are served in El Charro lounge as well as on the terrace.

The guest rooms are spread out in several one-and two-story buildings, all reflecting their New Mexico heritage. In a wide assortment of sizes and configurations, they are especially spacious, well lit, and well furnished. The decor is ranch-style southwestern with kiva fireplaces, simple wooden furniture, and earth-tone fabrics with splashes of color. Some rooms have beamed ceilings, some have private balconies or terraces. The bathrooms are larger than average and designed for convenience. Air conditioning, TVs, and telephones are standard features.

The Bishop's Lodge has an impressive roster of recreational choices. There are ample facilities for horseback riding, tennis, volleyball, swimming, and skeet shooting as well as lots of extras: a playground (complete with a tepee), fishing pond for children (stocked with trout), maps with hiking trails, and lists for bird watchers (over 110 species can be observed on the grounds). Golfers are welcome at any of three private courses in the area.

The lodge also offers an abundance of special activities such as a newcomer's cocktail party held by the Thorpes, exercise classes, fashion shows, storytelling on the front lawn, steak fries, children's cookouts—the list goes on and on. The resort also keeps guests informed of events in the area.

In the summer, there's an excellent program for children aged 4 to 12 that includes hiking, swimming, pony rides, and arts and crafts. The cost is part of the Modified American Plan during July and August and is available for an extra fee in June.

Teens get special attention. In the summer there's a dining table especially for them, and events such as swim parties are planned, depending upon the number of young guests.

Horseback riding is important here. Most of the guests ride, whether they are experienced or have never mounted a horse before. With more than 60 horses, the resort offers daily guided rides ($20 per person), plus special breakfast and picnic rides.

Since 1918, when James R. Thorpe developed the Bishop's Lodge as a ranch resort, three generations of the family have owned and run the lodge. Previously, the property had belonged to the newspaper publisher Joseph Pulitzer, who established the Pulitzer Prizes.

Grant Corner Inn
122 Grant Avenue
Santa Fe, New Mexico 87501
505-983-6678

Innkeepers: Louise Stewart and Pat Walter
Accommodations: 13 rooms (9 with private bath)
Rates: $55–$65; double, $55–$135
Included: Full breakfast
Added: 4% room tax
Payment: Major credit cards
Children: Over 8 welcome
Pets: Not allowed
Smoking: Not permitted
Open: Year-round

One of the nicest inns in the Southwest is at the corner of Grant Avenue and Johnson Street in Santa Fe. Walk through the latticed archway to a nostalgic world of pinafores and quilts, warmth and hospitality. Whether your childhood included visits to Grandma's house or not, you'll feel as if it did when you visit this inn, run as a B&B.

The Colonial manor home two blocks from the plaza was built in 1905 by a wealthy ranching family, and was opened as an inn in 1982 by Louise Stewart (daughter of Jack Stewart, the founder of the Camelback Inn in Scottsdale) and her husband Pat Walter. Guests pass a white picket fence and softly swaying weeping willows through an etched glass front door to a living room furnished in antiques. From the Wedgwood blue ceiling and walls to the gleaming wood floors and the Oriental carpets, the house exudes warmth. The adjoining dining room gets lots of use, for the inn serves breakfast to the public as well as its guests. It only takes a moment to start noticing the rabbits—calico rabbits, wooden rabbits, furry rabbits, porcelain rabbits, even rabbit napkin holders on the dining room table.

Throughout the house, there are other touches that give the inn its special charm. Hanging on the door of each guest room is a stuffed heart with the word Welcome printed on it. Arriving guests find in their room a small fruit basket, a carafe of wine, fresh flowers, chocolates on monogrammed pillowcases, and a welcoming note from their hosts.

Eleven guest rooms are on the first three floors. Each has its own decor, with brass and four-poster beds, quilts and tieback curtains. Some rooms have small refrigerators, covered in frills. Every room has a private phone, TV, air conditioning, and a ceiling fan. The rooms aren't large, but the overall ambience makes up for any loss of space. Adjoining rooms with a shared bath are a good choice for families. The bedrooms range from one twin bed to one king-size and have enough space for a roll-away. Room 11 is perfect for a child since it has a single brass bed and is filled with stuffed toys.

Five blocks away is Grant Corner Inn Hacienda, an adobe condominium with two guest rooms upstairs and a living room, dining room, and kitchen downstairs. Its modern decor includes cathedral ceilings and skylights. The entire unit can accommodate up to eight; each guest room can be rented individually. Both have queen-size beds; one has a beehive fireplace. Rates range from $90 for one room to $250 for eight people renting the entire unit.

Guests in both the main house and the condominium eat a breakfast feast in the inn's dining room or on the front porch, draped with hanging plants. There are two entrées—perhaps pumpkin raisin pancakes or artichoke mushroom crêpes with sour cream sauce—along with homemade jellies and breads, fruit frappes, a selection of fine teas, and fresh coffee. Breakfast is so special that even fried eggs, bacon, and home fries taste like elegant treats. Brunch is served on Saturdays (7:30 A.M. to noon) and Sundays (8 A.M. to 1 P.M.). These meals are so popular that the inn sells its own cookbook, along with jellies and country crafts. (If you're in the area and want to eat at the inn, be sure to make reservations.)

Guests at Grant Corner can use a nearby sports club (a 10-minute drive), which offers tennis, racquetball, indoor and outdoor pools, a whirlpool, sauna, and massage.

Hotel St. Francis

210 Don Gaspar Avenue
Santa Fe, New Mexico 87501
505-983-5700
800-666-5700
Fax: 505-989-7690

General manager: Michaleen Sawka
Accommodations: 82 rooms
Rates: $60–$135; double, $75–$150; $15 additional person; suites, $175–$300
Added: 10.25% tax
Payment: Major credit cards

Children: Under 12 free in room with parents
Pets: Not allowed
Smoking: Nonsmoking rooms available
Open: Year-round

In a town dating from 1610, the St. Francis, built in 1924, is a relative newcomer. The St. Francis was renovated in 1987, adding charm and flavor to the cultural capital of the Southwest.

A wide front porch with white wrought-iron furniture, great for people-watching, opens onto Don Gaspar Avenue, only a block and a half from the Plaza. The hotel's high-ceilinged lobby has the look of elegance, with classic white columns, Queen Anne furniture, Oriental rugs, and Saltillo tile floors. In keeping with the mood, afternoon high tea is served in the lobby in front of a roaring fire during the winter months or on the verandah in warm weather. The hotel's restaurant features a changing menu from a variety of cuisines. In the summer you can dine in the pleasant garden courtyard.

There's a hint of romance and history throughout the St. Francis. The halls leading to the guest rooms are wide and grand, with white walls, deep blue carpets, and sitting areas next to the stairwell. There's an old-fashioned switchboard right next to the modern pay phones.

The guest rooms, although relatively small, are delightfully decorated, featuring white iron and brass beds, period furniture, and matched petit floral fabric bedspreads and curtains in blue and rose tones. The beds have pillow shams and dust ruffles. The bathrooms, also on the small side, are adorned with marble. Other amenities include safes and small refrigerators.

In order to maintain the hotel's original flavor, the decision was made during renovation not to add a swimming pool, as it would have required altering the building's structure too much. With all Santa Fe has to offer, you probably wouldn't have much time to swim anyway.

Inn of the Anasazi

113 Washington Avenue
Santa Fe, New Mexico 87501
505-988-3030
800-688-8100
Fax: 505-986-9005

General manager: Robert D. Zimmer
Accommodations: 59 rooms
Rates: $150–$200; double, $175–$275; suites, $275–$400

Added: 10% tax
Payment: Major credit cards
Children: Under 12 free in room with parents; $10 additional
  for roll-away
Pets: Not allowed
Smoking: In bar only
Open: Year-round

The Inn of the Anasazi was developed by Robert Zimmer, a well-known hotelier who also had a hand in creating the first-class Bel-Air, Mansion on Turtle Creek, and Hana Maui hotels. With the Inn of the Anasazi, Zimmer wanted to build a luxury hotel, but one that was in keeping with the values of the Native American Anasazi culture.

As you walk past the large terra cotta pots filled with native and flowering plants at the inn's entrance, the smell of cedar incense greets you. The lobby, whose fireplace is ablaze in winter, sets the tone for the rest of the inn. The flagstone floor, potted cacti, and overstuffed leather chairs have a down-to-earth feel — you'll find no pretentious objects here.

The rooms are decorated in earthy colors with pine four-poster beds, down comforters, easy chairs, basket lamps, hand-woven rugs, and folk art made by local artisans. The unusual Do Not Disturb signs — Anasazi motifs painted on blocks and strung on bolo tie cords — have confused more than one guest. While a great effort has been made to create an age-old flavor throughout the hotel, modern comforts have not been forgotten. All rooms have coffeemakers, gas lit fireplaces, safes, televisions, and VCRs. Suites come with a stereo and CD player. A video library is available through room service, and if the hotel does not have a film you want, they'll send someone out to rent one for you.

On the ground floor, guests are welcome to use the library (where the bookshelves interestingly enough are filled with artifacts rather than books), and the living room. There's a wine cellar in the basement that can be rented out for private parties. The inn's restaurant, which serves all three meals, puts an inventive southwestern and Native American spin on such dishes as chile glazed duck with mango cilantro vinaigrette ($16.75) and grilled lamb loin with tomatilla-serrano vinaigrette and a spring squash tart ($19). For a truly unique dining experience, the inn's concierge, who is a Navajo, can arrange special meals at local pueblos for guests.

In-room massages are available, as is aromatherapy. Valet parking is $10 per day.

Inn on the Alameda

303 East Alameda
Santa Fe, New Mexico 87501
505-984-2121
800-289-2122
Fax: 505-986-8325

General manager: Gil Martinez
Accommodations: 42 rooms
Rates: $145; double, $155; suites, $250
Included: Continental breakfast
Added: 10.125% tax
Payment: Major credit cards
Children: Free in room with parents
Pets: Allowed with $50 deposit
Smoking: Nonsmoking rooms available
Open: Year-round

A small, conveniently located hotel offering personal service —that's the Inn on the Alameda. Only two blocks from the Plaza, this pueblo-style adobe lodging is a quiet retreat, secluded from the hubbub, yet within easy walking distance of many attractions. The inn opened in 1986, and in a short time it has become one of the most popular in Santa Fe. Some of its buildings are as old as 80 years, yet the inn has a fresk look throughout.

The rooms are spacious and airy, reflecting their southwestern locale but with a modern flair. Much of the furniture is handmade, such as aspen-pole beds, flagstone tables, and mirrors framed in hammered tin. Wood is an important accent, from pine ceilings to latilla chairs. Most of the rooms have a private patio or balcony, and all have air conditioning, cable TV, terrycloth robes, and phones. The rooms have either one king-

or two queen-size beds, some angled for a distinctive look. Six casitas have private entrances, wet bars, and sitting areas in front of cozy fireplaces. The bathrooms are above average for the area, with theatrical bulb lighting and full-length mirrors.

Breakfast is served buffet style next to the library, or you can have it brought to your room for a $2.50 service charge from 7:00 to 11:00 A.M.. Typical fare is coffee cake, croissants, blueberry muffins, raisin rolls, bagels, fresh fruit, fresh juice, and coffee. At night the breakfast room becomes a gathering spot where drinks are served at the latilla bar. Out in the courtyard, an enclosed blue tile whirlpool is shaded by apricot trees— truly a romantic nook.

But the best thing about Inn on the Alameda is its service. The general manager visits with guests at breakfast, and the desk clerks are sincere when they ask how they can help you.

Hotel parking is free.

La Fonda

100 East San Francisco Street
Santa Fe, New Mexico 87501
505-982-5511
800-523-5002
Fax: 505-982-6367

General manager: James Bradbury
Accommodations: 160 rooms
Rates: $125–$155; double, $135–$165; suites, $225–$365
Added: 10.125% tax
Payment: Major credit cards
Children: Under 12 free in room with parents
Pets: Not allowed
Smoking: Nonsmoking rooms available
Open: Year-round

If you like to be at the center of activity, La Fonda is the place. Its motto, "The world walks through our lobby," has more than a ring of truth to it during busy periods. Right on the Plaza, it's a nucleus for tourists. Step outside to an ongoing Indian market. Walk a half block to St. Francis Cathedral. Cross the Plaza to the Palace of the Governors and the Museum of Fine Arts.

At the hotel you can sign up for sightseeing tours, river rafting, the Cumbres and Toltec Scenic Railway, even trips to the Grand Canyon. You can also start your Santa Fe shopping; there's an art gallery and many fine shops right in the hotel.

While town records show that Santa Fe has had a fonda, or inn, since it was founded in 1610, the present La Fonda was built in 1920 on the site of an earlier hotel. Today's version is a rambling adobe filled with local flavor and a festive spirit.

The guest rooms come in standard, deluxe, mini-suites, and suites. Color spills from the rooms in the form of gaily painted headboards, rich teal or rose carpeting, bright white old-fashioned bedspreads, and hand-decorated Spanish colonial furniture. Sofas and small refrigerators add to your comfort while carved wood molding adds to each room's individuality.

Standing in the halls, you'll swear that a band of elves had a marvelous time decorating everything in sight. Look in one direction to see a flock of birds in midflight. Turn the other way: the air-conditioning vents are trimmed in bright designs. Even the elevator entrance didn't escape.

La Plazuela, the hotel's main restaurant, is in a festive courtyard, where brightly painted windows screen diners form the busy lobby. You'll feel as though you're in Mexico as you eat New Mexican specialties under a skylit viga roof. La Plazuela serves all three meals. Lunch entrées range from $5.95 to $7.95; dinner entrées start at $7.95.

La Terraza, overlooking St. Francis Cathedral, offers rooftop dining during the summer. Weather permitting, lunch is served from 11:30 A.M. to 5:00 P.M. and cocktails from 5:00 P.M. until closing, occasionally with entertainment. The Belltower, with magnificent city and mountain views, serves cocktails seasonally. There's also a French pastry shop and crêperie at La Fonda, and La Fiesta lounge offers nightly entertainment just off the lobby.

An outdoor pool, two indoor hot tubs, and a cold plunge pool are on the first floor. Massages are available by appointment. Covered garage parking is available for guests at $2 per night.

If you're interested in the history of Santa Fe and the area, be sure to stop by La Fonda's newsstand. From outside, it looks like any hotel gift shop, but inside is one of the best selections of regional guides around.

La Posada de Santa Fe

330 East Palace Avenue
Santa Fe, New Mexico 87501
505-986-0000
800-727-5276
Fax: 505-982-6850

General manager: Michael Swanson
Accommodations: 119 rooms
Rates: $110–$295; suites, $185–$395
Added: 10.125% tax
Payment: Major credit cards
Children: Over age 12, additional $10 room charge per night
Pets: Not allowed
Smoking: 35 nonsmoking rooms
Open: Year-round

Only two blocks from the bustling Plaza, La Posada is a world unto itself. Its rooms, spread over 6 acres surrounding a pleasant central courtyard, offer respite from the nearby summer crowds, and each opens on to its own patio. You never feel as if you're at a city hotel.

The Staab House, named for the well-to-do merchant who built it in 1882, is the focal point of the hotel. The main dining room specializes in New Mexican cuisine and features abundant Sunday brunches. The house also has an impressive oak bar for cocktails, a guest library with burgundy leather couches that's perfect for curling up with a book, an elegant private dining room for small groups, and a number of Victorian guest rooms.

The rest of the guest rooms are in adobe buildings that were built from the 1930s to 1987. Decorated in Santa Fe style, the rooms are all different. Those at the lower end of the price scale can be small and dark, while the deluxe suites are spacious and beautifully furnished with ornamental tinwork, handmade furniture, flagstone floors, skylights, colorful Mexican ceramic tile bathrooms, viga ceilings, and kiva fireplaces, all made by local artisans. Eight rooms have refrigerators, and most have fireplaces. Since the accommodations vary so much, be specific about what you want when making a reservation.

During the summer, guests can enjoy the outdoor swimming pool and a leisurely meal on the sunny garden patio. In the winter, guests enjoy the Santa Fe Ski Basin, 18 miles from the hotel. Of course, Santa Fe's renowned art galleries are open year-round.

Service at the hotel can be less than courteous at times, but if you like to be able to walk to the city's sights, La Posada is a good choice.

Rancho Encantado
Route 4, Box 57C
Santa Fe, New Mexico 87501
505-982-3537
800-722-9339
Fax: 505-983-8269

Owners: The Egan Family
Accommodations: 22 rooms, 29 condominiums
Rates:
  Main lodge rooms: $110–$175
  Casitas and cottages: $125–$245
  Condominiums: $100–$300
Added: 10.125% tax
Payment: Major credit cards
Children: Free in room with parents
Pets: Not allowed
Smoking: Allowed
Open: Year-round

When you turn into the driveway at Rancho Encantado, you may wonder whether this is really where such celebrities as Jimmy Stewart and Robert Redford choose to vacation. Don't be deterred by the unassuming sign and unpaved road—in Santa Fe, the best addresses are on dirt roads. Rancho Encantado, in operation since 1968, is no exception.

From the gate, a network of dirt roads winds through fragrant piñon and ruddy arroyos on the 168-acre property. Nestled in the high desert beneath the Santa Fe Ski Basin and Sangre de Cristo Mountains, Rancho Encantado is designed to harmonize with the existing terrain rather than intrude upon it. Although it is only 15 minutes from Santa Fe, 10 minutes from the opera, and 5 minutes from the artists' community of Tesuque, its location feels remote and private.

The main lodge also seems modest compared to similar resorts, but the unpretentiousness of Rancho Encantado is part of its appeal. The lodge's large, dark, southwestern furniture, comfortable sofas, ceramic tile floors, viga ceilings, and small dining room make you feel as though you're visiting someone rather than checking into a hotel. The ranch's "Wall of Fame," featuring photographs of its most famous guests, is in the back sitting room.

The handful of guest rooms in the main lodge are decorated in soft pastel colors and blend marble-topped Victorian tables with simpler southwestern pieces. These rooms tend to be more formal than those in the rest of the resort.

Adobe casitas are the primary accommodation here. Each casita has a refrigerator, kiva fireplace (amply stocked with firewood in colder weather), and a cozy sitting area furnished with traditional southwestern pieces in rich earth tones that complement the landscape. All of the casitas have terraces, but Numbers 25–32 have the best views of the spectacular sunsets over the distant Jemez Mountains.

Twenty-nine luxury condos, with full kitchens, have been built across the road, more than doubling the size of the original resort. Some of them may be rented by guests, based on availability. Rates are determined by the number of bedrooms and guests in your party.

The superb desert vistas and memorable food make dining at the ranch a rewarding experience. Considered one of the best restaurants in the area, the dining room is popular with Santa Feans and guests alike. The menu consists of New Mexican, fresh seafood (a rarity in the Southwest), and Continental specialties. A special menu features meals that are low in fat, cholesterol, and sodium, including a delicious Rocky Mountain trout with sun-dried tomatoes, garlic, and basil.

Breakfast has a decidedly New Mexican accent. Dishes are named for local Indian pueblos, such as Santa Clara and Nambe, and include a number of variations of huevos rancheros, some made with the Mexican sausage chorizo.

Sports play an important role at Rancho Encantado. There is a full-time tennis pro, 3 tennis courts, including one with a basketball net and backboard for pickup games, an outdoor swimming pool and hot tub that are covered and heated in the winter, and a pool table in the cantina. Perhaps the most popular activity is horseback riding, and trail rides leave from the corral twice daily year-round.

Rancho's helpful and friendly staff, many of whom have been here for a number of years, add to the relaxed environment.

Seattle

Alexis Hotel

1007 First Avenue at Madison
Seattle, Washington 98104
206-624-4844
800-426-7033
Fax: 206-621-9009

General manager: Bruce Parmly
Accommodations: 54 rooms and suites
Rates: $145–$310; double, $160–$320; suites, $205–$325;
  weekend and corporate rates available
Included: Continental breakfast
Payment: Major credit cards
Children: Welcome
Pets: Allowed
Smoking: Nonsmoking rooms available, no smoking in Café
  Alexis
Open: Year-round

Subtle elegance is the theme at the Alexis, where city noise fades as you enter the small peach and green lobby. There are no crystal chandeliers here. Recessed lighting, a few club chairs, and a clean-lined counter emphasize the understated motif. The hotel is a polished gem of a quality that has been recognized through numerous awards.

Built in 1901, the classic building went through several hands before it was renovated in the early 1980s. Everything in the present-day Alexis is new except the outside walls and courtyard. Now owned by Kimco Hotels, it's listed on the National Register of Historic Places, as is the Arlington Building next door, which houses the hotel's suites for extended stays.

Located in an area of downtown redevelopment, the Alexis is midway between Pike Place Market and historic Pioneer Square. It's a block from the ferry terminal and close to business centers and shopping. But when you enter the hotel, you leave all that bustle behind.

Rooms are quiet, air-conditioned (though the arched casement windows can be opened), and tastefully furnished in residential style. Suites are unusually spacious. Several have wood-burning fireplaces, down comforters, and wet bars stocked with complimentary juices and sodas. There are 18 room styles on each of three floors. Baths are dramatic in black tile and marble, with toiletries that include such thoughtful extras as sewing kits and travel toothbrushes.

Service is paramount at the Alexis. The no-tipping policy has not had a negative effect on the all-round courteous, friendly attitude that guests encounter. Among the complimentary services are breakfast in the hotel restaurant, your choice of morning newspaper (*Wall Street Journal, New York Times,* or *Seattle Post Intelligencer*), evening shoeshine, turndown service with chocolates, and evening sherry in the lobby. There is no fitness facility other than a steam room, but for $20 you may use the nearby Seattle Athletic Club.

The major change under the new Kimco ownership is in the hotel's restaurants. The Bookstore . . . A Bar, at the First Avenue entrance, remains the same, serving light lunches and appetizers in a bar with shelves full of books (the site once harbored a bookstore). Around the corner, on Post Alley, the Volcano Café is scheduled to open in 1992 with a casual atmosphere and a menu that combines Asian and American regional cookery.

Chambered Nautilus Bed & Breakfast Inn
5005 22nd Avenue N.E.
Seattle, Washington 98105
206-522-2536

Innkeepers: Bunny and Bill Hagemeyer
Accommodations: 6 rooms (4 with private baths, 2 share 1 baths)
Rates: $65.00–87.50; double, $72.50–$95; $15 additional
person; long-term and winter rates available
Included: Full breakfast
Payment: Major credit cards
Children: Under age 12 by arrangement
Pets: Not allowed
Smoking: Outdoors only
Open: Year-round

The Hagemeyers left the East Coast corporate world in 1988 to open a bed-and-breakfast just a block from the University of Washington campus. It's a long way from Connecticut to Seattle, but Bunny and Bill brought a touch of New England with them. Their big blue Georgian Colonial house has the classic atmosphere of a casual, inviting home where the rugs are a bit worn and books are scattered about.

Wingback chairs stand by the fireplace, and coffee and tea are set out on the sideboard. Wicker furniture and shelves of games and cards give the sun porch a summery ambience. Breakfast is served here or in the dining room. Bunny and Bill offer a varied menu of homemade muffins, fresh fruit, cereals, and main dishes, such as quiche or baked eggs. On Sundays, guests linger over a buffet and the newspaper as chamber music plays softly.

The second-floor rooms are furnished with antiques. The smallest room, Northwest Chamber, has a double bed; all others are queen-size. Garden Chamber and Rose Chamber share a flower-bedecked porch and a bath.

Up on the third floor, Crow's Nest is a fir-paneled hideaway with little eyebrow windows above the antique bed. The bath has a clawfoot tub with a shower. Scallop Chamber is the spacious former library, with a private porch overlooking the maple trees and ferns on the hillside behind the house. The third floor rooms are the only ones that accommodate more than two people.

The inn is half a block from the bus stop; it's a 20-minute bus ride to downtown Seattle. Several good ethnic restaurants are within walking distance. Bunny and Bill will make recommendations and are happy to point out nearby jogging and biking trails.

Four Seasons Olympic

Seattle, Washington 98101
206-621-1700
800-332-3442 in U.S.
800-268-6282 in Canada
Telex: 00-152477
Fax: 206-623-2271

General manager: Peter G. Martin
Accommodations: 450 rooms
Rates: $175–$205; double, $205–$235; suites, $235–$1,150; seasonal rates and packages available
Payment: Major credit cards
Children: Under 18 free with parents
Pets: Allowed
Smoking: Nonsmoking floors available
Open: Year-round

There are many reasons for staying at this historic Seattle hotel —the rooms are comfortable, the lobby and ballroom are wonderfully opulent, the list of amenities seems endless—but the best reason is the least tangible: service. It is superb. As one regular guest puts it, "I can arrive at any hour of the day or night, tired from traveling or a late meeting, and know I'll be taken care of perfectly, every time." With a ratio of 1.8 staff members to every room, and with a concierge on duty 24 hours a day, very few mistakes are made in dealing with guests' needs.

The Four Seasons Olympic, in the heart of downtown Seattle, has all the accoutrements of a major urban hotel. There's a brick circular driveway with a fountain and valet parking; brass panthers flank doors of brass and glass; the lobby is stately in gray and rose and marble. At one end of the lobby, a curving staircase leads to the Spanish Ballroom, which has banquet seating for 400. The hotel's original chandeliers, dripping with crystal, hang from a 30-foot ceiling.

At the other end of the lobby are the Georgian Terrace and Georgian Room, where orchid-graced tables stand in low alcoves punctuated with tall palms and stately palladium windows. Black armchairs are covered with tapestries in shades of green, the colors of a northwestern forest. Power breakfasts are the trend here, but are somewhat disappointing—cool toast, ordinary jams, muffins wrapped in so much linen it's an effort to find them. The service, of course, is excellent.

Dinner is much more significant. For formal classic dining and an extensive wine list, the Georgian is renowned. In 1990, the cuisine took an inspired turn with the arrival of Kerry Sears, a noted award-winning chef from Canada. Kerry's trendsetting menus have included such innovative dishes as white truffle pasta with truffle sauce, abalone risotto, and curried banana strudel.

As executive chef, he works closely with all three hotel restaurants: the Georgian, Schucker's, and Garden Court. Shucker's is a more casual San Francisco–style eatery. An oyster motif at the dark, carved cherrywood bar hints at the house specialty—a dozen kinds of oysters, along with other seafoods. Shucker's was recently named the best oyster bar in the city by a regional magazine.

The Garden Court is a green and glittery high-windowed room that is just right for a proper English tea or for a nightcap and whirl around the dance floor after an evening on the town.

When the old Olympic Hotel was first built in 1924, it was the elegant hub of Seattle's social and cultural life, where benefits and debuts and banquets for international heads of state were held. The Italian Renaissance building of buff brick was filled with crystal, antique mirrors, Italian and Spanish oil jars, and bronze statuary; the terrazzo floors were laid by Italian workers brought to Seattle for the project. But after those glory days, the Olympic, like so many big-city hotels, began to fade.

In 1980, a $60 million restoration began, and when the hotel reopened in 1982 as part of the Four Seasons chain, it was again established as a major site for social and business events. It is now listed on the National Register of Historic Places.

A few of its offerings today: interpreters for more than 100 languages, a swimming pool in a solarium, massages, whirlpool and sauna, mending and pressing, complimentary shoeshines, evening turndown, and 24-hour room service.

Guest rooms are commodious and uncluttered, mixing plain beige with splashy floral designs in residential furniture, thick carpets, and heavy drapes. A subdued Oriental theme is evident, as in many Northwest hotels, with brass hardware, porcelain jars, Chinese paintings, and white crysanthemums. There are televisions, telephones, stocked mini-bars, and an array of complimentary toiletries.

Along with careful attention to business travelers and tourists, Four Seasons Olympic caters to children. There are children's menus and crayons to color them, clown dishes, finger foods, and drinks in oversize glasses in the Georgian Room. Child-size robes are available. Car seats, bottle warmers, games, babysitters, and even water wings at the swimming pool are provided at this hotel worth visiting in all seasons.

Gaslight Inn

1727 15th Avenue
Seattle, Washington 98122
206-325-3654

Innkeepers: Trevor Logan and Steve Bennett
Accommodations: 9 rooms (5 with private baths, 4 share 2 baths)
Rates: $58–$88
Included: Continental breakfast
Payment: Major credit cards
Children: Not appropriate
Pets: Not allowed
Open: Year-round

Neither private home nor hotel, this urban inn fills the gap between the two. It's a blocky house, built as a family residence in 1906, with a sense of solidity that is emphasized by the owners' choices in furnishings.

In the wide entry hall, a big potted plant on a pedestal stands squarely in the center of the carpet. Sitting rooms on either side contain sturdy maple and oak antique furniture. The leathery black couch, old-fashioned gramophone with wooden horn, fluted glass fixtures, and green tile fireplace add character.

All the guest rooms have sinks, television sets, coolers, and clock radios. Those with modern bedsteads are queen-size; the antiques are double beds. You can count on comfort, but rooms differ in size and decor. Number 7 is the most whimsical, with brass bed and frontier artifacts—heirlooms from Trevor's grandfather's cabin in the Yukon. Deer and bear heads gaze from the wall, the mirror is framed with deer hooves, and an intriguing leaded lamp shows modes of travel painted on colored glass.

There's an inviting swimming pool in the enclosed backyard.

You'll be well cared for at Gaslight, and the active innkeepers enjoy visiting, but don't expect to be coddled. The inn makes a handy headquarters for independent business travelers and tourists planning to explore Seattle. Many guests are returnees.

A do-it-yourself buffet breakfast of croissants and fruit is served in the dining room. Coffee and tea are available all day.

The Capitol Hill neighborhood, where Gaslight is situated, is a lively, trendy area, full of shops and restaurants—well worth exploring.

Inn At The Market

86 Pine Street
Seattle, Washington 98101
206-443-3600
800-446-4484
Fax: 206-448-0631

General manager: Joyce Woodard
Accommodations: 65 rooms
Rates: $100–$150; $15 additional person
Payment: Major credit cards
Children: Under 17 free with parents
Pets: Allowed
Smoking: Nonsmoking rooms available
Open: Year-round

Open, airy, designed with elegant simplicity, this inn overlooking Elliott Bay has become one of the region's great little urban places to stay. A sense of festivity pervades the atmosphere, partially because of the hotel's proximity to one of Seattle's liveliest, most interesting attractions, Pike Place Market, and partially because of its fresh, bright decor.

You enter the inn through a brick courtyard edged with shops to a white-walled lobby with a fireplace and conversation area. For a more casual atmosphere, you might prefer the deck on the fifth floor, with its greenhouse full of herbs and orchids. There's a panoramic view of the bay, and lemonade and tea are served in the afternoon under the wisteria-covered trellis.

Each of the inn's seven suites has a view of the street and the busy bay. Pickled pine armoires conceal television sets, and delicate watercolors and botanical prints grace the walls.

There's a strong sense of balance and harmony in the hotel's rooms. Custom-made furniture was designed for each individual room, and there are few odd pieces or awkward angles; everything fits.

As a small hotel, Inn At The Market can provide a gratifying level of personal attention to each guest's needs. If you want a private party or a catered celebration, the staff will oblige with imagination and verve.

The Inn has a health room, where weary travelers can get a massage or lie in the flotation tank. Floating in 150 gallons of water mixed with 800 pounds of Epsom salts is said to help recovery from jet lag; there is no doubt that it is relaxing.

Across the courtyard is an excellent restaurant, called Campagne, which serves French country cuisine.

MV Challenger

1001 Fairview Avenue
Seattle, Washington 98109
206-340-1201
Fax: 206-621-9208

Owner/captain: Jerry Brown
Accommodations: 7 staterooms (4 with private bath, 3 share 1 bath)
Rates: $55; double, $65–$125
Included: Full breakfast
Payment: Major credit cards (discount for cash or check payment)
Children: Well-behaved children welcome
Pets: Allowed by arrangement
Smoking: Outdoors only
Open: Year-round

The MV Challenger was built in 1944 as a tugboat for the U.S. Army and then sold to a Victoria, B.C., tug company. The 96-foot vessel with a 765-horsepower engine was used as a working tug until 1981. Now, restored and remodeled for "bunk and breakfast" guests, it's cabled to a wharf on Lake Union, in the heart of Seattle.

You'll never see a tugboat more luxurious than the Challenger. It has a mahogany and oak interior, carpeting, a cozy salon with a granite fireplace and conversation pit, a convivial bar, and comfortable cabins on two decks. Jerry Brown, who opened his waterfront hostelry in 1986, provides ice, glasses, and drink mixes at the bar; guests bring their own beverages. Weather permitting, you'll have breakfast on the deck; crab omelette, French toast with "piggy parts" (bacon and sausage), strawberry pancakes, and fresh fruit are among the dishes Jerry prepares.

Every cabin has its own appeal. Biggest and most expensive is Captain's Cabin, which has a sitting room filled with nautical gear in the former pilothouse, a bedroom with TV, VCR, remote control phone, and refrigerator. Its portholes overlook the lake and the city skyline.

Since the tug was recently moved to a new position on the lake, all rooms now have outstanding views of Queen Anne Hill, Capitol Hill, the Space Needle, and downtown Seattle, as well as the lake shore and boat traffic.

Every room has a phone and nautical clock; most have television. The Challenger has five VCRs for guests' use, and more than a hundred movies. Other entertainment includes an electric piano, guitar, and numerous books and brochures on Seattle attractions.

If you're a qualified boater, your host will lend his skiff, or you can rent boats from several outlets on the lake. They range from classic wooden sailboats and canoes (the tug is near the Wood Boat Center) to sleek yachts.

Lake Union is 7.2 miles around and has numerous restaurants along its shores, some within easy walking distance. Jerry will assist you with reservations.

Roberta's Bed & Breakfast
1147 16th Avenue East
Seattle, Washington 98112
206-329-3326

Innkeeper: Roberta Barry
Accommodations: 5 rooms

Rates: $68–$88; double, $75–$95
Included: Full breakfast
Payment: Major credit cards
Children: Over age 10 welcome
Pets: Not allowed
Smoking: Not permitted
Open: Year-round

When you stay at Roberta's, you are greeted with enthusiasm, told to make yourself comfortable, and offered tea and conversation. This innkeeper loves people and knows what B&B visitors like: a quiet room, a good breakfast, someone who knows the area, and the chance to meet other, like-minded travelers.

The inn, a typical Seattle home with camellia bushes and flowers in the front yard, is in the Capitol Hill district, near downtown and within walking distance of Volunteer Park and several shops and cafés. Four of its guest rooms (Peach, Madrona, Plum, and Rosewood) are on the second floor, and the fifth, Hideaway, is under the eaves on the third floor. Hideaway is a cozy spot to curl up on the window seat with one of Roberta's many books.

Each room has its own bath (though Rosewood's is across the hall), some of them very small and cleverly designed to maximize the space. The rooms are furnished with antiques, but the decor is simple and homey.

Downstairs, in the parlor, there's a piano that guests are welcome to play. The New York Times is delivered daily, books and magazines fill the shelves, and there's a supply of brochures on Seattle sights. Talk is a big attraction here, for the outspoken, good-humored innkeeper enjoys sharing ideas with her guests.

Roberta serves a sizable, satisfying, meatless breakfast at the long dining room table. It often includes huge Dutch babies drizzled with powdered sugar and lemon, along with baked apples and muffins or breads with homemade jam. Some guests hurry off to morning appointments; others linger over a cup of coffee before heading out with a marked map and the cheery reminder to enjoy Seattle and come visit again.

Sorrento Hotel

900 Madison Street
Seattle, Washington 98104
206-622-6400
800-426-1265
Telex: 244206 SORRUR
Fax: 206-625-1059

Manager: Alex de Toth
Accommodations: 76 rooms and suites
Rates: $140–$160; $15 additional person; suites, $170–$325;
  penthouse suite, $700; weekend rates available
Payment: Major credit cards
Children: Under 18 free in room with parents
Pets: Not allowed
Smoking: Allowed
Open: Year-round

You know this hotel is different as soon as you arrive at the entrance and see palm trees swaying in the breeze off Elliott Bay. Palms are decidedly uncommon in this northern climate. The Sorrento keeps them, however, by heating underground pipes in winter—an unusual solution typical of an unusual hotel.

The Italian Renaissance building stands on a hill a few blocks from the heart of downtown Seattle. Its octagonal lobby is quiet and dusky, with indirect lighting creating a relaxed mood. A soft couch curves around a pillar by the Rookwood fireplace, an elaborate period piece of curved tiles with flowers and an Italian garden scene.

Off the lobby is the Hunt Club, a restaurant with brick walls and intimate booths. With Barbara Figueroa as its widely acclaimed executive chef, the Hunt Club is considered one of the region's top dining spots. Barbara, who came to Seattle from Spago's in Los Angeles, offers an imaginative Northwest menu that typically includes oyster mushroom timbales with smoked duck and hazelnuts, rack of Ellensburg lamb with loganberry wine demi-glace, and king salmon served with a ragout of rock shrimp and a corn, avocado, basil and lobster sauce. The menu changes seasonally.

The Sorrento was completely refurbished in early 1990 and won the prestigious Gold Key Awards grand prize in the Luxury Suite category. Antiques and art lend European style to the suites, which were redone in burgundy, gold, and soft beige hues.

Standard rooms have been lightened and brightened in the seven-story hotel, which first opened in 1909. Traditional residential furnishings, goose down pillows, bathrobes, oversize cotton towels, and vases of fresh flowers create an atmosphere of warm, understated luxury. Snacks from Pike Place Market, Seattle's festive, eclectic shopping complex, are placed in every room. You'll also find a jogging map, chocolates in the evening, and even a bed warmer for chilly nights.

The penthouse, with a view of and over downtown skyscrapers, is a good spot for groups and meetings. It has pink walls and ceiling, walnut bookshelves backed by mirrors, a baby grand piano, and a powder room all in black with exotic pink flowers.

The Sorrento is a low-key, livable place, favored by those who like an intimate atmosphere and a front desk staff that remember your name & — personal yet unobtrusive service.

The concierge will supply courier, translation, babysitting, and secretarial services and handle more unusual requests, such as chartering an airplane, if you wish. Whether you need a crib or bedboard, drycleaning or complimentary limousine service, the Sorrento is happy to provide it.

St. Louis

Adam's Mark Hotel
Fourth and Chestnut Street
St. Louis, Missouri 63102
314-241-7400
Fax: 314-241-6618
Reservations:
Adam's Mark Hotels
800-444-ADAM

General manager: Maurice Briquet
Accommodations: 910 rooms, including 96 suites
Rates: $145–175; double, $160–$190; suites, $350–$410;
packages available
Minimum stay: None
Added: 9.475% tax plus $2 occupancy per day
Payment: Major credit cards
Children: Welcome
Pets: Not allowed
Smoking: Nonsmoking rooms available
Open: Year-round

In the shadow of the Gateway Arch, the Adam's Mark is the largest hotel between Chicago and Atlanta. While it doesn't provide the service or grandeur of many large hotels, it successfully combines the old and the new. The hotel is in what was once part of the Pierce Building, a turn-of-the-century office complex. Extensive reconstruction on the site led to the creation of twin towers, designed to provide all rooms with sweeping views of the Arch and the Mississippi River. Many of the antique fixtures were carefully preserved, including ten sets of bronze elevator doors with enamel medallions. A pair of life-like bronze horses, nostrils flaring and heads held high, preside over the lobby.

For convention groups, the Adam's Mark features the 20,000 square-foot St. Louis Ballroom, as well as 21 conference suites, 44 meeting rooms, and three boardrooms. Faust's, the hotel's formal dining room, serves Continental and American cuisine. Try the private library for special occasions. Chestnut's offers a more casual dining experience while a quartet of lounges join the hotel restaurants on the first floor.

Standard rooms are functional. For a room with a view, ask for one ending in 01, 02, and 97. The 96 rooms on the hotel's Concorde Level have access to a lounge with concierge service and other special amenities for business travelers. These include desks, phones, fax machines, copiers, and secretarial services.

The Adam's Mark fitness center has a heated indoor and glass-enclosed outdoor swimming pool, whirlpool, sauna, two racquetball courts, and a fully equipped exercise room. A gift shop, florist, barber shop, beauty shop, shoeshine, and underground parking are also available.

Coachlight Bed and Breakfast

P.O. Box 8095
St. Louis, Missouri 63156
314-367-5870

Innkeepers: Susan and Chuck Sundermeyer
Accommodations: 3 rooms (all with private bath)
Rates: $65–$80
Included: Full breakfast
Minimum stay: None
Added: 5.725% tax
Payment: Major credit cards
Children: 3 years and older
Pets: Not allowed
Smoking: In living room only
Open: Year-round

St. Louis's Central West End is a perfect spot for an evening stroll. It teems with unusual shops, galleries, and outdoor cafés. Nearby, on a well-tended street of historic town houses, is the Coachlight Bed and Breakfast. The original stained glass windows and green glazed brick fireplace are just two of the clues to the home's past life as a elegant urban residence, built to coincide with the World's Fair in 1904.

Baskets of dried flowers and Laura Ashley wallpaper and fabrics mix with thoughtful amenities throughout the inn. All the rooms are carpeted, with ceiling fans, telephones, and televisions tucked into armoires. Excellent bedding includes firm mattresses, lacy sheets, and quilts on antique beds. The Mahogany Room has fabric swags of blue and white over a mahogany bed and a full-length mirror by the dressing table. The Oak

Room has a pair of twin beds (which can be transformed into one king) and exposed brick in the bathroom. The Brass Room has a brass bed and white wicker accents.

Susan Sundermeyer has worked at luxury hotels downtown, so she knows how to treat her guests. Complimentary soda, ice, and a basket of candies can always be found on a table in the common room, along with fresh popcorn. You will find home-made cookies in your room. She knows the St. Louis area intimately, so don't be afraid to have her arrange theater tickets or dinner reservations.

Breakfast, with silver and patterned china set on a lacy tablecloth, starts with a fruit bowl of melon slices and strawberries. A grapefruit half topped with kiwi is followed by Dutch apple pancakes. Add croissant, muffins, coffee, fresh juice, and morning light streaming through arched windows, and you have one of the best morning meals the Midwest has to offer.

Hotel Majestic

1019 Pine Street
St. Louis, Missouri 63101
314-436-2355
800-451-2355
Fax: 314-436-2355
Reservations: 800-678-8946 or 800-544-7570

General manager: Richard Deutsch
Accommodations: 91 rooms, 3 suites
Rates: $155; suites, $200–$500
Included: Continental breakfast; all meals available
Minimum stay: None
Added: 9.475% tax, $2 per room occupancy fee
Payment: Major credit cards
Children: Welcome
Pets: Not allowed
Smoking: Nonsmoking rooms available
Open: Year-round

There is no check-in desk here. Instead, arriving guests are seated with a concierge who personally arranges every aspect of their stay. The elegant touches only begin here, which is why the Majestic remains synonymous with luxury travel in downtown St. Louis.

The circa 1913 hotel, formerly the DeSoto, was refurbished in 1989, reducing its 200 accommodations to 94 spacious rooms and suites. The exterior renovation included restoring the wood windows, awnings, and terra cotta tile. Heavy brass doors lead to the small lobby's wainscoted walls and trim, chintz fabrics, and Italian marble floors covered by Oriental rugs. Fresh flowers and a bowl of red apples pose artfully on an antique side table.

The guest rooms resemble small apartments, boasting turndown service with chocolates, a complimentary newspaper, overnight shoeshine, mini-bars, a fruit basket upon arrival, morning coffee served on a silver tray, along with 24-hour concierge, valet, and room service. There's even a telephone in the bathroom, which has marble-topped vanities, top-of-the-line toiletries (even toothpaste), and terrycloth robes.

The hotel's Richard Perry Restaurant is distinguished by its huge antique clock over a gleaming red oak and brass bar and Toulouse-Lautrec variations in mural form against a back wall. The lengthy menu here includes beef and seafood dishes, sometimes prepared by a celebrity chef. If it's available, try the grilled swordfish steaks or Norwegian salmon, the latter poached in white wine and fresh lemon and served with citrus beurre blanc and tomato fennel fondue. Visit the Just Jazz Bar and Lounge, which features local and national musicians along with a house pianist and singer.

Another plus is the hotel's central location. The Majestic is within easy walking distance of the famed Gateway Arch, Busch Stadium, Union Station, and the St. Louis riverfront.

The Ritz-Carlton St. Louis
1 Ritz-Carlton Drive
St. Louis, Missouri 63105
314-863-6300
Fax: 314-863-3525
Reservations:
    Ritz-Carlton Hotels
    800-241-3333

General manager: Hal Leonard
Accommodations: 301 rooms, including 33 suites
Rates: $140–$215; suites, $350–$1500; packages available
Minimum stay: None
Added: 12.975% tax
Payment: Major credit cards
Children: Welcome
Pets: Not allowed
Smoking: Nonsmoking rooms available
Open: Year-round

The long entry drive of St. Louis' swanky new Ritz-Carlton is flanked by greenery and fountains. Arched windows and wrought-iron balconies distinguish the newly constructed brick and limestone facade. Inside, Italian marble floors, rich wood paneling, jewel-toned tapestries, and fresh-cut flower arrangements blend with a collection of antiques and art objects worth well over $5 million.

Oversized, elegantly furnished guest rooms evoke the feeling of a country home, with mahogany beds, overstuffed club chairs and writing tables, private balconies, and marble bathrooms. Each room comes with the amenities you expect from a Ritz-Carlton: terry bath robes, fancy toiletries, blow driers, and second telephones in the bathrooms. Rooms on the front of the building offer the best views of downtown Clayton, the fashionable St. Louis suburb where the hotel is located.

The fitness center here offers a hot tub, a sun deck, personal trainers and massages by appointment. Even the pool is classy, with its wrought-iron furniture and elegantly draped windows. The Ritz-Carlton Club is located on the 17th and 18th floors, offering its own complimentary food and beverage service and a private concierge.

For meetings, guests can choose from two boardrooms, six conference rooms, and a 200-seat amphitheater. The ballroom hosts up to 1,000 for receptions.

About 15 miles from downtown, Clayton is home to St. Louis' financial district and also some of its finest eateries. The Ritz's own Restaurant has richly enameled walls and serves on crisp damask linen, fine china, and heavy silver. Meals here include fresh Maine lobster, steaks, and specialties such as Baked Rabbit Lori with Spinach and Woodland Mushroom Mustard Glaze. The mahogany panelled Grill offers more casual fare.

Seven Gables Inn

26 North Meramec
Clayton, Missouri 63105
314-863-8400
800-433-6590
Fax: 314-863-8846
Reservations: 800-243-1166

General manager: Dennis Fennedy
Accommodations: 28 rooms, 4 suites
Rates: $98–$126; suites, $155–$250
Included: Continental breakfast weekends only
Minimum stay: None

Added: 13% tax
Payment: Major credit cards
Children: Welcome
Pets: Check with manager
Smoking: Allowed
Open: Year-round

The Seven Gables Inn looks a bit out of place among the glass and concrete office towers of Clayton, the government and financial center of downtown St. Louis. The Tudor inn was built in 1926, inspired by the pen and ink sketches used to illustrate Hawthorne's House of Seven Gables.

Today the inn properly promotes itself as a small hotel that caters to the business traveler, but don't anticipate a luxurious stay. The guest rooms are well appointed, and even the smallest are quite spacious, but the carpeting and paint need touching up since the renovation in 1985. Country French antiques are found many rooms, and cable television, desks, and dual phone lines for conference calls keep you in touch with the outside world.

A nice personal touch is the hand-milled French soap and thick terrycloth robes found in each bathroom and the fine chocolate left on the bed during turndown. Room service brings morning coffee, juice, and breakfast pastries on fine French china. There's also complimentary valet parking and passes to the neighborhood health club.

The inn really shines in its dining rooms. Chez Louis, just off the lobby, is an award-winning French restaurant famous for its wine list; it was a fixture here before the inn opened. The menu changes daily, but seafood dishes with rich herb sauces are always recommended. For lighter fare, Bernard's boasts an informal turn-of-the century bistro and bar, decorated with framed posters.

In warmer months, lunch and dinner are served on the enclosed patio in the landscaped Garden Court, with umbrella-covered tables and window boxes filled with geraniums. Clayton is known for its excellent restaurants, so you may want to venture beyond the inn as well.

Tampa/ St. Petersburg

Don CeSar
3400 Gulf Boulevard
St. Petersburg Beach, Florida 33706
813-360-1881
Telex: 523496
Fax: 813-367-6952
Reservations:
  Registry Hotels & Resorts
  800-247-9810

General manager: Jerome Thirion
Accommodations: 277 rooms, suites, and penthouses
Rates: $115–$245; suites, $205–$600; penthouses, $750–
  $1,000; packages available
Included: Complimentary shuttle service to golf course;
  Kids, Ltd. program; meal plans with some packages
Minimum stay: With some packages
Added: 10% tax; $15 additional person; $15 roll-aways
Children: 18 and under free in room with parents
Pets: Not allowed
Payment: Major credit cards; personal check
Smoking: Nonsmoking rooms available
Open: Year-round

First-time visitors to the St. Petersburg/Tampa area may be unsure of how to find the Don CeSar once they drive west of the two cities into St. Petersburg Beach, but the skimpiest directions would suffice, for the grand pink palace is visible for miles. It's such a distinctive landmark that the National Maritime Association charts this beachside hotel on their maps as a navigational aid.

Opened in 1928, the Don CeSar hosted F. Scott Fitzgerald, Franklin D. Roosevelt, and Al Capone, among other celebrities. When the banks failed in 1931, the founder of the resort, Thomas Rowe, rallied his close-knit staff and they managed to survive the Depression, often working at half-pay. When Rowe died in 1940, after finally getting the hotel out of debt, more trouble lay ahead. After the bombing of Pearl Harbor, the Don CeSar rented out fewer than 100 rooms during the entire winter season. The resort was sold to the United States Army and converted to a hospital. The penthouses became operating rooms, the third and fourth floors became dental clinics, and what is now the Bistro Restaurant served as a morgue.

After World War II, the resort became an Air Force convalescent center, a hurricane shelter, and a Veterans Administration office. At this time, whatever had been preserved of the hotel's grandness was almost totally destroyed. Rooms of Oriental rugs, expensive furniture, and elegant drapes were loaded onto government trucks and carted away. All the walls were stripped of their bronze light fixtures and other appointments and painted a drab green. Some residents of St. Petersburg bought the beautiful furnishings and fixtures, but others were destroyed or sold out of state.

When the Veterans Administration moved out in 1967, there was talk of tearing the hotel down and building a public park. A "Save the Don" committee was formed, and the property was bought by hotelier William Bowman, Jr., who had tons of debris shoveled out of the hotel and hired an architectural consultant to return the Don CeSar to its former glory. The hotel was reopened in 1973 and has since had an additional refurbishment. In 1975, the resort was added to the National Register of Historic Places.

In 1988, during the 60th anniversary of the St. Petersburg Beach landmark, some of the old fixtures salvaged by St. Petersburg residents in the 1940s were brought in by them or, in some cases, their children or grandchildren. Elderly people who'd worked or played at the Don, as it's affectionately called, reminisced about the old days.

Today, the Don has been restored to much of its grandeur. Its architecture is Mediterranean, with a red tile roof, white trim accenting the pink stucco exterior, bell towers, and archways on the Gulf side that lead to terraces and curved white balustrades. A stately vehicular ramp has been built over the highway in front of the hotel, so guests can disembark at the elegant second-floor lobby entrance. Inside are pale marble floors, Axminster rugs, high ceilings, tall arched windows with fanlights, and tapestries, etchings, and original paintings.

A refurbishment prior to the Don's 60th Anniversary replaced heavy Moorish-style furniture with light oak pieces upholstered in pastels. The dark wrought-iron chandeliers and wall sconces were replaced with Italian crystal and with ceramic table lamps in a shell design. The shell motif is repeated in the guest rooms and throughout the hotel. Great care has been taken to recreate the graciousness of decades ago and to restore what remains of the original. This is nowhere more evident than on the fifth floor, where the grand ballroom and conference rooms are located. The hallways and rooms have been redone with elaborate window treatments, large crystal chandeliers, and sumptuous carpets.

In the middle of the marble reception room off the ballroom is a touching remnant of the past, the original fifth-floor fountain. While the original fountain in the downstairs lobby was apparently destroyed or carted away, the fifth-floor fountain was only covered over. It was uncovered and cleaned in the first renovation in the 1970s. Although the origin of this fountain is unknown, it looks Irish, with a woven plaster base encircling a ring of monklike figures, their hands folded piously in front of their robes and water shooting out of their mouths in a most undignified way. This charming, whimsical piece gives a taste of the humor, as well as the beauty, that still grace the Don.

All rooms have thick wall-to-wall carpeting and either a soft blue or a pink decorating scheme. The plaster walls are painted or have subtly textured wallpapers. Furniture is French country, upholstered in designer fabrics and kept scrupulously clean. Forty of the rooms have balconies; others have windows that overlook the pool and the Gulf or Boca Ciega Bay. The walls have interesting angles accented by brightly painted moldings.

The marble bathrooms are of delicately veined Carrara marble, with fixtures of polished chrome. Above the extra-long vanity is a mirror that covers the entire wall. Bath amenities include thick terrycloth towels and stenciled apothecary bottles of shampoo and lotion.

The suites have the same light furniture and pretty pastels, with opulent light fixtures and lamps. Window treatments are elegant, with swags and scalloped valances coordinating with designer drapes. The duplex penthouses are impressive, with spiral staircases and access to enormous rooftop terraces overlooking the Gulf and St. Petersburg. The indoor-outdoor carpeting on the terraces is worn and a little buckled. Perhaps ceramic tile would be better here. But the penthouses are a fine place for a gathering or a corporate reception.

Sunsets at the Don are legendary. Providing the perfect backdrop is the Italianate terrace of tropical trees and bright flowers overlooking the water. Dramatic white balustrades curve from the terrace garden and pool to double stairways that ascend to the French doors of the lobby. Pink stucco shelters with arched doorways and tiled roofs provide guests with poolside drinks and light meals. These small shelters look as if they came out of the 1920s; you can almost see Fitzgerald in a white linen suit, ordering a drink.

The best restaurant at the Don CeSar is the King Charles, which has won awards including the Trans-Culinaire Five-Star. The presentation, service, and ambiance are as outstanding as the food itself. Also at the Don is Le Jardin, a more casual restaurant catering to those who love seafood. Le Bistro is an informal café in a gardenlike setting, and doubles as a nightclub in the evening. Zelda's is a brand-new restaurant at the Don that seeks to bring back the heady days of the Roaring Twenties.

Downstairs, in what was once the original lobby of the hotel, is an old-fashioned ice cream parlor and sundries store. The red broken-tile floors are the same ones that the Fitzgeralds walked on. If you ask the staff behind the counter, they may show you the original staircase, now a storage area, that is hidden behind a door.

Though service has slipped a little recently, especially at the front desk where personnel are a bit cold, the overall performance of the staff is good. Particular effort is put into the children's program: a huge room in the basement is set up like a nursery school, with every kind of activity imaginable during the course of a year. The program is headed by a former schoolteacher.

Visitors who poke around the basement and the restored fifth floor will notice some of the hotel's eccentricities. There is something about the Don that makes it more than a place where famous people once came. It wasn't well-preserved; it was neglected and nearly destroyed. But the Don is a survivor—a grand lady who came through war, Depression, and hurricanes, and was just barely saved from the jaws of the wreckers. Many of the staff have a strong proprietorial feeling about it.

Hyatt Regency Tampa

Two Tampa City Center
Tampa, Florida 33602
813-225-1234
800-233-1234

Manager: Dennis O'Flannery
Accommodations: 517 rooms
Rates: $150–$170; suites, $265–$490; reduced weekend rates and packages available

Minimum stay: None
Added: 10.5% tax
Payment: Major credit cards
Children: Under 12 free in room with parents
Pets: Seeing eye dogs only
Smoking: Nonsmoking rooms available
Open: Year-round

The Hyatt Regency Tampa is a dramatic high-rise of mirrored glass and black steel located in the heart of the city's downtown. It's on the east side of the bay and within walking distance of the City Convention Facilities and the Performing Arts Center. A monorail connects it to the newly developed Harbour Island complex, where Hyatt has another hotel. The whole area has had a recent resurgence with a good deal of civic and private development and redevelopment. With the airport just six miles away, this is an outstanding business location.

The hotel is contemporary and high-powered, the kind of place where people who get things done hang out. A recent redecorating has rooms freshly papered and painted in dominate tones of green, rose, and soft gray. All corporate rooms are on a special second floor. The hotel's 14,500-square-foot Regency Ballroom is Tampa's largest, with a capacity of 2,800, and there are several smaller meeting rooms. A garage-size elevator can accommodate automobiles and boats for commercial exhibits and shows.

The endeavor to make the Hyatt the ideal business hotel is further carried out in the Regency Club, the hotel's special VIP accommodations. These lovely rooms, on two floors accessible only by private elevator key, include Regency Club privileges. Here any special needs are taken care of by a concierge on duty 24 hours a day. Services include hors d'oeuvres and cocktails in the evening and continental breakfast in the club room.

All rooms are fresh and modern, with wall-to-wall carpeting, a choice of two doubles or a king-size bed, comfortable furnishings, and well-designed ceramic tile bathrooms. Some of the rooms are spectacular, with sweeping views of the bay, the river, or downtown Tampa.

At Saltwaters Bar and Grille, seafood is the specialty. Pralines Cafe offers casual eating inside or on the outdoor Patio under the trees. The Hyatt's Breezes Lounge is a gathering place for businesspeople and professionals staying at the hotel, but also for Tampa area executives. It's a convivial spot, made more so by the spectacular atrium, eight stories high with a two-story waterfall, which dominates the lobby.

Although many guests are too busy to engage in a great deal of recreation, there is a healthy dose provided for those who want it. The fourth floor has a health club that includes an exercise room with a variety of Bally equipment, a locker room, and a sauna. On the fifth floor there is a special outdoor deck with a swimming pool, lawn tables and chairs, and chaise longues. This is an attractive area, with the magnificent glass and black steel tower of the hotel rising behind the pool.

Hyatt Regency Westshore

6200 Courtney Campbell Causeway
Tampa, Florida 33607
813-874-1234
800-233-1234

General manager: Gunter Stannius
Accommodations: 445 rooms
Rates:
　Rooms: $89–$145
　Casita Villa rooms: $115–$185
　Weekend discounts and packages available
Minimum stay: With special packages
Added: 10.5% tax; roll-away, $10
Payment: Discover, MasterCard, Visa
Children: Under 18 free in room with parents
Pets: Seeing eye dogs only
Smoking: Nonsmoking rooms available
Open: Year-round

Just 4 minutes from the airport, the new Hyatt Regency Westshore has much to recommend it. Only a few minutes' drive from downtown Tampa, it is an ideal location for the business traveler, yet its 35-acre nature preserve and Old Tampa Bay location give it a relaxing ambiance.

The Hyatt's two excellent restaurants (both on Tampa's Five Best Restaurants List) and the Casita Conference Center make the hotel ideal for meetings. Participants can fly into the airport, stay at the Hyatt Westshore for a week of business, and leave for the airport at the end of that week without ever needing to go downtown. One drawback to the hotel is its location in an area that was for years a marshy territory of struggling businesses. Hyatt and other developers are doing everything they can to change that image.

Tampa's recent surge in hotel construction has resulted in some interesting high-rise architecture. The Hyatt Westshore has a serpentine design of glass and concrete. Its 448 guest rooms and suites have some lovely views of the bay and the hotel's nature preserve. The grounds include two-story, white-washed Casita Conference Center villas, with eight conference rooms and 40 guest rooms.

Both the villas and the hotel rooms are decorated in soothing pastels and French provincial or traditional furniture. The best rooms for business travelers are those on the Regency Club floor. These are quite spacious, organized well for work, and include 24-hour concierge service. A limousine to Tampa's business district is available for Regency Club guests.

There are two freshwater swimming pools on the property, as well as a health club, tennis courts, whirlpool spas, and sailing. Cruises and golf can be arranged through the hotel. The Hyatt Westshore is an ideal place for couples and families, with cosmopolitan Tampa and attractions like Busch Gardens nearby.

Off-hours relaxation centers around the Hyatt's four lounges and three restaurants. The rooftop restaurant, Armani's, serves northern Italian cuisine; Oystercatchers has mostly seafood. Both are frequented by discerning Tampa residents as well as hotel guests.

The Hyatt's lobby is another favorite gathering place. It is a pleasure simply to walk across the floors, which are made up of different kinds and colors of marble laid out in patterns and borders. Throughout are sitting areas of light French provincial chairs, and sofas upholstered in pastels. With massive pillars and archways and a trompe-l'oeil ceiling of leafy ferns, this lobby almost takes your breath away.

Sheraton Grand Hotel

4860 W. Kennedy Boulevard
Tampa, Florida 33609
813-286-4400
800-325-3535

Accommodations: 325 rooms, 23 suites
Rates: $138–$190; suites, $260
Minimum stay: None
Added: 10% tax
Payment: Major credit cards; personal check
Children: Free in room with parents
Pets: Not allowed
Smoking: Nonsmoking available
Open: Year-round

A complex of massive glass and steel cylinders and cubes, the Sheraton Grand Hotel is one of Sheraton's new "world-class" hotels. Only a few minutes' drive from downtown and the airport and connected to Tampa's Urban Centre offices by two eleven-story atriums, this is an excellent convention and business hotel. Its J. Fitzgerald's restaurant has made the Sheraton popular with local gourmands, and recently received a Mobil 4-star rating.

Convention and conference facilities are functional and beautiful, with a professional planning staff on hand to help organizers plan events. The 5,000-square-foot grand ballroom, which can be divided into three separate rooms, opens into a reception area with a spectacular view of one of the atriums. Other amenities are a theater with built-in audiovisual equipment, a boardroom, and eight executive meeting rooms. Sheraton has provided a functional and inspirational place to work.

But this is also an excellent place to unwind and play. Colors of the rooms and suites are restful, with soft grays and pastels. Windows have double drapes to block out the sun on those mornings when you want to wake up late or slowly. Furniture is dark-stained bamboo or traditional. Standard rooms include a desk and have good lighting. Suites have a comfortable, elegant parlor with deep-cushioned chairs and a sofa, ideal for a private conference or for relaxing.

Accommodations include a Grand Club Floor, which caters to the business traveler and includes amenities like calculator telephones. The club room has a homey ambiance and elegant decor, with a mushroom and rose color scheme, carved bentwood and wicker chairs, and vases of orchids and other exotic flowers on the glass tables. A complimentary Continental breakfast is served here every morning and cocktails are offered every evening. A staff is on hand to give directions to downtown businesses, make arrangements for theater tickets, suggest places to eat downtown, and, in general, make a guest's stay hassle-free. Most people enjoy sitting on the couches to relax and work when they're tired of working alone in their rooms.

For unwinding in a lounge setting, The Bar is atmospheric and intimate, with rich, dark woods, soft lighting, and welcoming armchairs. Those who want to people-watch will find the Lobby Lounge a favorite spot. There's piano music here and the soothing rush of waterfalls and fountains from the atrium.

The hotel's Courtyard Café has this same airy, garden feel to it, with a view of the fountains and green plants in the adjacent patio. French doors open out for al fresco seating in balmy weather. Sunday brunch is popular with Tampa families arriving after church or an early tennis game. J. Fitzgerald's, the

Grand Hotel's gourmet restaurant, is an even bigger hit, with expensive and excellent international cuisine. Fresh seafood is a specialty, and the wine list is extensive.

For more vigorous recreation, the heated outdoor swimming pool on the pool deck overlooks Tampa Bay. Enhanced by its airy, lushly planted atrium, the Sheraton is also one of those big hotels that is fun just to walk around in.

Wyndham Harbour Island Hotel

725 S. Harbour Island Boulevard
Tampa, Florida 33602
813-229-5000
800-822-4200
Fax: 813-229-5322

Accommodations: 300 rooms and suites
Rates: $159–$199
Minimum stay: None
Added: 10.5 % tax
Payment: Major credit cards
Children: Free in room with parents
Pets: Not allowed
Smoking: Allowed
Open: Year-round

In Hillsborough Bay, adjacent to downtown Tampa, is 177-acre Harbour Island, a complex of businesses, condominiums, boutiques, a marina, and a luxury hotel. Developed several years ago, it has just begun to catch on. The Harbour Island Hotel is an excellent meeting place for business groups. Views of both the city and the water are beautiful.

Harbour Island is accessible by either car or an air-cushioned launch called a people-mover. The complex shares many elements with the Jacksonville Landing harbor development: brick walkways, exuberant fountains, and a festive mix of boats, shops, and busy people. Across the bridge from Harbour Island is the impressive new Tampa Convention Center, overlooking Garrison Channel.

The hotel itself is beautifully furnished and decorated: the floors are of dark green marble with deep-pile area rugs. Furniture in the lobby lounge is upholstered in rich green wool or variegated tapestry. The massive doors into the ballroom off the lobby are of tiger maple, with distinctive brass handles. Oriental vases with dramatic flower arrangements accent the tables.

The 300 guest rooms and executive suites are geared primarily toward business executives, though they are spacious enough for a family. A standard room has two double beds or a king-size bed, with traditional mahogany furniture, an armoire hiding the TV, flowered chintz drapes, a matching channel-quilted spread with coordinated dust ruffle, wall-to-wall carpeting, and beveled glass mirrors above the bureau. Bathrooms have a marble countertop, a ceramic tile shower/bath, and a large pink shell of soaps, shampoo, and lotions.

Executive suites have traditional or Oriental furniture, a comfortable sofa and chairs, and the same attention to fabrics and amenities as is found in standard rooms. The bedroom and parlor are separated by double-glass and louvered doors. Luxury suites are even more lavishly appointed, and have a dining room table and chairs. The spacious bathrooms include hair dryers and a vase of fresh flowers. All suites have panoramic views of the water, downtown Tampa, Davis Island, and the new Convention Center. The restaurants at Harbour Island Hotel were not well frequented by Tampa residents until recently, but the Sunday brunch at Harbourview Room has become popular with locals and guests alike. Serving American cuisine, it's also popular for breakfast meetings among local executives and professionals. The atmosphere and dress are casual, but sometimes the service is a little too casual. Gourmet Continental and American cuisine is served in the more formal Island Room. The white china and napery on the tables is accented with interesting brass and glass candle holders. Guests are seated at comfortable black leather chairs. Food here is good and service attentive. Garrison's Bar is the favored meeting place for cocktail fans. It has a tropical feel, with potted palms and good views of the waterfront.

The hotel has a large pool overlooking the marina. For those who want more vigorous activity, the hotel has an affiliation with the Harbour Island Athletic Club. State-of-the-art facilities include lighted, all-weather tennis courts, glass-backed racquetball and squash courts, Nautilus and Hydrafitness equipment, and an aerobics studio. At the Market at Harbour Island, shoppers will find 70,000 square feet of clothing boutiques, restaurants, and specialty shops. Subtropical landscaping and festive flags and kites hang from the atrium ceilings.

These upscale attractions provide some enjoyable distractions, but the Harbour Island Hotel is also an excellent place to get business done. The attractively appointed ballroom can accommodate up to 500 for banquets or be subdivided into smaller meeting spaces. There are seven conference rooms connected by a spacious foyer. Services for conferences and small conventions include professional planning and catering.

Tucson

Arizona Inn
2200 East Elm Street
Tucson, Arizona 85719
602-325-1541
800-933-1093
Fax: 602-881-5830

General manager: Patty Doar
Accommodations: 80 rooms
Rates: $52–$150; double, $62–$160; suites start at $120
Added: 9.5% tax
Payment: Major credit cards
Children: $10 additional for children over 10
Pets: Not allowed
Smoking: Allowed
Open: Year-round

A mourning dove sits on the tennis court net and watches two players approach down the walk lined with hedges. Near the fountain surrounded by flowers, a young couple sips coffee. Palms and oleander, cypress and citrus trees, grace the grounds of this estate.

The Arizona Inn is a lady—classic in her beauty and refined in her taste. She seems mature, having acted as grand hostess of the Southwest for six decades. Many of the employees are students from the nearby University of Arizona, and their youth and enthusiasm add spirit to the lady.

From the very beginning, the inn was designed to have a residential feeling and a sense of privacy. Now on the National Register of Historic Places, it opened in 1930 as the creation of Mrs. Isabella Greenway, a sophisticated, dynamic community leader. She was Arizona's only congresswoman, serving from 1933 to 1936, and established a furniture company to employ disabled World War I servicemen. One of the original purposes of the inn was to serve as a market for their furniture, and their craftsmanship can be seen throughout the inn today.

Mrs. Greenway had a hand in every aspect of the inn. She wanted to be sure that her guests could wake up and look out at the flowers, birds, and trees, so she went around the construction site with a makeshift bed to check that each windowsill was at just the right height; if it was wrong, she'd have the workmen change it. It is that kind of attention to detail that makes this place so special. The inn is still owned by the same family (Patty Doar is Mrs. Greenway's granddaughter), and Mrs. Greenway's commitment to quality and service is still at the heart of its operation.

The pink adobe inn is surrounded by vine-covered walls that screen it from the rest of the world. Inside those walls, there is such a feeling of peace and tranquillity that you forget you're just a hop, skip, and a jump from downtown Tucson. Low, residential buildings sprawl over 14 acres of beautifully landscaped grounds connected by winding paths.

The public rooms are grand and gracious. The library, with a vaulted ceiling and polished wood floors, comfortable seating and shelves of books, feels like a lodge. It's the type of place where guests—many of whom return year after year—borrow a book and return it on their next visit. (Notice the large photograph taken of the inn in 1935. You'll see how little it has changed—but the vegetation has gotten taller.) The Audubon Bar, with a white piano and a skylight encircled by a vine, is decorated with 19th-century Audubon prints. One of the dining rooms has hand-colored George Catlin lithographs from Mrs. Greenway's collection.

But the guest rooms themselves are at the heart of the Arizona Inn's charm. Spacious and well furnished, they feel like home. Since the pieces were individually selected and many were made by the servicemen, each room has its own character. Handpainted windows with delicate patterns, writing desks, overstuffed chairs, and sofas are just a few of the special touches in some of the rooms. Guests often become attached to particular rooms. It is said that one guest was so disappointed when his "regular room" was already booked that he asked that all its furniture be moved to the room he was staying in.

The rooms are designated as standard, midrange, and deluxe. Some have fireplaces, many have private patios with comfortable patio furniture, and all have TVs, radios, and air conditioning. The closets are bigger than average because in the 1930s, guests settled in for a season with their trunks, so the closets had to accommodate them.

The inn's swimming pool is a private world next to glassed-in gardens and a bar beneath vine-covered arbors. The porches alongside the pool can be heated on cooler winter days; ceiling fans circulate the air in warmer weather. The pool itself always seems to be just the right temperature. The nearby Har-Tru clay tennis courts give an extra touch of class to an already classic inn. Guests need only sign up on a chalkboard to reserve court time.

Dining at the inn is also a pleasure, especially on the romantic, open-air courtyard. Entrées such as swordfish steak with pesto ($12.95), smoked chicken breast ($9.50), and linguine with sun-dried tomatoes and herbs ($7.95) are deliciously healthful and attractively presented.

Because of the inn's popularity, reservations should be made well in advance—even in summer; and fall weekends fill up very quickly for the University of Arizona's home football games.

Canyon Ranch Spa

8600 East Rockcliff
Tucson, Arizona 85715
602-749-9000
800-726-3335
Fax: 602-749-0662

Owner: Mel Zuckerman
Accommodations: 153 rooms
Rates: Start at $300 per night; 4-, 7-, and 10-day packages
available; rates lower in summer
Included: Meals, airport transportation, medical screening,
local calls, and spa programs
Added: 18% service charge; 6.5% tax
Payment: Major credit cards
Children: Over age 14 welcome
Pets: Not allowed
Smoking: Nonsmoking rooms available
Open: Year-round

Canyon Ranch is a place where people go not to relax but to change their lives. Geared to the health of the body and mind, it's a coed fitness resort and spa that offers a combined program of exercise and nutrition with an amazing array of facilities, classes, and services, selected by the participant instead of the staff. Guests have different goals—to lose weight, to reduce stress, to become more fit, to stop smoking. Unlike some spas, this one attracts as many men as women, all seeking rejuvenation through a healthier lifestyle.

In the Sonoran Desert on the edge of Tucson, the spa offers exercise options that take advantage of the area's beauty, such as hikes to nearby waterfalls and bike rides through Sabino Canyon. The entire complex is connected with paths flanked by desert landscaping.

The spa building itself pulsates with energy. The locker rooms overflow with amenities and are decorated with energy-evoking yellow, red, and orange. More than 30 classes are taught here, from water aerobics to yoga. Personal services are all-encompassing, including massage, herbal wraps, life change counseling, nutrition counseling, astrology, and biofeedback. Facilities include a weight room, gymnasiums, and racquetball courts. Three swimming pools and six lighted tennis courts are also on the grounds.

At mealtime, guests dine in soothingly beautiful surroundings on such delicacies as lamp chops Dijon, paella, and blueberry cheesecake. Menus come with a calorie count and guests choose what they eat. Whole grains, fresh fruits and vegetables, the absence of refined flour and sugar, and small portions are at the heart of the cuisine. Meals are low in salt and have no additives or preservatives, and no caffeine or alcoholic beverages are served. To help guests continue healthy eating habits when they leave, there's a demonstration kitchen to teach food preparation the Canyon Ranch way.

Accommodations are in small buildings scattered over the resort's 28 acres. The standard rooms are fairly small, while executive kings have a sitting area, and casitas have a living room and kitchen in addition to the bedroom. The furnishings are modern and plush.

La Posada del Valle
1640 North Campbell Avenue
Tucson, Arizona 85719
602-795-3840

Innkeepers: Debbi and Charles Bryant
Accommodations: 5 rooms (all with private bath)
Rates: $90–$115
Included: Full breakfast on weekends, continental plus on weekdays
Added: Tax
Payment: Major credit cards
Children: Over age 12 preferred
Pets: Not allowed
Smoking: Not permitted
Open: Year-round

In a fine residential section of Tucson, behind a gray stucco wall, stands this pristine gray adobe with a red tile roof. A fountain adds grace to its courtyard, and orange trees, palms, and colorful container plants are scattered about the manicured grounds. Designed in 1929 by a renowned Tucson architect, Josias T. Joesler, the home exemplifies the early Santa Fe style of architecture. Inside, it sparkles with art deco furnishings.

La Posada del Valle opened as a B&B in 1986, one of the city's first, setting a high standard. The extra touches make it special, from stained glass art to peach potpourri. Breakfast, served in the dining room or on the patio, features fresh fruit, fresh bread, eggs, and French toast or waffles. Guests gather for afternoon tea in the living room, and turndown service is provided in the evening.

Each room honors an illustrious woman of the 1920s. Isadora's room is decorated in pale green, with swirls of geometric designs. Claudette's is mauve, featuring a maple burl king-size bed. Sophie's, done in peach, is one of the prettiest, with a Victorian bedroom set, fainting couch, and an 1818 king-size bed. (The bedroom suite once belonged to a fan dancer at the notorious Crystal Palace in Tombstone.) Each room has a private entrance.

The University of Arizona and University Medical Center are an easy walk from La Posada.

Loews Ventana Canyon Resort
7000 North Resort Drive
Tucson, Arizona 85715
602-299-2020
800-234-5117
Fax: 602-299-6832

Managing director: Johnny So
Accommodations: 398 units
Rates: $95–$305; double, $105–$325; suites, $135–$1,400; golf, tennis, spa, and holiday packages available
Added: 6.5% tax
Payment: Major credit cards
Children: Welcome
Pets: Not allowed
Smoking: Not permitted
Open: Year-round

The setting could hardly be more dramatic. Ventana Canyon, with an 80-foot waterfall in the center, is the tranquil backdrop or the hotel, which is built of deep taupe cement block to blend with the mountains behind. In fact, the natural landscape has been kept very much intact around this new resort.

Loews, with 94 acres of facilities, is part of a 1,000-plus-acre planned community. Next to the hotel is the Lakeside Spa and Tennis Club, with ten championship tennis courts, a lap pool, fitness trail, exercise center, and a spa. Also nearby is Ventana Canyon Golf and Racquet Club, with a 27-hole Tom Fazio PGA golf course. Loews guests have privileges at both clubs.

Behind the hotel itself there's a large, attractive pool (luncheon buffets are served there), a croquet lawn, and a shallow lake at the base of the mountain. Best of all, a path leads to the waterfall—an invitation to explore the mystical desert landscape. Desert lizards scurry in front of you, stately saguaros cover the hillside above, and within minutes you've forgotten there's a world somewhere with traffic jams and deadlines.

The guest rooms, with views of either the mountains or the city, have private balconies or terraces, mini-bars, and armoires with concealed TVs. The bathrooms, accented in marble, feature double whirlpool tubs.

Art is integral to the hotel's decor, from Arizona landscapes in the foyer to original lithographs in the guest rooms. The Ventana Restaurant, serving dinner only, specializes in new American cuisine. Entrées such as range-fed hen with a pecan crust in a honey-mustard sauce and grilled quail with roasted garlic sauce and foie gras range from $17 to $26. Canyon Café has all-day service. The Flying V Bar and Grill serves lunch and dinner overlooking the golf course. After 9:00 P.M., it's transformed into a video disco.

Sheraton El Conquistador Resort and Country Club
10000 North Oracle Road
Tucson, Arizona 85737
602-544-5000
800-325-STEC
Fax: 602-544-1222

General manager: Alan Fuerstman
Accommodations: 434 rooms
Rates: $85–$275; $15 additional person; suites, $110–$1100
Added: 8.5% tax
Payment: Major credit cards
Children: Under 17 free in room with parents
Pets: Allowed

Smoking: allowed
Open: Year-round

Spread over 150 acres of high rolling desert about 10 miles north of Tucson, the Sheraton El Conquistador looks up at the 2,000-foot Pusch Ridge cliffs directly beyond. A resort with a Mexican theme, it's a composite of one- to three-story buildings. The lobby itself is expansive, with many sitting areas and a desert scene above the front desk that is said to be the largest copper mural in the country.

The guest rooms have traditional furniture and southwestern decor in attractive cool colors. All the rooms have private patios or balconies. Junior suites are spacious, with writing desks, cushioned bancos and sofas for extra seating, tie racks and wooden valets in the closet, makeup mirrors, coffeemakers, and telephones in the bath. The most luxurious accommodations are the Casita suites which have their own fireplaces.

A variety of recreational facilities are available, highlighted by El Conquistador's 45 holes of championship golf. Its 30 tennis courts are excellent. There's a stadium court, pro shop, and tennis instructors. About 40 horses are stabled on the grounds for trail rides into Coronado National Forest. Cookout and sunset champagne rides can be scheduled upon request. For groups, hayrides, barbecues, and square dances can also be arranged. Of course, there's a large central swimming pool and a smaller one in the midst of the casitas, along with such extras as ten racquetball courts, jogging paths, and fitness centers.

The summer is an excellent time to get top value for your dollar, with prices for both rooms and recreation at the low end of the rate schedule. There is a Kid's Club during the summer, with supervised activities such as tennis, arts and crafts, swimming, and movies.

El Conquistador's five restaurants and poolside snack bar (the Desert Spring) give dimension and variety to dining choices. The casual Sundance Café serves breakfast and lunch; it has a children's menu, and kids under 6 eat for free. The Last Territory is a rustic steakhouse with entertainment and dancing. Dos Locos, fashioned after a Baja beachside cantina, serves Mexican food and turns into a lively disco after 9:00 P.M. The White Dove is El Conquistador's newest restaurant. Gourmet pizzas, grilled meats, and seafood are prepared with Southwestern flair and spice. La Vista atop the clubhouse at El Conquistador's country club offers panoramic views while dining.

Other services such as a concierge, 24-hour room service, a morning newspaper at your door, free self-parking, a weekly

ewsletter of events at the resort and in Tucson, and a friendly
taff contribute to El Conquistador's appeal.

ucson National Golf and Conference Resort

727 West Club Drive
ucson, Arizona 85741
02-297-2271
00-528-4856
ax: 602-297-7544

eneral manager: Charles V. Dyke
ccommodations: 167 units
ates: $75–$175; spa and golf packages available
dded: 6.5% tax
ayment: Major credit cards
hildren: Under 18 free in room with parents
ets: Not allowed
moking: Allowed
pen: Year-round

'his resort wears many faces. Designed as a private golf club, its
7-hole USGA championship golf course featured the Tucson
)pen for 15 years. As a family resort, it has a large attractive
ool, tennis courts, two restaurants, and several lounges as well
s beautifully designed rooms and suites. As a spa, it has few
quals, offering a variety of services, professional attention, and
exibility in its program.

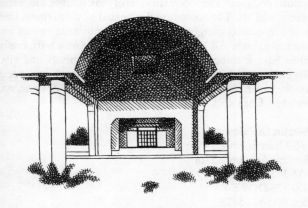

The club opened to the public in 1986. The spa, downstairs in
ne main building, is extremely well equipped. Of course it has
erbal wraps and massages, loofah rubs and body facials, hy-
rotherapy pools and tanning beds. Special services on the

women's side include Swiss showers (water ranging in temperature from 60 to 105 degrees comes from 14 shower heads and sprays from all directions, activating the capillary nerve endings in the skin and stimulating circulation) and orthion machines (back manipulation machines that help adjust the spine through gentle stretching and massaging with rollers). There's also a panathermal (one of the few in the U.S.) that is designed to break down cellulite, along with a Finnish sauna on the women's side.

The men's spa features a Scottish water massage (16 needle-spray shower heads and two high-pressure hoses controlled by an attendant, with varying pressure and temperature) and a Russian bath (a special steam room that opens pores and reduces toxicity, hence reducing tension).

Both men and women have inhalation rooms (eucalyptus and other herbs that help open sinuses and allow freer breathing). The lounges are plush, quiet, and relaxing. Exercise classes include aerobics, water exercise, stress management, and creative movement. The weight and exercise room is adequately equipped. The spa program is extremely flexible: you can enjoy just one of its services, sign up for a whole day, or buy a five-to seven-day package that includes room, meals, and an abundance of spa services.

About 15 miles north of downtown Tucson, the resort is surrounded by 650 acres of saguaro-studded desert. An appropriate setting for a spa dedicated to fitness and beauty, it is artfully designed. The lobby is a swirl of pink marble, fountains, plants, and art. The rooms are designated as villas (hotel size), poolside, casitas (ranging from hotel size to near suites), and executive suites. All have a patio or balcony and a refrigerator. Some have fireplaces. The interiors are large, plush, and visually exciting. While the rooms differ in decor, each has special touches such as beamed ceilings, hand-painted designs, and matched fabrics.

Westin La Paloma
3800 East Sunrise Drive
Tucson, Arizona 85718
602-742-6000
800-876-DOVE
Fax: 602-577-5878

General manager: Tom Cortabitarte
Accommodations: 487 rooms
Rates: $120; double, $140; suites, $175

Added: 6.5% tax
Payment: Major credit cards
Children: Under 18 free in room with parents
Pets: Not allowed
Smoking: Nonsmoking rooms available
Open: Year-round

The Westin La Paloma is a pink palace in the desert with first-class facilities—some of the best in the Southwest. The arched entryway is dramatic, as are the massive arched windows in the lobby that frame the distant mountain view. Just beyond the lobby, a small waterfall cascades over rocks into a lily pond.

The resort's 27-hole championship Jack Nicklaus golf course is challenging, with an unusual layout. It takes advantage of its Sonoran Desert setting while making a minimal impact on it. (Indeed, the developers were so sensitive to the landscape that with careful planning, they were able to save more than 7,000 of the 8,000 saguaro cacti on the site of the resort.)

The tennis courts (8 hard-surface, 4 clay) are top quality, in a scenic setting, and next to a good pro shop. La Paloma's free-form pool, with bridges, waterfalls, and lagoons, is like pools at Caribbean resorts. Hot tubs are tucked away invitingly among the shrubs. And there's more—a health club with racquetball, Nautilus equipment, and aerobics; a spa with massage, facials, waxing, and body wraps; a game area with croquet, volleyball, and bike rentals.

At mealtime, choose from the gracious and elegant La Paloma Dining Room (part of the private La Paloma Country Club), La Villa (in a charming hacienda), and Desert Garden (in the main building). Entrées at La Paloma ($17–$21) feature escalope of duck breast with apples, Dover sole with avocado and crayfish, and grenadins of lamb with asparagus and morels.

Throughout the resort, the look is refined Southwest with a modern flair. Accommodations are in two-and three-story buildings arranged in a semicircle facing the mountains. All are painted La Paloma rose, a color intended to suggest the sunset. The interior colors reflect the desert—sage green, cobalt blue, mauve, and gray.

While the rooms tend to be small, they are cleverly decorated and arranged with angled beds and other interesting layouts. Each has a patio or balcony, a refrigerator, and a remote control TV in an armoire. The bathrooms are also on the small side but have a separate tub and shower, phone, and robes.

Day-care is available for children aged 6 months to 12 years.

Westward Look Resort

245 East Ina Road
Tucson, Arizona 85704
602-297-1151
800-722-2500
Fax: 602-297-9023

General manager: John Dailey
Accommodations: 244 rooms
Rates: $80–$200
Suites: Start at $145
Added: 6.5% tax
Payment: Major credit cards
Children: Welcome
Pets: Allowed
Smoking: Nonsmoking rooms available
Open: Year-round

Westward Look, about 8 miles north of Tucson, glistens on the high desert landscape. It has a wide assortment of sports, a highly rated restaurant, and well-designed lodging, plus a friendly atmosphere conducive to family vacations.

Spread over 84 acres, the resort has three swimming pools and hot tubs, eight Laykold tennis courts, basketball and volleyball courts, a fitness center, and a fitness trail with desert plants identified, plus such extras as horseshoes and shuffleboard. Tennis gets lots of attention at Westward Look. There's a pro shop, a clubhouse, and viewing deck. An hourly fee is charged for court time, but tennis packages are frequently offered. There is no golf course, but the staff can arrange for you to play at one of seven courses in the area.

The Gold Room restaurant, specializing in seafood, veal, and Continental dishes, has beautiful views of Tucson and the mountains to the west—hence the resort's name. Entrées range between $6.95 and $12 for lunch, $16.50 and $22 for dinner. A twilight menu, from 5:30 to 6:30 P.M., offers smaller portions and smaller prices. For light meals, there's the lobby café. The Lookout Lounge has a jazz festival on Sunday afternoons and live music nightly except Monday.

The lodgings are sprinkled over the grounds, with nearby parking for each unit. The decor is pure Southwest, from beamed ceilings to desert art. Each unit has a private balcony or patio, small refrigerator, stocked mini-bar, coffeemaker, wet bar, cable TV, and a choice of one king-size or two double beds. The baths are attractive, decorated in yellow or terra cotta and accented with painted tiles.

Washington, D.C.

Four Seasons Hotel
2800 Pennsylvania Avenue, N.W.
Washington, D.C. 20007
202-342-0444
800-332-3442

Proprietor: Four Seasons Hotels
General manager: Stan Bromley
Accommodations: 197 rooms, including 30 suites
Rates: $250–$295; suites, from $675; weekend and corporate rates available
Included: Shoeshine
Minimum stay: None
Added: $30 each additional guest; 11% tax; $1.50 room tax
Payment: Major credit cards
Children: Welcome
Pets: Allowed
Smoking: 4 of 6 floors nonsmoking
Open: Year-round

Washington is teeming with elegantly refurbished grand old hotels that blend in with the embassies and beaux-arts government buildings of this landmark city. For those who have come to visit the White House—and not stay in it—or for business travelers who appreciate contemporary comforts more than crown moldings, there is the Four Seasons. This brick building nestles up to the edge of Georgetown, just over the C&O Canal and Rock Creek Park. It features one of the finest fitness facilities of any Washington hotel.

The Four Seasons lobby is paneled with light wood and carpeted with a thick pile extending down the wide hall in neutral geometric patterns. Geometric designs are used often at the Four Seasons, and spaces feel wider than they are tall, making the rooms expansive and relaxing. Along very wide, carpeted hallways, the guest rooms are furnished in unsurprising themes with floral carpeting and bedding. Rooms, serviced twice daily and given a full turndown, have three possible views of Rock

Creek, the M Street Canal, and the courtyard. Baths have a telephone and a scale. With children's packages, kids are loaned Nintendo games for their stay. The rates reflect not the unusual aspects of the guest rooms but the emphasis on the impeccable service.

Facing the woodsy C&O Canal at the end of the main corridor are several restaurants, including the Four Seasons formal Aux Beaux Champs, which serves classic modern French cuisine. A waiter is responsible for only one table during the five-course meal. The Garden Terrace is a sunny, tiered area with myriad cozy sitting areas divided by lush plants, where guests enjoy light fare, cocktails, and afternoon high tea accompanied by piano music; the Plaza Café courtyard is yet another option. Downstairs, the Desiree nightclub is a twelve-year Washington veteran of nighttime entertaining, with banquettes and living room seating.

Business facilities include a fax, computer station, and messenger service. The Fitness Club features state-of-the-art equipment, and its three levels have sweeping views of the canal and its foliage through large picture windows. Among the facilities are a heated skylit lap pool, whirlpool, sauna and steam baths, massage, aqua aerobics, personal trainers, and fitness evaluations. Guests receive complimentary workout attire. A nice alternative to the treadmill is the jogging path along the C&O Canal.

The Hay-Adams Hotel
One Lafayette Square
Washington, D.C. 20006
202-638-6600
800-424-5054

Proprietor: David H. Murdock
General manager: William N. Trimble
Accommodations: 143 rooms, including 18 suites
Rates: $150–$375; suites, from $475
Minimum stay: None
Added: $25 each additional guest; 11% tax; $1.50 room tax
Payment: Major credit cards
Children: Welcome
Pets: Not allowed
Smoking: Nonsmoking rooms available
Open: Year-round

Arguably Washington's most beautiful hotel, the Hay-Adams certainly has the city's best location, facing the White House and Lafayette Square. Although this grand old building looks as if it has held a position of prominence since it was built in 1928, its glory days have been recent, since June 1983 when David H. Murdock undertook a massive restoration and renovation of the formerly mediocre hotel. With the help of his wife, Gabriele, who did a magnificent job of interior design, Murdock opened the Hay-Adams to a vastly appreciative Washington audience in 1985.

The history of the hotel predates the building and rests on this landmark site. In 1885, world-renowned architect Henry Hobson Richardson designed adjoining homes on a lot across from the White House for John Hay and his longtime friend and Harvard classmate Henry Adams. Adams, the direct descendant of two presidents, and Hay, a millionaire who had been at one time the private secretary to President Lincoln, were great friends and certainly the hub of Washington's inner circle. Their houses were done in a classic, heavy Richardson Romanesque style and served as the gathering spot for the country's most important guests, including President Roosevelt, who would often stop by for lunch.

The houses were purchased by Washington developer Harry Wardman in 1927 for $600,000. With an additional $900,000 investment, Wardman razed them and erected an eight-story 200-room hotel. Turkish architect Mirhan Mesrobian designed the building after the river elevation of the Farnese Palace in Rome. Faced in Indiana white limestone, the hotel featured intricate plaster moldings on nearly every ceiling and balconies accessible through French doors, and it made tribute to John Hay by copying the Tudor detailing and coffered paneling from the foyer of his home.

Like a quick-burning flame, the hotel fell into the lurches of the Great Depression, and after only four years of prosperity, the Hay-Adams was sold at public auction. The Manger Hotel Company owned the property for nearly forty years, operating it as a transient hotel, followed by several other owners, until David Murdock came along in 1983. The result of the Murdocks' work is a breathtakingly beautiful, fully restored interior introduced by a new porte cochere supported by four polished columns approached by a circular drive. The rich walnut paneling of the lobby is adorned by gilded pilasters, above which are light molded arches and an elaborately coffered ceiling with 16th-century motifs, from which hang several brass chandeliers. A 17th-century Medici tapestry adorns one wall at the entry, complemented by tasseled royal red velvet club chairs and varied precious antiquities.

Up a half flight of stairs, guests have breakfast and lunch in the sunny Henry Adams Room, or afternoon tea and dinner in the several sections of the John Hay Room. The latter is one of the most magnificent public rooms in this book, with heavy carved walnut paneling, brightened by a gilded and light plaster coffered ceiling. Archways are hung with heavy red patterned drapery tied back with tasseled cords, revealing lavish floral bouquets. While one area is done in casual couches and Martha Washington chairs, the other formal dining area has patterned tapestry chairs around tables covered in white linen, dressed with delft pottery holding flowers. Brass sconces decorate walls, echoed in large chandeliers hanging from ceiling medallions. Tea is a beautiful event here, a must on any Washington visit. Tea master Chow, a fixture at the Hay-Adams for years, presents an array of delicacies and teas in the height of etiquette.

The guest rooms are unique; nearly each has intricate plaster moldings and ceiling designs. Gabriele Murdock intended the rooms to feel like lavish private residences. Window treatments are done in light florals or geometric patterns, as is the bedding. The chairs, some wing, others bergères, are beautifully upholstered in silk prints or cotton chintz. The reproduction furnishings vary from room to room — some Queen Anne, some Chippendale — with an occasional antique chair or mirror. Some have structured canopy beds reached by wood steps. Rooms facing the White House have the best views in the city, some of which feature balconies through French doors, some carved mantels. Guests are greeted with bottled water and fruit, and are provided with rich terry robes.

The service is formal, discreet, and high quality, and the excellent concierge service rises to every challenge. The Eagle Grill Bar is a relatively new offering, downstairs from the lobby, a fabulous clubby setting of dark leather chairs and leaded glass under a carved wood ceiling. Nooks under arches are filled with bookshelves, and tables are candlelit.

The Henley Park Hotel
926 Massachusetts Avenue, N.W.
Washington, D.C. 20001
202-638-5200
800-222-8474

Proprietor: RB Associates
General manager: Michael Rawson

Accommodations: 96 rooms, including 17 suites, all with
private bath
Rates: $145–$225; suites, from $325
Added: 11% tax; $1.50 room tax
Payment: Major credit cards
Children: Welcome
Pets: Not allowed
Smoking: Nonsmoking rooms available
Open: Year-round

The Henley Park is Washington's small European Hotel: understated with intimate public space that includes a romantic
restaurant, Coeur de Lion. While 16th Street serves as the gallery for grand old Washington hotels, the Henley Park sits apart
in a rather wanting area near the Convention Center, brightened by the Morrison Clark across the street.

The Henley Park underwent restorations in 1982 that returned the original elements of its 1918 Tudor architecture, including some 119 gargoyles. A pretty brick courtyard welcomes
guests, a white awning stretched overhead forming a carport.
While the eight-story brick and limestone building has a rather
straightforward neo-Gothic exterior, the Tudor features greet a
guest in the low-ceilinged, Mercer-tiled foyer.

The Wilkes Room, to the right of the foyer, is used as a common room and library. Guests lounge in leather wing chairs
and tapestried sofas. Neutral drapes fall from crown moldings,
covering floor-to-ceiling French windows.

Through an archway is Marley's, where, while the afternoon
sun filters through thick leaded glass windows, guests take high
tea of eight varieties. Tea is complemented by scones and finger
sandwiches, sweets, ports, and sherries. Nighttime jazz and
cocktails are enjoyed at the marble-top bar or in tapestried
banquettes and chairs.

The Coeur de Lion is reputed to have one of Washington's
more romantic dining rooms, named for Richard the Lion-
hearted, whose crest hangs above the threshold. The dining
rooms are three separate spaces which begin in the Atrium,
with exposed brick and a gathered beamed glass ceiling centered in a crystal chandelier, laced in greenery. French doors
open to a bilevel dining area with stained glass windows and
mirrored pillars, lavish crystal sconces on gray walls, a background to the strong mauve upholstered chairs. Chef Joseph
Nguyen's French cuisine is peppered with Asian influences.
Entrées range reasonably from $13.50 to $17.50. In addition to
medallions of beef, escalope of veal, and duck, the seafood

offerings are quite strong, including perhaps Florida red snapper, Norwegian or baby coho salmon, or a specialty of baby lump crabmeat cakes with smoked sweet peppers in lemon butter sauce.

On the upper floors, the guest rooms retain the feeling of apartments, with about 12 rooms per floor along a winding corridor. The suites have interesting configurations, and some have kitchens. Rooms are furnished very traditionally, with reproduction Queen Anne and Chippendale furniture, linens and window treatments in soft chintz, with a light color borrowed for the walls. Among the niceties are Lord and Mayfair amenities, nightly turndown, complimentary newspaper, and a stocked mini-bar. Service is quiet and helpful, like every aspect of the Henley Park.

Hotel Washington
15th Street and Pennsylvania Avenue
Washington, D.C. 20004
202-638-5900
800-424-9540

Proprietor: Gal-Tex Corporation
General manager: Muneer Deen
Accommodations: 350 rooms, including 16 suites, all with
    private bath
Rates: $157–$197; $69 family plan offered seasonally and
    weekends
Minimum stay: None
Added: $18 each additional guest; 11% tax; $1.50 room tax
Payment: Major credit cards
Children: Welcome
Pets: Allowed
Smoking: 2 of 10 floors nonsmoking
Open: Year-round

Among the attractive aspects of the Hotel Washington are its location overlooking the White House, its relatively low rates, and the wonderful eleventh-story rooftop café, one of the best places from which to view this planned city.

The Hotel Washington was built in 1918 and has been owned for the last half century by the Gal-Tex Corporation. Maintaining its reputation as the oldest continually operating hotel in the city, the Washington remained open during its two-year $12 million renovation, completed in time for its seventieth anniversary celebration. One of the most costly projects was the restoration of the colored facade, one of the few examples of

Italian sgrafitto in North America. An Austrian artisan painstakingly restored the arabesque sgrafitto designs around the perimeter and between the upper windows, medallion portraits of Washington, Jefferson, and Lincoln, emblazoned in bold red and white on the brick and limestone exterior, at a cost of $300,000.

The two-story lobby features fabulous arched floor-to-ceiling windows which run the entire length of the building, decorated with white Roman shades and framed by dressy pink tasseled drapes. Lit by lavish chandeliers, the wooden molding is richly carved with friezes, columns, and capitals, its themes reproduced in the authentic Corner Bar of the lobby. The furnishings are upholstered in busy chintz and thick fabrics, separated by lots of plants and a set of nine marble urns from the late 19th century.

The Two Continents restaurant on the lobby floor is a lovely room of historic merit. Murals above the windows feature not-so-pithy quotes from George Washington that once served as incentive when the room was used as the Bache Stock Exchange: "Timely disbursements to prepare for danger frequently prevent much greater disturbances to repel it." The Empire chairs and geometric carpeting are formalized by the lush Corinthian columns supporting the ceiling.

Any Washington visitor ought to whisk up to the eleventh floor to have a bite or a drink on the Sky Terrace, which runs the length of the building. From period reproduction wicker chairs, guests can gaze at the lovely city panorama. Ceilings in the Sky Room are 15 feet high, under which enormous windows display views across the Potomac. Three wallpaper panels decorate the walls, by Jardin d'Armide, painted in the mid-19th century.

The guest rooms retain their original doorbells and are now decorated with 18th-century reproduction mahogany furnishings. Behind muslin curtains are old-fashioned lace panels, and cranberry carpeting and light wallcoverings contribute to the traditional feel. The pretty baths are appointed in Italian marble, and amenities include a sewing kit.

The Washington Hotel offers quite special packages for families.

The Jefferson

Sixteenth and M Streets, N.W.
Washington, D.C. 20036-3295
202-347-2200
800-368-5966

Proprietor: Lancaster Group Hotels
Managing director: Elmer Coppoolse
Accommodations: 100 rooms, including 32 suites
Rates: $245; suites, from $275; weekends $145, $180
Added: $25 each additional guest; 11% tax; $1.50 room tax
Payment: Major credit cards
Children: Welcome
Pets: Small pets allowed
Smoking: Nonsmoking rooms available
Open: Year-round

The Jefferson is most certainly a refuge for gourmets, with the new Virginia cuisine of its extremely young award-winning chef Will Greenwood; yet it is also a memorably romantic retreat, with its plush, individually decorated rooms, intimate, nearly residential scale, and its standing as one of Washington's great grand old hotels.

Four blocks from the White House, next to the National Geographic Society, the Jefferson is the height of Washington sophistication imbued with European grace. Originally built as a residence in 1923, the U-shaped beaux-arts building is eight stories of light stone. The subtle entrance is marked by wood doors under a single-story portico of intricately carved stone, topped by a Palladian fan window and wrought-iron detailing. The understated reception desk introduces the Atrium Court, one of the more beautiful reception halls in Washington. The long single-story barrel-vaulted corridor, the open part of the U shape, looks rather like a lost wing of the National Gallery. This main breezeway is flanked by two small atriums with fountains, where guests may have breakfast in a cool, shaded light. The elaborate plaster moldings and trim, from the Doric columns to the arched vaulting, are painted a soothing ecru, contrasting well with the light cream walls. Three formal Federal parlor sets divide the Atrium Court into separate areas, with brushed velvet sofas, attenuated wing chairs, linked by classic benches along the wall. The back of the Atrium Court is marked by a faux marble fireplace flanked by green faux marble Ionic columns under a portrait of Lafayette. The marble floors are covered with Oriental carpets.

The hallways on the guest floors are graced with beautiful lithographs and architectural drawings. Each of the 100 guest rooms is decorated in surprisingly different and boldly successful colors and patterns, all with unusual antiques, classic reproductions, and creative window and bed treatments. While Room 810 is decorated in soft champagne tones, Room 811 is done in a splashy but classic orange plaid, with a fitted crown canopy over the king-size bed. Some beds have upholstered headboards matching their linens, and others have rich wood sleigh beds. Some have French doors leading to bedrooms, others have working fireplaces or whirlpool baths. While televisions and VCRs are in each room, the suites are furnished with armoires housing mini-bars and compact disc players. Among the amenities are robes and hair dryers in the baths, which have charming flowered porcelain fixtures. Guests are greeted with a half bottle of red wine, and rooms are serviced with nightly turndown.

The Jefferson Lounge, to the right of the Atrium Court, is a clubby place, with leather chairs, red walls, and a fireplace under a nautical oil painting. The intimate, L-shaped restaurant is quite striking, with wood floors and tufted leather banquettes. The wall rounds slightly between the classic white crown moldings, textured in an interesting faux burl finish and graced with historic 18th-century prints, some of which hung in the White House and Blair House at one time.

Will Greenwood's menu changes daily. A choice of appetizers might include plantation corncake with smoked salmon and chive cream, wild rice and pheasant cakes with shiitake mushroom essence, or crab hush puppies with red pepper marmalade. Entrées, all below $20, could include venison escalops with lingonberry sauce and chestnut spoonbread or smoked pork chop roasted with cider honey glaze served with sweet potato hotcakes. The desserts are highly acclaimed, as is the extensive wine list.

Service is impeccable. Beyond the formality, the staff is genuinely friendly, personable, and solicitous.

The Mayflower—A Stouffer Hotel
1129 Connecticut Avenue, N.W.
Washington, D.C. 20036
202-347-3000
800-468-3571

Proprietor: Stouffer Hotels
General manager: Bernard Awenenti
Accommodations: 680 rooms, including 68 suites
Rates:
  Weekdays: rooms, $210; suites, $375
  Weekends: rooms, $135; suites, $185
Included: Coffee and newspaper with wake-up call
Added: 11% tax; $1.50 room tax
Payment: Major credit cards

Children: Welcome
Pets: Small pets allowed
Smoking: 1 of 9 floors nonsmoking
Open: Year-round

Two weeks after its opening, the Mayflower hosted 6,000 guests at Calvin Coolidge's inaugural ball on March 4, 1925. This event exemplifies the enormity of scale and richness of history that the Mayflower represents in Washington. This historic property completed a $10 million renovation that focused on accommodations in 1991.

The construction of the hotel was delayed three years because of such unplanned obstacles as fossilized tree stumps, quicksand, and an underground stream. In 1925, at a cost of $12 million, the block-long neoclassic Mayflower opened with 1,057 guest rooms, furnished with 25,000 pieces of furniture that took three months to install. The ten-story brick building was designed by Warren and Wetmore of New York, who also designed Grand Central Station. A promenade one-tenth of a mile long served as a public hallway between blocks, with Oriental rugs, sculpture, and more gold leaf than any building in the country outside the Library of Congress. Upholstery and carpentry shops were instituted in the hotel, as well as a medical clinic for its one thousand employees.

The 1950s ushered the Mayflower into a self-conscious era during which it scaled down its glories to appeal to the masses: the 24-karat detailing was covered by paint, wood paneling replaced the lobby's marble pillars, the chandeliers were stored, and the bronze doors were traded for stainless steel and glass.

A caring group of Washingtonians bought the underappreciated Mayflower in 1965 and invested $65 million in its resurrection. By 1985, the hotel was once again the grande dame it was born to be. The reproduction trim and crown moldings measured more than 50 miles. Bathrooms received 46,800 square feet of marble. The capitals and ceiling glimmered in gold once again. Most recently, Stouffer Hotels bought the Mayflower and completed its most recent refurbishments.

On Connecticut Avenue taking up the entire block between L and M streets in the center of businesses and shops, the Mayflower seems to urge guests not to leave. Its famous promenade holds an arcade of shops, as well as the formal Nicholas restaurant offering new American and mid-Atlantic cuisine, the informal Café Promenade, the Town & Country Lounge for entertainment, and the Lobby Lounge. The two-story lobby has the grandeur of a ballroom, with marble flooring, plaster pillars topped by gilded capitals and crown molding, observed from a second-floor balcony that wraps around the room.

The guest rooms needed a face lift and are quite lovely today, with custom-made Henredon reproduction furnishings and upholstery and fabrics consistent with the Federal period. For such a large property, service is surprisingly available at every turn.

Morrison Clark

Massachusetts Avenue and Eleventh Street, N.W.
Washington, D.C. 20001
202-898-1200
800-332-7898
Restaurant: 202-289-8580

Innkeeper: Lorraine F. Lucia
Accommodations: 54 rooms, including 12 parlor suites in
   addition and 12 Victorian suites in older portion
Rates: Weekday, $115–$195; weekend, $99–$135
Included: Continental breakfast
Minimum stay: None
Added: 11% tax plus $1.50 occupancy
Payment: Major credit cards
Children: Welcome
Pets: Not allowed
Smoking: Nonsmoking rooms available, no smoking in
   restaurant
Open: Year-round

In a town dominated by large hotels, the Morrison Clark stands alone as a boutique inn of unusual refinement and luxury. The reasons for its outstanding nature are twofold: the creativity of Albert Massoni and his partner Royce LaNier, who masterminded the project from its outset to its 1989 opening and saved a crumbling piece of history, and the talents of chef Susan McCreight Lindeborg, who oversees lunch and dinner every day but Sunday. The food is exceptional.

The historic property, twin three-story brick houses that served for years as the Soldiers and Sailors Club, was built in 1864 by business partners David Morrison and Reuben Clark. As the club attracted a greater following, the property was enlarged in 1876. In 1917, the distinctive Chinese-influenced verandah was sewn onto the front, and from 1923 to 1980, the club was used as the Woman's Army and Navy League gathering spot. The houses then fell into sad disrepair until preservationist Albert Massoni came to the helm in 1987, undertaking a massive and laudable restoration effort. Today, the inn nearly gleams with pride, the old part renewed to its former glory and a new addition with 42 guest rooms complementing the historic lines in postmodern understatement.

The original mansion has twelve Victorian suites on the second and third floors, with wonderful high ceilings, enormous windows, some with heavy brocaded window treatments, colorful reproduction Victorian wallpaper borders, some stunning armoires containing televisions and stereos, and beautiful period furnishings including antique chairs, writing desks, marble-top dressers, and lavish carved wood headboards. The baths are elegantly appointed with marble and sophisticated amenities. Some of these rooms have porches. Quite notable is the artwork on display in the hallways and rooms.

The rooms and parlor suites in the new L-shaped wing have a strikingly different feel in two different decor schemes: a simple country French wing at the back of the inn, and a neoclassic wing that parallels Eleventh Street. The custom-designed furniture in the neoclassic wing is quite intriguing, with clean, masculine, modern lines, Roman shades, and complementary artwork. Service is exceptional, with nightly turndown, twice-daily maid service, morning newspaper, room service, and in-room movie rentals.

The common rooms and dining rooms at the Morrison Clark are simply beautiful. The foyer is a parquet marble, with a huge floral centerpiece on a precious round table, set off by deep rust-colored walls. Daunting, heavy mahogany doors lead to the breakfast room and bar, one of five dining areas, with floor-to-ceiling windows, and carved marble fireplace mantel. An intimate dining room follows, with a circular banquette, high ceilings, and enormous windows covered in diaphanous white curtains, lending a soft light to the room. Other dining areas are in the exterior courtyard between the wings of the houses, on the Chinese verandah, and in the sunny solarium.

Dinners in this eclectic and elegant setting are orchestrated by Susan Lindeborg, a noted pastry chef whose talents have expanded to great acclaim. Her vegetables and side dishes are called sensational, memorable, and luscious by local reviewers. A dinner might begin with an appetizer of goat cheese and roast garlic flan with tart tomato fondue, or stuffed quail with grilled polenta and ancho chili sauce. Warm leek salad with pommery mustard and honey dressing might follow; or perhaps a salmon chowder with tomato and ginger. Entrées are quite reasonably priced for the capital, under $20. Among the baffling choices are beef tenderloin with two-mustard Laphroaig Scotch sauce; tuna steak with grilled vegetables and semolina gnocchi; grilled salmon with green lentils, applewood bacon, and horse-radish; or grilled lamb leg with coriander sauce and couscous. The setting is a lovely backdrop to the delicious meal.

Park Hyatt
24th and M Streets, N.W.
Washington, D.C. 20037
202-789-1234
800-922-7275

Proprietor: Hyatt Regency Corporation
General manager: Paul Limbert
Accommodations: 224 rooms, including 130 suites
Rates: $285–$310; suites, from $405; weekends, $159 and $199
Added: $30 each additional guest; 11% tax; $1.50 room tax
Payment: Major credit cards
Children: Welcome
Pets: Allowed
Smoking: Nonsmoking floors available
Open: Year-round

While 16th Street is the bastion of grand old Washington hotels, a cluster of grand new hotels has opened on the corner of 24th and M streets. Its finest offering is the Park Hyatt, which opened in 1986, designed by Skidmore, Owings, and Merrill. Its first two stories of stone and plentiful glass house the public spaces and Melrose restaurant. The ten higher stories for guest rooms rise above in stone, culminating in a green copper roof.

Guests enter a massive double-height lobby, with floors in two-toned herringbone marble, walls in softer beige and brown marble decorated with contemporary paintings from the Washington Color School and Oriental sculpture, and several precious works by Pablo Picasso and Frank Stella. Glimmering brass, rose and mauve-toned wool carpets, and furnishings upholstered in velvet, silk, and mohair create a grand contemporary space, enjoyed best during afternoon high tea where visitors listen to piano music and muse over French pastries, finger sandwiches, and individual pots of tea over candle warmers. A palm reader circulates Wednesdays and Thursdays — her most certain prediction being that evening caviar and champagne will be served in this setting several hours hence.

On the ground floor, in two stories of enclosed glass, is the Melrose restaurant. Chef Kenneth Juran prepares contemporary American cuisine, in a $34 prix fixe or and à la carte menu, which could include appetizer of angel hair pasta with fresh Maine lobster, mascarpone cheese, tomato, and herbs; or an entrée of Lake Superior whitefish with olive paste and wild mushroom risotto. Melrose overlooks the outdoor café, where guests may enjoy light fare to the sounds of the fountain and scents of surrounding flowers — as late as 3 A.M. on weekends.

The rooms at the Park Hyatt were designed larger than the average, with a majority of suites to which all guests will be upgraded on availability. Contemporarily furnished with light pecan wood, in a pasteled decor of rose, seafoam green, and peach walls and beige and peach carpeting, all rooms have at least a separate dressing area as well as a sitting area and full writing desks. The baths are quite luxurious, done in full marble, with brass and chrome fittings, a phone and television, hair dryer, terry robes, and Crabtree & Evelyn amenities with the bonus of toothbrushes and paste. In addition to evening turndown, guests receive a morning newspaper. Among other amenities are complimentary shoeshine and foreign currency exchange.

Guests have full use of the Health Club, with Nautilus, pool and Jacuzzi, and massage, steam, and sauna rooms. The Rendez-Vous in the Park Salon is well recommended by First Lady Barbara Bush, who has her hair done here. The salon also offers manicures, pedicures, and massages. In addition, the mezzanine level of the Park Hyatt has a full business center, the Write Choice.

The Ritz-Carlton

2100 Massachusetts Avenue, N.W.
Washington, D.C. 20008
202-293-2100
800-241-3333

Proprietor: The Ritz-Carlton Hotel Company
General manager: Marcos Bekhit
Accommodations: 230 rooms, including 23 suites
Rates: $195–$380; suites, from $500
Added: $30 each additional guest; 11% tax; $1.50 room tax
Payment: Major credit cards
Children: Welcome
Pets: Not allowed
Smoking: Nonsmoking rooms available
Open: Year-round

This property was once the grande dame Fairfax Hotel — the Fairfax had been a sophisticated Washington fixture since it was built in 1927 and was home to the famous Jockey Club restaurant for more than 20 years. The Ritz-Carlton Hotel Company adopted the hotel and has incorporated its Old World sophistication. The two-story portico on the corner of 21st Street and Massachusetts Avenue rests on a brick drive, separated from traffic by a sculpted hedge. Six columns support the flat stone facade, part of a pentagon, and guests enter under a white awning, repeated in domed forms across the ground floor windows. Sister Parish was brought in from Great Britain to redecorate the entire property as an English country manor house, with dark wooded librarylike parlors, formal Federal hallways, and bright yellow and blue accommodations decorated in chintz. The extensive art collection begs a guest to meander through the hallways gazing at the 18th-and 19th-century oil paintings. In true Anglophile fashion, the themes are often nautical or equestrian — of the races, the hunt, or portraits of beloved hunting dogs poised at attention.

At any Ritz-Carlton, the reception desk is warm and understated, here leading to elevator banks and the Fairfax Bar at the back of the hotel. This wonderful lounge and gathering spot is the setting for afternoon high tea. Sweets and scones, salmon, and cucumber and tomato sandwiches are served in front of the wood-burning fireplaces. Decorative shadow boxes rest in the neighboring Potomac Room, plush with tapestried pillows, banquettes, and leather wing chairs.

Since it opened in 1961 on the eve of President Kennedy's inauguration, the familiar Jockey Club has been an insider's restaurant. It has the atmosphere of an English tap room, with dark paneled walls, sporting art, and white and red linens. Recently, the sophisticated menu was appended to accommodate children in the form of a coloring book featuring Carlton the lion, and offering suitable choices like peanut butter and marshmallow, spaghetti and meatballs, and banana splits.

The rooms are done in the height of British good taste, with bright chintz fabric covering the club chairs, the beds, and the floor-to-ceiling drapes. The two-poster custom-designed beds in dark wood match the end tables and writing desks. The walls are either a buttery yellow or robin's egg blue. Guests can expect such luxuries as 24-hour room service, nightly turndown, and terry robes. The top two floors denote the Ritz-Carlton Club, with special concierge service, use of the Federal parlor, and five complimentary food presentations, including Continental breakfast, a midday snack, tea, cocktails and hors d'oeuvres, and chocolate and cordials.

The staff is reliably professional and highly trained in Ritz-Carlton etiquette at this classic property. For aficionados, new Ritz-Carlton properties opened in 1991 in two Washington suburbs, Tysons Corner and Pentagon City. Each has a deluxe fitness center and pool, and both are in the heart of suburban shopping.

The Sheraton Carlton
923 16th Street at K Street, N.W.
Washington, D.C. 20006
202-638-2626
800-325-3535

Proprietor: The Sheraton Corporation
General manager: Michel J. Ducamp
Accommodations: 197 rooms, including 13 suites
Rates: $210–$240; suites, $340–$875
Included: Complimentary shoeshine and newspaper
Added: $25 each additional guest; 11% tax; $1.50 room tax
Payment: Major credit cards
Children: Under 17 free in room with parents
Pets: Check with manager

Smoking: 2 nonsmoking floors
Open: Year-round

The Sheraton Carlton is one of those classic buildings that has been a quiet, consistent fixture of elegance for years—like the Junior League or the country club. Two blocks from the White House, the Carlton hotel was built in 1926 to resemble an Italian Renaissance palace, eight stone stories high. It has been the flagship property of the Sheraton Corporation since the 1950s. Just recently, between 1988 and 1990, $20 million was invested in the Sheraton Carlton's restoration and renovation.

Guests enter a semicircular drive to a gilded carport. Domed awnings cover the Palladian windows that span the first floor. Inside, the grand lobby is the hotel's treasure, the backdrop for afternoon tea, set to the music of a harpist. Classic and intimate parlor settings cluster over an expansive Oriental carpet. Most breathtaking is the open-beamed, dark wood ceiling, magnificently carved, lit softly by two crystal chandeliers. Four mullioned arched windows stretch to the ceiling, framed by heavy drapery.

Some grand architectural details are echoed in Allegro, the Carlton's restaurant around the corner from the lobby, featuring fine Italian food. The dark beamed ceilings are done in similar deep wood, with less ornate carving, complementing the mahogany bar. The original sconces and freestanding lamps are wonderful art deco specimens, their smoky glass shades in the shape of flower petals. The Palladian windows continue around the perimeter, made into mirrors on the back wall.

The guest rooms, benefiting from the recent renovation, are unusually elegant. In addition to stocked mini-bars, terry robes on satin hangers, a safe, and a television hidden in an armoire, the rooms have been decorated with care in several different schemes. The suites are especially nice, decorated to fit the original period of the hotel in neutral and pale blue shades. All the baths have marble walls and floors, makeup mirrors, hair dryers, and television speakers.

Special touches at the Sheraton Carlton add convenience: exercise equipment will be delivered to a guest room if one doesn't wish to trudge to the Exercise Room. The hotel is one of the few in the city with a special welcoming service to its younger guests, who, under 17, are free in parent's room in existing bedding. In the Carlton Kids program, children are greeted with a variety of toys and games, including Nintendo, Trivial Pursuit, and board games. Nightly turndown consists of milk and cookies. Infants receive a basket of Pampers and a stuffed animal. The lower level of the hotel houses a salon, and also a celebrity of sorts: resident barber Milton Pitts has been cutting hair for presidents, except Carter, since 1969.

The Watergate Hotel
2650 Virginia Avenue, N.W.
Washington, D.C. 20037
202-965-2300
800-424-2736

Proprietors: Trustehouse Forte and Cunard Hotel Group
Managing director: Ibrahim Fahmy
Accommodations: 235 rooms, half of which are suites
Rates: $240–$350; suites from $450; weekends, $145–$185, suites from $225
Included: Use of health club facilities
Minimum stay: None
Added: $25 each additional guest; 11% tax; $1.50 room tax
Payment: Major credit cards
Children: Under 14 free in room with parents
Pets: Allowed
Smoking: Nonsmoking rooms available, no smoking in restaurant
Open: Year-round

Most people would recognize the Watergate Hotel, but perhaps not from the newest face it puts forward. Though the exterior looks the same—still a modern collection of scalloped buildings trimmed with balconies that overlook the Potomac—the interior is impressively improved. The Trustehouse Forte Hotel Group acquired the landmark hotel in the spring of 1990 and redecorated all the guest rooms to their current state of elegance. In addition, the hotel was given a fantastic new health club, the plushest in Washington hotels. Most exciting is its two-star Michelin chef Jean-Louis Palladin, Washington's only chef to have earned five stars from the Mobil guide for his culinary mastery.

The Watergate has quite an international clientele, with half of its guests from overseas. The staff prides itself on its linguistic versatility. The lobby is a glistening display of polished marble, the setting for afternoon high tea. Guest rooms hover above, and about half have balconies and views of the Potomac River on whose banks the hotel sits, next to the Kennedy Center. Not including the deluxe suites, there are three tiers of regular guest rooms at the Watergate in several types of traditional decor.

The rooms are furnished with dark wood reproduction furniture, and chintz fabrics in light colors, rusts, or blues decorate the windows and beds. Period reproduction highboys contain remote televisions, videos, and tape decks, and all rooms have stocked mini-bars. The baths are appointed in light marble, with dryers and a basket of Gilchrest and Soames amenities.

In a fairly glamourous marbled setting, the health club offers several rooms equipped with a Nautilus gym, a 25-by-30-foot lap pool, a whirlpool, and saunas. The lockers are done in light oak, and adjacent rooms offer massages.

Jean-Louis's dining room is an incredible spot, with only twelve tables in a mystical, dim setting, lit obliquely behind swatches of silk which hang from the walls under a smokily mirrored ceiling. The menu is boldly handwritten in flourishes by the chef in French, with a typed English translation, and it changes like the palette of a working artist. Jean-Louis offers two fixed price selections at $85 or $95. The experience might proceed as follows: a crab soup with small crabcakes and quenelles; a salad of fresh seaweed, macerated with sesame, smoked salmon, and ginger; roasted saddle of rabbit with herbs and marrow flan, a julienne of celery root and truffles; followed by tiramisu with coffee coulis and cacao ice cream.

The plusher menu offers six courses, which proceed as follows: celery root soup with rabbit sausage, truffle quenelle, and fresh truffle; Santa Barbara abalone with enoki mushrooms; fresh American duck foie gras with rhubarb; fresh salmon wrappped with a leaf, concassée of tomato and black olives, butter of epazote; followed by mignon of Pittsburgh lamb with cheese ravioli and spices; finishing with a symphony of pears.

The Willard Inter-Continental

1401 Pennsylvania Avenue, N.W.
Washington, D.C. 20004
202-628-9100
800-327-0200

Proprietor: Willard Associates and the Oliver Carr Company
General manager: Graham K. L. Jeffrey and
   Inter-Continental Hotels
Accommodations: 365 rooms, including 65 suites
Rates:
   Weekdays: rooms, $265–$355; suites, from $500
   Weekends and winter: $145–$165
Added: $25 each additional guest; 11% tax; $1.50 room tax
Payment: Major credit cards

Children: Welcome
Pets: Not allowed
Smoking: Nonsmoking rooms available
Open: Year-round

The Willard is basking in the relatively new limelight of its third incarnation. After sitting vacant and boarded up since 1968, the Willard received $74 million worth of attention and was reintroduced to Washington society in 1986 with great fanfare.

The site on which the glorified Willard now sits, catercorner from the White House, has served as a hostelry since 1816. In 1850, the land was bought by Henry Willard, who transformed the property into a 100-room hotel with the help of his brothers Edwin and Joseph. The Willard sat at the focal point of political activity. After receiving death threats, Abraham Lincoln lived secretly at the Willard from February 23 until his inauguration on March 4, 1861. The same year, Julia Ward Howe wrote the "Battle Hymn of the Republic" in her Willard guest room.

When the Willards decided to expand their accommodations, they hired famed architect Henry Janeway Hardenbergh, who had designed such treasures as the Waldorf-Astoria, the Plaza, and the Dakota apartments in New York. Completed in 1904, the Willard was one of the city's first skyscrapers, twelve stories of lavish French Second Empire beaux-arts architecture, reinforced in steel. The hotel prospered, though gradual decline came after the Second World War, when the Willard family sold the property for $5 million. Under new ownership, the hotel survived until 1968. Just several months before the hotel closed its doors, Martin Luther King wrote his "I Have a Dream" speech in his guest room.

In 1976, the Pennsylvania Avenue Development Corporation paid $8 million for the decrepit Willard, inviting bidders in 1978 to propose a fitting restoration. The project was begun in 1981 by the Oliver Carr Company, and in 1983 Inter-Continental Hotels was asked to oversee hotel operations. Since it had been abandoned for 15 years, nearly all of the interior work had to be reconstructed, and five of the original public spaces were painstakingly restored during three years of intensive and academic research, completed in 1986.

The restored public spaces included the lobby, the 189-foot Peacock Alley, the Willard dining room, the F Street Lobby, and the Crystal Room. Originally, the 7,000 square feet of flooring in the lobby and Peacock Alley had been hand-set with marbled mosaic tiles, three-quarters of an inch wide. These were reproduced after several trips to Italy to locate the original marble and hand-set once again. Altogether 35 different marbles were excavated from six countries. Layers of paint were scientifically matched to contemporary hues. Archival photos of the interior were used as documentation to replace millwork, marble flooring, chandeliers, plaster molding, as well as the grand lobby carpet. The intricate craft of scagiola, an elaborate faux marbling, was restored and matched in the columns of the lobby and the Willard dining room. Replicas of the 12 original chandeliers were handmade by the grandson of the original craftsman.

Eclectic antiques carefully decorate the Willard's lobby, but the true treasure lies overhead, in the 48 state seals adorning the coffered ceiling. Hawaii and Alaska have since been added. Other public spaces are the Round Robin Bar, a clubby, masculine space with green fabric walls lined with more than a dozen portraits of well-known guests, like Charles Dickens, Warren Harding, Walt Whitman, Nathaniel Hawthorne, John Philip Sousa, Calvin Coolidge, and Alice Roosevelt Longworth, daughter of Teddy, who created a stir by smoking publicly in the dining room. Above was, at one time, the ladies' lounge, now the Nest, where high tea is served daily.

Guest rooms hover above on 11 floors. Compared to the lavish public areas, the accommodations are subdued, in a muted brown scheme and a more attractive blue. The suites, done in Federal simplicity, are quite nice and worth an upgrade if possible. All rooms have a marble-top mini-bar, a bath with a telephone, hair dryer, and television speaker.

The Willard is a most exquisite dining room, overseen by executive chef Peter Schaffrath. For afternoon fare in a pretty setting, the hotel has the European-style Café Espresso. The service at the Willard is quiet and formal, and the location, of course, is ideal.

Index

Best Places Report

We appreciate any information you can supply about the quality of the lodging. Detailed information about the building, furniture, service, food, and setting is most important. Describe as many rooms as you can, including living rooms, dining rooms, other common rooms, and of course bedrooms. A note about activities and nearby sights would be helpful. Tell us what category you think the place belongs in and why. Finally, how did you hear about the place, and how long have you been going there?

We will be happy to send you a free copy of the next edition of the book if we use your suggestion.

To: Chris Paddock
    Best Places to Stay in America's Cities
    The Harvard Common Press
    535 Albany Street
    Boston, Massachusetts 02118

Name of hotel _____

Telephone _____

Address _____

_____ Zip _____

_____

Description _____

_____

_____

_____

_____

_____

_____

Your Name _____

Telephone _____

Address _____

_____ Zip _____

_____

Best Places Report

We appreciate any information you can supply about the quality of the lodging. Detailed information about the building, furniture, service, food, and setting is most important. Describe as many rooms as you can, including living rooms, dining rooms, other common rooms, and of course bedrooms. A note about activities and nearby sights would be helpful. Tell us what category you think the place belongs in and why. Finally, how did you hear about the place, and how long have you been going there?

We will be happy to send you a free copy of the next edition of the book if we use your suggestion.

To: Chris Paddock
Best Places to Stay in America's Cities
The Harvard Common Press
535 Albany Street
Boston, Massachusetts 02118

Name of hotel _____

Telephone _____

Address _____

_____ Zip _____

Description _____

_____

_____

_____

_____

_____

_____

Your Name _____

Telephone _____

Address _____

_____ Zip _____

_____

Best Places Report

We appreciate any information you can supply about the quality of the lodging. Detailed information about the building, furniture, service, food, and setting is most important. Describe as many rooms as you can, including living rooms, dining rooms, other common rooms, and of course bedrooms. A note about activities and nearby sights would be helpful. Tell us what category you think the place belongs in and why. Finally, how did you hear about the place, and how long have you been going there?

We will be happy to send you a free copy of the next edition of the book if we use your suggestion.

To: Chris Paddock
    Best Places to Stay in America's Cities
    The Harvard Common Press
    535 Albany Street
    Boston, Massachusetts 02118

Name of hotel _____

Telephone _____

Address _____

_____ Zip _____

Description _____

_____

_____

_____

_____

_____

_____

Your Name _____

Telephone _____

Address _____

_____ Zip _____

_____

Best Places Report

We appreciate any information you can supply about the quality of the lodging. Detailed information about the building, furniture, service, food, and setting is most important. Describe as many rooms as you can, including living rooms, dining rooms, other common rooms, and of course bedrooms. A note about activities and nearby sights would be helpful. Tell us what category you think the place belongs in and why. Finally, how did you hear about the place, and how long have you been going there?

We will be happy to send you a free copy of the next edition of the book if we use your suggestion.

To: Chris Paddock
     Best Places to Stay in America's Cities
     The Harvard Common Press
     535 Albany Street
     Boston, Massachusetts 02118

Name of hotel _____

Telephone _____

Address _____

_____ Zip _____

_____

Description _____

_____

_____

_____

_____

_____

_____

Your Name _____

Telephone _____

Address _____

_____ Zip _____

_____

Best Places Report

We appreciate any information you can supply about the quality of the lodging. Detailed information about the building, furniture, service, food, and setting is most important. Describe as many rooms as you can, including living rooms, dining rooms, other common rooms, and of course bedrooms. A note about activities and nearby sights would be helpful. Tell us what category you think the place belongs in and why. Finally, how did you hear about the place, and how long have you been going there?

We will be happy to send you a free copy of the next edition of the book if we use your suggestion.

To: Chris Paddock
      Best Places to Stay in America's Cities
      The Harvard Common Press
      535 Albany Street
      Boston, Massachusetts 02118

Name of hotel _____

Telephone _____

Address _____

_____ Zip _____

_____

Description _____

_____

_____

_____

_____

_____

_____

Your Name _____

Telephone _____

Address _____

_____ Zip _____

_____

Best Places Report

We appreciate any information you can supply about the quality of the lodging. Detailed information about the building, furniture, service, food, and setting is most important. Describe as many rooms as you can, including living rooms, dining rooms, other common rooms, and of course bedrooms. A note about activities and nearby sights would be helpful. Tell us what category you think the place belongs in and why. Finally, how did you hear about the place, and how long have you been going there?

We will be happy to send you a free copy of the next edition of the book if we use your suggestion.

To: Chris Paddock
       Best Places to Stay in America's Cities
       The Harvard Common Press
       535 Albany Street
       Boston, Massachusetts 02118

Name of hotel _____

Telephone _____

Address _____

_____ Zip _____

_____

Description _____

_____

_____

_____

_____

_____

_____

Your Name _____

Telephone _____

Address _____

_____ Zip _____

_____

Best Places Report

We appreciate any information you can supply about the quality of the lodging. Detailed information about the building, furniture, service, food, and setting is most important. Describe as many rooms as you can, including living rooms, dining rooms, other common rooms, and of course bedrooms. A note about activities and nearby sights would be helpful. Tell us what category you think the place belongs in and why. Finally, how did you hear about the place, and how long have you been going there?

We will be happy to send you a free copy of the next edition of the book if we use your suggestion.

To: Chris Paddock
      Best Places to Stay in America's Cities
      The Harvard Common Press
      535 Albany Street
      Boston, Massachusetts 02118

Name of hotel _____

Telephone _____

Address _____

_____ Zip _____

_____

Description _____

_____

_____

_____

_____

_____

_____

Your Name _____

Telephone _____

Address _____

_____ Zip _____

_____